Perceiving in Advaita Vedānta

Perceiving in Advaita Vedānta:

Epistemological Analysis and Interpretation

Bina Gupta

MOTILAL BANARSIDASS PUBLISHERS
PRIVATE LIMITED • DELHI

First Indian Edition: Delhi, 1995

ISBN: 81-208-1296-9

Also available at:

MOTILAL BANARSIDASS
41 U.A. Bungalow Road, Jawahar Nagar, Delhi 110 007
120 Royapettah High Road, Mylapore, Madras 600 004
16 St. Mark's Road, Bangalore 560 001
Ashok Rajpath, Patna 800 004
Chowk, Varanasi 221 001

[redacted]

PRINTED IN INDIA
BY JAINENDRA PRAKASH JAIN AT SHRI JAINENDRA PRESS,
A-45 NARAINA, PHASE I, NEW DELHI 110 028
AND PUBLISHED BY NARENDRA PRAKASH JAIN FOR
MOTILAL BANARSIDASS PUBLISHERS PRIVATE LIMITED,
BUNGALOW ROAD, DELHI 110 007

For Madan, whose faith turns possibility into reality

Contents

Abbreviations

AB	*Āśubodhinī*
AS	*Advaitasiddhi*
Bhāmatī	Vācaspati, *Bhāmatī with Kalaptaru and Parimala.* Nirnayasagar edition.
BP	*Bhāṣā-Pariccheda with Siddhānta-Muktavalī.* Advaita Ashrama edition.
BSB	*Brahma-Sūtra-Bhāṣya of Śrī Sankarācārya*
BU	*Bṛhadāraṇyaka Upaniṣad*
Catussūtrī	*The Bhāmatī of Vācaspati on Śaṅkara's Brahmasūtra-bhāṣya.* Madras: Theosophical Publishing House ed.
CU	*Chāndogya Upaniṣad*
KU	*Kena Upaniṣad*
MU	*Muṇḍaka Upaniṣad*
NS	*The Naiṣkarmya Siddhi of Śrī Sureśvara:* London: Shanti Sadan edition.
NVTT	*Nyāyavārtikatātparyaṭīkā*
PP	*Paribhāṣā Prakāśikā.* University of Calcutta edition.
PPD	*Pañcapādikā. Gaekwad Oriental Series*
PPDV	*Pañcapādikāvivaraṇam.* Madras Govt. Oriental Series.
PU	*Praśna Upaniṣad*
SB	*Siddhāntabindu of Madhusūdana with the Commentary of Purushottama. Gaekwad Oriental Series*
SBT	*Siddhāntabinduṭīka*
SLS	*Siddhāntaleśasaṅgraha.* Madras University Series edition.
SM	*Śikhāmaṇi*
SS	*Saṃksepaśāriraka of Sarvajñātman.* Radhakrishnan Institute, University of Madras edition.
TP	*Tattavapradīpikā*
TU	*Taittirīya Upaniṣad*
TSD	*Tarka-Saṃgraha of Annaṃbhatta with Dīpīka.* Calcutta: Progressive Publishers.
TSDNB	*Tarka-Saṃgraha of Annaṃbhaṭṭa with Dīpīkā and Govardhana's Nyāya-Bodhinī.* Bombay Sanskrit and Prakrit Series edition.
VP	*Vedānta Paribhāṣā*
VPS	*Vivaraṇaprameyasaṅgraha.* Kumbakonam edition.

Foreword

Professor Bina Gupta gives us in this volume an English translation of the chapter on perception (*pratyakṣa*) of *Vedāntaparibhāṣā*, a well-known work on Advaita Vedānta epistemology. The text of *Vedāntaparibhāṣā* needs no introduction. Generations of Indian philosophers have been introduced to Indian epistemology by this work. In this book, the chapter on perception is especially noteworthy; it succeeds in presenting an account of perceptual cognition that was present in the earlier works by the great Advaita masters but was never available in such a succinct manner. Professor Gupta's translation, I am sure, will enable scholars not well versed in Sanskrit to follow the presentation closely and faithfully. We should be grateful to her for this help.

She does not give us only a translation. The notes that she adds introduce the major interpretive issues as well as references to the major commentaries in the Advaita Vedānta theory of consciousness and knowledge.

The theory of perception that *Vedāntaparibhāṣā* develops is basically an identity theory: in perceptual cognition, the subject and the object achieve a sort of identity. But, on the Advaita metaphysical theory, the only reality is the all pervading differenceless consciousness. In that case, the subject of cognition is the same consciousness as limited by the cognitive mechanisms belonging to the empirical person under consideration, just as the object of cognition is also the same consciousness as *limited by* what ordinarily one would regard as the external thing. In perceptual cognition, the inner sense assumes the form of the object (a very Aristotelian picture); there is a sort of identity between the consciousness as *limited by* the subjective cognitive mechanism and the consciousness as limited by the thing that is known: this identity is the perceptual cognition. Within this general theory, Advaita Vedānta introduces the idea of a modification of the inner sense, which is called *vṛtti*, whose function is to remove the veil of ignorance that conceals the thing to be known. Although in all cognition, the object is manifested by consciousness in its role as the witness-consciousness, external things are not directly manifested by the witness consciousness. An appropriate modification of the inner sense mediates.

This is a complex but highly interesting picture. I would recall here only another side of the picture. If the object perceived is manifested by the appropriate modification of the inner sense (which by removing the veil of ignorance saves it from the status of being unknown), the mental modification itself is directly manifested by the witness consciousness. One does not need another such modification of the inner sense for the original modification of the inner sense to be known. What this means is that when I have a perceptual state, I *eo ipso* know that I have that perceptual state, I do not need another perceptual state in order for the first perception to be known. The Advaita epistemology recognizes several types of such states that are directly manifested by the witness-consciousness: besides all first-level cognitive states, such states as pleasure and pain are also directly manifested (meaning that when I have a state of pleasure, I at once know that I have one, there being no unknown pleasure). But what became important for Advaita epistemology and metaphysics is the thesis that I likewise have an immediate awareness of my own ignorance (of whatever I am ignorant). If one held that a state of ignorance is known only when there is an appropriate modification of the inner sense that objectifies it, one would also have to say that this alleged modification of inner sense would have the function (which it always has) of destroying the veil of ignorance which conceals that original ignorance, but the idea of an ignorance being concealed by ignorance seemed to entail a sort of infinite regress that threatened to be vicious. So the Advaita epistemologists held that one's own ignorance is directly manifested by the witness-consciousness without the meditation of a modification of the inner sense.

Thus we have a marvelous theory that not only accounts for my knowledge of such things as pots and pans, but also takes into account the fact that I immediately know that I know, as also for the fact that I am immediately aware of the fact that I am ignorant of such and such thing.

A short step leads us from the above account to the conclusion that everything whatsoever is an object of consciousness—whether as known *or as unknown*. All objects are not merely objects of knowledge (as the Berkeleyan thesis *esse est percipii* seems to entail), they are also objects of ignorance; but since both being-known and being-unknown are two ways of being presented to the witness-consciousness, all things are objects of that consciousness. The result is a form of idealism that curiously enough makes room for the realistic intuition that there are unknown (e.g., unperceived) things.

We must be indebted to Professor Gupta for having made the details of this theory, along with the various interpretive possibilities that the tradition explored, available to the western readers.

The comparison with phenomenology—Husserlian or of some other brand—is temptingly at hand. But that is a large and intricate topic on which I will desist from making any remarks. Professor Gupta's work contains many hints at such a comparison. Let us listen to her.

It is always a pleasure, one of the satisfactions of a long teaching career, to find one's pupils producing scholarly works of distinction. The author of this work was a member of a class I taught at the Visva Bharati University at Santiniketan, India. By asking me to write a foreword to her book, she has added to that pleasure and to that satisfaction.

JITENDRA MOHAN MOHANTY

Preface

Vedānta has been recognized as the most important and the most well-known philosophical system of Indian thought. Vedāntic texts have been the subject of numerous commentaries, which have given rise to several schools of Vedānta. Advaita Vedānta is the nondualistic school of Vedānta primarily explicated by Śaṃkara (ca. 788–820). It was commented upon, elaborated on, and developed by several generations of scholars. It is one of the most widely known and recreated systems of Indian philosophy; it makes the most enigmatic assertion about the nature of the world and our perception of it—*brahma satyaṃ jagan mithyā jīvo brahmaiva nāparaḥ* (Brahman is real, the world is false, and the individual self is none other than Brahman)—an assertion that western scholars find difficult to comprehend. Thus, it is not surprising that Advaita Vedānta is the most pervasive and enduring Indian perspective, and continues to be the most challenging and provocative philosophical position the world over.

In recent times a great deal of attention has been paid to the divergent facets of Advaita Vedānta. Little attention, however, has been paid to its epistemology. As Professor Deutsch points out, "except in the later phases of the tradition, and even here to only a limited extent...there is little awareness of epistemology as a distinct philosophical discipline" (*Advaita Vedānta: A Philosophical Reconstruction,* 81). One possible explanation for this phenomenon that comes to mind is Advaitic taxonomy. Śaṃkara does not discuss epistemological issues separately, but rather intermingles them with the metaphysical issues.

There are two forms of knowledge: *parāvidyā* (higher knowledge) and *aparāvidyā* (lower knowledge). *Parāvidyā* is the knowledge of Brahman, the Absolute, and *aparāvidyā* is the knowledge of every other kind, bearing on the empirical world where the plurality of names and forms is manifested. These two forms of knowledge, Śaṃkara maintains, are incommensurable. The *parāvidyā* is *sui generis:* it is attained all at once—immediately, intuitively. It is neither mediated nor conditional. Such a knowledge is self-certifying, because no other form of knowledge can either confirm or disconfirm it. When Brahman is realized, nothing remains to be known. However, until the attainment of *parāvidyā*—the Brahman realization—the *aparāvidyā* holds sway as the 'ultimate', but it can never claim the ultimacy that belongs to *parāvidyā*. In other words, before Brahman realization, all transactions of the phenomenal world are real and true as far as they go; that is, to the extent that they refer to phenomena *per se*. One of the more enduring aspects of the Advaita Vedānta explication is to demonstrate how the two incommensurable spheres nevertheless interpenetrate and yield to a unifying vision, presenting itself as the solution implied in the problem.

The purpose of this study is to undertake an analysis of the epistemological issues inherent in the Advaita Vedānta theory of the knowing and the known, to explicate their two-tiered theory of knowledge from a phenomenalistic perspective, and at the same time to make sense of the overarching unity that prevails over the duality and division. My interpretation and analysis will be based on the first two sections of Dharmarāja's *Vedānta Paribhāṣā* (*VP*) and its commentary *Paribhāṣā Prakāśikā* (*PP*).

It seems important to note that prior to the appearance of *VP*, neither metaphysical nor epistemological issues were treated separately and apart from all other philosophical issues and themes. *VP* is a classical work on Advaita epistemology. Because of Dharmarāja's effort in the seventeenth century, epistemology began to be treated as an independent discipline, although to a limited extent. This book, for the first time, provides a systematic exposition and defense of the Advaita theory of knowledge. It deals exhaustively with the different means of valid knowledge and epistemological issues inherent therein. The departure from the tradition in this respect, represented by the text of *VP*, affords a modern and hence helpful mode of access to the classical spirit of Advaita literature. The work to a large extent follows the Vivaraṇa tradition, one of the two major 'highways' (*prasthāna*-s) to interpretations of Śaṃkara.

VP has been the subject of numerous commentaries that attest to its importance. The most notable among them is by the author's son, Ramakṛṣṇa Adhvarīndra, entitled *Sikhāmaṇi*(*SM*). *Āśubodhinī* (AB) of Śrı Kṛṣṇannāth Nyāyapañcānana's and *Paribhāṣā Prakāśikā* (*PP*) of Anantakṛṣṇa Śāstrī's are some of the well-known commentaries on it. Amardasa's *Maṇiprabha* is a gloss on *Sikhāmaṇi.*

I have made *PP* the basis of my exegetical commentary, which incorporates in its analysis the distinctive points of other commentaries on *VP*. It not only discusses the issues raised in *VP* but also the questions not anticipated in the text of *VP*. The virtue of the particular commentary relied upon in this work, in contrast with many other extant analyses, is that it not only incorporates perspectives drawn from several divergent subsequent developments in Advaita thought, but that it also appreciates the other schools of Indian thought. For example, it clearly brings out the differences between the Vivaraṇa and the Bhāmatī traditions, the two main developments of Advaita tradition, while incorporating in its discussion viewpoints of the different schools of Indian philosophy, namely, Nyāya and Mīmāṃsā. The distinction of *PP* lies in its resolute attempt to adhere to a textual interpretation securely anchored in the Advaita perspective instead of sliding into the Nyāya camp.

Indian philosophy may be considered to be a living tradition alive to the positions and the points of view at odds with what is held as one's own, and also moving forward. The latter aspect is often imperceptible and slow, judged from the standpoint and pace of the history of western philosophy, but nevertheless it is there in its classical and the neoclassical forms. One has only to skim through the five volumes of S. N. Dasgupta's *History of Indian Philosophy* to see the contours and detours of its growth and development. Vedānta in a sense spearheads the process through its simultaneously performed operations of rejection, incorporation, and transformation. One may see this at work in the Classical Vedānta and in the contemporary reincarnation of it in the form of neo-Vedānta with its windows opened to the outside world. The present work is a modest attempt falling under the latter category. In recreating and reappraising Vedānta in contemporary idiom, the author at the same time felt the need for a direct indepth acquaintance with how the tradition itself sought to carry it forward at the hands of its living exponents and exegetes, continuous with the past, and yet discontinuous in its novel and creative reconstruction. It is in answer to this need that a contemporary exegetical writing on an important Advaita text was chosen as the basis for recreating the central insights of Vedānta . The document chosen, while not exactly a model of clarity, is nevertheless comprehensive and discernful. It is incisive, analytical, and eminently intraphilosophical with respect to the leading Indian philosophical traditions of India. The present author of the commentary, Anantakṛṣṇa Śāstrī, at times is overslanted in his approach, especially in his critique of the commentaries, entitled *Śikhāmaṇi* and *Āśubodhinī*. The aim of this book is not to assess these commentaries independently as it would needlessly enlarge the scope of the task addressed, namely, a phenomenological reconstruction. Accordingly, the writer has confined herself to a selective and critical use of the commentary *PP* in interpreting the tract of *VP* chosen for analysis.

Indianists from the west working on the Indian texts often tend to ignore the living stream represented in the oral and written materials originating from the class of specialists called Pandits, for lack of both access and time. For these specialists, it is a total commitment and a full-time preoccupation. It is earnestly hoped that the present work, drawing from this mainstream, may succeed in giving the western reader at least an inkling of the manner and method in which philosophy is discussed and debated as an ongoing concern as integral to an ultimate concern. The west tends to consider all ultimate concerns as religious. However, in the Indian context, the concerns of religion and philosophy merge.

The primary focus of my attention is the chapter on perception of the text of *VP*. Perception is of special significance, because the *parā-vidyā,* Advaitins hold, is immediate, which is different from the mediate knowledge that results from the means whereby knowledge is obtained through inference and comparison. Brahman, the only reality of the system, has been articulated as that which is direct and immediate (*sākṣāt aparokṣāt*).

How do we account for this notion of immediacy? The immediacy of knowledge does not depend upon its arising from the senses as is generally believed, but on the presented object. What makes it possible for knowledge to be perceptual is the immediacy of the object presented to consciousness that apprehends it. The phenomenal world rests on a distinction between cognition and content. In the immediate experience of Brahman, no such distinction exists. Pure consciousness, however, involves the nondifference of cognition and content. Pure consciousness is the criterion of peceptibility. Accordingly, in a perceptual situation the object does not have any independent existence apart from the pureconsciousness. The cognizer-consciousness and the consciousness that is the substratum of objects, such as pitchers, partake of the common medium of pure consciousness. This is how, in the perception of a pitcher, the pitcher becomes 'immediate'.

The importance of the analysis of perception for the central task of Vedānta as an inquiry cannot be exaggerated. What is the central task addressed in Vedānta as a reflective inquiry? One may state it in most general terms as the task of the recovery of immediacy. The most arduous and sustained search that Vedānta represents is for recovering the ground on which one stands. The central insight of Vedānta cannot be expressed more adequately than in the form of a paradox: you are that which you seek. The task is not simple. The onus is on oneself to *discover* that one, in one's very core, represents the goal that one is striving to attain. This is immediacy. The Vedānta analysis of perceiving brings out the paradox of immediacy by demonstrating that in the knowing process, the two poles of knowing—the subject at one end and the object known at the other—meet on the common platform of consciousness.

The present work also includes a translation of the entire perception chapter of *VP* as well as the introduction and also a free reconstruction of the gloss provided on it by *PP*. Two translations of *VP* in book form presently exist. The first, by Śrī S. S. Suryanarayan Śāstrī, is opaque by virtue of its technicality and presumption of familiarity with the Advaitin terminological esoterica. Its inaccessibility thereby limits its utility for anything but the narrowest of purposes. The second, by Swāmī Mādhavānanda, as the author himself concedes, is written to "popularise the study of Vedānta among the English knowing people in all parts of the world" (xii). The very fact of its popularization, it seems fair to claim, trades accessibility for philosophical precision and technical accuracy. The translation provided here represents an attempt to preserve the full integrity of the Sanskrit text while clarifying or illuminating, as it were, the fundamental epistemological issues addressed in the chapter on perception. Additionally the book contains extensive critical notes clarifying some of the complex ideas contained in the two documents and also drawing from the vast and growing secondary writing on the subject. I have resisted the temptation to compare Vedānta with the terms and concepts of western philosophy in the body of the book. However, I have sought to provide constructive leads in this regard in the endnotes. The presentation is addressed mainly to specialists in Indian philosophy, although it is earnestly hoped that it may not be without some appeal to an open-minded thinker of western philosophy as well. Quotes have been used in the endnotes either for the purposes of elucidation of ideas not familiar to the readers, or because of the unavailability of so many of these writings, including translations of difficult Sanskrit texts. It is hoped that the notes provided will reduce the opacity of many of the points discussed and debated in the body of this work.

In contrast with the more or less standardized numerical system in and through which western scholars make reference to classical Greek texts (e.g., the writings of Plato and Aristotle), no universally accepted and sequential textual numbering system has won acceptance among classical Indian commentators. Reminiscent of the numerical system appearing in Wittgenstein's *Tractatus*, the procedure used here for referencing the specific text is partially chronological and partially thematic. That is, relevant exposition has been assigned a number, followed by a subdivision designating the objection to the thesis, followed by another subdivision to designate that portion of the text containing the response and rejoinder to the objection, and so on. Essentially, this is the system used as consistently as possible throughout. In addition, the commentary as a whole, lacking the equivalent of chapters or similar divisions, has been so provided, again in the interest of exegetical clarity.

I am under no illusion that the present effort will qualify as a definitive exposition of Advaita epistemology. Rather, the more modest aspiration has been to contribute elements out of which a comprehensive and systematic interpretation may emerge one day. It also may hopefully stimulate interest in comparative philosophy and contribute in a small way to stimulating interest in contemplating philosophical issues as a global inheritance sharing common quests and envisaging goals that are relevant for humankind as a whole. It is toward this expectation that an introduction has been appended, which explores the specifics as well as the more general dimensions of the problems of perception relevant to the text undertaken for study.

I wish to thank Professors N. Veezhinathan and Revati Srinivasan of the University of Madras for studying the commentary *PP* with me. I also wish to thank Professors Joel Brereton of the University of Missouri at Columbia and Madhav Deshpande of the University of Michigan, Ann Arbor, for helping me with the transliteration of *VP*. I also am grateful to Ms. Trish Love and Ms. Angie Heckman for the graciousness with which they carried out the many tedious tasks involved in the preparation of this manuscript. I want to acknowledge my gratitude to the Research Council of the University of Missouri-Columbia, and the American Institute of Indian Studies for providing me with the funds to help defray costs involved in this project. I would like also to thank Professor Krishna Sivaraman for his advice, insightful suggestions and for introducing me to Śāstrī's commentary, and William C. Wilcox for his support, assistance, and encouragement throughout this project. Finally, I would like to thank my husband, Madan, and daughter Swati, for believing in me and being there for me when I needed them.

Perceiving in Advaita Vedānta

Introduction

Perception as a Problem in Philosophy: Its Role and Significance

The problem of perceiving or knowing is intrinsic to a determination of what is the case and what we are to do, the two well-known domains of ontology and ethics, respectively. These domains represent the heart and essence of a philosophical tradition, at least in the pre-modern sense of the term. 'Seeing' is integral to perceiving and knowing things and also to any kind of doing that accompanies knowing. It is not simply seeing as a sensory function accomplished through the physical eyes, but 'seeing' with the inner eye. The bridge between perceiving in the ordinary sense as a sensory function and perceiving of the true or the real must be crossed. In some extended sense, sensory perceiving itself must point to contemplation.

In all philosophies, western as well as eastern, in which vision plays a vital role and is avowed as the terminal goal or as the condition that informs worthwhile living, the issue of perception provides a point of entry. Plato gives us the myth of the cave and speaks of 'seeing' with the inner eye. Whether one speaks of going out of the cave or returning to the cave, there is no doubt that perception is tied to seeing. There is a continuity in the function of seeing, between seeing with the eyes involved in the perception of objects or 'shadows', and 'seeing' with the eye of the mind, the eternal object.

In the eastern context, the philosophico-religious tradition that forms the subject matter and the focus of attention in the present work (namely, the tradition of nondualism, Advaita Vedānta), reiterates the same point. Whether one sees a pitcher or a piece of cloth, one is 'seeing' Brahman, the term of the tradition for ultimate reality or more simply, reality. What is perceived, or seen, is nothing but the reality or consciousness as conditioned or defined by the perceived object. In one sense, the reality *per se* is supersensible and indeterminate, defying all determinate relations to the senses. The real is not what is simply seen, heard, smelled, tasted, or touched and therefore is not 'perceived'. It is not literally perceived to the extent that a sensory function is a structural condition of perception. But, in another sense, the reality is perceived all the time when something is perceived. When a pitcher is perceived, the reality is *ipso facto* perceived. What makes pitcher-perception veridical is the entailment of reality. The 'experience' of veridicality that psychology addresses as a phenomenal datum on par with feeling or sensation is really what it is in virtue of being an experience of reality. The Upaniṣads—the foundational texts of the tradition—declare emphatically: "All this is Brahman."[1] Empirical perception and perception, hailed and hallowed as saving gnosis (vidyā), are continuous. They are not two self-enclosed spheres. There is continuity in the function of seeing, whether it be of objects *per se* or of objects as symbolic of something not present as objects, and seeing in the form of meditative reflection. The continuity, differently stated, is between seeing as a cognitive (i.e., a theoretic function) and seeing in the sense of realizing reality. Perception itself, when rightly understood, may be seen to be the portal to reality in the ultimate sense.

The conceptualization of philosophy in the context of the Indian tradition reveals that its notion of philosophy overlaps what has come to be called religion in the western context, in which the term earmarks a special sphere of activity. Philosophy as a theoretical function in the western tradition is never combined with the activities and forms of *praxis* that one generally associates with religion. Religious beliefs and philosophical traditions are two entirely different categories. The Indian tradition, however, presents an entirely different picture. True, the two sets of activities are culturally distinguished, but in the very nature of the case, as the Indian philosophical tradition comes to be self-consciously defined and refined, it becomes apparent that there can be no divorce between theory and practice. For example, while the conceptual elucidation and analysis at the core of the central function of 'discrimination' represents the proper sphere of philosophy, the expressed use of it in the service of a deepening of intuition or 'revelation' of what is real, and therefore also good, is the domain of religion.

Generally, although the term 'philosophy' may be used to describe a set of disinterested activities involving or calling forth pursuits for their own sake, for enlightenment as an end in itself, there is, however, a peculiar sense of the term that seems unique to the tradition of Indian thought. For the entire Indian tradition, philosophy evokes the same sense of awe and respect that 'religion' does in the west. Indeed, philosophy is perceived as an activity, but also with a striking consensus, as a sacred pursuit. It is sacred in that it represents an interested approach to truth, the truth that makes one free. It is not as if there is an either-or quandary about the possession of truth and conquest of freedom or liberation. The 'truth' in itself is precious and implies a state of liberation. The search for liberation presents itself as the search for truth, as what redeems one from a compulsive adherence to untruth. In the western context, needless to say, the truth that makes one free signifies salvation or redemption and is relegated to the domain of religion. Philosophy stands contrasted with this domain, and even when viewed as a kind of activity, it is seen as instrumental to obtaining knowledge. Definitionally, it is a noetic enterprise. For the Indian tradition, knowledge (*vidyā*), which is co-extensive with philosophy, is itself an insight into reality and redemption from bondage to non-knowledge (*avidyā*). It should be apparent how central to philosophy, understood as *gnosis,* as light that dispels the gloom of darkness, is the function of perception as a means as well as an end.

Perception as a philosophical problem enjoys its status as a general domain within epistemology. In the Occident, with the advent of modern philosophy, epistemology comes to be accorded a right of precedence over other inquiries, such as ontology and ethics. The reasons for this shift of interest are well-known, and at any rate should not concern us here. Perception, however, in the specific sense that is the focus in this study, is more urgent and claims an order of priority, because it is tied to the process of enlightenment. Such a process raises, or involves preeminently, a deepening or heightening of the consciousness that frees one from a previous servitude, an unreflective acquiescence in the experience of life and things. At the same time the raising of consciousness involves liberation from a previous servitude to a dogmatic and unjustifiable acceptance of the world in which one lives. This is philosophy in the existential sense, a sort of quickened inquiry, in which the questions of bondage, freedom, truth, and error all acquire an existential meaning. All this attests to the importance of perception in the tradition of Advaita.

The term for philosophy in the Indian context, used in apposition to Advaita, deserves to be noted. The Sanskrit term *'darśana'* directly imports 'seeing', or better yet, 'sight'. Sight has been used in a manner that is unique to the way verbal nouns are formed in the Sanskrit language; it has been used in two different senses: It signifies the product of a process, and it also names the process itself. The same is true of expressions such as knowing or knowledge, perceiving or perception, doing or deed. These may be understood in either of the two ways: in terms of their 'what,' that is to say, holistically; or in terms of their 'how', as the process whereby they come to be articulated. Seeing is 'sight' according to the first sense and the 'means' by which sight is accomplished in the second sense.

Philosophy in the technical sense of its self-understanding according to the tradition of Advaita focuses on the cognitive means by which what is true (i.e., real), is perceived. It is cognitive in that it involves intellect and results in a state of enlightenment or immediate realization, the structural meaning of perception. This explains why in Indian philosophy the final goal of liberation is articulated on the model of visual perception rather than on a process of thinking or reflection. Thinking or thought is subordinated as a means to the end of perception. The descriptive label used in the foundational text of Advaita for ultimate reality is 'that which is direct and immediate'.[2] The goal of liberation is likewise significantly described in the words: the knower of (ultimate) reality becomes ultimate reality.[3] Knowledge *is* the realization of identity.

Methodological Issues

The history of western thought acquaints us with a number of lines of approach. The great debates between realism and idealism, rationalism and empiricism, dogmatism and skepticism are well-known. What interests us about them is that they have their moorings, *inter alia*, in the issue of perception. Characteristic is the Kantian analysis of perception as a logical-epistemological question, which sets the stage for the more recent developments of Occidental thinking. In the context of Indian philosophy, in which perception is approached in its relation to the goal of philosophy and religion, the significant question arises: Is perceiving better comprehended in the light of an analysis of it as experience rather than as a case of logical or linguistic analysis? We shall revisit this question in the concluding section of this essay. However, some general remarks are in order now.

Anyone acquainted with the story of the unfolding of Indian philosophy is aware of its multifaceted character and its plethora of theories—logical, epistemological, grammatical, linguistic, hermeneutical, and phenomenological—on every philosophical issue that it addresses. The philosophical textual material on which the tradition of Advaita rests, almost from the moment of its inception and growth, purports to span all shades and schools of thinking that are later developed side by side, and which together constitute the spectrum of Indian philosophy. The general label used to refer to this foundational textual material, as well as to all the sustained attempts that were made later to recover the heart and essence of its teachings, is a blanket term 'Vedānta', literally the 'end of the Veda'. Veda is the general term used to refer to the material looked upon as the original source of wisdom about truth and therefore as laying intrinsic claim to be authoritative.

Vedānta represents thought, in a philosophically worthwhile sense, both as an ongoing attempt to recreate and reverbalize 'original' material and as the endeavor to approximate to the seeing of that original material that comes with the claim of being a timelessly unveiled mode of knowledge. In other words, philosophy in this context implies two inter-related activities:one is a hermeneutic of what is timelessly revealed as true—the truth that alone makes one free—involving the arduous exercise of discerning the text from within the framework of the text itself viewed as one and homogeneous. The comprehensive term that is particularly used to refer to this sort of activity is *'mīmāṃsā';*[4] the other is an analytic activity of the discursive mind implying logical and semantic rationality, interpreting the interpretation in light of our knowledge of the phenomenal world and of the structures of language and thought involved or assumed in such knowledge.

Needless to say, there is considerable overlapping between interpretation and analysis. Philosophy as a hermeneutic act cannot be carried out without reference to the world and to the spheres of language and thought. Likewise, philosophy as analysis must constantly fall back upon its source and direct its searchlight into hidden structures. Philosophy, in the sense in which one can significantly talk about Indian philosophy, and more particularly if also less equivocally about Vedānta as philosophy, means a conjunction of two interrelated activities, namely, intuitively acknowledging something as given, as the 'this' (*idam*) which is thematized as the ineradicable given in an investigation of perception, and as a cognitive self-explication that articulates it.

The treatment of perceptual experience in the Advaita Vedānta tradition exemplifies the aforementioned conjunction. The treatment may be described appropriately as phenomenological[5] in that it represents an attempt, in simple terms, to understand experience and its implications through an immanent inspection of introspection. Introspection is used in this context, not in its usual sense as a term of psychology, but in an extended manner. It points to an integral aspect of perception itself, its immediate self-perception: not a perception of the perception that structurally is no different from perception, but the self-awareness illuminating perception itself. The object as such is not the focus of attention, as is the case in a cognitivist analysis or even in a metaphysical account that seeks for the object behind the objects. The focus of attention *vis-à-vis* the object rather is consciousness, that functions as the medium in and through which one attends the object. This, as we shall see later, is not the idealism of western philosophy, although it shares with western phenomenology its inseparable links with idealism. To be more precise, it is consciousness with respect to its ways of referentiality, not the object as such, that is perceived as the main epistemological concern. Analysis of the perceptual mode of consciousness as the principal means by which one comes to know the world illustrates an orientation that may be described as phenomenological in a typical Indian sense of the term. Thus it is an orientation different, on the one hand, from a psychological-naturalistic account of origins and, on the other, from a logical-epistemological and metaphysical account involving the positing of judgments concerning realities.

A theory of perceiving, to be adequate to the importance and centrality of perception for philosophy, should be more than a simple analysis and a prescriptive definition of terms involved in the process. It should rest on an immanent inspection of the perceptual experience itself. The terms that we use to make distinctions in the cognitive sphere, like truth and falsehood, knowledge and ignorance, real and unreal, mediate and immediate, must arise and receive attestation from within the inspection of one's own experience. In one's own experience the occasion must present itself as the ground for such a usage. When we see objects or, alternately, when we apprehend a state of our own mind, we do not ask whether it is real or true. Rather, these metalogical expressions, acquire their meaning in one's experience from situations that entail a transition from an unquestioned affirmation of what is the case to its negation. The contrast that this experience of negation or cancellation forces on one's attention provides the true experiential edge for using the evaluative terms 'real' and 'unreal.' The real then is understood as the new semantic equivalent of that which resists being 'cancelled' (*bādha*).[6] To use the terminology of Advaita, the real is what abides unsublated (*abādhita*). And by the same token, what is not real would be that which is subject to being sublated by another experience. The unreal is yet another category that is neither sublated nor unsublated by any other experience. Unreality can never become an object of experience, actual or possible. In short, unreal objects in principle can have no objective counterpart, and consequently do not fall within the purview of phenomenological inspection.

The use of what has been described as a phenomenological method as intrinsic to the task of interpretation is implicit in the writings of Śaṃkara (8th century C.E.) and the later Vedāntins. The different stages in the analysis of cognitive error summed up under the rubric of what is termed the indeterminableness of the erroneous apprehension (*anirvacanīya khyāti*) have provoked the attention of some neo-Vedāntins of this century in India who sought to reconstruct the Vedāntic theory of 'appearance' (*adhyāsa*). The latter is a technical expression in Śaṃkara, who also describes it as erroneous apprehension (*mithyā jñāna*) and illusion (*avabhāsa*). The exact nature of the phenomenological method as a hermeneutical principle in the hands of Śaṃkara will presently be considered, but we may pause here to refer to his celebrated description of appearance in the opening section of *Brahmasūtrabhāṣya* (hereafter referred to as *BSB*): "the appearance elsewhere with a nature that is similar to recollection (*smṛti*) of what one perceived earlier." That such an appearance is illusory Śaṃkara deduces from what is intrinsic to its structure, namely, its terminability. It is like a dream cognition which, by definition, is what is terminated upon waking up. The appearance-experience, maintains Śaṃkara, is essentially a case of coupling the true and the untrue. The snake appearance, masquerading as given to cognition, is illusory. It is superimposed on the rope that is real, the truly given as 'this'. The snake thus experienced is not the snake that the experiencer recognizes as mere recollection. To recollect a snake previously perceived is not the same as actually seeing the snake in the substratum of the rope. In instances such as the rope-snake, the shell-silver, what is seen now is not the same as that seen previously. They are appearances very similar to, but not the same as, recollection. The important point to note here is that the content of appearance is not real but indeterminable.

The different stages involved in the case of an erroneous perception that typify all cases of knowledge are, as earlier observed, elaborated with great perspecuity by the contemporary Vedāntins . In simplified analysis, it involves stages discernible in a manner that lends itself to be arranged in chronological succession as earlier and later. When we thus state it, it must be borne in mind that it is not the fact of the successiveness of their occurrence that constitutes the essence of the experience of correction, which is structurally cognate with the erroneous perception (as wakefulness structurally is to sleep or dream). The sequence is logical rather than chronological. First, there is the presentation of the snake, then it is cancelled or corrected, and finally—the most significant stage from the perspective of interpretative inspection—contemplation, or hermeneutically speaking, interpretation of cancellation or correction. It is only at this stage that one becomes thematically aware of the distinction of the orders or levels of the real and the false. Cancellation brings in its wake the contemplation that the process that is involved here is not a simple suspension of belief in a previously believed content but a disavowal that the previous belief ever had a content. This is reflected in the question that inevitably is raised about the status of the 'snake', which could be corrected by knowledge. The rope and the snake cannot both be real; neither can both be false. The latter cannot be real like the former, as it does not stand out, but is cancelled. Neither can it be unreal, because it presents itself *de facto*. It is therefore explicated as a being that nevertheless is an appearance: it is a being that cannot be determined either as what is or as what is not. It is an indeterminable appearance.

The Vedāntic analysis of error seeks to isolate the element of 'appearance of one thing as having the attribute of another' as the phenomenological ingredient in all rival theories of error. Error arises, one may generalize, because of the failure to discriminate. Alternately, it may be explained as the outcome of an act of commission consisting in fictitious assumptions in a locus of the attributes that are contrary to the attributes of that locus. In whatever way one theorizes, there is the experiential denominator common to them that cannot be gainsaid. It is the implicit acknowledgment of the appearance of one thing as being of the nature of another thing. Such, in short, is the Vedāntic methodological thesis of error cognition, namely, a cognition not of the real but of what is not determinable as real.

This Vedāntic method is presupposed in the commentaries of the teachers of the tradition who examine rival theories and principles of knowledge with great polemical vigor. But it may be noted here that the scope of this analysis is not thematized as a method as such or extended to the application of the issues of logic or psychology or other sciences. It is in relation to these areas that the phenomenological method, as it is developed in the west, has been utilized. The method under consideration as part of Vedāntic analysis is spelled out more as a hermeneutical principle than as a method that illumines the different areas of knowledge and experience. As a hermeneutical method it is used in the service of assessing the relative weight of the seemingly conflicting verbalizations of experiences at the source of Vedānta, at the hands of its principal founder, Śaṃkara. Śaṃkara uses this method, but he disavows that it is his own invention. Nevertheless, it makes him and his exegesis of the principal text through its use, perhaps the most controversial figure on the Indian philosophical scene. The method, as we shall see, is intrinsic to Advaita itself, as a form of experience and its self-articulation. This is the method, in technical language, of 'initial superimposition and subsequent sublation." This method exemplifies what may most aptly be described as a phenomenological attitude, in the sense of probing or uncovering the deeper layers of experience as the implications of experience.

The use of this method by Śaṃkara, as both a hermeneutical principle and also as expounding the heart of Advaita as experience, is a long story and is spread over all of his writings. What is attempted here is an oversimplified sketch of it, mainly in support of the claim that it reflects what is herein described as a phenomenological method. In general, the Vedānta texts purporting to explain the nature of Brahman use the language of paradox: they derive the world from Brahman as its cause but then negate the world in Brahman. The elaborate discussion of cosmology does not have the intention of providing a creation theory explaining the coming to be of the world. Truly speaking, says Śaṃkara, they seek to establish an ultimate reality that is nondual. In a seemingly cosmological tenor the world is derived from Brahman as the creation or manifestation thereof. This created or manifested world, however, is subject to negation when Brahman is described as 'not this, not this'.[7] The negation of the world empirically experienced in Brahman, on the surface, may imply that it exists outside Brahman. Therefore, Brahman is first described as the source of the world, that from which it comes, on which it rests, and into which it resolves. This is done, however, to show that the world has no reality apart from the reality of Brahman. Although this is stated in cosmological and metaphysical terms, the object here is progressively to isolate and distinguish a new dimension of one's present experience, called pure consciousness. This is done through a process of deepening of reflection.

In other words, the method used purports to isolate an enduring but imperceptible dimension of experience itself through an analysis of that experience. To explain it any other way, as, for example, that it is an expression of distrust both in the universe disclosed through sense perception and of an urge for transcendence, is to miss the point. It is to overlook the significance that is intrinsic to the method of analysis of experience coming to understand itself. A quest for transcendence of being it surely is, but what is of significance here is how the quest itself is encountered. The quest arises in an answer to a requirement from within an inspection of experience.

Using the term 'phenomenology' to describe a method that has a central use in Advaita Vedānta, however, should not obscure the ontological commitment that defines the enterprise of Vedānta. Ontology, broadly speaking, is a concern for that which is and a probing of its nature. Vedānta is expressly ontological[8] in the sense that being alone, or being itself—labeled as Brahman—is the Alpha or the Omega. Being defines *gnosis* or true knowledge, differentiating it not only from all other noncognitive activities but also from cognitive activities of the discursive and the relational kinds. Such activities masquerade as true knowledge. *Gnosis* stands differentiated from them, not from a phenomenological point of view, as just one component of the structure of given experience, but ontologically, belonging to a different kind. In the language of Śaṃkara, *gnosis* is reality-dependent. He uses a method of immanent analysis of experience to uncover reality. The goal of my study is to expound this method. But the presupposition of this analysis is that cognitivity derives its essence from the reality of the cognized content. 'I know X but I do not know if X exists' will be a contradiction.

What is described here as the phenomenological approach of Vedānta has a feature distinctive to it, namely, its approach from within the sphere of negation. The approach through critical analysis of experience, characteristic of Vedānta, is an aspect of the *via negativa*. It is not a case of focusing on experience with a view to isolate from their concrete settings structures that are perceived as constants; not a case, in other words, of abstracting a form from the content. The Vedānta approach from within negation rather aims at isolating an element that was previously fused in experience and focusing one's attention on it. The language of form and content may be used as a kind of analogy. In a given situation, at the pre-discriminative level, neither form nor content stand distinguished; they are given as a homogenous mass. When subtler forms progressively unfold, every lower stage is understood as one in which these forms had stood indiscriminatedly fused.[9]

The body, for example, may be considered as just one object among others in space and time before the process of discrimination begins. But when discrimination sets in, the body stands isolated from objects in general. Phenomenologically looking at it from inside, the body is not simply an object in space and time but a means by which we relate to objects in space and time. One may therefore say that the body is relatively more subjective than other objects. If the world is an object of experience to a subject that experiences it, then the body, as the medium of this experience, is on the side of the subject that uses it as a means. What is meant by saying that it is on the side of the subject is that even though the body, outwardly considered like any other object, is a part of the world, nevertheless as 'me' or 'you' it transcends the world. Anything that is called 'this' is so only in relation to my body, and so phenomenologically speaking, the body is subjective relative to everything. This is what lends plausibility to one's body and the senses, which are functions of the body, to be considered as the prime candidate for one's self-identity.

The mind and mental states may likewise be seen to be more subjective than the body and bodily functions. How does discrimination separate the mind from body? Here again, one comes to recognize through an inner inspection of experience that mind has a special status in relation to the body. To state it differently, it is with the help of mind that we are able to objectify the body as a given 'this'. Mind, in this context, is more inward than the body and the senses. Mind and the mental functions have a subjectivity that is freer than that of the body and the senses, just as the body and the senses have more subjectivity and freedom than other objects.[10]

Likewise, mental functions in turn can be objectified in relation to something that is more inward and freer, mind considered in isolation from its functions: "These states are mental, but they are objects at the same time. Felt, in themselves, as relatively more subjective than either body or physical things, they are.... Mental states which are primary objects are said to be objects to introspection, and other states which are non-cognitive—feelings and wills, for example—are objects for mental perception."[11] The mental functions, in other words, can themselves be objectified as 'what are experienced' (*dṛśyam*), as when we say 'I am happy' or 'I am unhappy'. Happiness or unhappiness, although immediately experienced, are, truly speaking, objectifications of experience. Could we extend this analysis and speak of a possibly more inward dimension, to which mind itself, as well as its states, is an object? The Vedāntic answer to this question is in the affirmative. It says not only that it is possible but that it can be experientially (i.e., in its most meditative reaches), isolated from mind and mental functions.

It is of interest to note here that the act of isolating itself has to be performed by the operations of mind. Somewhere along the line we have to replace the language of content becoming an object with the language of manifestation. This procedure leads to the witness-consciousness (*sākṣin*),[12] and finally to consciousness itself. What thus comes last in the order of knowing is not last in the order of being.[13] It has been present and functioning from the very beginning. In Vedānta such an analysis does not amount to an act of abstracting, like abstracting colorless from color, but is of the kind in which a factor previously unattended becomes the focus of attention. What was previously fused through ignorance is now distinguished with clarity. The factor of ignorance itself thus emerges into the orbit of thematic attention.

The Emergence of Vedānta as a Theory of Knowledge

The term 'Vedānta' in its original sense refers to a feature or aspect of the Vedic scriptures in either a trivial or in a deeper sense. The suffix in the compound literally means 'end' (*anta*); Vedānta means that the terminal section of the Veda, and in this sense Vedānta simply means the Upaniṣadic texts are the final portions of the composition of the Vedas as a recital and as a document. One may compare this trivial sense of the term with the sense that is attached to the label *metaphysics* that came to be applied to a book of Aristotle. The more significant sense of the term 'Vedānta' derives from understanding 'end' as conclusion and goal. Vedānta carries the sense of the intended goal and destiny of the Vedas. It is as if the entire corpus of the Vedas is intended to lead one, spiritually speaking, into a discussion of the self and a meditative-reflective inquiry into the nature of being: the being that alone was in the beginning, one only, without a second.[14]

Vedānta as a philosophy is crystallized in this original sense as interpretive knowledge of being (*sadvidyā*). *Sat* is the Upaniṣadic expression for being. It is of interest to note that, in this most initial sense of Vedānta as philosophy, according to the self-understanding of the Upaniṣads, the issue of knowing is integral to the nature of being. The teaching about being, referred to above, is introduced as an answer to the question about teaching "whereby what has not been heard of becomes heard, what has not been thought of becomes thought, what has not been understood becomes understood."[15] It should be noted that the question about the teaching in this context is not simply a case of hearing or thinking or understanding of something, but of a 'hearing' of something in which what is not heard becomes heard, what is not thought is thought, and the un-understood becomes understood. The intertwining of knowledge and being that has been mentioned in this context must not be lost from sight.

Inquiry into the nature of knowing precedes that of being in the order of the enterprise of discovering it, although in the order of the way things are, being precedes knowing. The Upaniṣadic affirmation that the knower of Brahman becomes Brahman formulates the paradox, leaving it open for two interpretations. In a straightforward sense, it simply means that knowing results in a realization of being. But it lends itself to being understood the other way around as well; that is, one who becomes Brahman itself, alone is the knower of Brahman. Knowledge is identity with Brahman. The epistemological priority in Vedānta nevertheless should not be underrated. It is what invests the system with its unique feature as a cognitive discipline.

This epistemological priority in Vedānta should, however, be understood as different from the precedence that came to be accorded to epistemology as a separate and autonomous discipline in modern western philosophy.[16] For Indian philosophy, especially in its crystallization as Vedānta, being is the transcendental reality, and is accordingly the condition of the possibility of knowledge. Being thus comes first as it logically precedes all knowing, although from the standpoint of the knower, knowledge comes first. It is the process of knowing and its inner dynamics that discloses its ontological ground. It is through an introspection of knowing or the perceiving process that one also comes to 'perceive' the revelatory light that renders possible the very perceiving process. The self-effulgent, self-luminous light (*cit*) is also the unlapsable, never varying ground of being (*sat*). Vedānta, in its original sense of revelation, discloses the reality of being, not as a mere datum to be accepted as the starting point but as the solution implied in the question: 'What is that which, when known, everything else becomes known?'[17]

The evolution and growth of Vedānta as a doctrine that became crystallized as a noetic discipline by bringing to the forefront the implications of the question raised above may be set forth briefly. From its original form, as the name for a significant layer of what is accepted as the scripture, embodying 'discourse' or 'discussion' about the nature of being as nondual, the term 'Vedānta' slowly and imperceptibly extended to apply to a meditative inquiry into what is being discoursed about as the Vedānta. The term, in other words, comes to be applied to what presents itself as the exegesis of Vedānta in the original sense. Such exegesis, being called forth to make intelligible the paradoxical statements of the Upaniṣads about the nature of being, marks the earliest denoted sense of the term 'Vedānta' (first level, 1000 to 500 B.C.E.). Inquiry into the Vedānta, as the new meaning of Vedānta, also incidentally names the most influential, the most well-known, and the most diverse of the philosophical traditions of India.

The second level (1st century C.E.) of Vedānta is a continuation of this spirit of inquiry and implies a program, a striving for a system of knowledge internally coherent and logically defensible against positions or perspectives that are at variance with it. At this level, Vedānta still remains a comprehensive theory of being, including and transcending similar theories of being that are either imperfectly derived from an understanding of the scriptures or elaborated outside the framework of the scriptures.

Vedānta as represented at this level of evolution is outlined in the *Vedāntasūtras* of Bādarāyaṇa, also known as *Brahmasūtras.* It was a complex development, open-ended, indecisive, and comprised of vague statements harboring within it many seeds of discussion. But it affirms without equivocation a monistic view, interpreting being as 'one only, nondual' literally and without entailing negation of any kind. It simply accepts the two views of being as indeterminate pure consciousness and as determinate and personal. It asserts that being as consciousness develops itself into the world of experience and yet remains transcendent. The importance of the problem of knowing does not emerge as integral to the quest at this level.

It is only at the third level (7th to 8th century C.E.) of the evolution of Vedānta, represented by Gauḍapāda and Śaṃkara, that the potential epistemological dimension unfolds. The role and influence of philosophical Buddhism with its deontological emphasis on Vedānta becomes apparent. Although both Gauḍapāda and Śaṃkara formulate theories of appearance, Śaṃkara more self-consciously makes it a necessary preliminary to an inquiry into the nature of Brahman. Vedānta as philosophy at this level moves beyond its earlier monistic and pantheistic vision of being to a truly nondualistic one. Brahman is undifferentiated being, the nonpersonal ground of being.

If such is the nature of reality corresponding to and meant by the term 'Brahman', then Vedānta is confronted with the fact that we do not realize Brahman, so conceived, in our normal, rational, sense-based consciousness. What is the relation, then, that obtains between Brahman, the nondual being, and the world of multiplicity? Again, Vedānta is confronted with the problem of how may Brahman, undifferentiated and nonpersonal consciousness, be known? If Brahman is unknowable by means of ordinary conceptual-perceptual knowing, by what other means of knowledge is it known?

The more specific epistemological questions that are bequeathed to Vedānta at this level concern the means by which knowledge is validated. How does valid perceptual knowledge stand differentiated from an erroneous perception? How does valid perceptual knowledge allow room for error? The answer to all these issues is embodied in the theory of appearance and that of a primordial superimposition of the real upon the nonreal that spearheads the domain of appearance.

At this point, however, we must keep in mind that Śaṃkara's 'notorious' diversion of interest and attention to the negative side of being is only a pedagogical device (in our language a phenomenological ploy), and he balances this novel epistemological requirement with a more positive theory of being, which admittedly represents the heart and essence of Vedānta. The epistemological preamble of Śaṃkara, seemingly a detour, is a response to a requirement to approach the question from within the vantage point of experience. The attempt does not mark a failure of nerve, or disenchantment with a positive theory of being, but rather its opposite. It is an attempt to secure a deeper foundation to it by relating it to the existential nature of the inquirer.

The situation changes slightly when we go to the fourth and final level (8th to 17th centuries C.E.) of the evolution of Vedānta. At this level, which may be called 'later Vedānta', the theory of appearance, that is, the sphere of nescience, and of those aspects of cognitive experience that typify the nature of appearance, namely, the false, become more central, and considerations of Brahman themselves tend to be relegated to the background. Not that Brahman as pure consciousness is ignored, but rather it is approached obliquely as the ground, as well as the object, of the covering nescience. This shift of interest can be attributed to the polemics of non-Vedānta schools, which, on the basis of the undisputed givenness of the experience of the world of differentiation and duality, question the viability of the theory of appearance. Vedānta thus becomes exercised on epistemological grounds to combat the theory of experience to which the world of duality and plurality is allegedly disclosed.

The polemics of non-Vedānta schools, seek to vindicate the experience of a world of difference and duality in defiance of the claims of Advaita or nondualism. The chief advocate of the point of view from which these non-Vedānta schools draw their material for defending the positions from the onslaughts of nondualistic analysis is the logical school of Indian philosophy called Nyāya.[18] This school, which also has a history stretching back to the early Common Era, develops a new and philosophically sophisticated position under the caption of Navya-Nyāya, 'the new logic'. It is a kind of counterblast to the nondualistic thesis. The Naiyāyikas maintain that whatever is known has or must have a well-defined existence. The Vedānta response to the Nyāya takes two forms. A destructive response, trying to prove that all that is known is indefinable, nonreal, and has being, but only of pragmatic significance, recalls the destructive dialectic of the great Buddhist scholar Nāgārjuna of the first century C.E.[19] The best known exponent of such a response is Śrī Harṣa of the eleventh century,[20] who is sometimes acclaimed by scholars as the philosophical successor to Nāgārjuna. The second strategy is that of diffusing the realist's perspective on knowledge and experience by taking a more positive stand, and even participating in the realist's discourse, but ultimately with the object of undercutting realism. The Nyāya definitions and views are criticized and used as providing the occasions for establishing positive definitions of their own. Epistemological questions thus come to assume an important position in the Vedānta literature of their times, countering the epistemological position of the Nyāya.

The Vedāntic text that is chosen here for a detailed notice, particularly of its section on perception, belongs to this class. Acclaimed both by the tradition, as well as by those outside it, as perhaps embodying the most precise summary of Advaitic epistemology is *Vedānta Paribhāṣā* (henceforth abbreviated as *VP*).[21] It has an admirable focus on the theory of knowledge in Vedānta and especially on the centrality of perception. All the important problems of Advaita philosophy that overlap between epistemology and ontology and ethics and religion, such as the nature of the means of knowledge and the grades of reality and/or nonreality, are lucidly explained and analyzed. The nature of reality, God, self, and the world, their relationship to individual ignorance (*avidyā*), cosmic ignorance (*māyā*), and liberation (*mokṣa*) as well as the means to liberation are discussed with great insight. The book is also unique for using the language of Nyāya, while explaining the Advaita theory of knowledge. In the case of the writings of its contemporaries and predecessors, we find in-depth discussions of logical problems carried on with great skill and dialectical power, but they make no attempt to give a systematic exposition of Advaita epistemology. The author of *VP* was one of a very small number who, using the language of Nyāya, succeeded in giving an epistemological twist to the conclusions of Advaita.

Dharmarāja Adhvarīndra, the author of the text *VP*, was a scholar in his own right, of proved worth in the traditions of Nyāya as well as Vedānta. Hailing from South India, the author probably lived and wrote *VP* around the seventeenth century. He was a contemporary of some of the greatest thinkers of the Advaita tradition.

The text has been published several times with many commentaries. The most important of them is entitled *Śikhāmaṇi* (henceforth abbreviated as *SM*), and is by the author's son.[22] Mention also must be made of the commentary *Āśubodhinī* (henceforth cited as *AB*).[23] Both of these commentaries are drawn upon by the document mentioned below. The text *VP* has been the subject of several commentaries, but the most important commentary in Sanskrit in the twentieth century is *Paribhāṣā Prakāśikā* (hereafter abbreviated as *PP*) of Śrī Anantakṛṣṇa Śāstrī, a renowned Advaitic scholar.[24] The distinction of *PP* lies in its resolute attempt to interpret the text from within the standpoint of the Advaita tradition instead of sliding into the Nyāya camp, a temptation many of the earlier commentators of the text could not resist. Of significance also is the consideration that *PP* explores the different schools of Advaita in support of the views of the text of *VP*. This preeminence makes it the basis of my exegetical analysis attempted in this book.

The Centrality of Perception in the Scheme of *pramāṇa*-s

Perception is the name for valid knowledge (*pramiti)* and at the same time is also the means or the method of acquiring such knowledge. In the latter sense of the term it is called *pramāṇa* and it can readily be seen how central or foundational perception is to all other means or methods of acquiring knowledge, such as inference, comparison, and verbal testimony. Indian philosophical thought, particularly in its theory of knowledge, deals with the following questions: what is the nature of the means of valid knowledge (*pramāṇa*-s), the resulting perceptual cognition (*pramiti)*, the cognizer (*pramātā*), and the object of cognition (*prameya*)? These related notions in a sense derive their meaning from the more basic and pervasive use of the first of the four terms, *pramāṇa*-s, which has been articulated in the Indian philosophical systems again in terms of four basic questions: the specific nature of *pramāṇa*-s, their object, the number, and the result they lead to. There is no unanimity with regard to the conception of *pramāṇa*-s , and even at the risk of oversimplification, one might say that all the varieties and doctrines of Indian philosophy are mirrored in the diversity of interpretations of the precise sense and the nature of *pramāṇa*-s. There is, however, a consensus about the use of the term understood as a determinate sort of means, technically called *karaṇa*, which leads to or serves as an instrument of right knowledge. What is the proper candidate for the role of *karaṇa* has been the subject of endless debates: Is it a sense organ or is it knowledge itself leading to another knowledge? This, however, is to anticipate what is to follow.

The conception of perception, it was observed earlier, carries the sense of the most fundamental *pramāṇa,* in the sense that all other *pramāṇa*-s are based on it. The Indian materialists,[25] who are also admitted to the fellowship of philosophers in the sense in which philosophy has been explained earlier, deny in the name of positivism the validity of inference and of all other means of knowledge. Their point of view amounts to questioning, a strictly cognitive feasibility of moving from the known to the unknown. Their critique of all other *pramāṇa*-s is a vindication of the primacy of perception as a means of knowledge.

Perception is also central in the scheme of *pramāṇa*-s in a much deeper sense. It is the presupposition of all other *pramāṇa*-s, not merely genetically in the sense that the latter are based on the knowledge derived from perception, but also morphologically. Perception represents a structure that overlaps into all other means of knowledge. It is the paradigm of nonmediate knowledge, while also being intrinsic to mediate knowledge.

The issue before us is: How is perception to be defined consistently with its central place in the scheme? The Advaitins define perception as immediacy of consciousness. It is not a product of the conjunction of a sense organ and its object. The definition proposed by the Advaitin, who thematizes perception, is striking. Quite frankly, and without much ado, he maintains that perception is simply immediacy of consciousness, perception not as a general name for valid knowledge, but as a *pramāṇa* in the epistemologically determinate sense of the term. In other words, perception is immediate knowledge which is not mediated by any instrument. The senses have to operate, of course, but to provide avenues of manifestation for consciousness, and not to bring into existence anew a knowledge-occurrence. The senses are only a more internalized and relatively less variable set of instruments like the external accessories; for example, optical lens, light, and so on. They do not generate or produce perception. Consciousness needs avenues to manifest the world, because consciousness is shrouded under the veil of ignorance. The perceptual mechanism, the sensory complex as well as the outer accessories merely facilitate, in a partial and limited manner, in the removal of the shroud. The resulting knowledge, although partial and limited, is nonetheless immediate, like the illumination of light. The association of perception with sense-stimulation induced by the object undoubtedly is necessary, but in a trivial sense. From the standpoint of consciousness, however, it is more accidental than essential, more of a limitation than a defining characteristic.

The most interesting aspect of the treatment of perception in Advaita is its fundamental insight, reflected in its recognition of the distinction between two sets of facts: perception as valid perceptual knowledge-event, and valid perceptual knowledge itself. The two are to be conceptually distinguished even though, ontologically speaking, they are one and the same. Valid perceptual knowledge has been defined unequivocally in the Upaniṣads as consciousness that is direct and immediate. This serves as a clear mandate for epistemology, and therefore it is not surprising that even a highly discursive treatment of the subject, such as the one given in *VP*, begins with a preamble citing the abovementioned Upaniṣadic text.

Although according to the general theory of *pramāṇa*-s knowledge and methods of knowing are recognized as interrelated, in Advaita the interrelationship ultimately collapses into identity. Knowledge and the means of knowledge are one. Knowledge here stands for cognition that is true, uncontradicted, and unfalsified. False knowledge, or 'falsity', itself is a contradiction in terms. However, true knowledge, which is uncontradicted in this context, points to the original structure of consciousness in its immediacy; it serves as the evidential basis of knowledge and only derivatively refers to a particular instance of cognitive act that can be either true or false. When *VP* speaks of the instruments of valid knowledge, such as perception, it refers to the cognitive act that is phenomenally given and whose truth or falsity is a matter of verification through experience.

One must not forget, however, that the perception of a pitcher is still pure consciousness reflected in or defined by a mental mode. It is asked: how can the perception of a pitcher claim to be valid knowledge as reflecting pure consciousness, when such a perception is patently contradicted by another perception that 'it is not a pitcher'? It is answered by saying that such a contradiction exists only within the twilight zone of relative existence, a state when one, being unaware of one's true identity as pure consciousness, falsely identifies with the 'I' as the cognizing subject. But when one experiences pure consciousness, perception, *qua* a cognitive act as structured through reference to objects, stands contradicted. Pure consciousness is experienced through an abrogation of the particular and contingent nature intrinsic to any cognitive act.

Earlier we made a distinction between a state of relative existence, when one is oblivious to one's identity with pure consciousness, and a state when one experiences pure consciousness. The peculiar standpoint of Advaita is that all modes of knowledge, including even perception, are empirical and relational; therefore they do not qualify literally as knowledge. The only virtues of perception are its self-transcending character and the help that it renders in making this distinction. The very posture of cognizership, underlying several empirical cognitions, carries the sense of the 'false'. What this means precisely will soon be explained. However, at this point we must keep in mind that its falsity derives from the relation that a cognizer bears to the witnessing consciousness in which the false is grounded. The relation that is constitutive of falsity, in the technical language of Advaita, is 'one of superimposition'.[26]

The conception of cognizership carries with it certain notions that make it generically different from the consciousness that plays the role of a witness in a cognitive relation. Let us first focus on the sense of cognition that is intrinsic to the idea of cognizership. The concept of a cognizer (*pramātā*) implies among other things that there is something to be cognized and that can be cognized. The functions of a cognizer are relational. A cognitive relation is nothing but the cognizer being related to the object of cognition. It is the latter circumstance that makes it possible for a cognition to be either true or false. Accordingly, a choice or preference is exercised in keeping with this distinction. The true-false distinction that is structural to a cognition is not only an awareness of difference but also implicitly an exercise of preference or choice. The true means 'I accept it' or 'I desire it', and the false implies its opposite.

One wonders whether such an understanding of cognition does justice to all known cognitive modes in our experience. Is there not implicit in this notion of cognizing or knowing as judgmental, a preunderstanding of knowing as simpler and more immediate? Is there not behind knowing something as true or false a simpler nonmodal, non-preferential knowing? If cognition is an exercise of choice between true and false, should not then the two alternatives be known before the choice is exercised? And, if yes, should not the alternatives be known simply and not as *either* true *or* false?

One may wonder whether a case for positing such a 'knowing behind knowing' can find confirmation from within our cognitive experience itself. Is it a theoretical construct that we use to explain a given set of data, or is it a part of the datum of experience itself calling only for a special kind of attention to be noticed? The Advaitins say 'yes' to the second alternative. Knowing behind knowing is a cumbersome way of explaining a simple cognitive relation that is ulterior to knowing as true or false. When we know pleasure or pain, and when we 'introspect' into our own cognitive states, the presence of such a simple, more ulterior cognitive relation is evident. By introspection here we do not mean, as explained earlier, psychological introspection that is on par with ordinary cognitions. The introspection which attests to the presence of a prototype cognitive relation is the one which reveals or manifests its 'object', in this case a cognitive state. In other words, a cognitive state itself is its object. It differs from a cognition in that it cannot itself be an object again to another external awareness.[27]

A more unequivocal instance of such a proto-cognitive relation as a commonplace of our cognitive life is the apprehension of an illusory object entailed in an erroneous cognition. This will be discussed at greater lengths, but what may be noted here is the approach that is uniquely characteristic of the Advaitin in his analysis of error. The object apprehended in an erroneous cognition is immediate (i.e., nonrelational, nonjudgmental), despite appearances to the contrary, and the seeming nature of the judgment in which such cognitions are often uncritically verbalized. The point to note here is that no process is involved in knowing, because consciousness as it were immediately possesses the object.

The conception of cognizership in cognition, we have observed, entails the exercise of choice among the known, in terms of an implicit norm. The norm itself, although implicit, is set up by the relationship of the mind and the body to the objects. The mind or the internal sense sets up the standard in terms of the requirements of the body. Those that can satisfy its requirements are called real. The object given in error, such as the illusory silver, although directly given, is nonreal because it does not satisfy this standard. From the standpoint of pure consciousness, the elevation of the accidental standpoint of the internal organ might appear quite arbitrary. In fact, pure consciousness does not represent a standpoint. To know is to be the thing. In cognizership, in contrast, what looks unjustifiable and arbitrary from the perspective of pure consciousness becomes the essential condition of the empirical and relational modes of knowledge. Only on the hypothesis of identification with the internal sense can the operation of perception as a means of knowledge be explained. What is in immediate contact with my body and senses is alone perceptual to me at that time. In empirical perception, what is produced as a result is perception as a cognitive relation, and the *karaṇa,* or the instrument, is the intuition of the witness-consciousness which possesses the object immediately and directly.

The general thesis that runs through all the detailed statements about perception that *VP* makes, which will be explained selectively in the sections that follow, is that without the lustre of pure consciousness, all objects, physical and mental, apparent and actual, merge in the darkness of nescience. Things are manifest in the universe through the light of consciousness, because everything shines through its radiance. It is through this light that the subject knows the object and the object becomes known to the subject. The cognizing subject and the object alike are manifested through its radiance. Where there is no consciousness, there is no manifestation of any kind. Strictly speaking, pure consciousness can know of no absence, as there is nothing else beside it. However, we must keep in mind that we are only referring to its expression as self-awareness, not to consciousness as such. It is in this sense that it is permissible to speak of the light of consciousness and a state of darkness where it is not manifest. Consciousness is what manifests all variations of empirical existence:

> As the morning sun lights up the stained glass of a memorial window, the multicoloured paintings that never appear in the darkness of night, immediately become vivid. The various forms and figures in different hues seem to be aglow. The blue sky, the fleecy clouds, the grey mountains, the trees and shrubs with green foliage, the sparkling streams, and green meadows, the dusky cottages, the yellow and red robed human forms—all come into full view. Each and every painted object appears distinct and manifest in its own way. But, as a matter-of-fact in and through the entire picture all that is manifest is the light of the sun. That shining, all else appears to shine. As the sunlight gets dim, the whole painting gets dim. With the disappearance of sunlight the painting vanishes. The very window is hardly noticeable in the absence of light.[28]

The analogy of physical light that makes things visible is very appropriate to indicate the nature of consciousness as revelation. Physical light is an apt model for understanding something appearing to be self-manifest. Everything else is manifest through it, and no other light is needed to manifest it. Nothing appears when the light goes out and the light shines through all that appears. However, it should not be overlooked that the physical light is not consciousness. The physical light cannot help where there is no manifestation of consciousness. It is true that nothing can be seen without external light, but external light only helps the eyes when they are associated with consciousness. When illumined by the light of consciousness, external light unveils things and objects. It is the light of consciousness, shining within sentient beings that illuminates things, including the light itself, as it approaches them through the vehicle of sense organs. This self-effulgent omnipresent consciousness is the light of all lights.

The Identity of Cognition and Content: The Criterion of Perceptuality in *Vedānta Paribhāṣā*

Pure consciousness, epistemologically speaking, involves non-otherness or the identity of cognition and content. This notion, as central for the phenomenology of perception, serves as the criterion for perceptibility. The central thesis of *VP* in this regard is its categorical affirmation of the identity of cognition and content entailed in the general idea of pure consciousness. The text contemplates this thesis in a manner that is unique to it, in respect of terminology, although not with regard to the idea. It is described as the identity of consciousness defined in terms of the object and the same but defined in terms of the subject, and consciousness defined by both the cognitive act (*vṛtti*)[29] and the content.[30]

The underlying idea behind this formulation is simple. Perceptual knowledge is direct, immediate apprehension. Knowledge is direct (i. e., perceptual), when the object is known directly. What makes the light immediately known is the immediacy of self-awareness. Perception rests on the object known here and now, that is to say, concurrently in space and time. This is what is meant by saying that it is marked by immediacy. It does not derive from the knowledge of anything else. One may contrast inference with perception in this regard. Inferential knowledge is not immediate: knowledge of fire on the distant hill derives from the knowledge of smoke and its invariable association with fire.

The self-awareness that is direct and intuitive is what accomplishes the immediacy of perception. The immediacy of perceptual cognition by which the content becomes direct to it may be explained in this way: the principle of consciousness is the only reality, and hence the object that presents itself as the content is not 'another' to consciousness existing in its own right, as maintained in systems like Sāṃkhya-Yoga, [31] Nyāya-Vaiśeṣika, and others. Accordingly the language that is used to describe a material object *qua* object of knowledge is 'the consciousness falsely limited by the superimposed object'—*viṣaya caitanya,* in the language of *VP*. In perceiving an external object, the alliance of the object with the percipient is effected by the outgoing mind. The mental modification which is a description of the outgoing mind unveils the object, becomes united with it, assuming as it were its form, and eventuating in its immediate cognition. In external perception what therefore serves as its direct cause is the cognitive mode of mind (*antaḥkaraṇa vṛtti*), which is technically to be distinguished from a 'mental state', which is used as a more generic term to describe all modifications of the mind, affective and conative, as well as cognitive. In terms of the underlying reality of consciousness, the language that is used in *VP* to refer to it is *antaḥ-karaṇa vṛttyavacchina caitanya,* that is, 'the consciousness falsely limited by the superimposed [cognitive] mental mode'. Insofar as this mental mode is accepted as the instrument that brings about knowledge in the sense of manifesting the hitherto nonmanifest object, it is also called 'the consciousness defined by the means of valid knowledge,' that is, *pramāṇa caitanya.*

As a mental modification, knowledge is directly cognized by the consciousness. Knowledge is intermediate between the subject consciousness (*jīva*) and the object known. With reference to consciousness, knowledge is invariably a direct cognition, but with reference to the object it can be either direct or indirect. If the object is indirectly known, the knowledge is indirect or mediate, as when one infers the existence of fire on the hill. Even here the knowledge is direct as far as the hill is concerned but indirect with regard to the fire. Although the hill has fire, *VP* maintains that even in such a case the cognition is strictly to the effect, 'I see the hill and infer the fire'. An external object is directly known when it is presented to the appropriate sense organ and is unified with the mental mode, which again unites it with the knowing self. Even the percipient ego becomes manifest through a mode of mind such as 'I'. In other words, the assertion that all knowledge or cognitions are either mediate or immediate acknowledges that a modification of the mind is entailed therein.

The coincidence of the mental mode with the object of cognition is the structural precondition of perceptual knowledge. In internal perception, where the objects are the states of the mind, the mind does not go out to assume the form of the object but naturally coincides with it. As the mental mode arises, it is revealed by the witness-consciousness and the percipient has the direct knowledge 'I am happy'. The perceptual judgment, 'I am happy', is an expression of a direct experience of the state of happiness because of the coincidence of the cognitive mode with it. It is important to remember that the coincidence of the cognitive mode in this context is really the coincidence of the consciousness underlying it, which is the fundamental reality acknowledged. Such then is the criterion of perceptuality, even of internal perceptions.

What distinguishes perceptual knowledge from nonperceptual modes of knowledge is that the mind in perception must be united with the object. To perceive an object means that the object is manifest to subject consciousness. In nonperceptual knowledge, such as inference, there is surely the involvement of the mental mode approximating the object, but there is no contact between the two. In internal perception, as has already been observed, the mental mode is invariably one with the object, which is a state of the mind. In visual and auditory perception, however, the mind conjoined with the sense organ reaches out to the object and becomes united therewith. The mind, conjoined with the sense organ, operates from the locus of the body as a function of the psycho-physical organism. In visual, auditory, and olfactory perceptions, however, their 'going out' is involved. In other forms of perceptual experiences (i.e., the gustatory and the tactile experiences), the mind and the senses function without the implication of going out.

Despite these differences in how perception arises, the common agreement is that perception is wholly presentative: the object must be present to the subject through the appropriate sense organ. There is no representative theory of perception. Even examples of complex perception cited as cases of complication by psychologists are not viewed as cases of perception partly presentative and partly representative. 'I *see* a fragrant sandalwood,' or 'snow appears cold', are examples not of internal visual perception but cases involving coordination of immediate and mediate modes of cognition. They are not instances of single perception.

We have seen that in the cognitive process involved in the perception of an object, the object becomes known through its association with the immediacy of subject consciousness. We also have observed that a mental mode affects such an association. The importance of the theory lies in the recognition that no object is cognizable without the manifestation of the consciousness underlying it. The objects, whether of internal or external perceptions, have no light of their own. They are shrouded, according to the doctrine and terminology of Advaita, in the darkness of ignorance. They are the transformations of *māyā* or *ajñāna*,[32] and must be understood cosmologically as the matrix of the phenomenal world, like the primordial nature of Sāṃkhya-Yoga as well as, in epistemological terms, darkness. It is the latter sense that is unique to Advaita. The Advaitins maintain that an object becomes manifest through the manifestation of consciousness that underlies it. This may be understood on the analogy of an object becoming visible. An object becoming visible implies the condition of the visibility of the light associated with the object: the object emerging from the shroud of its darkness. Manifestation of an object likewise means the manifestation of consciousness underlying it. No object can be perceived until the veil of *ajñāna* hiding it from the perceiver is withdrawn and the underlying consciousness becomes manifest. The veil of ignorance that hides the object before its perception is but a derivative phase of the nescience that is primal and cosmic (*mūlāvidyā*), the nescience of which the entire cosmos is a transformation. Nescience conceals Brahman, which also is its locus. But the individual, derivative, subsidiary, modes of nescience conceal or shroud each of its products. Withdrawing of individual modes of nescience is necessary for uncovering what is perceived by an individual so that the underlying consciousness may become manifest. This is what is meant by saying that in perception the object becomes manifest by the percipient-consciousness that reveals it (*pramātṛ caitanya*). In the absence of contact with the perceiving self, the object lies shrouded by ignorance. Nescience as unknowing and unknown envelops all things, living and nonliving. The perceptuality of the percipient and the perceptibility of the perceived object,[33] therefore, means the temporary removal or the withdrawal of the two aspects of nescience. What is unperceived remains veiled by nescience.

The mental mode conforms to its object in the way the sense organ does and removes the partitioning veil of nescience with reference to the perceiver. The mental mode conjoined with the particular sense organ removes the corresponding veil of nescience. It is with the aid of the organ concerned that the mind contacts anything physical. The important thing to add here is the conjoint functioning of the mind and the sense in effecting the connection between the percipient and the object perceived. The mind acts as a transparent foil for the reflected light of consciousness, and the mental mode, as the bearer of the radiance of light, coincides with the object and removes the veil of nescience that hides the object from the percipient. The consciousness that underlies the object, because of its manifestation by the transparent mental mode, reveals the object:

> A modification of Nescience called the Antaḥkaraṇa (inner organ) residing in the body and pervading it throughout, which is a product of the five subtle elements having therein at that time the predominance of the Sattwa (guṇa), being extremely clear like a mirror &c., having gone out (of the body) through the eyes &c. and pervaded the appropriate objects such as pot &c. assumes the forms of those individual objects like molten copper &c.[34]

The entire cognitive process of external visual perception consists of the following five steps:

1. The mind in contact with the organ of vision reaches out to the object and coincides with it.
2. The mental mode removes the veil of *ajñāna*, which conceals the object from the perceiver.
3. The consciousness that underlies the object, being manifested by the mental mode, illumines the object.
4. The mind effects a connection between the consciousness that underlies the object and the one that underlies the subject.
5. As a result, the subject perceives the object.

In other words, the consciousness that becomes manifest through the process thus described, namely, of the mental mode coinciding with the object, serves as the perceptual knowledge of the object. The resultant knowledge is what is technically called *pramiti.* It is useful here to restate the triple distinction made with respect to one self-identical consciousness in terms of mind and the mental mode involved in perception. Because mind is a transparent foil of consciousness, the consciousness that underlies it, although one and self-identical, finds expressions through the different parts of the mind in three different ways. We can make three functional divisions with respect to the mind: the mind that remains as a mere part of its locus, the body; the mind that connects to the object by extending from the body; and the mind that coincides with the object. Consciousness manifests in the first of its functions as the cognizer, in the second as the cognitive means, and in the third as the resulting cognition.

The account set forth thus far amounts to saying that the subject knows and the object is known because of pure consciousness. Mind functions as the instrument of knowledge because of the transmission of pure consciousness. The same consciousness shines through all the various parts of the mind and the mental modes through the knower, the object known, the knowledge, and the instrument of knowledge.

Although there is a difference of opinions among the Advaitins as to how an object becomes manifest to the subject, most of them recognize the twofold function of a mental mode entailed in an external perception: the removal of the veil of ignorance that hides the object from the subject, and the association between the subject consciousness and the object.[35] What has been given above is a general explanation of the Advaitic thesis of the conforming of cognition and content entailed in any cognitive process. A slightly modified account of the process involved in perception, however, is set forth in *VP* and explained and defended with great phenomenological support by the author of *PP*. The position stated above explains how the functioning of the modification of mind leads to perception by effecting a connection between consciousness underlying the sense object and the cognizer-consciousness. In this process there is no coinciding or identity; the perceiver dwells in the body apart from the object.

The view that is propounded in modification of the above account espouses a more literal coincidence of the object-consciousness and the cognizer-consciousness. The cognizing subject is here understood to be co-extensive with the mind, which is the limiting adjunct of the cognizing subject. In a perceptual process, the subject co-extensive with the mind and its modes extends itself to the object and coincides with it. This is possible because the consciousness limited by the mind is the cognizer-consciousness. The consciousness limited by the mental mode and the consciousness limited by the object become one or united. The oneness, however, should not be understood to mean coalescence insofar as the limiting adjunct of each endures.[36]

The author of the text himself explains exactly what this absence of difference means:

> The perceptuality of the content, like pitcher, etc. (is a case of) its nondifference from the cognizer (i.e., the perceiving subject).
>
> [Objection]: Now, how can a pitcher, and the like, be non-different from the consciousness conditioned by the internal organ, since it contradicts the experience of difference in 'I see this'?
>
> The answer is: What is termed nondifference from the cognizer does not mean [a literal] oneness or identity [with it], but rather not having any existence apart from that of the

> cognizer. Accordingly, since pitcher, and the like, are superimposed on the consciousness conditioned by them [pitcher and the like objects], the existence of the pitcher is the existence of the consciousness conditioned by the pitcher, because the superimposed objects do not have any independent existence apart from the reality of its substratum. And since the consciousness conditioned by the content is the content-consciousness in the manner described above, and since the cognizer-consciousness alone is the substratum of the pitcher, and the like, the existence of cognizer is itself the existence of pitcher, etc., and not any other, hence the immediacy of pitcher, etc., is as proved.[37]

The object not being different from the cognizer-consciousness means having no independent existence apart from that of the cognizer. Because objects such as pitchers are superimposed on the consciousness limited by them, their existence is indeed the existence of the consciousness associated with the objects. Superimposition implies that the existence of what is superimposed is not admitted to be something over and above that of its substratum. Because the consciousness associated with the object is not different from the consciousness associated with the subject, the latter consciousness alone is the substratum of objects, like the pitchers, and hence their existence is identical with the existence of the cognizer-consciousness. *VP* states very clearly that this is how, in the perception of a pitcher, the pitcher becomes 'immediate'.

PP analyzes the statement of *VP* given above and throws new light on it, particularly on *VP*'s assertion that the superimposed objects, by definition, cannot have any independent existence apart from the ground on which they are superimposed. *PP* provides a phenomenological interpretation and articulates it in terms of the identity of an object that has no independent existence apart from the ground on which it is superimposed.[38] The author of *PP* maintains that it must be understood more in the way that Brahman in the substratum of ignorance is understood, without any conflict with the cognitive expression, 'I am ignorant'. *PP*'s resolution of the latter is that both the internal organ and ignorance are superimposed on one and the same consciousness.

The illustration that is given to explain this phenomenon is that of the ether. The ether, a material substance like light and yet finer and more pervasive than light, presents itself as an ideal illustration of an understanding of the impartite nature of consciousness. The ether within a jar coincides with the ether in a hall without becoming identical. They are in a sense identical but allow themselves nevertheless to be distinguished because of the limiting adjuncts. It is as a result of the three forms of consciousness that the object becomes manifest to the subject, being unveiled by the mental mode transmitting the light of consciousness.

The process of perceptual knowledge is picturesquely described in *VP* against this setting of the identity of consciousness:

> Just as the water of a tank, having come out of an aperture, enters a number of fields through channels assuming like those [fields] a quadrangular or any other form, so also, the internal organ, which is characterized by light, goes out [of the body] through the door [sense] of sight, etc., and [after] reaching the location of the object, say a pitcher, is modified in the form of the objects like a pitcher. This modification [of the internal organ] is called a mental mode (*vṛtti*). In the case of inferential cognition, etc., however, there is no going out of the internal organ to the location of fire, since fire, etc. [other inferred objects], are not in contact with the sense of sight, etc. [other sense organs].
>
> Thus, in the case of perceptual cognitions such as 'this is a pitcher,' since the consciousness conditioned by the pitcher and the consciousness conditioned by the mental mode in the form of pitcher are located in one and the same place [outside the body], the consciousness conditioned by both [the object perceived and the *vṛtti*] is one. This is because the modification of the internal organ and the object like pitcher, though having the capacity of differentiation [between the consciousness conditioned by the *vṛtti* and the consciousness conditioned by the object], do not give rise to any difference on account of their being located in one and the same place [where the object exists]. For this very reason, the ether conditioned by a pitcher in a monastery is not different from the ether conditioned by a hall in the monastery [inspite of being two distinct limiting adjuncts].[39]

One may wonder about the language of realism used here and also about the example that is adduced. If a mental mode assumes the form of the object, it follows that the object exists before the mental mode's stretching to it and taking its form. We observed earlier that the object as such does not exist except as superimposed on consciousness and as such falsely limiting it. The position taken by *VP* and elucidated at great length by *PP* exhibits great insight. The object that is expressed in awareness is expressed as a material object rather than the substratum on which it is superimposed. The consciousness defining the object as such does not stand as the object of awareness. Nescience in its cosmic aspect veils the substratum-consciousness through the false projection (*vikṣepa)* of the material object. Empirical knowledge cannot effect its removal. What it can remove is only the individual derivative form of nescience which, like darkness, has been hiding the consciousness of the particular object. The object becomes manifest through the removal of the temporary ignorance of the object accomplished by the mental mode. The mental mode, as illumined by consciousness, thus acts technically as the means of valid knowledge.

A general objection to the thesis of the manifestation of the object as nondifferent from consciousness may be raised at this juncture. If a pitcher is perceived as nondifferent from the cognizer-consciousness, why does not the cognizer have an experience such as 'I am a pitcher' instead of 'there is a pitcher'? The important thing to consider here, and to determine from a careful analysis of one's experience, is the exact nature of the mental modification of the 'I-ness'. The 'I' is a state of mind or the mental mode that is inevitably associated with the physical body. In the waking state, the perceiver of objects like pitchers always identifies himself/herself with his/her body and not with the mind. Consequently, he/she cognizes the pitcher located away from him/her as 'this'.

Moreover, as the author of *VP* clarifies, identity, from the epistemological perspective, does not mean 'oneness' in a numerical sense, but rather means having no independent existence apart from the underlying reality of the cognizer. *PP* clarifies it further. The perceptual evidence, as attested by the experience 'I see this' and not as 'I am this', assumes the existence of difference between the witness-consciousness and the object. The fundamental position of Advaita, when stated in ontological terms, is that objects, such as pitchers, do not exist in their own right. The 'existence' present in consciousness conditioned by the pitcher is superimposed upon the pitcher. This results in a false identity between the pitcher and the existence, irrespective of whether one views the status of the object pitcher in this way, or more simply, as the transformation of *māyā*, which the author of *PP* favors. The important point here is that there is identity between the pitcher and the consciousness conditioned by the pitcher.

Witness-Consciousness (*sākṣin*) : History and Evolution

As stated earlier, all the later theoretic developments of Advaita can be traced back to the Upaniṣads, which represent Vedānta in its original sense. The concept of *sākṣin,* whose morphology will be analyzed in the next section, is a case in point. Here an attempt will be made, even at the risk of what may seem like a digression or detour, to trace the evolution of the conceptual formulation of *sākṣin* and the growth and early crystallizations of the epistemological ideas associated with the notion of *sākṣin.*

The most important idea, which provides an ambiance to the epistemology of Vedānta, the horizon in which the play of the notion of *sākṣin* takes place, is the nondual character of reality. Reality in the ultimate sense is at once of the nature of being and consciousness. But it is also the reality of the empirically given world. The nondual nature of reality implies that empirical existence, indeed empiricality itself, has no reality of its own. Reality is the indwelling essence of everything that appears to be, inclusive of knowledge. The philosophical tradition of Vedānta explains this feature of nonduality in terms, as it were, of an initial involvement of the real in what is nonreal and a subsequent withdrawal or retracing of the real from the nonreal. Such involvement is addressed as a problem in the context of the epistemological question of knowledge. From the noetic perspective, being in the world is confrontation between what is present as an object (*viṣaya*) and that to which it is thus present (*viṣayī*). These are the objective and the subjective poles of a knowledge relation. Although appearing as two different sorts of entities with natures apparently opposed to each other, like light and darkness, they are essentially one and the same reality. The platform on which the two meet and make one relevant to the other is reality in the ultimate sense (Brahman). This is sought to be reached by the respective analysis of the knower and the known. But in the Advaita literature, as ancient as the Upaniṣads and as modern as *VP,* Brahman is approached through an analysis of the knower in relation to the known. In other words, it is realized through a transcendental analysis of knowledge and the conditions that make it possible.

What is distinctive of the epistemological approach is that the knower is not accorded the sole reality. The order of the known is also equally real. The general standpoint of Vedānta epistemology is that both the knower and the known in a knowledge relation are ascriptions of the same reality. The great insight of the Upaniṣads consists not in a simple assertion of a transcendent reality but of its nondual character. The reality to be known and the knower coalesce into one, that is, *ātman* is Brahman.

The epistemological inquiry then takes the form of an investigation into the nature of the ground on which all duality, including the duality of the knower and the known, is based. What is sought here as the basic epistemological principle is something that helps unearth at once the ground of the world of phenomena that is experienced and also the ground of the notion of 'I'. Such then is the notion of *sākṣin,* or the witness-consciousness, which stands behind what is known as well as what is unknown on the one side and also behind the 'knowing itself'.

The gradual evolution of the idea of *sākṣin*, in the precise sense, and the epistemololgical role assigned to it in later Vedāntic works like *VP*, is a subject of great interest in its own right. What is being attempted in this section is only a brief sketch that aims at highlighting key ideas associated with the concept in a few Upaniṣads. Scattered terms and concepts that approximate to the notion of *sākṣin* are found in the Upaniṣads. These concepts serve as a basis for the later development of the notion of *sākṣin.* The passage "that Brahman is direct (*sākṣāt*) and immediate (*aparokṣāt*)" is the one the text of *VP* cites at the very beginning as providing its point of departure for explaining perception.[40] The descriptive term used here for Brahman as direct may be taken as almost verbalizing *sākṣin* and also hinting at its nature as unconditional immediacy.

BU, from which the above citation was made, also contains the most detailed account of knowing and its presuppositions. It is not surprising that the Advaitins like Sureśvara and Madhusūdana adduce many texts from *BU* in support of the thesis of *sākṣin.* *BU* clearly states: "He entered in here, even to the finger-nail tips, as a razor would be hidden in a razor case, or fire in a fireholder. Him they see not...."[41] What this statement means to say, when translated into the epistemological key, is that the self is not knowable by any empirical means of knowledge. The self is also described as the all-knower, who, in turn, cannot be known by anything else. Again, the passage: "You could not see the seer of the seen, you could not hear the hearer of hearing, you could not understand the understander of understanding,"[42] is an anticipation of the theory that cognitive functions are apperceived by the seer, and the seer himself/herself in turn is not an object of a more ultimate awareness.

The most important and well-known section of *BU*, which foreshadows the concept of *sākṣin*, is the one that discourses on the self as its own light. It is interesting to note in this section that the question that is asked, in answer to which the above reply is given, takes the form, 'what light does a person here have'? It seems that 'light' in this context means not merely consciousness and its conditions in an abstract sense, but that in the light of which 'one sits, moves around, does his/her work, and returns.'[43] The epistemological question about the light of knowledge comprehends both the domains of ontology and ethics, as stated at the outset of this introduction.

In waking life objects are illuminated by the light from external sources, such as the sun, the moon, and fire. But in dreams and deep sleep this source of illumination, external as it is, is no longer available. And yet dreams and sleep represent subwakeful levels of experience, and objects are revealed in them as well as in the waking state, entailing the presence of light. What, then, is the real and invariable source of illumination in all these states? The answer that is given here is that the self is that which is not illuminated by anything else but still illuminates everything else. "As a great fish goes along both banks of a river, both the hither and the further, just so this person goes along both these conditions, the condition of sleeping and the condition of waking."[44] What is stated here is obvious. The self is what continues in the three states of waking, dreaming, and deep sleep and is therefore not identical with any of them. This is a clear description of the notion of self as witness standing behind everything that is known—known discursively in wakeful life, known dreamingly in dreams, and known as unknown in deep sleep—shining forth in its own light revealing eternally and continuously.

These three states of the self become the subject matter of the entire *Māṇḍūkya Upaniṣad* (hereafter cited as *MAU*). The self in these three states is different. These three states are taken to be three different forms of the embodied self. The self in itself *is* beyond these states (*turīya*). The wakeful self, the enjoyer of the gross objects, is the first 'part' (*pādam*) of Brahman. The dreaming self, the experiencer of dream contents, is the second 'part' of Brahman. The dreamless sleeper, in whom consciousness is dense and undifferentiated, like objects in darkness, is the third 'part' of Brahman.[45]

Gauḍapada, the celebrated predecessor of Śaṃkara, elaborates on the epistemological implication of the threefold distinction. What successively moves into the three spaces is independent of them all. The self in itself is pure and unrelated. The three spheres, or spaces, really stand for three states of the embodiment of the self. Even the dreamless sleeper is embodied in a primitive and undifferentiated condition: if one becomes freed from the embodiment in sleep, one would not be able to reawaken as 'I'. When it is without embodiment even primitively, the real, unconditional nature of the self becomes manifest.

The notion of the dreamless sleeper, the self of dreamless sleep in whom the notion of 'I' is absent as an explicit term, comes close to the idea of the witness-consciousness. The self in that state is not aware of itself, or of others, and is therefore shrouded by undifferentiated darkness in which duality is absorbed. Consciousness is intrinsically unaffected, even by this potential darkness, and is therefore described as the 'fourth'. But it is only the self in the third state that is epistemologically significant as containing the potentiality for a cognitive relation characteristic of wakeful life.

What is significant for understanding the cutting edge of *sākṣin*, as it is developed to explain perception, is not merely an understanding of the self in its true nature. The latter as such does not enter into a cognitive relation. It is the distinction between the self in its true nature and the self as immanent within empirical experience that really counts.

The important landmark in the evolution of the Vedāntic idea of knowledge, however, is represented in the rationalistic and the systematic writings of Śaṃkara. A reference was made to his celebrated theory of appearance (*avidyā*) and superimposition of the real upon the nonreal, which helps him to read coherence into the diverse philosophical teachings of the Upaniṣads. More relevant to the present context of understanding the *sākṣin* ideal and its evolution is Śaṃkara 's exegesis, especially in its attempt to situate *avidyā* in a nondualistic framework. It may be taken as setting the stage for later epistemological questions. What is distinctive of the general treatment of the subject in his hands is his constant reiteration of a relation of polarity and identity between self as pure consciousness and self as associated with ignorance. The terms 'Brahman', '*Īśvara*', and '*sākṣin*' are often used interchangeably as denoting the same awareness of the differences with respect to their 'sense'. In the very opening section of his *magnum opus*, the commentary on *Vedāntasūtras*, the idea of self experienced as immediate and inward (*pratyagātman*) is introduced.[46] Corporeality, sensory, and even psychic orientations are falsely ascribed to the self, which essentially is the witness-consciousness. 'I am fat', 'I am dumb', 'I am miserable' are all consequences of a primordial relation of a false ascription between two categories that are not only different but opposed to each other as radically as darkness and light.

The idea of self or *sākṣin* as what is not discovered empirically but experienced as residual through some transcendental reflection is also found in Śaṃkara's writings. In his commentary on *Praśna Upaniṣad* (henceforth cited as *PU*), Śaṃkara takes note of several theories of consciousness that strike a different note from the Advaita insistence on the foundational character of knowledge.[47] The most radical of the positions mentioned and criticized is the nihilistic position. The Advaita response to nihilism, although not the most significant refutation of rival theories, is still an appropriate preamble for any epistemological discourse. Śaṃkara criticizes nihilism on the ground that it is impossible to establish the absence of consciousness at any time, for the absence itself is an object of some form of consciousness. 'Anything that is known in any way emerges to consciousness, only as an object of knowledge.'[48] To deny this obvious fact would be a contradiction. "For the nonexistence of knowledge, being itself a knowable object, cannot be cognized unless there is knowledge of it."[49] What is especially significant in this seemingly trivial refutation of nihilism must be noted. Denial of things and denial of consciousness are two very different things. This is what is taken up in the Advaita writings in the form of the paradox of the denial of knowledge. Denial of things is conceivable, but denial of knowledge of things, without the denial itself claiming to be knowledge, is not conceivable. This understanding of consciousness as what remains, even when you negate it, accounts for the very certitude implied in any knowledge activity.

In his commentary on *Brahmasūtras*, Śaṃkara again interprets the discourse on the nature of the 'inner controller' (*antaryāmin*).[50] Who is this *antaryāmin*? It is the indwelling essence of the individual. That in which it resides and controls, however, does not know it. The *antaryāmin,* for example, resides in the sun, but the latter does not know it (*na veda*). Śaṃkara here understands the sun to symbolize the knower. What indwells and grounds the knower, the knower himself does not know.

The self in its inwardness appears unconscious during deep sleep, not because it is really absent but because it is unmanifest in the absence of objects to be revealed. It remains awake even while the sleeper sleeps and discloses the dream contents improvised by *avidyā*. In itself, however, it remains unknowable until it enters the 'cave' of the internal sense (*antaḥkaraṇa*).

The inward self strictly speaking cannot be evidenced by perception, as perception depends on the objects that are constituted by limiting adjuncts (*upādhi*). But it can be transcendentally apperceived as what is implied in the activity of perception. What is perceived in the I-consciousness is the limited self as reflected in the conditions of the intellect; for example, the 'I' in 'I am happy'. The inward self itself, however, is not really conditioned by the quality of happiness. It can be described as having qualities, but only as ascriptions. It is known as *dṛṣterdraṣṭā*, that is, 'the seer of seeing'. Śaṃkara explicates with clarity what this expression means when articulated as statements about the complexity of the function of knowing. At least two ideas seem to be conjoined here: the seeing self cannot itself be seen, and the seer of the seen itself is 'everseeing' with no break in its seeing function. In this respect it is different from the normal empirical kind of seeing of the objects that has gaps in between any two of its moments. The distinction thus drawn between the unseen seer of the seen as identical with selfhood, and the transient seer of the seen, which figures from waking to dreaming, is crucial, epistemologically speaking, to bridge the gaps between the two acts of seeing of the objects. The two kinds of seeing or the seer, however, are experienced as fused, and the first kind as witnessing the other kind of seeing, presents itself as its background. When the background of intrinsic seeing is associated with empirical seeing, the character of empiricality becomes ascribed to it.

The most interesting and intriguing proposal about consciousness and its evidence, distinctive of this earlier phase of the evolution of the concept of *sākṣin*, is the statement that consciousness cannot know its own absence. It is the light that never goes out. It is there all the time. One can readily see that it is there in all of our wakeful activities. With some imagination, we can understand it as also pervading dream awareness. The dream consciousness is also a kind of experience attesting to the presence of the illumination of some kind. But can one talk about illumination in the state that follows dreams? In deep sleep, apparently, there is no evidence for believing that there is consciousness. Logically, one may be involved in a contradiction in saying that consciousness can know its absence, and experientially one is unaware of consciousness during sleep.

The whole analysis of the deep sleep state, or of 'deep sleep ignorance' (*sauṣupta ajñānam*), is one of the interesting topics of early Advaita which provides a phenomenological basis for the construction of a theory of knowledge. The deep sleep state does not represent absence or disruption of experience. It is, itself, an experience. It is the experience of 'nothingness'. An experience of "nothing"' however, does not mean no experience. The person on awakening says, 'I slept happily and

I did not know anything'. This statement represents an experiential basis for construction and conceptualization of nescience in Advaita. There are apparently two conjunct assertions made in this statement, so that if you deny a part of it, you deny the whole of it. The statement, in other words, means 'I slept happily', such that 'I did not know anything'. Analysis of this statement reveals that it is based on the memory of deep sleep. On waking up we attest to our memory of the darkness of deep sleep. The observation that is of special interest here is that 'I did not know anything' is a memory judgment. Śaṃkara rejects the suggestion that it is an inference by demonstrating the contradictions that will arise in holding to such a position if one were to subject it to scrutiny. He appeals to the verdict of actual experience here: on waking up, we have an actual memory of our experience of the darkness of sleep, as 'I knew neither myself nor anything outside'. It is a case of recollection precisely because it is of a previous cognitive experience. All 'recalling' implies the identity of past and present experience. Memory glosses over the time gap in experience by appropriating a past experience to the present mode. Śaṃkara, claiming the status of memory for the above statement, implies the existence of an identical experience both during deep sleep and wakefulness. Memory is similar to perception, although technically, not itself a perception. It lacks an important ingredient of perception, namely, 'previous unknownness'. Memory is a cognitive activity, but distanced by one remove from cognition proper. It is not an immediate experience, but the recall of an immediate experience.

Śaṃkara's refusal to consider the retrospective experience of sleep as some kind of mediate cognition, like inferring the fire on the yonder hill on perceiving the smoke, is experientially plausible. A merely logical refutation of the hypothesis that it is some kind of inference (as is held by the classical Naiyāyikas)[51] is undertaken by the later Vedāntins like Madhusūdana. But Śaṃkara's insightful observations already adumbrate it, just as they do the general thesis of *sākṣin.*

Absence of knowledge during sleep may be inferred from the circumstance of the nonavailability of the necessary conditions of knowledge at hand. This position may be held for the reasons stated above. The Advaitins question such a reasoning: How is one to know the nonavailability of the conditions of knowledge during sleep? It might be replied that one infers that the senses did not function during sleep because of some other middle term like the 'felt refreshedness' of the senses after sleep or some other factor. The Advaitins would ask, on what basis can one establish a relation between the freshness of the senses and a previous nonfunctioning of the senses? This can be substantiated only by an appeal to an experience that knows them both. In other words, any attempt to prove it by another instance of mediate knowledge will be self-contradictory. My present knowledge cannot be used as a middle term to prove the absence of something in the past. Every suggested middle term has to be inferred with the help of some other middle term and this launches one into an *infinite regress*. The Advaitins maintain that on waking up there is a memory of the darkness of the deep sleep that would not be possible if darkness had not been the object of consciousness. The argument therefore seems to be circular: it is memory because it is an object of consciousness, and it is an object of consciousness because without it there cannot be any memory. The point that the Advaitins are trying to make, however, is this: one can only remember what has been experienced in the past. The presence of consciousness in sleep is as indubitable as its presence in the waking and dreaming states of consciousness. Accordingly, the Advaitins maintain that consciousness is an invariant in all three states. These states themselves are variant—that is, they come and go—but there is an invariant that spans these states. What is constantly present in these states, apperceiving even their sequence, is consciousness in its aspect as the witness. Senses, because they do not operate in the dreaming state, cannot be described as present in all three states. Mind or the ego-sense cannot be said to be present either, because there is no operation of mind in deep sleep. The ego-sense also does not function in deep sleep, because there is no awareness identifiable as 'I am having deep sleep now'. What is being thus argued amounts to a kind of transcendental proof, because one becomes retrospectively aware of the different states of the dream and sleep and of their difference from the waking state. It is only in the waking state that one knows about one's dream and sleep condition, things which cannot be known through introspection either in the state of dream or the state of sleep itself.

In the opening section of his commentary on the *Kena Upaniṣad*, Śaṃkara makes a distinction between pure consciousness, the ground of all other forms of knowledge, and the empirical cognition.[52] The first is the very essence of selfhood. It is transcendental, pure, and foundational. The second appears in relation to particular objects, subject to mutations and change, where one can speak of an increase and a decrease of knowledge and its variability as erroneous, doubtful, or true cognition. In keeping with the consensus of the Indian philosophical tradition, the Advaitins also analyze the empirical level of consciousness in terms of the distinction of knowledge, the knower, and the known. The Advaitins call the first of the two kinds herein distinguished *svarūpa jñāna* and the second one *vṛtti jñāna*.[53] *Svarūpa jñāna* is consciousness without differentiation of the knower, the known, and the knowledge. It is self-luminous. Self-luminosity means that a cognition does not depend on another cognition to be known.[54] If it is maintained that a supporting inference is necessary to sustain the validity of one's cognition, then one would find oneself in the absurd situation of making an infinite number of inferences, with each supporting inference requiring another one and so on *ad infinitum*:

> If even on the birth (appearance) of conception, the object thereof be not comprehended, until the purity of its cause has been the production of another conception from a new source; for until its purity has been ascertained, the conception would be equal to nothing (i.e., false). And this second conception too, would be true only on the ascertainment of the purity of its cause; and so on and on, there would be no limit (to conceptions upon conceptions).[55]

This amounts to saying that a cognition, although cognized, cannot itself be the fruit or the object of another act of cognition. Additionally, if the character of being self-revealed was not intrinsic to the nature of consciousness itself, if one did not have the knowledge of the cognition simultaneously with the illumination of the object, one would not be certain in the next moment that he actually cognized the object. In this respect, the Advaitins differ from the Buddhists, who only recognize cognitive states and not consciousness. These cognitive states for them are 'phosphorescent'. Although self-knowing, they are discrete and momentary. There is no apperception of them. Whatever apperception is required for the ordinary practical life is supplied by the links and their succession. All non-Buddhist philosophies of India, including pre-eminently Advaita, accept consciousness. But there is an important difference between the Advaita and the other non-Buddhist schools. The latter maintain that consciousness, like an object, must be known by another act of consciousness. Consciousness intrinsically is not unlike any object. The Advaitins, however, do not accept this interpretation as an adequate understanding of the notion of consciousness. Their thesis rests on an analysis of experience. Such an analysis, in effect, asserts that, at some stage of knowledge, its becoming aware of itself must yield to a recognition of its character as self-evident or self-luminous. The point emphasized by the Advaitins, while affirming the self-evident or self-luminous character of consciousness, is its immediacy. One can say that these assertions are implicit anticipations of the later notion of *sākṣin*.

To substantiate their theory of consciousness as immediacy, the Advaitins reject positions that are at variance with it. For example, they reject the Prābhākara view that consciousness is its own object, that consciousness indeed is subject as well as object rolled into one.[56] The Advaitins reject this and other theories on the ground that consciousness is unobjectifiable and therefore cannot be known objectively. Although not knowable objectively, it is not unknown. It is unconditionally immediate. The uniquely defining character of knowledge is that it has the capacity of immediate presentation without being an object of knowledge. This conception of consciousness is systematically developed by Citsukha, a later Advaitin, in the formula "what is fit to be described, despite its unknownness as unconditionally immediate."[57]

Although this appears like a later doctrine, it is not peculiar to later Vedānta. One finds it in Śaṃkara at many places, and in the *Kena Upaniṣad* itself, where it is stated that consciousness is different from the known as well as the unknown: it is known because it is immediate, and yet it is unknown in the sense that it can never become an object of knowledge, not even to itself. "I do not think that I know it well, nor do I think that I do not know it."[58] Again: "To whomsoever it is not known, to him it is known, to whomsoever it is known, he does not know."[59] Although the Advaitins analyze the experience of consciousness through the interposition of the discursive concept of 'knowledge by the mental mode', it is by enunciating the real and the ultimate nature of consciousness manifesting itself in the triple distinction of the knower, the known, and the knowledge that they seek a grounding for the phenomenon of knowledge.

The difficulty of explaining empirical knowledge, considered to be a knowledge-event, while also taking cognizance of the transcendental nature of consciousness was felt by the Sāṃkhya system, which perhaps represents the earliest speculative effort of the Indian philosophers. The changing form of the ego—what the Advaitins call 'knowledge through the mental mode'—has been called 'intellect' (*buddhi*) in Sāṃkhya. *Buddhi* is an evolute of what is in itself nonconscious, namely, 'nature' (*prakṛti*). It is rendered conscious through the reflection of pure consciousness that is from without nature. The Sāṃkhya also subscribes to a reflection theory; the reflector or the agent of reflection is *buddhi*. Intellect effects the light of consciousness. There is a similar reflection theory in Vedānta, which was later developed by the Vivaraṇa school under the rubric of 'reflection proto-type theory'. The difference between these theories is worth noting. According to Advaita Vedānta, what effects such a reflection is consciousness in its pure form, epitomized as God in the Vivaraṇa school. In other words, the initiative comes from the side of consciousness and not from the nonconscious, as is the case with the Sāṃkhya school. Pure consciousness, according to Sāṃkhya, is devoid of initiative and only provides the background of light in which the reflection takes place. The reflector, as stated earlier, is intellect, and the reflected is the individualized self. The earlier formulation of Advaita as nondualism, in the hands of Śaṃkara, is a reorientation and reconstruction through an in-depth critique of Sāṃkhya. God, or alternately, the witness-consciousness, while approximating to pure consciousness, also partakes of (freely one may say), the character of the nonconscious. Like Sāṃkhya, the Vedāntins believe that one cannot attribute change to pure consciousness, but only to the 'internal sense', which is an evolute of nescience. Empirical knowledge is a modification of the internal sense appearing in different forms through perception, inference, and so on. It is made conscious through the agency of the individual 'I', the cognizing subject, through a mutual superimposition of the self and not-self. Thus, while the dualism of Sāṃkhya was a major influence on the formulation of a nondualistic cognitive theory, it is also true that the theory in all its essentials is prefigured in the Upaniṣadic idea of 'that which is immediate and direct'.

Finally, to complete the account of the evolution of the notion of *sākṣin,* we must bring it to the more immediate context of ideas in which *VP* reformulates the questions of epistemology. This context is provided by *Pañcapādikā,*[60] Padampāda's most important work, the next landmark in the history of Advaita after Śaṃkara. In this work, the important theoretical issues pertaining to knowledge are raised for the first time. One can almost say that the surfacing of the epistemological interests of Advaita takes place only at this stage of development.[61] The most significant contribution of *Pañcapādikāvivaraṇa* is its understanding of *avidyā* and the inferential proof that Vivaraṇa provides in support of *avidyā,* with its distinct epistemological overtones. In this essay, we are not going into the scholastic details surrounding this inference. We are only concerned with the implications of such a conception of inference for a theory of knowledge. All knowledge takes place by destroying the 'previous unknownness'. This is the general assumption behind the attempt to provide a proof for *ajñāna.* What is meant by saying that an object is revealed in knowledge? Revelation does not imply that something is added to the object. Revelation only amounts to the removal of the cover. Such an understanding of knowledge is occasioned by the following considerations: If consciousness is universal and continuous, how does one account for statements such as, 'I do not know anything'? The Vivaraṇa text reiterates that consciousness, by its mere presence, does not amount to knowing an object, because it is under cover. Consciousness becomes a knower when it is associated with the 'I' sense (*ahaṃkāra*), and knowledge occurs when the veil is partially removed by the 'I' sense.

The question might be raised: Can one meaningfully speak of ignorance (nonknowledge) residing in consciousness (knowledge)? This is indeed the principal objection posed by the non-Advaitins against the Advaita theory of ignorance. The answer that Vivaraṇa proposes underscores the need for recognizing the category of the witness-consciousness. Ignorance co-exists with, without being cancelled by, consciousness. Consciousness in this aspect is called the witness-consciousness. The difference between the two consists in consciousness considered in itself, both with and without reference to *ajñāna*. The witness-consciousness itself remains uncovered, and everything remains manifested to it all the time. The known, and even the unknown, in some way or other, is revealed by the witness-consciousness. Its revelation knows of no temporal disruption. It follows then that the variations in knowledge are not due to the witness-consciousness, but due to the modification of the internal sense as 'I', which is a superimposition on it.

Knowing something from the perspective of the internal sense is not possible without having known the 'previous unknownness' of that something. What was previously unknown (i.e., under cover), now becomes uncovered (i.e., known), thanks to the knowing process initiated by the internal sense. The latter is called 'valid knowing' (*pramāṇa jñāna*), and its function is to destroy or dispel the cover under which the objects remain shrouded. The point that is made here by the Vivaraṇa school about the illusory object, in contradistinction to the actual object uncovered by *pramāṇa jñāna*, deserves our attention. For example, there is no 'previous unknownness' with respect to the illusory silver. The illusory silver did not exist before the moment of its illusory perception. Nor was there a cover for it. The illusory silver therefore is not an object of *pramāṇa jñāna*, but it is what is immediately manifested by the witness-consciousness without the interposition of 'valid knowing'. What happens in an erroneous cognition is explained in the Vivaraṇa tradition as follows: nescience is transformed in a twofold way with respect to the illusory silver; namely, as the object 'silver' and as the illusory perception of that silver. Both, it must be kept in mind, are manifested by the witness-consciousness. Here we must not lose sight of the fact that the witness-consciousness co-exists with nescience, while at the same time manifesting it.

The manifesting function of the witness-consciousness is present even in the waking experience, but remains obscured. In deep sleep, however, this function is unambiguous and nescience is directly experienced. As there is no 'I' consciousness in this stage, happiness (e.g., in the deep sleep stage), is not a mental mode but it is identical with the witness-consciousness.

Witness-Consciousness and Perception

The Advaita concept of the witness-consciousness (*sākṣin*) is the single most important postulate of the principle of revelation operative in experience, cognitive and noncognitive alike. A phenomenological exploration leads to the recovery of this principle as a necessary ingredient of the perceptual process and provides an interesting sidelight on the issue of perception. The text of *VP* is well aware of it, although it details the idea after enunciating the central thesis of the identity of consciousness as underlying the threefold aspects of the cognitive relation: the knower, the known, and the knowledge. The revelatory principle of the witness-consciousness is intrinsic to the notion of the empirical percipient, and yet is more fundamental than the merely empirical. We have already made a case for distinguishing a stratum of knowing that underlies and transcends all cases of knowledge, a knowing that is simpler than knowing something as true or false. It is a form of apprehension, direct, non-relational, nonpropositional, prejudgmental, and most characteristically, non-preferential, that is, nonevaluative, both in cognitive and practical affairs.

What has been described as providing an experiential basis for the notion of the witness-consciousness simply means that such a notion alone can do full justice to the data of experience. If a *sākṣin* were not admitted as the constant, inalienable background of the individual knower, all our usages would fall to the ground. All discourse, relating not only to the noncognitive spheres of existence like volition, feeling, and ego-sense, but also to the region of cognition itself, derives its justification from the idea of the witness-consciousness. The question of how internal phenomena as facts stand on a par with external objects has been answered with the help of the notion of the witness-consciousness.

In our account of perception, the factors of the cognizer, the cognized object, the cognition, and the sources of cognition were recognized. Opponents ask: can we not explain with the help of these factors alone perception directed toward internal phenomena as well as external objects? This is the standard approach of epistemological realists like the Naiyāyikas, to whose position we referred earlier. The Advaita critique of this position, both implied and expressed, was already indicated in connection with the investigation of the question of the meaning of *pramāṇa*-s. How is cognition as a fact to be known? To assume that it is known by an act of introspection, revealing original cognition, will create problems. Knowledge of one cognition will require an infinite number of cognitions. Aside from the logical difficulties connected with the infinite regress, there also is the problem of conceiving an infinite number of cognitions, operative either at the same or at different times. A simultaneous origin of many cognitions is contradictory to experience, which presents itself to inspection as only a temporal structure. To hold then that many cognitions may be admitted sequentially with regard for their temporal nature, one perishing and manifesting the succeeding one, also will not do. The difficulties inherent in the doctrine of momentariness[62] are well-known, and the Advaitins reject it on the evidential basis of consciousness as over-reaching and underlying discrete cognitions.

The Naiyāyikas, on the other hand, maintain that a cognition simply manifests the object. It does not manifest either the cognizer or the cognition itself. A cognition, although itself unknown, reveals the object. The Advaitins find such an understanding of cognition no different in principle from an understanding of the function of a sense organ, like the eye, because it makes a cognition no different from the senses. Like the senses, a cognition also becomes a revealer through another cognition. Cognition is not merely a means of manifestation, but is at once what is manifested and that by which something is manifested. The Nyāya theory does not therefore secure the principle of revelation for cognition.

The Advaitins maintain that in a cognition, when we cognize an object, the object is indeed manifested. However, it is not the only thing that is manifested. When we apprehend things, there is also an immediate self-awareness of our apprehension. When an object is known through a mental occurrent involving the function of sense, for example—in an external perception—the occurrent is also known by the knower without the mediation of another mental mode. The particular cognitions are not themselves literally self-aware but are grounded in a continuous principle of self-awareness.

The author of *VP* expresses the same point in a somewhat different language:

> It cannot be argued that if the internal organ and its attributes are admitted to be the contents of mental modes, there would be contradiction with the admission of their being known by the pure witness-consciousness. For, being cognized by the pure witness-consciousness alone does not consist in being the content of witness-consciousness without [the aid of corresponding] mental modes; rather it consists in being the contents of the witness-consciousness without [the functioning of] the well-accepted means of valid knowledge, like sense organs, inference, etc. [other *pramāṇas*].[63]

The mental states as well as the outgoing mental modes, subsumed under the expression mental occurrent, are not themselves self-aware but are revealed only by the witness-consciousness. This, however, should not be taken to imply that they are manifested by the witness-consciousness without the mediation of any mental mode, but rather that they are known without the functioning of the well-accepted means of valid knowledge, such as perception, inference, and so on. The mental occurrents that are entailed here, further contends the author of *VP*, are not fresh occurrents. They themselves are, thanks to the *sākṣin* , their own objects.[64]

So far we have discussed some of the experiential grounds that the Advaitins adduce against their opponents for admitting a revelatory principle of consciousness called the witness-consciousness, over and above the individual cognizer. Opponents raise a number of questions regarding the nature and essence of such a witness-consciousness: Is it the essence of a subject or an object? If the latter, it becomes a knowable entity and cannot serve as the principle of revelation. If the former, it must either be the individual self or Brahman. If it is the individual self, it becomes the cognizer and, if Brahman, it is simply another name for pure consciousness. The witness-consciousness, on the other hand, cannot be apprehended in empirical perceptual situations that belong to the sphere of *avidyā*. The Advaitins themselves state:

> Though the character of the 'Perceiver' (Witness) belongs to Brahman as conditioned by Nescience, yet 'Nescience' does not enter into the constitution of the 'Perceiver' (Witness) for the simple reason that Nescience is something totally devoid of consciousness (while the character of the 'Perceiver' is consciousness itself); in fact 'Nescience' forms a factor in that which is perceived or witnessed (the object cognised); in the same manner, though the character of the 'object' belongs to Brahman as conditioned by the Vritti, yet the Vritti does not enter into the constitution of the 'object'; for the simple reason that it could not form its own objective; in fact though not an 'object' itself, the Vritti imparts the 'objective' character to the Consciousness (of Brahman); and there can be nothing incongruous in this.[65]

The witness-consciousness is relevant only in reference to the world. How, then, can it also function as the revelatory function?[66]

The viability of the thesis of the witness-consciousness is brought out by the Advaitins against these objections through an analysis of the nature of erroneous cognitions. The question arises: Does 'thisness' in an erroneous experience of 'this is silver' belong to the shell or the silver? If it belongs to the silver, then the sublating cognition, 'this is not silver', cannot arise. In the sublating experience of silver, the thisness that belongs to the silver is also sublated. It cannot be argued that thisness pertains to the shell. If 'this' in 'this is silver' really referred to the shell, then thisness could not have been revealed along with the cognition of the illusory silver. What, then, is the solution? It is said, although thisness really belongs to the shell, it also appears with the illusory silver, because thisness is identified with the silver that is cognized instead of the shell. The same is the case with the nature of *sākṣin.*

Brahman is said to possess the *sākṣitva* of all objects (*sarva-sākṣin*). Although the essence of *sākṣin* is really pure consciousness, it also is identified with the individual cognizer, who in the epistemological situation is a cognizing subject. Pure consciousness, as the essence of the witness-consciousness, is enveloped by cosmic or primal ignorance. Cosmic nescience, however, is not a veil *really* hiding pure consciousness, but is, in a manner of speaking, eternally cancelled or sublated. When this fact is recognized, along with the realization on the part of *jīva* in the form 'I am Brahman', the *sākṣin* in its essence reverts to the original position of pure consciousness.[67]

The *sākṣin* is the principle of revelation and, to the extent that it reveals objects, it does not depend on either *antaḥkaraṇa* or *māyā.* It is the changeless element that does not cease to exist even in dreamless sleep, sleep, or swoon. Śaṃkara states:

> Just as a person who experiences a dream is never affected by the illusory nature of the dream vision, in as much as it does not persist during the conditions of deep sleep and wakefulness, even so, this one unchanging, constant and immediate witness of all the three conditions (viz. The Highest Self i.e. Brahma) is not affected by the three changing transmigratory conditions (of creation, preservation, and resorption).[68]

In the state of deep sleep, the mind is merged in nescience, but the ever present *sākṣin* is there, manifesting nescience and the inherent bliss of the self.

VP makes an important distinction in connection with the notion of the witness-consciousness, between individual-defining-consciousness (*jīvasākṣin*) and God-defining-consciousness (*Īśvarasākṣin*).[69] The individual and the witness are both forms of consciousness, although qualified in different ways:

> The internal organ is...by nature unconscious, *jaḍa*, but reflects the light of pure consciousness. Being itself unconscious, the internal organ is not capable in itself being *about* anything. So the relation between consciousness and internal organ is just that the internal organ residently qualifies consciousness, limiting it in such a way that it *constitutes* what we call the individual self. By contrast when we speak of an individual's self being aware of something or other, we are identifying that self not through its constitutive character—that particular internal organ—but rather through its experiences, the contents it 'witnesses,' and since these contents are actually the contents of consciousness *per se*, and not the contents of the internal organ which differentiates this self, the witnessing self is being identified through an *upādhi*, through an accidental rather than a resident feature of it.[70]

Thus *jīva* is the consciousness that is essentially tied to the intellect (*antaḥkaraṇa*). *Sākṣin*, however, is the eternally unchanged spectator of all the changes of the *jīva*. What comes within the experience of one witness-consciousness does not necessarily come within the experience of another witness-consciousness. If this is not accepted, then we would have to admit that what is cognized by one person is recollected by another person.[71] This, however, is not the case. In other words, the individual-defining consciousness is different in each individual.

The point of distinction between *jīva* and *sākṣin* is very crucial for an adequate understanding of the Advaitic theory of knowledge. *Sākṣin* stands for the pure element of awareness: it is all knowing; it is self-luminous. Its presence is co-eval with its revelation. On the other hand, *Jīva* is known like any other object, because of the objective element it includes. It is an object of self-consciousness. Explaining the distinction, Professor Hiriyanna says: "the *jīva* is spirit as immanent in *antaḥkaraṇa* while the *sākṣin* is spirit as transcendent."[72] In short, *sākṣin* and the *jīva*, although not identical, are not quite distinct either. *Jīva* as the doer, or the enjoyer, changes and cannot be a witness to its own changes. *Jīvasākṣin's* association with the intellect only differentiates one *sākṣin* from another and does not enter into the constitution of the *sākṣin*. With regard to the *jīva*, the intellect is the attribute (*viśeṣaṇa*) that not only distinguishes one *jīva* from another, but also enters into the very being of the *jīva*. Likewise, as cosmic, the *sākṣin* is the psychical element associated either with the *māyā* or *Īśvara*.

The text also distinguishes between *Īśvara* and *Īśvarasākṣin*:

> Consciousness conditioned by *māyā* is *Īśvara* or the supreme lord. When *māyā* is a qualifying attribute, it is the state of being a God (*Īśvaratva*); and when it is a limiting adjunct there is the state of being a witness (*sākṣitva*). Such is the difference between the state of being a God (*Īśvaratva*) and the state of being a witness (*sākṣitva*), and not between God and the witness-consciousness possessing these attributes.[73]

In other words, in one case, the cosmic *māyā* is an attribute of *Īśvara*, while in the other, it is its limiting adjunct (*upādhi*).[74] Substantially there is no difference between the two. But so far as the attributes and the limiting adjuncts are concerned, the state of being a God (*Īśvaratva*) and the state of being a witness (*sākṣitva*) are distinct states. It must be noted in this connection that *jīva* is the one who *attains* the status of *sākṣin* when it directly realizes its nature as consciousness by dispelling nescience once and for all. But *Īśvara* is eternally free.

We have already seen that the function of *sākṣin* does not obviate the need for the intervention of a mental mode. To be an object of *sākṣin* is to be known without a *pramāṇa* and not necessarily to be known without a mental mode. There are two kinds of mental modes:

one pertaining to mind and the other to nescience. The first corresponds to the 'I-consciousness', while the silver, perceived in the erroneous cognition, is of the second kind. The illusory silver is superimposed on the object-consciousness, but because this is essentially identical with the witness-consciousness, the illusory is also at the same time superimposed on it. That is why the Advaitins maintain that the object of an erroneous cognition, such as silver, is revealed only by the *sākṣin* and that it is not revealed to some other person or *sākṣin.* The same is true of internal states such as happiness and pain.

It might be asked: Why does the knowledge of the witness-consciousness require the mediation of a mode of nescience (*avidyā vṛtti*)? The answer is simple. Although it is true that the illusory silver is directly revealed to *sākṣin,* the latter does not become identical with the illusory silver. The erroneous cognition does not generate an identity judgment of the form 'I am silver', which we have in the case of internal states like 'I am happy'. The identity between them cannot be established using the mental mode. In the case of 'I am happy', the intervention of the mental mode in the form of 'I' is required.

Finally, the *sākṣin* is aware of everything either as known or unknown.[75] The immediate illumination of mental states such as cognition, feeling, and willing shows that whatever occurs in the mind also is directly related to the *sākṣin.* But a cognition always refers to an object. The object of cognition is revealed by the *sākṣin* and the required relation is obtained by the mediation of the *vṛtti.* The *sākṣin* is aware of the objects when it is aware of their cognition. This is what is meant by saying that *sākṣin* is aware of everything as known. It is also aware of the objects as qualified by nescience. One of the conditions of knowledge is that the object itself must have existed unknown before the means of knowledge could be directed upon it. Before the knowledge of an object arises, the *sākṣin* must be aware of the fact that the object is unknown. This is another way of saying that the *sākṣin* is aware of nescience and the object attached to nescience. The object at this stage is known by the *sākṣin* but known as unknown, because there is no mental modification with respect to it.

Perceptuality and Immediacy: Vivaraṇa and Bhāmatī Points of View

VP's thesis expresses the Vivaraṇa point of view, as distinct from the school of Bhāmatī, the two great polarizations of later Vedānta.[76] The representations of these two as polarizations, however, may be an overstatement. Constant efforts have been made since the time of *Advaitasiddhi* of Madhusūdana to present the views of the two lines of development, not as representing systematic differences, but as creative distinctions that are intrinsic to the efforts of later Vedāntins to recover and reconstruct the various shades of doctrines and opinions that are found scattered in the writings of Śaṃkara. The effort of the author of *PP* in this regard is very much in line with this trend, although the text of *VP* speaks from the Vivaraṇa platform, as one may see on a quick reading of the comments gleaned in the second part of this work. These two lines of developments originated as streams of interpretations of Śaṃkara. Most scholars agree that Padampāda (9th century C.E.) was Śaṃkara's youngest contemporary and his student. It was he who started a tradition of interpretation and understanding of Śaṃkara. Several commentators belong to this tradition, including Prakāśātman, who wrote a commentary called Vivaraṇa, the name by which this school of Advaita is identified. The views expressed in Vivaraṇa and Padampāda's significant work *Pañcapādikā* have come to be known as the tenets of the Vivaraṇa tradition.[71] The views of Maṇḍana Miśra, a contemporary of Śaṃkara, developed in considerable detail and subtlety by Vācaspati Miśra (9th century C.E.), incorporating Maṇḍana's ideas but interpreting Śaṃkara, passed as the tenets of the Bhāmatī tradition. Writers coming later have tended to hold fast to the views of either of the two schools, even though, as indicated above, efforts were not lacking to harmonize the differences between the two traditions.

Speaking strictly from the point of view of an analysis of perceptual experience, the points at issue between the two schools may be said to hinge on the extent to which immediacy may be avowed as intrinsic to the nature of perception. Both avow immediacy, but the more conservative Bhāmatī school does not understand it as the immediacy of perception. Instead it transforms what is a case of percept-ion into a state different from perception, some kind of yogic realization. The transformation is effected through a noncognitive process. The sensory perception involved in the hearing of the scripture is only a beginning. It has to culminate, through yoga, in a meditative realization in which the subject/object distinction becomes obliterated. Scripture is indeed acknowledged as the final authority, but it has to be helped by reasoning, as an auxiliary, to remove the doubts that attack the mind so that one can contemplate the ultimate reality uninterruptedly and with faith and realize it in the immediacy of experience.

Why does the Bhāmatī school hold to this position? The main

argument is that *avidyā* can be removed only by immediate knowledge. Verbal testimony cannot accomplish it. Hearing of the *śruti* signifies relation and mediateness. Vedānta texts can only provide an indirect knowledge of Brahman. Therefore the realization in practice requires training of the mind, through meditation;[78] hence, the need of meditation to convert mediate knowledge into immediate intuition.

The Vivaraṇa point of view, however, upholds the theory of immediacy of cognition through hearing of the revealed word, the only means by which the experience of Brahman as pure consciousness becomes possible: "The self is of the form of pure consciousness which is devoid of any defect. It is naturally immediate as heat is (natural) to fire. So from the statements of the Upaniṣads which are faultless, there arises the immediate knowledge of the self."[79] This has been generally known as the theory of the immediacy of verbal knowledge (*śabda aparokṣavāda*). The Vivaraṇa view is radical in holding that immediate intuition or knowledge can arise through a sensory experience, in this case, hearing: "Nowhere indeed has meditation been found to be the cause of the immediate perception of the object of meditation. Even admitting that the immediate perception of the object of meditation results from meditation, what evidence is there that the object of meditation is real (i.e., of that character, viz., identity of the jīva with Brahman)?"[80] Accordingly, it rejects the viewpoint of the Bhāmatī school, which maintains that in the case of the perceptual cognition of a content, whether external or internal, the sensory contact with the object accounts for the immediacy of consciousness. The difference between the ordinary cases of perception and the immediate intuition of the impartite (i.e., Brahman), maintains Bhāmatī, is not qualitative. It is only a matter of degree, a case of less or more, more being accomplished through a cleansing of the sense, or the mind, or the internal organ, by means of *yoga.*

The Vivaraṇa school rejects this position as unphilosophical, in the sense that such a position is not true to the spirit of Vedānta as a cognitive discipline:

> The scriptural texts such as: "The knower of Brahman becomes verily Brahman"—Mund. III. 9, which promise liberation immediately after the cognizance of Brahman, repel the interposition of any action, since simultaneity of time as to cognizance and the attainment of Brahman is specified. Hence Brahman cognised (from verbal testimony) is not related (as object) to (a meditative) act.[81]

Therefore, it questions the very assumption that immediacy is brought about through sense contact, whether with respect to empirical perception or the knowledge of Brahman. For example, in the case of internal perceptions such as someone's introspection of one's own mental states (e.g., 'I am happy'), no sense-contact is involved, as Bhāmatī labors to demonstrate. *VP* demonstrates that such a perception is a clear case of consciousness itself, in its role as the witness manifesting mental states. In the case of external perception, the consciousness as witness still manifests, but it is fused with the cognitive act which serves to rend the intervening veil separating it from consciousness as defined by the object. *VP* thus makes use of the Vivaraṇa thesis of the immediacy of cognition through *śabda* (words) as support for its more general thesis about perceptual immediacy.

The basic difference between the two orientations, however, should not blind one to the point of agreement between the two. Both agree that scripture is an authoritative means of valid knowledge and that the path to *mokṣa* lies in and through such knowledge. In fact, both also agree even over the issue of the primacy of scripture over perception as a means of valid knowledge. This is clearly brought out by the commentator of *PP*, who interposes questions and answers in this regard at the appropriate places in his commentary. The assumption that the Advaitin of both the Vivaraṇa and the Bhāmatī persuasions reject is that perception is the first and basic means of knowledge. What is first and basic surely cannot be rejected. The Advaitins, however, maintain that perception, although first chronologically, is not necessarily basic in the sense of unsublatable. Where a subsequent cognition arises validly, the earlier one should be taken to be sublated. The cognition of the rope could not arise if the first cognition as snake had persisted. Therefore, the rope-cognition is admitted to sublate the snake-cognition. What is distinctive about the Vivaraṇa position, which *VP* represents, may be noted: It brings the sense of the experience of the immediacy that arises through verbal testimony into the deeper structure of perception itself.

The abovementioned point may be illustrated by the extensive importance accorded to a discussion of the realization of impartiteness as the sense of the expression 'thou art that' in the Vivaraṇa tradition and a relative paucity of it in Bhāmatī. The doctrine is of such vital importance for Advaita that the author of *VP* incorporates the cognition generated by the text 'thou art that' into a perception and speaks of it as an example of perception of the indeterminate variety, on a par with the recognitive perception 'this is that Devadatta'. Observations made by *PP* in this regard are valuable: they are to the effect that identity statements are not atypical verbalizations unique to verbal testimony, but are similar to ordinary perceptual statements even though the sense of identity remains obscured in the latter case.

In the Bhāmatī school, Vācaspati does not seem to recognize the vital importance of impartite statements.[82] One of the reasons may be that verbal testimony is not by itself the cause of immediate knowledge. While agreeing that scriptural testimony is the supreme *pramāṇa,* they maintain that the cognition resulting from such a testimony is only a mediate cognition that sets into operation a continued process of meditation (*prasaṅkhyāna*) before there arises the final intuition of Brahman. Thus the Upaniṣads, by themselves, cannot make the true nature of Brahman known to us. They merely supply a tentative conception of Brahman and convince us to discover its real nature for ourselves. *Prasaṅkhyāna* is essential for this discovery.

There is no doubt that the need for *prasaṅkhyāna* is admitted by all the Vedāntins, including the followers of Śaṃkara. However, it has been assigned a subordinate role.[83] The followers of Śaṃkara, with the single exception of Vācaspati, hold that Brahman can be known directly from the Upaniṣads. Because Brahman is one with our immediate self, major texts such as 'thou art that' can very well be the means of imparting the immediate knowledge. Upaniṣadic knowledge therefore does not need any assistance from *prasaṅkhyāna.*

The point of contention here is that knowledge generated by verbal testimony can only be mediate. Vācaspati inherits this view from Maṇḍana. The later followers of the Vivaraṇa school, following Sureśvara and others, reject this view. They do not claim that verbal testimony by its very nature gives rise to immediate knowledge. They maintain that mediacy or immediacy of knowledge derived from verbal testimony depends on the character of the object of knowledge.[84] Words give rise to the mediate knowledge of a mediate object, but they can also cause immediate knowledge if the object is immediate. Brahman is immediate and self-luminous and that is why it is conceivable that impartite statements by themselves can give rise to immediate knowledge of Brahman. Verbal testimony is a valid *pramāṇa,* while *yoga* and meditation are not. "To attach so much importance and value to *prasaṅkhyāna,*" maintains Sureśvara, "is as absurd as making the eye the organ of taste."[85]

What makes it easy for *VP* and the Vivaraṇa school of thought to bridge the gulf between verbal testimony and perception is their understanding of the essence of perception as consisting in its immediacy. The perceptual character of knowledge is not determined by contact of the senses with the object. The immediacy of cognition is not sense-generated, because in that case a form of cognition, like inference which is mediate and mind-generated, will pass for immediate cognition. This objection, of course, is directed against equating immediate cognition with a cognition that is not sense-generated. The opponent here assumes that mind is a sense organ. This, however, as we will presently see, is a point at issue between the two schools.

According to Vācaspati, the mind is a sense organ, whereas for the Vivaraṇa tradition it is not. The ground for the former's position is that we cannot otherwise account for the validity of the knowledge of mental states, such as happiness, which are generated by the internal sense. In internal perceptions the activity of external senses is not involved. It only involves the functioning of the mind. Therefore, it follows, so runs the argument, the mind should be regarded as a sense organ. If the mind is not regarded as a sense organ, then we must either maintain that the perception of mental states, such as happiness, is not an instance of perception or that a sense organ is not the instrument of perception. The Vivaraṇa school, on the other hand, considers knowledge of mental states, such as happiness or misery, as valid, but not in an epistemologically significant sense, precisely for the reason that it is not sense-generated but manifested by the witness-consciousness. Senses are the instruments only in cases of external perceptions. The mind is merely the locus of valid knowledge; it is not its instrument. In the case of the experience of pleasure, for example, a perceptual character accrues to it for the following reason: the circumstance of the consciousness defined by pleasure as a content, and the consciousness defined by pleasure as a mental mode (*sukha vṛtti*) should be identical, because the two adjuncts are present in the same locus. This circumstance, while justifying it as perceptual, does not account for its validity. The validity of a knowledge-event involves the operation of an outgoing mode, and the object thus perceived becomes unveiled from a previous state of unknownness.

In this context the author of *VP* comments on the texts from the *Bhagavadgītā*, *Mahābhārata*, and *Kaṭha Upaniṣad*.[86] To the objection that mind, being imperceptible, cannot become an object of perception, the author of *VP* responds:

> There is no proof that the internal organ is a sense organ. It is said that the evidence is the statement of the *Bhagavadgītā*:

> "The sense organs with the mind as the sixth one" (XV), the answer is "no," because there is no contradiction in filling mind as number six, though it is not a sense organ. There is no hard and fast rule that the completion of a number [in the list of organs] must be done by an organ alone; for in "those with *yajamāna* (sacrificer) as the fifth, eat the *iḍā*," we see that the number five relating to the priests is completed by the sacrificer who is not a priest. In the same way, in "he taught all the Vedas by rote with *Mahābhārata* as the fifth (Mbh. I. lxiv. 131, xii. ccil. 20), the number five is completed by the *Mahābhārata* which is not a Veda; furthermore, *śruti* such as: "Objects are superior to the sense organs, the mind is superior to objects" (*Kaṭha*, 3.10), prove that the mind is not a sense organ.[87]

Additionally, it cannot be maintained that there would be no immediacy for the perception of pleasure if mind is not taken to be a sense organ, because immediacy is generated by the fact of nondifference between the consciousness and the consciousness conditioned by the object.

The reason why the Bhāmatī school sets great store on according recognition to mind as a sense organ has already been stated: immediacy can result only through a functioning of the sense organ. The sense organ with respect to Brahman-knowledge, which arises as the culmination of a continued meditation, can only be the mind: "The final intuition cannot be effective in destroying ignorance which is immediate unless it is itself immediate, that the immediacy can come only from the functioning of a sense organ, and that, since no other sense organ is operative in the process of intuition by contemplation of the truth of nondualism, the mind must be admitted to be a sense organ."[88]

If it is objected that the mind is involved in mediate cognitions also, the reply is that such an admission does not prejudice recognition of its status as a sense organ. There is no correlation between immediate cognition and the sense organs. A defect in the sense organ may obstruct immediacy. Likewise, on the positive side the trained sense like that of a *yogin* can have immediate cognition of what an untrained sense cannot perceive. The fact that discipline is needed for the mind does not detract from the character of mind as a sense organ.[89] In other words, the immediacy cannot arise except through the functioning of a sense organ or its equivalent. The Upaniṣadic texts like 'thou art that' give us only indirect and mediate knowledge, like all verbal cognitions. This indirect cognition turns into immediate realization through a process of meditation.

Śaṃkara, in his *BSB*,[90] clearly states that while scriptures do not consider mind to be a sense organ,[91] some *smṛti* texts mention eleven sense organs and include mind in the list of eleven.[92] In this context, commenting on a passage from *BU*[93] that attempts to establish the existence of mind as different from the senses, Śaṃkara simply mentions different views, without trying to reconcile these views or reject one in favor of the other. Vācaspati interprets Śaṃkara's silence as supporting his view that mind is a sense organ. The followers of Vivaraṇa, on the other hand, maintain that mind is not a sense organ. Whenever there is a conflict between *śruti* and *smṛti*, *śruti* prevails. The obviousness of this fact accounts for Śaṃkara's silence.

The standpoint of the Vivaraṇa school, as the author of *PP* pointedly observes, is not to focus on something as the instrument of cognition (i.e., whether it is a sense organ or something else), but rather on the object. The perceptibility of an object does not depend upon the instrument of cognition but rather on the nature of the object. If the object is perceptible (the text of *VP* gives a set of qualifications that must be fulfilled for rendering an object perceptible), then the knowledge also is perceptual, and it does not matter by what means such a knowledge arises. This position, to which *VP* adheres and which is defended by *PP*, shows greater phenomenological insight than a theory that perception must entail a sense organ.[94]

Another of the well-known points of difference between the two streams of Advaita tradition, which bears significantly on the question of perceiving, is the one relating to nescience. There are some superficial differences that may be ignored in the face of the substantial agreement, but there are also deep differences which have been treated by the author of *Advaitasiddhi* in detail. *PP* maintains that these distinctions do not undermine the integrity of the doctrine.

In both the traditions the need for distinguishing between primal and modal nesciences has been recognized. The text of *VP* itself, and the commentary *PP* even more elaborately, uses this important distinction to explain empirical perception. Vācaspati interprets the beginningless character of superimposition to mean a streamlike beginningless, looking for the cause of superimposition in an earlier superimposition, without positing an absolute beginning. The Vivaraṇa school, on the other hand, resorts to primal nescience as the original cause of all superimpositions. But both the traditions, and especially Vācaspati with characteristic incisiveness, recognize a primal nescience as logically entailed by modal ignorance.

Vācaspati holds that the statement '*avidyā* is one and not many', means that *avidyā*-s differ in each and every individual self, each of whom has his or her own personal *avidyā*. This is his famous theory of 'multiple nescience located in many individual souls' (*aneka jīvāśrita anekāvidyā vāda)*. Individual illusions and errors are products of the modal nesciences and are sublatable by other appearances of the same grade of reality. Modal ignorances are sublated by cognition of the objects veiled by them; for example, ignorance about silver is cancelled by the knowledge of the shell. Primal nescience, however, is removable only by the knowledge of ultimate reality and hence endures up to the realization of Brahman.

As stated above, the distinctive feature of Vācaspati's doctrine in this regard is his emphasis on the plurality of nesciences. Some scholars maintain that the assumption of a multiplicity of nesciences indeed has greater explanatory value than the assumption of one nescience with multiple powers. The latter is the device by which the other schools of Advaita seek to reconcile the singleness of *avidyā* with a plurality of individual selves. The seeming adequacy of this view is that it is only one among many powers of nescience that becomes destroyed when a particular *jīva* attains freedom. Nescience itself, however, is not destroyed because it would result in the contingency of the simultaneous release of all *jīvas.* In this position it will be difficult to show how the power itself becomes susceptible to destruction without the possessor of power himself becoming likewise susceptible to destruction. Power and the possessor of power are one. That is why the Bhāmatī tradition maintains that nesciences are many, and that one of these is destroyed when a particular *jīva* attains freedom.[95]

The need for emphasizing many nesciences should be obvious. Otherwise one will be forced to maintain that when one nescience is destroyed on the release of a single finite self, it is destroyed for all other individual selves as well. There will be no other ground for making a distinction between the bound and the released selves. If the distinction between the bound and the released is not based on ignorance, then a plurality of individual selves must be conceded. To the extent that Vācaspati insists on the reality of the other individual selves and of their duties and obligations to each other, to that extent his position could be treated as realistic. But there is also a traditional Vedānta solipsism holding to the view that perception of things is either the creation of oneself or simultaneous with one's creation.

What lends some basis for solipsistic Advaita is the view

associated with the Vivaraṇa school that Brahman is both the content and the locus of nescience and that it is one. Brahman through its own nescience seems bound and through its own knowledge seems released. It is doubtful whether the Vivaraṇa tradition perceived itself as logically entailing some form of solipsism, but the fact remains that thinkers like Madhusūdana were inclined to be as accommodating to solipsism as to its opposite.

The important issue in this context, and the one that clearly demarcates the two traditions, pertains to the locus of nescience. The Vivaraṇa tradition maintains that the same self-identical pure consciousness is the ground as well as the content concealed by nescience.[96] What this means, as *PP* elucidates, is that it is undifferentiated consciousness, not differentiated as God or the individual self, that serves as the ground of nescience.[97] God or self are consequential to nescience and therefore cannot serve as its locus or content. It must be noted here in defense of the Vivaraṇa tradition that no contradiction is perceived in locating nescience in Brahman. Nescience is opposed not to consciousness but to consciousness reflected in the mental mode. Consciousness reflected in the mental mode serves to sublate nescience relating to a particular object. In response to the objection (such as the one raised by Rāmānuja)[98] that if pure consciousness is not opposed to nescience, how could its reflection in the mental mode conceivably be opposed to it, *PP* maintains that the opposition of consciousness reflected in the mental mode to nescience lies not in the aspect of consciousness as such, but in the relation of consciousness to the mental mode. *PP*'s reply in this context displays the characteristic discernment the commentary exhibits at many places.

The Bhāmatī school, however, holds to the position that the individual self is the locus of nescience, which obscures the true nature of Brahman, thereby making Brahman an object.[99] This view cannot be dismissed on the trivial ground that the individual self is not different from Brahman. The individual self is indeed different from Brahman because of nescience, although when the latter ceases to exist, the two are recognized as nondifferent. This, of course, gives rise to the charge of reciprocal dependence between the two: the individual self as the result of nescience and nescience depending on the individual self as its locus. Bhāmatī 's reply to this charge is that they are beginningless and that they are like the chicken and the egg or like the seed and the tree series.[100] The point of defense is that both nescience and individual self rest in the same delimitation of consciousness, so that it is conceivable that each is a determinant of the other.

The author of *PP* even provides a phenomenological defense of the position of Vācaspati while he himself veers to the position of Vivaraṇa which the text of *VP* upholds. Mind has the power to reveal ignorance, as when one says, 'I am ignorant'. The nature of the revealing medium is such that it reflects the object as if it were present inside it, as the mirror reflects one's face as if it is present inside the mirror. Thus the mind, while revealing nescience, reveals it as it shows itself signifying consciousness reflected in it, namely, as the individual self.

The commentator finds the statement that the individual self is the locus of ignorance compatible with the view that ignorance is grounded in pure consciousness which constitutes the essential nature of the individual self. Pure consciousness comes within the empirical usage as the 'I' when it serves as the supporting ground of ignorance.[101]

Toward a Reconstruction of Perceptual Experience: A Summary Statement

In conclusion, we may raise and discuss some of the more general questions that arise from the account of perception that has been set forth so far. In what precise sense does this account of perceptual experience, especially as crystallized in *VP*, differ from other theories of Indian philosophy contemporary to it? Does it strike a new path, a departure perhaps from the classical position held by Śaṃkara and the earlier Advaitins? What sense, if any, can we make of the assertion that perception involves a 'going out' of the inner sense and an assuming of the form of the object—a notion unique to the text of *VP*? Finally, is the notion of the identity of subject and object logically viable?

Although it has been explained how immediacy is asserted as the constitutive core of perceptual experience, it has not been made precise how this assertion stands distinguished from other conceptualizations of immediacy or its equivalents in the other well-known philosophical traditions of Indian philosophy. The object is not to see how Advaita represents other positions at variance with it, but to underscore what is maintained as unique to the position defended. For example, immediacy, or nondifference, is affirmed in Advaita in a manner that sharply differentiates it from the way it is done in the Mahāyāna Buddhist school of Vijñānavāda, the Indian paradigm of an idealistic theory of knowledge. The main plank of idealism is the primacy of consciousness and the derived nature of its content. Śaṃkara's position is often interpreted as idealism,[102] but his sustained and unequivocal critique of Vijñānavāda Buddhism should give one pause. Vijñānavāda idealism not only scouts the idea of the externality of the object but even applies this idealism to the case of erroneous cognitions. Vijñānavādins maintain that error in cognition is essentially misperceiving the given as what is external when in fact it is only an idea (*vijñāna*). Cancellation of error, which provides the context, phenomenologically speaking, for a thematic awareness of error in retrospect merely removes the externality and restores it to its nature as an idea.

The truth about cognition consists precisely in that there is no external reality corresponding to it. If the generality of the Buddhist philosophical tradition represents the idealist shift—idealist in the epistemologically significant sense—in the otherwise even tenor of the scene of Indian philosophy, Vijñānavāda stands for its radicalization, and thus provokes a nonidealistic articulation of knowledge and reality at the hands of the 'orthodox' and the Jaina philosophers of the Indian tradition. At the opposite extreme stand other theories of Indian philosophy, seeking to explain immediacy either as a relation or as a quality of the percipient, a quality that may be either perceived or inferred from the knownness of the object. We may describe these theories as responses to counter idealism by making the object a necessary term of the cognitive relation, and even deriving the idea of a cognizing subject from it. The object provides the model for understanding knowledge and its terms and even for understanding reality. The presupposition, articulated and often unarticulated, seems to be that only what is known is objectively real. For want of a better word, we may describe it as realism.

The point of view of Vedānta represents a position that seems to partake of some of the characteristics of both the extremes. The approach that is characteristic of their point of view is from the vantage point of the occasion of a live cognitive operation. The mind, as the subjective pole of the operation, and the operation itself as the process both become enlivened or illumined by pure consciousness. By means of this contact with the cognitive operation, the object also becomes revealed. What is significant in this account of perception as immediacy is the admission, which not only occurs in the text of *VP* but also is reflective of the general trend, that the object becomes thus revealed not merely as a content of awareness but as an objective fact.

The question that may be raised here is: Does this formulation of epistemological realism accord with the classical position of Advaita, or, as many think, does it strike a new path, a departure maybe, for example, from Śaṃkara? The question is addressed here not merely because of its historical interest but with a view to seeing how intrinsic a concern with realism is to a theory of knowledge from the Vedānta perspective. It is well-known that Śaṃkara advocates and defends the view of knowledge, in the common acceptance of the term, as entailing the givenness of the object, against the attacks of Vijñānavāda Buddhists. The position of the Buddhist idealists is that what is known or experienced is nothing but knowledge or experience. How do they arrive at this conclusion? They do this with great argumentative skill, and some of their efforts in this regard represent the high-water mark of developments in logic in Indian philosophy. But these arguments themselves rest on an appeal to experience. In experience, ask the Buddhists, is it not the case that the object and the mind always appear together? Their appearance together without variation is a proof of their nondifference.[103]

Śaṃkara rejects the abovementioned position on the very ground that such an analysis offends the nature and verdict of experience itself:

> Our perceptions point out to us external things like pillars and walls. We are aware in perception, not of perception but of the objects of perception. Vijñānavāda admits it when it says that the internal object of cognition appears like something external. If we have independent experience of the external world, how can we say that it seems like something external? We apprehend things through means of knowledge.... Objects are apprehended as external and distinct from ideas. Between the idea and the object there is not identity but only causal connection. We have knowledge of different attributes black and white as also of different ideas.[104]

Whatever is actually perceived is not nonexistent. The external entities exist because they are actually perceived. Accordingly, Śaṃkara maintains that in all noetic experience the separation of subject and object cannot be denied. Additionally, it is only in the context of the functioning of our consciousness in relation to an external world that we can legitimately speak of the 'possibilities and absence of possibilities' in experience:

> [B]ecause the possibility or the absence of possibility of the existence of an entity, depends upon the antecedent operation, or the absence of operation, of the means-of-proof (with regard to such entity) and not vice versa, viz., that the operation, or

> the absence of operation, of the means-of-proof depends on the possibility or the absence of possibility (of the existence of such an entity). That which is actually perceived by the operation of one or other of the means-of-proof is possible (of existence), and that which is not perceived by any of the means-of-proof whatsoever, is not possible (of existence), and that which is not perceived by any means-of-proof whatsoever, is not possible of existence.[105]

Perceptual experience clearly demonstrates that ideas are different from the objects which are known through them. Śaṃkara observes that their simultaneity only means that they have a relation of cause and effect between them, not that they are one and the same: "It is not that because cognitions have the form of the objects of such cognitions, that destruction of such objects results, for cognition cannot have the form of external objects if such external objects themselves did not exist, and also because, such objects are as a matter of fact perceived to be external."[106]

The opponent appeals only to the circumstance of the object and the mind appearing invariably together in experience, but he overlooks, says Śaṃkara, the important fact, again a verdict of experience, that the object that appears 'invariably together' also appears as external. In every specific cognition of objects as pitchers or otherwise, the objects are given to us, not created from inside ourselves. If there were no external objects, even the illusion of externality would be impossible."No one would say," observes Śaṃkara humorously, "Visnumitra appears as if he is the son of a barren woman,"[107] "a barren woman's son" being a contradiction in terms. This observation, incidentally, is not a simple confession of faith in naive realism but a phenomenological refutation of a position that does not truly report on actual facts but only elucidates an *a priori* truth.

Viewed against this background, the explanation of *VP* that mind 'goes out' to meet its object and assumes its form apparently seems to underscore the same element of realism[108] that is presupposed in Śaṃkara's refutation of idealism. The crucial element of the theory of *VP* in this context is the explanation of the nondifference of the mental mode with the object. The mental mode, or the cognitive operation, is the primary datum in perception, at least insofar as the phenomenal experience is concerned, and it presents itself as a continuum only to such an experience. Its presentation as a continuum provides the basis for discerning not only itself, as a phenomenal cognition, but also at its two extremities, the phenomenal cognizer and the phenomenally cognized content. This is, of course, only one side of the coin so far as Vedānta is concerned. In the realm of epistemology, what gives edge to the Vedānta approach is its distinction of levels. It begins with the level that represents a straight line with the even tenor of cognition and discourse of natural, unreflective life, but from there moves on to a level of depth that remains veiled or concealed by the initial level. What, in other words, is distinctive of its standpoint is its theory of nescience and the attendant concept of two truths, two modes of knowledge, and two levels of life:

> *Māyā* does not mean denial of the world. The ultimate non-being of the world does not have to be stated as a theory, as it is strictly implied in the very definition of *Brahman* itself. As a theory it only seeks to translate the implicit into the explicit, thereby necessitating the complete phenomenological tracing, or retracing of the paths through which the world appearance has come into being. *Māyā*, therefore, is a provisional recovery of the world so that its ultimate non-being, along with *Brahman*'s being may be spoken.... *Brahman* stands over against the world, and *māyā* is the ground of this provisional distinction between the world and *Brahman*, all distinctions being provisional. Out of the distinctions surely arises *Brahman* as the real but it is not the ground of distinction but of non-distinction.[109]

More relevantly from an epistemological point of view, the theory implies that the cognitive operation itself is of the nature of a superimposition upon pure consciousness, which provides the ontological focus of philosophical reflection for the Advaitins.

Pure consciousness is pure existence or being, and what is said in the context of the latter is equally applicable in the context of the former. The general standpoint of Advaita about pure existence is that all effects with different names and forms are real only as pure existence but are in themselves nonreal. Just as a clay pitcher has no existence apart from the clay, similarly the manifold has no existence apart from Brahman, its source. As identical in essence with Brahman, the phenomenal world is real. Likewise, it may be said about pure consciousness that all the referents of the terms in a cognitive relation, such as subject, object, and their relation, are real only as pure consciousness but nonreal in themselves. As identical in essence with pure consciousness, all three terms of a cognitive relation refer to reality.

Pure consciousness in such an exigency becomes threefold: the cognizer-consciousness, the means-of-cognition consciousness, and the object-consciousness. From the perspective of pure consciousness, these divisions are only apparent, and none of the three as such has any substantive being. From that perspective, the object is only apparently independent of the subject, but not truly independent.

Śaṃkara, even where he refutes Buddhist idealism, does not deny or suggest that the object of knowledge is independent of the knowledge of it:

> It is not possible that cognition can be conscious of itself as apart from an (external) entity, precisely because a thing cannot act on itself. If you (the follower of Buddha) say that in case a cognition were to be apprehended by means of a thing apart from the cognition itself, that again will have to be apprehended by something else, and that again by still some other thing and so a *regressus ad infinitum* will result.[110]

Thus to claim that an idea knows itself and to deny that an external thing is known through an idea is absurd. The main thrust of his critique is to affirm the dualistic structure of empirical knowledge. To interpret it in any other way is to look the other way from experience. Realism, in other words, in an experientially grounded epistemology, is inescapable. When it is explained as obtaining under the sway of superimposition and a primordial nescience that accounts for it, what is suggested is that realism is germane only to that portion of human experience that functions or operates at the surface level, oblivious to its own hidden depths.[111]

The phenomenological approach, in the sense in which it has been understood in this essay, is not a theory of appearances with studied restriction to what presents itself only on the surface level. A phenomenology should help one to uncover the implications of what appears, through close attention to experience, and should help one 'see', that is, directly realize the depth-dimension. To realize the depth' may not be taken metaphysically as an exhortaton to believe in some extra-empirical revelation. 'To realize the depth' is another way of saying 'unrealize the surface, the flat, and the one-dimensional world of unreflective experience'.

From an inside understanding of perceptual experience, what is disclosed is that the essence of experience is constituted by its conformity to a cognized content. Analysis itself is in the service of helping one see that the world truly is synchronous not only with the infinite mind but also with finite minds. Both the percipient and the perceived object, as they appear on the surface, are but the modes of ignorance caused the presence of a common stuff of ignorance, covering a common self-identical consciousness.

The picturesque image, used to bring home the key epistemological idea of conformity of cognition with the content, that the text of *VP* distinctively uses is well-known. The operation of mind in perception consists in 'going out' to the object to be perceived and assuming its form. Should it be taken literally or metaphorically? That it is often taken literally should not come as a surprise to anyone acquainted with the basic assumptions about matter in Indian thought. Mind or internal sense is generally believed to be a product of matter. Mind structurally participates in the collection of the raw material of perception: "The function of mind is to go out to the object through the senses and manifest it. This it is able to do because of its capacity to reflect intelligence. Since mind is considered in Indian thought to be a product of primal nature (*prakṛti*) and therefore material, the 'going out' of the mental psychosis is not metaphorical, but actual."[112] Professor Sundaram reiterates the same point when he says: "The Advaitic theory is that it is the function of mind to go out to the object, take on its form, and manifest it. This 'going out' is not metaphorical, but actual, as the mind in the Indian thought is a product of the matter."[113]

In a recently held symposium on "Spirituality and Science" in India which assembled scientists and Sanskritists in the same forum, it was maintained that the expression 'reaching out' used in *VP* can only be a figure of speech. It is similar to the phrase "eyes falling on the object."[114] In the published proceedings of the symposium, however, the writer of the Foreword, a scientist of repute and also a monastic of the Śaṃkarite order, writes that modern science is veering round to a position where the *indriyas* 'reaching out' is not totally figurative, but somewhat substantive.[115] He refers to recent research in auditory perception to substantiate his claim. Even in visual perception, he observes, what is transmitted to the brain is an optical hologram of the object.[116]

The causal theory of perception that will follow on a literal understanding of the phenomenon of 'going out' will lead to many philosophical problems. One will not be able to avoid representationalism. The gulf between the subject and the object will never be bridged. There also will be the problem of directly knowing the object cognized, independently of the cognition of it, and of being able to verify the mind's conformity to it. The immediacy assumption will be reduced to saying that sensing the sense-datum is all that there is in knowledge by acquaintance.[117] Moreover, the definition offered of the perceptibility of an object in terms of the mode of the mind 'going out' and conforming to the object must be understood against the background of the thesis of consciousness. What becomes perceptual is only the consciousness conditioned by the superimposed object and the consciousness conditioned by the mode of the mind assuming the form of the object. Contact of the mind with the object is a case of the transformation of the mind in the service of effecting the removal of modal ignorance unveiling the object.

All that the phenomenon of 'going out' seems to suggest is that the initiative in perception must be from the mind, that the sense or its equivalent must somehow approach the object. D. M. Datta echoes the same point, when he says: "An approach must be made from the side of our organism towards the object. Our senses must somehow approach the object itself. This direct approach will explain better the directness of perception."[118] Moreover, taking it in this light conforms to our stipulation that the explanations that are offered should be from within the order of experience. We should not abdicate it in favor of a naturalistic account and seek for a 'scientific' explanation.

The Advaitic perspective on perception easily lends itself to misunderstandings and vulnerable to the charges of either saying what is trivial or tautologous or something that is logically contradictory. For example, take the description of valid perceptual knowledge as a state of consciousness. This looks trivial and seems to convey nothing significant about perception. One may see in it little more than a tautology, saying knowledge is knowledge or consciousness is consciousness. That this is not so should become obvious to anyone who may have the patience to comprehend a whole set of epistemologically significant statements that the Advaitin unpacks from this observation. The admission that consciousness is knowledge does not preclude him from recognizing the varieties and forms of valid knowledge and of means thereof. Likewise, when he equates perception with consciousness, the equation does not inhibit him from recognizing the different aspects of the questions of perception, such as those relating to the percipient and the object perceived, as well as to the mechanics and the dynamics of the process of perception itself. Instead, the seemingly tautologous equation helps him to answer the most central question of knowledge, the relevance of the object known to the knowing subject.

The Advaita thesis of perception stated in a somewhat oversimplified form gives rise to the question whether the identity of subject and object is logically coherent or viable. The following observations may be made in response, keeping in mind the assumptions underlying the question and the possible ways of answering it. To begin with, to characterize the position of Advaita in this regard as one of the affirmation of identity of the subject and object is not accurate. Speaking specifically with reference to the answer that is provided in *VP*, Advaita does not simply affirm the identity of subject and object, but the nondistinction of the cognizer-consciousness, the consciousness conditioned by the mental mode, and the consciousness conditioned by the object. Even in this context, as the commentator of *PP* often reiterates, what the text asserts is not the identity or nondistinction of the cognizer and the mental mode assuming the form of the object, but rather the mental mode assuming the form of the object with the object itself. Even assuming that the position of Advaita may be represented loosely, without technical precision, as affirming the oneness of the subject and the object, the question still remains whether it is meaningful. A subject is what the object is not and *vice versa.* According to the opening statement of Śaṃkara in his philosophical *summa*, the object, and that to which it is an object, at least seem reciprocally opposed to each other. What logical sense then can we make of the assertion of identity? Before answering this question, we may have to translate these terms into their phenomenological equivalents, namely, as cognition and content, and then seek to answer the question whether the identity between the two is viable from the standpoint of lived experience. This, of course, raises questions about the distinction between logical and phenomenological analysis. Although there is no clear awareness of the distinction between the two approaches in the philosophical debates that have been going on for centuries in India, it is permissible for one today who seeks to reconstruct the Advaita theory of perception to make such a distinction.

One of the disturbing aspects of Indian philosophical discussion that particularly intrigues someone looking at it from without is that debates and dissents between schools often seem to be carried on with no apparent consensus on the precise nature of the issue involved. Whether this is really the case cannot be discussed here. However, it cannot be denied that it leaves one with that impression. Some look at it from a phenomenological perspective while others look at the issues with more objective eyes—in the interest of logical distinctions. It is not as if the two are exclusive of each other, or that one has to exercise a choice between the two. The questions that are posed here, rather, are whether the common logical method, with its implicit reference to the pregiven actual world, can be adequate for philosophical investigation, and whether the method of using definitional statements relating to concepts as logically entailing propositions about the empirical world does justice to the spirit of Indian philosophy. In defense of the Advaita thesis, restated in our terminology as affirming the identity of perceptual cognition and content, the following may be said: without acknowledging that the two are identical in some sense or the other—identity admittedly having a wide variety of meanings ranging from relation in its most externalized form at one end, to absolute oneness of the kind that cannot even be verbalized—there can be no accounting for the experience of immediacy that is distinctive of perception.

The point of view herein advocated is not another kind of approach to experience in a presuppositionless manner. Such a procedure is futile. That philosophical reasoning should free itself from all presuppositions, even if conceivable, certainly does not represent the sense in which the Advaita method of analyzing has been explained. Instead it may even be said that such a method may be viewed as representing the attempt to expose the presuppositions that make knowledge and experience possible. Beginning from the level of experience as given, we seek out the presuppositions that ground experience and its layers. In the last resort, the content that we arrive at through such a process of transcendental reflection may not be other than the consciousness of it. What has been attempted here is not to look at experience in light of metaphysical assumptions, but rather to see whether a sensitive and scrupulous inspection of all experience—veridical and erroneous, wakeful and sub-wakeful, cognitive and noncognitive, linguistic and extra-linguistic—may not help one to approach the so-called presuppositions of a new metaphysic of experience with a conviction born of experiential verification.

NOTES

1. *Muṇḍaka Upaniṣad* (henceforth cited as *MU*) describes Brahman as omnipresent: "Brahma, indeed, is this immortal. Brahma before, Brahma behind, to right and to left. Stretched forth below and above, Brahma, indeed, is this whole world, this widest extent." *The Thirteen Principal Upanishads*, trans. Robert Ernest Hume

(Oxford: Oxford University Press, 1967), 2.2.11, 373. *Bṛhadāraṇyaka Upaniṣad* (henceforth cited as *BU*) describes Brahman as "the Truth of the truth" (*satyasya satyam*). Splitting the word *satyam* into three syllables, *sa, ti*, and *yam*, the Upaniṣad maintains that the first and the third syllables mean *truth* that the second means *untruth*, and that the entire world signifies the enclosure of untruth by truth on both sides. In other words, the world is not to be rejected as unreal. It is derivatively true, being sustained by the Truth. *BU* 2.1.20.

2. *BU* 3.4.1.

3. *sa yo ha vai tat paramam brahma veda brahmaiva bhavati*. *MU* 3.2.9.

4. *Mīmāṃsā* literally means *inquiry* or *investigation* into the text of revelation or the scriptures. It focuses upon rules for interpreting the scriptures as a body of injunctions rather than as religious statements about God, soul, and the world. Mīmāṃsā as a school of Indian philosophy undertakes a systematic study of the *brāhmaṇas* (guidelines for the performance of sacrifices) and subordinates the other parts of the Vedas (relating to hymns in praise of various deities and philosophic interpretations) to them. Vedānta, generally referred to as *Uttara* Mīmāṃsā, primarily analyzes the last (*uttara*) section of the Vedas, that is, the Upaniṣads, which provide the philosophic interpretation.

It might be noted as a matter of interest for philosophy that there is a common assumption underlying the *genre* of Mīmāṃsā, both Pūrva and Uttara, namely, that Vedic terms and concepts must be explicated in light of an understanding reflected in the language of the world. This has been discussed under the rubric of *loka vedādhikaraṇa.* For a short and incisive analysis of the history of this school, see P. V. Kane, *A Brief Sketch of the Pūrva-Mīmāṃsa System* (Poona: Aryabhushan Press, 1924).

5. Although I am using the term 'phenomenology' to describe a method that has a central use in Advaita Vedānta, I am not applying the intentions avowed by phenomenology as a movement to the task of interpreting Vedānta. Phenomenology, as a twentieth-century movement, is part of a program of philosophy as a rigorous science. It is an attempt to lay a foundation for science in experiential terms and is avowedly restricted in its application to empirical experience. The essential goal of Husserl's phenomenology was to arrive at philosophy as a rigorous science: "Philosophy...does not want to leave anything unsolved; it wants to reduce everything to primary 'presuppositions' which do not need to be clarified because they are immediately evident and cannot even be clarified. It is only in this sense that philosophy as the the 'science of ultimate grounds' is a rigorous science." J. Kockelmans,"What is Phenomenology?" in *Phenomenology*, ed. J. Kockelmans (Garden City, NY: Doubleday, 1967), 27. See also "Philosophy as a Rigorous Science" in Edmund Husserl, *Phenomenology and the Crisis of Philosophy*, trans. Quentin Lauer (New York: Harper Torchbook, 1965), 71–148.

6. The Sanskrit term, '*bādha*', literally means 'cancellation.' In the context of Advaita ontology, it is usually translated as "sublation.' Sublation implies that when one attains the state of identity with Brahman—the Absolute—the world as such disappears. However, for the sake of clarity and for the purposes of understanding its meaning fully, Professor Deutsch translates '*bādha*' as 'subration.' He states: It "is the mental process whereby one disvalues some previously appraised object or content of consciousness because of being contradicted by a new experience.... It is an axio-noetic process that involves, psychologically, a withdrawal of attention from an object as it was originally judged to be and the fastening of attention either to the same object as reappraised or to another object that replaces the first object as a content of consciousness; and the placing of a higher value upon the content of the new judgment

.... "In short, subration involves three things: initially, a judgment about some object or content of consciousness; the initial judgment is recognized as faulty in the light of another judgment that is incompatible with the first judgment; and the acceptance of the new judgment as valid. *Advaita Vedānta: A Philosophical Reconstruction* (Honolulu: East-West Center Press, 1968), 15–16.

Professor Deutsch's analysis of *bādha* as 'subration' highlights that the point of distinction of the Vedāntic use of phenomenology as a method is the inseparability of value and existence. For Vedānta, the very sense of real existence originates, through the act of negation or cancellation, which is therefore as much an act of denial in the ontological sense as it is devaluation.

Using the criterion of *bādha*, Śaṃkara arrives at his ontological hierarchy. Anything that is in principle negated has a lesser degree of reality than that which replaces it. In light of this, to say that the experience of reality itself cannot be subrated amounts to saying that the experience of reality cannot be denied or disvalued by anything else. It is the highest experience we can have.

7. *BU* 2.3.6.

8. Phenomenology, as a contemporary movement like other philosophical movements of the times, represents a general retreat from ontology. The important point about phenomenology is its studied disavowal of any ontological commitment. Ontology, broadly speaking, is a concern for that which is and a probing of its nature. A phenomenologist suspends or brackets that which is and its presence. In Husserl's own words: "This means suspending all beliefs characteristic of the 'natural attitude', the attitude of common sense and science; in short, everything that is not 'apodictic'. Our perception of a chair, for instance, involves the belief that a physical chair is present 'out there'. This belief is neither necessarily true nor necessarily false. In the phenomenologically reduced state of the given we are to hold in abeyance every such belief." Edmund Husserl, *The Idea of Phenomenology*, in *Readings in Twentieth Century Philosophy*, ed. William P. Alaston and George Nakhnikian (London: The Free Press of Glencoe, 1963), 627.

Marvin Farber explains the basic phenomenological method of bracketing as follows: "Instead of the universal doubt of Descartes, then, Husserl proposes this universal 'epoche'. A new scientific domain is thus determined. All the sciences which refer to the natural world are also eliminated: no use is made of their propositions and results. They may only be 'assumed' in brackets, and not as propositions presuming validity. That which remains when the entire world is eliminated (including us with all 'cogitare') is 'pure' or 'transcendental' consciousness. That is the phenomenological residuum." Marvin Farber, *Foundations of Phenomenology* (Cambridge, Mass: Harvard University Press, 1943), 527. For Husserl, then, to do phenomenology amounted to returning to the transcendental ego (the pure subject) as the ground for the foundation and constitution of all objectivity. Only then is a person able to grasp intuitively how the pure subject constitutes the objects and at the same time serves as the source of all objectivity.

Whether the deliberately adopted attitude of bracketing is calculated in the end to evolve a new perspective of experience and to lay a new foundation for what we call experience or not, and if the former, whether it succeeds in carrying out that project, are matters for dispute.

9. Kalidas Bhattacharyya, in an illuminating analysis of this thesis, notes: "The relation between body and the world, between mind and body and between pure consciousness and mind ... is unlike any ordinary case of distinguishing where when X is distinguished out the remainder is understood as a clear positive definite Y equivalent to the given situation *minus* X. Dissociation of the stages of freedom, as

thus of a different sort, can be best represented by saying that what is now dissociated had earlier, by an inscrutable act of self-negation, deformed itself positively as the given that was started from. This is the Advaita principle of *ajñāna*." Kalidas Bhattacharyya, *A Modern Understanding of Advaita* (Ahmedabad: L. D. Institute of Indology, 1975), 1–2.

10. The transcendental subjectivity of Husserl, it may be noted, does not aim at pointing beyond experience. Thus the transcendental subjectivity of Husserl is only the core of the purified region of experience, the home of essences. It represents a standpoint or principle on which all possible forms of knowing and experience are functionally grounded. However, it cannot be used to describe the notions of spirit, self, or reality as being of Vedānta, in which the goal is not to seek a foundation for science or empirical knowledge but rather to recover the transcendental depth to which the empirical experience points. It is true that there is a sense in which Brahman knowledge, as the goal of Advaitic inquiry, may be described as the foundation of all cognitive enterprises. But one must not forget, in this context, that the task of laying the foundation is understood rather in the paradoxical sense of showing all species of knowledge to be species of ignorance. Progress and indefinite expansion are conceivable in the sphere of the latter, but Brahman knowledge does not contribute to such progress except in an odd sense in which the knowledge of reality may be said to provide a grounding for the appearance of all knowledge in the empirical sphere.

True, the overall intention of phenomenology is to focus not on natural perception but on the experience in which the true forms are revealed. "Natural knowledge," maintains Husserl, "progressively takes possession of a reality at first existing for us as a matter of course and as something to be investigated further as regards its extent and content, its elements, its relations and laws. Thus the various sciences of the natural sort (*natürlichen wissenchaften*) come into being and flourish, the natural sciences... the sciences of culture (*geistes wissenschaften*) and, on the other side, the mathematical sciences, the sciences of numbers, classes, relations, and so on." Husserl, *The Idea of Phenomenology*, in *Readings in Twentieth Century Philosophy*, 14. Husserl contrasts the natural mode of reflection with the philosophical mode in the following words: "But *philosophy lies in a wholly new dimension*. It needs an *entirely new point of departure* and an entirely new method distinguishing it in principle from any 'natural' science." *Ibid.*, 19. Vedānta, however, does not rest content with a mere separation of things of natural attitude and experience. Rather, it is interested in recovering a deeper layer of experience than that experienced at the surface.

11. Bhattacharyya, *A Modern Understanding of Advaita*, 4–5.

12. The source of *sākṣin* as a philosophical concept is obscure. It is virtually nonexistent in the Upaniṣads, although compounds, such as *sarvasākṣin* (*Kaṭha*, 3.4) *nityasākṣin* (*MAU* 3.11) do occur. However, it is difficult to assign any precise referent to these concepts. These scattered references can undoubtedly be construed as anticipating the later systematic development of this concept.

As a philosophical concept, *sākṣin* is found in the later Upaniṣads such as *Śvetāśvatra* (6.11) and *Maitrī* (6.16). It also occurs in the *Sāṃkhya-Kārikā* (19), in which the *puruṣa* is said to be the witness of *prakṛti*. For a detailed analysis of the history and development of this concept, see sections 6 and 7 of this essay. For the most comprehensive survey and evaluation of the concept of *sākṣin*, see A. K. Chatterjee and R. R. Dravid, *The Concept of Sākṣin in Advaita Vedānta* (Banaras: Banaras Hindu University, 1979).

13. In this respect, the method used in Vedānta, although in many ways similar to phenomenology, is different. The reflective standpoint, while being recognized as distinct from the natural standpoint, is still deemed a part of the natural. The reflective

standpoint is valuable as paving the way for a perspective that only can be described as overnatural or transnatural. Intellect, in other words, in the context of Vedānta, as well as of religious traditions that are cognate with Vedānta (for example, Yoga), is still 'nature'. In the program of transcendental phenomenology avowed as integral to the philosophic culture of European rationalism, any effort to recognize something transcending 'intellect' will simply be ruled out. Although a natural standpoint is rejected, there is no concept of the transnatural.

14. *sad eva, saumya idam agra āsīd ekam evādvitīyam.* " In the beginning, dear boy, this was one alone, one only without a second." *Idam* signifies that before the multiplicity of names and forms, this world was pure being. The aphorism reinforces the ontological priority of Brahman over the world. *Chāndogya Upaniṣad*, 6.2.1. Hereafter this Upaniṣad will be cited as *CU*.

Also see *Taittirīya Upaniṣad* (henceforth cited as *TU*) 2.7.1; and *CU* 3.19.1; *Maitrī*, 6.17.

Pañcadaśī 1.19, a later Vedānta text also emphasizes the intention of the *CU* passage quoted above:

idaṃ sarvam purā sryṣṭer ekam evādvitīyakam
sad evāsīn nāma-rūpe nāstām....

"Prior to creation everything was being, one only without a second; name-forms were not."

15. *BU* 3.7.23.

16. Epistemology in modern western philosophy takes the form of a critique of knowing, its scope and limits, as a refreshing departure from earlier preoccupations with ontology, irrespective of whether it be of the order of nature or supernature, that is, God. Both rationalism and empiricism and the accompanying criticism of Kant arise in response to the skepticism with which Descartes inaugurates modern philosophy. When scholars use the notion of epistemology in an Indian context and assert its priority over the question of being, they often tend to overlook an essential difference between modern western philosophy and Indian thought, which is traditional and unencumbered by issues that originate with modernity.

17. *MU* 1.1.3.

18. The Nyāya school probably had its origin in its attempt to formulate canons of argument for use in debates, which pervaded the Indian philosophico-logical scene for a long time. The *Nyāya-Sūtras* probably date back from the third century B.C.E. These *sūtras* were variously commented on by Vātsyāyana (fifth century C.E.), Vācaspati (ninth century C.E.), Jayanta (tenth century C.E.), and others. By the time of Udayana (tenth century C.E.), the school of modern Nyāya, technically called Navya-Nyāya, was formed because of the efforts of Gangeśa. For a competent account of this system, see Bimal Krishna Matilal, *Nyāya-Vaiśeṣikas,* ed. Jan Gonda, *A History of Indian Literature* Series, vol. 6 (Wiesbaden: Otto Harrassowitz, 1977).

19. Nāgārjuna (second century C.E.) maintains that all perspectives about ultimate reality involve contradictions. He applies this dialectical method to all doctrines—causality, substance, attribute—to demonstrate that all judgments about the real are contradictory. Everything, being relative, is unreal. Illustrating the dialectical procedure in the case of causality, Nāgārjuna maintains that entities are neither produced out of themselves, nor from others, nor from both, nor from a lack of causes. Cause and effect, in other words, have a relative and dependent existence and, when taken as referring to absolute unconditional entities, can only lead to absurdities. The only appropriate thing to say is that everything is void or empty (*śūnya*). Nāgārjuna's, *Mādhyamika-Kārikā* ('Middle school verses'), the foundational text of the Mādhyamika school, dialectically expounds the above viewpoint. It is of special relevance that

Nāgārjuna addresses the question of the viability of *pramāṇa*, in a separate work entitled *Vigrahavyāvarttanī*, demonstrating the logical contradictions involved in the task of providing a *pramāṇa* for *pramāṇa*. For a detailed account of this issue, see Kamaleswar Bhattacharya, *Vigrahavyāvarttanī* (London: Routledge, & Kegan Paul, 1979). Candrakīrti, the sixth-century commentator of Nāgārjuna, in his *Prasannapadā*, also devotes a chapter on this issue. See Marvin Sprung, trans., *The Lucid Exposition of the Middle Way* (Delhi: Motilal Banarsidass, 1986).

20. Śrī Harṣa (1125–1180 C.E.), a staunch Advaitin of great dialectical skill, called his philosophical work *Khaṇḍanakhaṇḍakhādya* literally 'the sweetmeat of refutations'. Out of the three methods— *vāda*, *jalpa*, and *vitaṇḍā*—Śrī Harṣa preferred the last one as the most appropriate form of method for destructive criticism, because in this method it is not necessary for the debater to prove or defend his own view. He saw the goal of philosophy as consisting simply in the refutation of all rival views and theories. For example, in the context of refuting, the Naiyāyika contention that the difference is real, Śrī Harṣa states: "...if, on the one hand, difference is viewed as entering into the essential nature of the things that differ, the relation between the latter, if duly thought out, is found to be one, not of difference, but of identity. And if, on the other hand, difference is held to be something extraneous to the things that differ, the need of establishing a connection between difference on the one and the things differing on the other hand drives us into the assumptions of an endless series of relations—which explains nothing'." Śrī Harṣa, *Khaṇḍanakhaṇḍakhādya,* chap. 1, sec. 9, trans. Ganganath Jha, *Indian Thought* 1, no. 2 (April 1907): 138. Harṣa's critical analytical examination paved the way for the Neological school, technically known as Navya-Nyāya. Also see, Harśa *Khaṇḍanakhaṇḍakhādya,* trans. Phyllis Granoff (Dodrecht, Holland: D. Reidel Publishing Co., 1978), preface.

21. See Dharamarāja Adhvarīndra, *Vedānta Paribhāṣā*, trans. S. S. Suryanarayana Śāstrī (Adyar: The Adyar Library, 1942); and Swāmī Mādhavānanda (Mayavati: Advaita Ashrama, 1983).

22. Rāmakṛṣṇa Adhvarīndra, *Vedānta Paribhāṣā* and *Śikhāmaṇi*, ed. Swāmī Govindasinhasadhuna (Bombay: Shree Venkatashwar Publishers, 1968). Henceforth the book will be cited as *SM*.

23. Kṛṣṇanāth Nyāyapañcānana, *Āśubodhinī*, commentary on *Vedānta Paribhāṣā* (Calcutta: n. p., 1852). Hereafter the book will be cited as *AB*.

24. *Paribhāṣā Prakāśikā*, a commentary on *Vedānta Paribhāṣā* (Calcutta: University of Calcutta, 1927). Henceforth the book will be cited as *PP*.

25. The period from the sixth century or earlier saw the development of philosophical idealism, logical fatalism, and antireligious ideas, generally known as materialism or Cārvāka, whose origins can be traced as far back as the *Ṛg Veda*. No original writings of this school exist. The much later seventeenth-century *Tattvopaplavasiṃha* ('Lion assaulting all principles of reality') is the only extant work of this school. It is a polemical work directed against all the orthodox schools of Indian philosophy. Materialism is also known as *lokāyata*, that is, the doctrine that only this world exists: there is no world beyond it. See Jayarāśi Bhaṭṭa *Tattvopaplavasiṃha*, trans. S. N. Shastri and S. K. Saksena, ed. Sukhalalji Saghavi and Rasiklal C. Parikh, Gaekwad Oriental Series, 87 (Baroda: Oriental Institute, 1940).

26. In the introduction to his commentary on *Brahmasūtras*, Śaṃkara defines superimposition as the "apparent presentation (to consciousness) in the form of remembrance of something previously experienced in something else." In the example of rope and snake, the rope, the immediate datum of consciousness, is taken as a snake because the qualities of snakes perceived in the past are erroneously attributed to it. The point to note here is that the illusory judgment, 'this is a snake' is the result of a positive identification between what is remembered and what is perceived.

27. Compare this with M. Merleau-Ponty: "The act whereby I am conscious of something must itself be apprehended at the very moment at which it is carried out, otherwise it would collapse. Therefore it is inconceivable that it should be triggered off or brought about by anything whatsoever; it must be *causa sui*." *Phenomenology of Perception*, trans. Colin Smith (London: Routledge, Kegan & Paul, 1962), 371–72.

28. Swami Satprakashanada, *Methods of Knowledge* (Calcutta: Advaita Ashrama, 1975), 85.

29. *Vṛtti* at times has been translated as 'psychosis' (see S. S. Suryanarayana's translation of *VP*). Such a translation, however, having pejorative psychological connotations, is misleading. It should be construed in terms of an epistemic process or act. Briefly, a *vṛtti* is a mental modification that assumes the form of the object. After assuming the form of the object, it enters into *antaḥkaraṇa* (internal sense), which is a passive instrument illumined by the *sākṣin*. The internal sense effects the connection between the *vṛtti* and pure consciousness. In short, the perceptual process takes place as follows: the object is presented, the *vṛtti* goes out, assumes the form of the object, and transports it to *antaḥkaraṇa*, which presents the *vṛtti* to *sākṣin* which in turn illumines it.

30. The expression 'defined by' and other similar expressions such as 'conditioned by' and 'limited by' used in this work may be understood in the sense in which one may speak of 'space' as defined by the four walls of a room. These are only ascriptions, limiting adjuncts, and not literal delimitations.

31. For a detailed and philosophically articulated treatment of the Śaṃkhya school, see Jerry Larson, *Classical Sāṃkhya* (Delhi: Motilal Banarsidass, 1969).

32. In the writings of Śaṃkara , *māyā* and *avidyā* have been used synonymously. The term '*māyā*' can be traced as far back as the Ṛg Veda, in which it is mainained that Indra, with the help of *māyā* , assumes many shapes (6.47.18). The concept *māyā* does not occur in the Upaniṣads in a fully developed form. However, the idea was not entirely foreign to the seers of the Upaniṣads. Yajñavalkya, for example, implies such a notion when he states that there is duality 'as it were' (*BU* 2.4.14). 'As it were' in this context implies that the world of duality, the multiplicity of names and forms, is not real. It is a creation of *māyā*. In the later Upaniṣads (e.g., *Śvetāśvatra*), we come across *māyā* being used in the sense of illusion, where the Lord is said to be *māyin* (4.10). *Avidyā*, which is an equivalent of *māyā*, occurs in quite a few Upaniṣads (for example, *Kena Upaniṣad*, 2.5).

Although *māyā* and *avidyā* have been used interchangeably, *avidyā* has generally been accorded precedence over *māyā* in the matters of bondage and freedom. *Avidyā* has been regarded as the cause of a person's bondage. A distinction also is usually made between two forms of *avidyā* in Advaita Vedānta: *mūla* or primeval, and *tūla* or derivative *avidyā* . The Advaitins account for the empirical world in terms of *mūlāvidyā* and a personal world of illusions in terms of *tūlāvidyā*.

The terms '*māyā*' *avidyā*' '*ajñāna*' though having different connotations, are used synonymously in this book. *Ajñāna* is not absence of knowledge. It is opposed to knowledge, being removed by the direct experience of Brahman. It is contrary to Brahman, its locus. In short, the denotation of all three is nescience or ignorance: "By that element of plurality which is the fiction of Nescience, which is characterized by name and form, which is evolved as well as non-evolved, which is not to be defined either as the Existing or the Nonexisting, Brahman becomes the basis of this entire apparent world with its changes, and so on, while in its true and real nature it at the same time remains unchanged, lifted above the phenomenal universe." *The Vedānta-Sūtras of Bādarāyaṇa with the Commentary by Śaṃkara*, trans. George Thibaut (New York: Dover Publications, 1970), 2.1 27, 352.

33. Perceptibility and perceptuality, although often used interchangeably, should technically be distinguished as follows: perceptibility refers to the circumstance of the object being perceived, whereas perceptuality is the term used when speaking with reference to the percipient or the perceiving knowledge.

34. In this context, Devanji also mentions that Madhusūdana Sarasvatī in his other work, *Advaitasiddhi*, explains the modification of the mental mode with the help of the following example: "the Vritti of the inner organ is like the water of rivers or tanks which being carried through a channel to an adjoining field encircles the trunk of a tree requiring water and assumes the form of a water-basin around it and remains connected with the main source through the channel." Devanji, Prahlad Chandrashekha, trans., *Siddhāntabindu of Madhusūdana with the Commentary of Purushottama*. Gaekwad Oriental Series, vol. 64 (Baroda: Oriental Institute, 1933), n. 3, 235. Readers may wish to compare it with the example given in *VP* to explain the perceptual process. Hereafter this edition will be cited as *SB*.

35. Madhusūdana Sarasvatī further contends that the function of *vṛtti* , which manifests consciousness, would vary depending on the nature of the soul. In the case of the theory in which the soul "is a reflection in Nescience and is present everywhere the function of mind has for its objects the forging of a connection between the knowing-self and the object-self and the removal of the veil...and in the case of the theory in which the soul being limited by Nescience is omnipresent but covered over the function of the mind has for its object only the breaking of the veil on an object-self as in that case the soul himself being the material cause of the universe is already connected with all objects." *Ibid.*, explanatory and critical notes section, 107.

36. 'Identity,' 'nondistinction,' and 'coincidence' are all expressions with different nuances of meaning used essentially to describe the situation that serves as the distinguishing feature of perception. The Sanskrit terms used in this context are: *'abhinnatvam' 'abheda', 'ananya'*, and *'aikya'*, all of which are synonyms of *advaita* in the Vedāntic writings.

37. *VP*, passages 25 and 26.

38. *PP* on *VP*, passages 25 and 26.

39. *Ibid.*, passage 8.

40. *Ibid.*, passage 2; *BU* 3.4.1.

41. *BU* 1.4.2; Hume, *The Thirteen Principal Upanishads*, 82.

42. *BU* 3.4.2.

43. *Ibid.*, 4.3.6.

44. *Ibid.*, 4.3.18; Hume, 136.

45. By 'part' here is not meant spatial parts, of course, but rather an aspect or mode of Brahman. It is, so to speak, to understand Brahman in a certain way, or from a certain point of view.

46. At the outset of his commentary on *Brahmasūtras*, Śaṃkara contends that the subject, the self, and the object, the nonself, which are as opposed to each other as light and darkness, cannot be identified. Nonetheless, individual beings, because of ignorance, do not distinguish between the two and their respective attributes and superimpose on the one the nature and the attributes of the other.

Śaṃkara applies this notion of superimposition *adhyāsa* to the self. The superimposition of the self on nonself and *vice versa* constitutes *avidyā*. One superimposes the characteristics of the body when one says, 'I am fat' and 'I am thin', and the characteristics of the senses and organs when one says, 'I am deaf' and 'I am blind'. Similarly, one superimposes the internal organ, which possesses the characteristics of egotism, and so on, on the self, and superimposes on the internal organ, and so on, the self which is opposed to the non-self and which is the witness of everything.

47. *Praśna Upaniṣad* (henceforth cited as *PU*), 6.2.
48. *Ibid.*
49. *Ibid.*
50. *BU* 3.7.9; *BSB*, 1.2.18–20.
51. The Nyāya argument in support of its position that the self is a non-intelligent substance with momentary knowledge as its special quality is simple. The self exists in sleep but its knowledge obviously does not. One becomes aware of such an absence upon waking through a reasoning that takes the following form: the self in sleep is characterized by *jñānābhāva* because of the nonavailability of any other means of knowledge. If some other means of knowledge were available at the time of sleep, that would certainly be remembered upon waking. The Vedāntic analysis and refutation in this context is a model not only of rare logical astuteness but also of sensitivity to the verdicts of experience. The subject (*pakṣa*) of the inference, namely, the *ātman* existing in sleep, can itself be asserted only by a perception of it which, however, admittedly is not available in sleep. The nonavailability of the means of knowledge as the reason (*hetu*), again, can be known through an absence of knowledge. Cognition of the means of knowledge implies and is implied by knowledge. If it is maintained that a cognition of the means of knowledge is inferential in nature, arrived at through a reasoning from some other means, say, the nonfunctioning of the sense organs or even mind during sleep, then such non functioning itself again will have to be evidenced by yet another inference, for example, using as reason something like stimulation of sensory function. The problem, however, will not end here. One will be required to establish a connection between the nonfunctioning of the senses and their feeling of stimulation, which can only be substantiated by a direct experience to which both are present. The other reason adduced that there is a necessary and invariable loss of memory of any sleep experience is inconclusive. Without a direct knowing (that is, perceiving), of the sleep state itself, it cannot be asserted that there is a necessary nonremembrance of it in the wakeful life. G. R. Malkani, R. Das, and T. R. V. Murti, *Ajñāna* (London: Luzac & Co., 1933), 167–69.
52. *Kena Upaniṣad* (henceforth cited as *KU*), sec. 1.
53. Eliot Deutsch and J. A. B. van Buitenen list the conditions that render empirical knowledge (*vṛttijñāna*) possible: "All empirical knowledge (*vṛttijñāna*) must meet these conditions: (a) the consciousness must undergo a modification or assume a mode (*vṛtti*) which enables it to appropriate the form of the object to be known; (b) it must synthesize the formal sense-contents into a meaningful concept through the activity of the intellect (*buddhi*); and (c) the consciousness of the subject must, through the instrumentality of the 'internal organ' (*antaḥkaraṇa*) illumine the object." *A Sourcebook of Advaita Vedānta* (Honolulu: University Press of Hawaii, 1971), 311.
54. Paul Hacker very clearly explains what is meant by self-luminosity: "Self-luminosity is a special aspect of the self's freedom. It implies that the self is known in a manner different from the way in which objects become known. The self is not an object. It is not necessary to prove...that the self exists. On the contrary, the self's luminosity is the presupposition for any object's being known. One may say in a paradox that the self is unknowable because it cannot become an object of knowledge, but it is at the same time better known than any object inasmuch as no object can be cognized save in the light of the self." "Śaṃkara's Conception of Man," in *Kleine Schriften* (Wiesbaden: F. Steiner, 1978), 128. An interesting corroboration of the same point is provided from an entirely different orientation by M. Merleau-Ponty: "At the root of all our experiences and all our reflections, we find, then, a being which immediately recognizes itself, because it is its knowledge both of itself and of all things, and which knows its own existence, not by observation and as a given fact, nor

by inference from any idea of itself but through direct contact with that existence. Self-consciousness is the very being of mind in action. The act whereby I am conscious of something must itself be apprehended at the very moment at which it is carried out, otherwise it would collapse." *Phenomenology of Perception*, 371–72.

55. Kumārila, *Śloka-Vārtika*, trans. Ganga Nath Jha (Delhi: Sri Satguru Publications, 1983), 2.49–51, 28–29. These are the standard Mīmāṃsā arguments, which are also accepted by the Advaitins.

56. See Citsukha, *Tattvapradīpikā*, ed. Yogīndrananda, with *Nayanaprasādinī* of Pratyaksvarūpa's *Nayanaprasādinī* and editor's Hindi commentary, chap. 1, sec. 1.4 (Banaras: Shuddarsana Prakasan Pratisthana, 1956), 4–5. Hereafter the book will be cited as *TP*.

Citsukha, a later Advaitin, considers at least eleven definitions of self-luminosity, and one of the definitions he rejects is that it could be taken to mean that it is itself its own manifestation (*svasya svayam eva prakāsá itivā*). Prābhākara maintains that the very same conditions that lead to the origination of a cognition also lead to its manifestation. In a cognition of the form 'I know the pitcher', the cognition manifests itself, the object, and the self—the substratum of that cognition. The Advaitins, on the other hand, maintain that consciousness alone is self-luminous and that all the objects of the world are manifested by consciousness. Accordingly, they contend that consciousness and the objects are qualitatively different.

57. Self-luminosity, Citsukha maintains, has the fitness of being immediately known yet it is not an object of any cognition (*avedyatve saty aparokṣa vyavahāra yogyatvam svayam prakāśa lakṣaṇam*); *ibid*., sec. 2.1, 16. He further contends that the self is nothing but this self-luminous consciousness. Inference attests to its self-luminosity. "Consciousness is self-luminous, because it is of the nature of experience. A pitcher, for example, is not self-luminous" (*anubhūtiḥ svayamprakāśā anubhutitvāt yan naivaṃ tannaivam yathā ghatah*). *Ibid*., sec. 2.4, 21. *Śruti* also testifies to the self-luminous character of the *ātman*:

cidrūpatvād akarmatvāt svayaṃjyotir iti sruteḥ,
ātmanaḥ svaprakāśatvaṃ ko nivārayituṃ kṣamaḥ. *Ibid*., 1.3, 38.

58. *KU* 2.2.

59. *Ibid*., 2.3.

60. *Pañcapādikā* is a commentary on Śaṃkara's commentary on the first four *sūtras* of *Brahmasūtras*. See D. Venkataramiah, *Pañcapādikā*, Gaekwad Oriental Series, vol. 107 (Baroda: Baroda Oriental Institute, 1948). Here-after the book will be cited as *PPD*.

61. Karl Potter notes: "It is Padmapāda who pioneers the epistemology we most likely associate with Advaita. He provides the bridge between Śaṃkara and later Advaita, which is as obsessed with epistemology as Śaṃkara was with the contrast between knowledge and action." Karl Potter, *Encyclopaedia of Indian Philosophies*, vol. 3 (Delhi: Motilal Banarsidass, 1981), 73. Another well-known scholar, referring to the *Vivaraṇa* text, states: "This work marks a milestone in the history of the dialectical literature of Advaita Vedānta, for it deals exhaustively with different means of valid knowledge and the epistemological problems connected therein." Dr. Bratindra Kumar Sengupta, *A Critique on the Vivaraṇa School* (Calcutta: Dr. Bratindra Kumar Sengupta, 1959), 271.

62. Śaṃkara refutes the doctrine of momentariness on the same grounds on which he rejects the Vaiśeṣika atomism: "In the course of examining the Vaiśeṣika theory we said that this is not possible even on the assumption of permanent atoms and experiencing souls which can sustain the acquired merits; and can this be possible here, my dear friend, simply by assuming momentary atoms which have no experiencers and

which are not related with everything by way of being the abider and the abode (or the benefited and the benefactor)?" *Brahma-Sūtra-Bhāṣya of Śrī Saṅkarācārya*, trans. Swāmi Gambhirānanda (Calcutta: Advaita Ashrama, 1983), 405.

The Vedāntic critique of momentariness on the grounds that it does not account for remembrance and recognition shows great insight into the nature of experience underlying remembrance or recognition. The latter is not merely a revival of a past experience in the present but also implies the added consciousness that one has experienced previously. A strictly momentary mental state cannot cognize another mental state. However, the Vedāntic explanation of remembrance, in the context of a permanent self, is itself not free from difficulties. Remembrance is not a mere continuity of consciousness or an assertion of identity. There is also the added consciousness, the knowing of something as having been experienced in the past and as being related to the present experience. The question immediately arises: What is the relation between the unchanging awareness and the changing mental modes? *VP* makes a distinction between the functions of unchanging awareness (*ātman*) and changing mental modes (*vṛtti*). However, some relation between the two must be postulated to account for the coherence of experience. According to the Vedāntins, the relation between the two is one of false identification (*adhyāsa*). For a balanced presentation of the issue between the Buddhist and the Vedāntic traditions, see T. R.V. Murti, *The Central Philosophy of Buddhism*, 33–34.

63. *VP*, passage 30.

64. There is no substantial difference between the two interpretations outlined here. However, in speaking of mental modes as their own objects, it seems to me that the author of *VP* has somewhat departed from the original position of Śaṃkara. Śaṃkara, in his *BSB* (2.2.28), undoubtedly speaks of mental modes as objects but never their own objects. For a discussion of this issue and the concept of *sākṣin* in Advaita, see Tara Chatterjee, "The Concept of Sākṣin," *The Journal of Indian Philosophy* 10 (1982): 339–56.

65. Madhusūdana Sarasvatī, *Advaitasiddhi*, chap. 1, sec. 5, trans. Ganganatha Jha, *Indian Thought* 6, nos. 2 & 3 (1914): 287–88. Hereafter this edition will be cited as *AS*.

66. See Anil Kumar Ray Chaudhuri, "The Concept of Sākṣin," *Our Heritage* 1 (1953), 69–76.

67. *Ibid.*, 75.

68. Śaṃkara, *Brahma-Sūtra-Shānkara-Bhāshya*, trans. V. M. Apte (Bombay: Popular Book Depot, 1960), 2.1.9, 294. See *VP*, passages 28–32.

69. *VP*, passages 37–41.

70. Karl Potter, "*Vedāntaparibhāṣā* as Systematic Reconstruction," *Perspectives on Vedānta*, ed. S. S. Rama Rao Pappu (Leiden: E. J. Brill, 1988), 111.

71. *VP*, passage 40.

72. Mysore Hiriyanna, *Outlines of Indian Philosophy* (Bombay: George Allen & Unwin Pvt. Ltd., 1973), 343–44.

73. *VP*, passages 31.

74. A *viśeṣaṇa* (attribute) is an invariable distinguishing feature, as blueness in a lotus. *Upādhi* (limiting adjunct), on the other hand, is a limitation, a separable, distinguishable feature, as a red flower in the proximity of a crystal that appears to be red because of the presence of the red flower. The distinction between *viśeṣaṇa* and *upādhi* is one of the highlights of the Vedāntic thinking, marking its perspective off from the Nyāya and the other schools. For an illuminating account of this distinction, see Madhusūdana Sarasvatī, *AS*, chap. 1, sec. 24, *Indian Thought* 9, no. 1 (1916): 25–27.

75. *Sarvaṃ jñātatayā, ajñātatyā vā sākṣin caitanyasya viṣayah:* "All things are objects of the witness-consciousness, on account of their being either known or unknown." Srirama Śāstrī, *Pañcapādikāvivaraṇam, 1st Varṇaka* (Madras: Government Oriental Manuscript Library, 1958), 83–84. Henceforth this edition will be cited as *PPDV*.

76. Srirama Śāstrī, in the preface to the abovementioned volume in which *Pañcapādikā* also appears, lists ten principal differences between Padmapāda's and Vācaspati's philosophies, xviii–xix. Anantakṛṣṇa Śāstrī, in the introduction to his commentary on *Brahmasūtras*, provides a more detailed listing of the differences between the two. I quote them here in full both because it is the most comprehensive account to date of the differences between the two traditions and also because of the unhappy circumstance that the edition from which this has been taken is extremely difficult to obtain. Anantakṛṣṇa Śāstrī notices sixteen important points of divergence and similarity:

Bhāmatī	***Vivaraṇa***
"1. *Jīva* (individual self)—locus of both cosmic and individual .	1. (a) Cosmic *Avidyā* (*Māyā*) in Brahman. (b) Individual nescience (*avidyā*) has for its basis *Jīva*.
2. *Avidyā* is different in different jīvas. *Avidyās* are therefore *many* and not one.	2. (a) Cosmic *Avidyā* [*Māyā*] is one. (b) Individual *Avidyās* are manifold
3. *Avidyā* has for its object Brahman.	3. The same.
4. *Avidyā* is only the efficient cause (*nimitta-sahakārī*) in the capacity of being a fault.	4. *Avidyā* is the efficient cause in the capacity of a fault and is also the material cause.
5. *Avidyā* possesses the power of veiling (*āvaraṇa-śakti*) alone.	5. It possesses a twofold function (a) veiling (*āvaraṇa*), and (b) projection (*vikṣepa*).
6. Brahman alone is the appearing or illusory Cause (*vivartopādāna*).	6. Brahman and *Māyā* both are material causes: (i) Brahman is the illusory or apparent Cause, (ii) *Māyā* is the really transforming material cause.
7. Perception is only mental (*mānasa*) not verbal (*śābda*).	7. Perception is both mental and and verbal.
8. Mind is also an organ of sense (*indriya*).	8. Mind [*manas*] is not an organ.
9. Deep meditation (*nididhyāsana*) is factor in Spiritual Realization while study (*śravaṇa*) and deliberation (*manana*) are subsidiaries.	9. *Śravaṇa* (study) is the main factor in Realization, *manana* and *nididhyāsana* are auxiliaries.

10. Only the associated Absolute (*upahita Brahman*) is the object of Vedāntic knowledge and not *pure* consciousness.	10. Pure Consciousness (*śuddha Brahman*) also comes within the scope of Vedāntic knowledge.
11. Pure Consciousness is neither the object of mental mode (*vṛtti*) nor of the reflected consciousness (*phala caitanya*).	11. Pure Consciousness is the object of mental modification *akhaṇḍa-kāra (vṛtti)*
12. Knowledge is a form of mental action, but does not come under the scope of injunction.	12. Knowledge is not a mental action and does not come under the jurisdiction of Vedic injunction.
13. There is no injunction in the act of study (*śravaṇa*) in the Upaniṣadic text—*śrotavyo*, and so on.	13. There is restricting injunction (*niyama vidhi*) in the *śrotavyo* text.
14. Even the sense organs, superimposed as they are on the witnessing self (*sākṣin*),are perceptible.	14. Only the characteristics (dharma) of the sense organs are imposed on the witnessing self (*sākṣin*), and as such they are perceptible.
15. No mental modification is admitted in things directly illumined by the *sākṣin*.	15. Mental modification exists in such cases also; but such mind-modifications are not generated by any means of correct knowledge (*pramāṇa*).
16. *Īśvara* is the consciousness limited by a totality (samaṣṭi) limitations; while *Jīva* is consciousness with individual limitations (*vyaṣṭi*).	16. *Īśvara [God]* is the prototypal consciousness (*bimbacaitanya*) while *Jīva* is reflected consciousness (*pratibimba*) and *not* limited (*avacchinna*)."

Śaṃkara, *Brahmasūtra-Śaṅkara-Bhāṣyam*, ed. Anantakṛṣṇa Śāstrī, Calcutta Sanskrit series, vol. 1, part 3 (Calcutta: The Metropolitan Printing and Publishing House, Ltd., 1941), 9–10.

In this introduction, however, I have discussed at length only the distinctions that are relevant to a discussion of the issues in *VP* and *PP*. For a detailed account of differ-ences between the two traditions, readers may wish to consult the books mentioned above.

77. The other well-known dialectical works on Advaita philosophy are *Tattvapradīpikā*, by Citsukha (end of 12th century C.E.), *Khaṇḍanakhaṇḍakhādya* by Śrī Harṣa (end of 12th century C.E.), and *Pañcadaśī* by Vidyāraṇya (end of 14th century C.E.). All these works follow the tenets of the *Pañcapādikāvivaraṇa*.

Vivaraṇaprameyasaṃgraha of Vidyāraṇya is a lucid analysis of the conclusions arrived at by Prakāśātman in his *Pañcapādikāvivaraṇa*. The other two important works, *Saṃksepaśāriraka* of *Sarvajñātman* and *Prakaṭārthavivaraṇa*, follow the tradition initiated by Padmapāda. For an exhaustive listing of the commentaries on the *Pañcapādikā* literature, the readers might wish to consult E. P. Radhakrishnan, "The Pañcapādikā Literature," *Poona Orientalists* 6 (1941–1942), 57–73.

78. Vācaspati, *Bhāmatī with Kalaptaru and Parimala* (Bombay: Nirnayasagar Press, 1917), 1.i.1: *na caisa sākṣātkāraḥ śabdasya pramānaṣya phalam*. Hereafter this edition will be cited as *Bhāmatī*.

79. *The Saṃksepaśāriraka of Sarvajñātman*, ed. N. Veezhinathan (Madras: University of Madras, 1985), 1.341, 315.Hereafter the book will be cited as *SS*.

80. *PPD*, Fourth *Varṇaka*, 2.4, 298.

81. Ibid., 303–304.

82. *Vācaspati's* failure to discuss *akhaṇḍārtha* is one of the most perplexing features of the *Bhāmatī* school. Various explanations have been given to explain this perplexity. However, the explanation offered by S. Suryanarayana Śāstrī and Kunhan Raja appears most plausible. "...unlike Maṇḍana, Vācaspati does not hold to the sphoṭa–vāda, the doctrine that meaning is one and integral and that it is but revealed gradually in the spoken letters and words. He would seem to have more sympathy with the Associationist and the Behaviourist explanations of the acquirement of meaning than with an explanation like that of the Gestalt psychologist. The juxtaposition of such a doctrine alongside that of akhaṇḍārtha would have appeared, to say the least, incongruous." *The Bhāmatī of Vācaspati on Śaṅkara's Brahmasūtrabhāṣya*, introduction, ed. S. S. Suryanarayana Śāstrī and Kunhan Raja (Madras: Theosophical Publishing House, 1933), xxii. Hereafter this edition will be cited as *Catussūtrī*.

83. On this point, Sueśvara notes: " The author of Brahma–Sutras did not mean to inculcate *prasaṅkhyāna* when he said (at *Brahma–Sūtra* 4.1.1). 'There must be repetition and pondering, because it has been more than once taught'. All he meant was that what was partly or imperfectly understood could be understood if it were heard again later properly.' " *The Naiṣkarmya Siddhi of Śrī Sureśvara*, 3.125, trans. A. J. Alston (London: Shanti Sadan, 1959), 198. Hereafter the book will be cited as *NS*.

84. See for example, Sarvajñātman, *SS* 1.122–24; 1.341.

85. Sureśvara, *NS* 3.17.

86. *VP*, passage 15.

87. *Ibid.*

88. See S. S. Suryanarayana Śāstrī, introduction to Appaya Dīkṣita's, *Siddhāntaleśasaṅgraha*, vol. 1 (Madras: University of Madras, 1935), 58–59. Hereafter this book will be cited as *SLS*.

89. *Ibid.*, 59.

90. Śaṃkara, in *BSB* 2.4.17.

91. *etasmāj jāyate prāṇo manas sarvendriyāṇi ca*, "From this are derived the vital air, the mind, and all the sense organs." *MU* 2.1.3.

92. *mahābhūtāny ahaṃkāro*
buddhir avyaktvam eva ca
indriyāṇi daśai'kaṃ ca pañca ce ndriyāgocarāḥ. *Bhagavada Gītā*, 13.5. "The great (five gross) elements, the I-sense, understanding as also the unmanifested, the ten senses and the mind and the five objects of the sense," are the constituents of the 'fields' of '*kṣetra*', the contents of experience.

93. Upaniṣads establish the existence of the mind separately from the senses. Mind directs the senses. The functions of mind are desire, deliberation, doubt, faith, lack of faith, steadiness, unsteadiness, shame, intelligence, and fear. *BU* 1.5.3.

94. *VP*, passage 16.

95. Appaya Dīkṣita, *SLS*, introduction, 40.

96. In this context, the Vivaraṇa tradition clearly follows the line of thought held by Sureśvara. Sureśvara maintains that the *jīva* cannot be the locus of *avidyā*, because the *jīva* is a modification of *avidyā*. Therefore, *ātman* is the locus as well as the content of *avidyā*. Sureśvara, *NS* 111–17.

97. Passage 1.1.2.1 of this manuscript.

98. For a succinct, readable account of the formative ideas of Rāmānuja, see John B. Carman, *Theology of Rāmānuja* (Connecticut: Yale University Press, 1970).

99. Vācaspati, *Bhāmatī*: *jivādhikaraṇāpya avidyā*. 1.4.3.

100. The question is asked: How, if the *jīva* is a product of nescience, can it also be its locus? The answer of the *Bhāmatī* school in effect points to the beginninglessless nature of nescience. An earlier nescience produces the *jīva* who becomes the locus of subsequent nescience. The charge of infinite regress poses no specific threat to a believer of the *Bhāmatī* tradition. The very inability to provide ultimate explanation indeed constitutes the essence of nescience (*tad evā vidyānām avidyātvam*). Suryanarayana Śāstrī, *SLS*, introduction, 42.

101. Passage 1.1.3 of this manuscript.

102. Although there is no unanimity about what idealism means, idealists generally maintain that there can be no object of knowledge without knowledge. Consciousness is the prius of reality. This point has received undue attention from early interpreters of Advaita in this century, for example, A. C. Mukerji, interprets Advaita as a form of idealism: "The objects may change their essence, but consciousness cannot be said to change in as much as it witnesses all objects irrespective of the place where they may happen to be; the fact-of-being-known is there implied by all objects without exception. Even when something is supposed to be nonexistent, this very nonexistence cannot be proved in the absence of knowledge." *The Nature of Self* (Allahabad, India: The Indian Press, Ltd., 1938), 110.

There is no doubt that in Advaita the transcendental and pure form of consciousness is a necessary condition of all phenomena. The Advaitins, however, invoke *sākṣin* (witness-consciousness) for witnessing the object. An object then exceeds empirical experience. The being of things, from which things come, is merged, and there is a consciousness of this being of things which is called *sākṣin*. Additionally, the Advaitins accept *avidyā* (veil of ignorance). There is a consciousness of this veil, a consciousness that bears witness to the veil, and when this veil is removed, the consciousness and the object become one. One may call it consciousness (*cit*), or one may call it existence (*sat*). *Sat* and *cit* are not two modes of being, existing side by side in being. Being is alternately describable as *sat* or *cit*. *Sat* and *cit* are two names of the same thing. They have the same denotation but connote different things, much like Frege's "the morning star is the evening star." The morning star and the evening star have the same referent but different meanings. Likewise, *sat* and *cit* have different meanings but refer to the same being. Brahman is the object *par excellence*. It is so objective that the knowing act merges into it. It is not pure subject, because subjectivity is surrendered in the realization of the being. Revelation is the unveiling of being, the emergence of the being by the veil being removed.

Radhakrishnan, perhaps the greatest neo-Vedāntin of our times, in *An Idealist View of Life*, calls Advaita the Indian version of idealism, provided one keeps in mind that it is neither Berkeley's subjective idealism, *esse est percipii*, nor the objective idealism of Kant. It is an idealism that would use consciousness to describe the sense in which being and knowing are identified. Radhakrishnan says that he is using the term in a minimal sense, not in the epistemic sense of something, 'I know It,' but in the minimal sense of the identity of knowing and being. This identity of knowing and being has not been conceived anywhere in the western idealistic traditions. (*An Idealist View of Life*

[India: George Allen & Unwin Ltd., 1971], chap. 1). In short, one may call Śaṃkara's philosophy idealistic as long as one keeps in mind that it is not an epistemological idealism.

103. According to Vijñānavādins, ideas alone are ultimately real. "As to ontology," notes Junjiro Takakusu, "this school...adheres neither to the doctrine that all things exist, because it takes the view that nothing outside the mind (mental activity) exists, nor to the doctrine that nothing exists, because it asserts that ideations do exist." *The Essentials of Buddhist Philosophy* (Delhi: Motilal Banarsidass, 1978), 81. The things that exist in the outside world can be experienced through mental processes. Of the three factors—the knower, the object known, and the knowledge—the last one alone is taken to be true. All we ever perceive are our own mental forms, and even consciousness appears to itself as an external object. Consciousness is nothing but an everchanging stream. The forms of the objects of knowledge, which any cognition assumes at any particular instant, are not determined by the reality of the external world but by ideas. Accordingly, the differences between cognitions of a wall and a pitcher are mental in character. Independent existence of external objects cannot be demonstrated. Because our knowledge of objects in the form of ideas and of the objects themselves is presented simultaneously, they must be one and the same. In other words, no object is ever experienced apart from consciousness, therefore, they are one and the same.

104. S. Radhakrishnan, trans. *The Brahma Sūtra: The Philosophy of Spiritual Life* (New York: Greenwood Press Publishers, 1968), 2.2.28, 384.

105. *Ibid.*

106. *Ibid.*

107. *Ibid.*

108. Various explanations have been offered by modern interpreters of Śaṃkara to explain his realism. Some of them amount to an overinterpretation and even distortion of the position of Śaṃkara (for example (Kokileswar Sastri, *An Introduction to Advaita Philosophy* [Calcutta: University of Calcutta, 1926]). D. M. Datta's assessment by contrast is balanced and insightful: "In fact, epistemologically Śaṃkara can be classed rather with realists and the pragmatists, in so far as he admits the existence of an external world, outside and independent of the subject mind and judges the validity of knowledge by practical results.... Śaṃkara is not a solipsist or subjective idealist, as often he is thought to be. For he admits the existence of an external world. He is not, therefore, an acosmist, as well. He is rather a realist and a pragmatist, though in a limited sense. For he considers the universe to be real in so far as it is grounded in Reality itself." "Some Realistic Aspects of the Philosophy of Śaṃkara," *Recent Indian Philosophy*, ed. Kalidas Bhattacharyya (Calcutta: Progressive Publishers, 1963), 343–45.

109. J. G. Arapura, "*Māyā* and the Discourse about Brahman," *The Problem of Two Truths in Vedānta and Buddhism*, ed. Marvin Sprung (Dodrecht-Holland: D. Reidel Publishing, 1973), 119–20.

110. Apte, *Brahma-Sūtra-Shānkara-Bhāshya*, 400.

111. Eliot Deutsch's assessment in this context represents the most apt and perspicuous estimation of Śaṃkara's realism: "When a distinction between subject and object is a necessary condition for *someone* to know *something*, then, there is no way in which one can, without self-contradiction, deny either the subject or the object. What is peculiar about this 'soft realism' of Advaita is, of course, that the knowledge so obtained within the *necessary* dualistic structure of empirical knowledge is permeated with *avidyā*. A realistic epistemology is thus philosophically *necessary* but ultimately false. It is restricted to only a portion of human experience." *Advaita Vedānta*, 97.

112. T. M. P. Mahadevan, *The Philosophy of Advaita* (New Delhi: Arnold-Heinemann Publishers, 1976), 33–34. He further notes: "The Vedānta view that mind goes out to the object in order to grasp it, explains the perceptual process better than the impressionistic view of the West. Mind is not a mere *tabula rasa*, a recorder of impressions received from without. It is not at all passive in perception." *Ibid.*, 31–32.

113. P. K. Sundaram, *Advaita Epistemology* (Madras: University of Madras, 1968), 30–31.

114. *Sense Perception in Science and Śāstars*, ed. T. M. Srinivasan and B. G. Sreelakshmi (Sringeri: Sri Sharda Trust, 1986), 13.

115. *Ibid.*

116. *Ibid.*, 14.

117. For example, the following quotation from Price is typical of the British empirical tradition: "When I see a tomato there is much that I can doubt. I can doubt whether it is a tomato that I am seeing, and not a cleverly painted piece of wax. I can doubt whether there is any material thing there at all. Perhaps what I took for a tomato was really a reflection; perhaps I am even the victim of some hallucination. One thing however I cannot doubt: that there exists a red patch of a round and somewhat bulgy shape, standing out from a background of other colour-patches, and having a certain visual depth, and that this whole field of colour is directly present to my consciousness. What the red patch is, whether a substance, or an event...physical or psychical or neither, are questions that we may doubt about. But that something is red and round then and there I cannot doubt." H. H. Price, *Perception* (London: Methuen & Co., 1961), 3.

118. D. M. Datta, *Six Ways of Knowing* (Calcutta: University of Calcutta, 1972), 45. Jadunath Sinha also maintains, and rightly so, that in Advaita Vedānta it makes perfect sense to say that in the perceptual process mind 'goes out' to meet the object. For the Advaitins "the object does not break in upon the mind and imprint its form on it, but the mind goes out to the object and assumes its form. Thus, though both subject and object are necessary for perception, dominance is given to the subject, and the object is regarded as subordinate to the subject. Subject and object, therefore, cannot be regarded as co-ordinate terms in knowledge but the subject is always the dominant factor. The supreme importance of the *vṛtti* of the mind in perception proves the dominance of the subject-element. But the subject (mind) can pour itself into the object and incorporate it in itself.... It is much easier to conceive the *out-going* of the mind intelligized by the conscious self to the object than the *in-coming* of the unconscious object to the mind." *Indian Psychology*, vol. 1 (Calcutta: Sinha Publishing House, 1958), 136–37.

1

Truth and the Means of True Knowledge

Upodghātaḥ

yad avidyāvilāsena bhūtabhautikasṛṣṭayaḥ.
tam naumi paramātmānaṃ saccidānandavigraham [1.1]

Introduction

1.1 *Through the appearance of whose nescience—of which the creation of the elements and objects derived from elements are created—to that supreme self, whose form is being, consciousness, and bliss, I offer obeisance.*

1.1 The author of the text *Vedānta Paribhāṣā* (*VP*) begins his text with a benedictory verse, in conformity with the time-honored practice of Sanskrit writers. A benediction (*maṅgalam*)[1] is invoked expressing a hope that the work attains to completion in all respects, and that it has the sanction of tradition. Tradition does not refer to something hallowed and ancient, but rather signifies a category of knowledge. Anantakṛṣṇa Śāstrī, the author of *Paribhāṣā Prakāśikā* (*PP*), speaks of tradition as a source of valid knowledge in its own right. The authority of the grammarian Patañjali is cited. Patañjali states that religious texts (*śāstras*) are, as it were, set on their feet thanks to the invocations at the beginning, middle, and end.[2] The reader's attention is drawn to three kinds of invocations: the bodily prostration, vocal prayer, and inward contemplation or reflection. The third one consists of an insight in the form of acknowledging that there is something or someone greater than 'me.' Śāstrī maintains that meditation on nondual reality should be the true auspicious act of invocation to the deities that one makes at the commencement of one's project.[3] It is indeed true that *smṛti*[4] maintains that those desirous of accomplishment shall worship the sun, or the Preceptor, Great Gaṇeśa, and others. But such mandates of *smṛti* must be understood in light of the *śruti* declaration that he who worships God as another, 'I am this, he is another', is indeed ignorant.[5] In other words, *smṛti* must be understood in light of *śruti*.[6] It is as if indicating that a true benediction has for its content nothing else but the essence of supreme self that the author of *VP* begins the treatise offering obeisance to supreme self construed as reality or being, consciousness, and bliss.[7]

1.1.1 The expression 'through the appearance of whose nescience' (which accounts for the creation of the world of elements and things made of the elements, i.e., elementals) becomes the occasion for the discussion, among other things, of a central issue of Advaita Vedānta, germane for comprehending the notion of 'object-defined consciousness' (*viṣaya avacchinna caitanya*) developed later in the chapter on perception.

The genetive case used in the expressions 'whose nescience', 'nesciences' appearance', and 'whose appearance' is significant.[8] It indicates a 'substratum-located relation' (*āśraya āśrayībhāva*). The cause of the world's manifestation is *māyā* (used synonymously with nescience), which in the final analysis is none other than the supreme self. The cause of the world's appearance, therefore and appropriately so, is said to be the supreme self. Similarly, the instrumental case, 'through whose', should not be taken in its literal sense as indicating an instrument-agent relation. The instrumental sense imports identity (*abhede tṛtīyā*). Everything, the elements as well as the objects made of these elements, is a manifestation of nescience. The manifold world of names and forms is the creation of nescience and, therefore, equally the creation of the supreme self.

1.1.2 The first of the issues raised concerns Brahman as the substratum as well as the content of nescience. The answer to the question, 'whose nescience, and nescience with respect to what', points to one and the same thing, namely, Brahman. Brahman is the subject or the agent of nescience as well as its object or accusative. In other words, Brahman is the ground of nescience as well as the content concealed by it. This distinctive viewpoint of the Vivaraṇa school was clearly anticipated by Sureśvara[9] and forcefully propounded by Sarvajñātman.[10] Even Śaṃkara admits it when he speaks of *mahāmāyā* as *mahāsuṣupti*, and as grounded in the supreme God.[11]

1.1.2.1 The theory stated above is explained with great clarity in *PP*: Pure undifferentiated consciousness, 'one only without a second', alone acquires the characteristic of being the locus as well as the content of *avidyā*. That is to say, it is not God or the individual self, but rather Brahman, not differentiated as God or self, that serves as the ground of *avidyā*. God or self are only consequential to *avidyā*.[12] Therefore, they can serve as its locus or its content. What comes into being subsequently cannot serve as the locus or the content of that which has been previously existent.

1.1.2.2 The position at variance with the view expressed herein is held by Vācaspati Miśra. He states that the individual self is the locus of *avidyā*.[13] This view comes closer to common sense and phenomenological verification. In an ordinary declaration, 'I do not know', it is surely the individual 'I' that is spoken of as ignorant, not pure consciousness.

1.1.2.3 The Vivaraṇa critique of the theory stated above, especially as formulated by *PP*, is very much on target: If *avidyā* is located in the individual 'I', then for *avidyā* to be manifest the 'I' also must be manifest. If the ground remains unmanifest, how can there be a manifestation of what stands on that ground?[14] In the state of deep sleep, the individual 'I' remains unmanifest, because mind provisionally merges in *avidyā*, although *avidyā* remains manifest. Upon returning to the waking state, one affirms 'I slept well', which testifies to the presence of consciousness in the state of deep sleep. If this were not the case, no affirmation of it in memory could be possible. 'I slept well', is a case of retro-cognition,[15] and not introspective cognition. The presumption that consciousness persists even without the instruments of sense and cognitive experience, that one rightly makes, therefore is the proof of the thesis herein maintained. Pure consciousness alone can be the substratum of ignorance.

1.1.2.4 After stating the Vivaraṇa point of view, *PP* seeks to defend the point of view of Vācaspati. The formulation of the defense exhibits great phenomenological discernment. How does one explain the veridical nature of the waking experience, 'I am ignorant'?[16] True, pure consciousness manifests *avidyā* in the state of deep sleep. Such a statement, however, lacks phenomenological verification, and is true only as an ontic statement. What is distinctive of waking consciousness is the circumstance that the state of mind is superimposed upon pure consciousness. Mind has the power to reveal *avidyā*, and the nature of the revealing medium, i.e., mind, is such that it reveals the object as if present in itself. The mirror reflects one's face as if present inside the mirror. In the same way, mind, while revealing *avidyā*, reveals it as it shows itself, signifying consciousness reflected in it, that is, the individual self. It is therefore the individual self that must be said to be the ground or the locus of *avidyā*, not Brahman. Brahman is the content of *avidyā*. The genetive compound 'whose *avidyā*' therefore signifies 'whose content is *avidyā* '.

Additionally, Brahman, as the locus of *avidyā*, is viewed as the 'transfigurative' (*vivarta*)[17] material cause of the world. Even Vācaspati, when he argues that the individual self is the locus of *avidyā*, does not suggest that the individual self is the material cause of the world. He clearly states that Brahman is the material cause of the world. Vācaspati's position therefore is not incompatible with the view of Vivaraṇa regarding Brahman as the ground or the locus of *avidyā*. Brahman is the material cause of the world for both Vācaspati and Vivaraṇa.

1.1.2.5 The author of *SM* finds this debate irrelevant at this juncture,[18] because only what is admitted here as beyond dispute, that is, Brahman as the content of *avidyā*, matters. The fact that they differ regarding the locus of *avidyā* should not concern us here. *PP*, however, maintains otherwise, and for good reason: the invocatory verse of *VP* is concerned with the creation of the world of elements and elementals; Brahman is said to be the creator of the world not because it is the content of *avidyā*, but precisely because it is the locus of *avidyā*. Reference to Brahman as the content of *avidyā* does not serve the purpose of explaining the material causality of Brahman with respect to the world. The point of defense that *PP* articulates is that the convergence between the schools of Vivaraṇa and Bhāmatī over the issue of the recognition of Brahman being the locus of the world, one explicitly and the other tacitly, is more significant than the commonplace agreement of Brahman as the content.

1.1.3 Finally, reconciling the position of Vācaspati with the thesis that Brahman is the locus, *PP* elicits the phenomenological meaning and significance of the statement that *avidyā* is grounded in the individual self. It is the individual 'I' that is said to be ignorant in the statement 'I am ignorant'. The experience underlying the verbalization of such ilocutionary state-ments must be subjected to careful analysis. Does the 'I' imply the consciousness conditioned by the intellect that makes the statement? This obviously cannot be the case, because the judging mind itself belongs to the realm of ignorance. The judging mind is a product of *avidyā* and does not precede it, standing without, owning it. Nor can the 'I' mean simply the consciousness conditioned by *avidyā*, as attested by the statement 'I am ignorant', which will be little more than a self-referring tautology. Therefore, the 'I' stands for pure consciousness, which serves as the essential nature of the individual 'I'. The individual *self itself*, in other words, also serves as the locus of *avidyā*. *Avidyā* is grounded in pure consciousness, which constitutes the essential nature of the individual self. Pure consciousness comes within empirical usage, as the 'I', when it serves as the supporting ground of *avidyā*. The 'I-consciousness' is that which is concealed by *avidyā* . There is no confusion between the two in the phenomenal realm.

yad antevāsipañcāsyair nirastā bhedivāraṇāḥ
taṃ praṇaumi nṛsimhākhyaṃ yatīndraṃ paramaṃ gurum [1.2]

1.2 *I salute my teacher's teacher, the [supreme] preceptor named Nṛsiṃha, whose lion [like] pupils put aside the elephant [like] opponents of the doctrine of dualism.*

śrīmadveṅkaṭanāthākhyān velāṅguḍinivāsinaḥ
jagadgurūn ahaṃ vande sarvatantrapravartakān [1.3]

1.3 *The inhabitant of Velāṅguḍi called Veṅkaṭhanātha , to that world teacher, the founder indeed of all sacred lores, I offer my salutation.*

yena cintāmaṇau ṭīkā daśaṭīkāvibhañjinī
tarkacūḍāmaṇir nāma kṛtā vidvanmanoramā [1.4]

1.4 *He, by whom has been written a commentary, that is pleasing to the mind of a scholar called Tarkacūḍamaṇi on the [Tattva] Cintāmaṇi in which he discards ten commentaries.*

ṭīkā śaśadharasyāpi bālavyutpattidāyinī
padayojanayā pañcapādikā vyākṛtā tathā [1.5]

tena bodhāya mandānāṃ vedāntārthāvalambinī
dharmarājādhvarīndreṇa paribhāṣā vitanyate [1.6]

1.5 *He, by whom has been written a commentary for the students of Śaśadhara and who also explained the Pañcapādikā by construing its word meanings—*

1.6 *By that Dharmarājādhvarindra is written this Paribhāṣā, for the instruction of dull persons.*

1.7 *iha khalu dharmārthakāmamokṣākhyeṣu caturvidha puruṣārtheṣu mokṣa eva paramapuruṣārthaḥ; "na sa punar āvartate" ityādiśrutyātasya nityatvāvadhāraṇāt; itareṣāṃ trayāṇāṃ tu pratyakṣeṇa "tad yatheha karmacito lokaḥ kṣīyate evam evāmutra puṇyacito lokaḥ kṣīyate" ityādiśrutyā ca anityatvāvagamāc ca. sa ca brahmajñānād iti brahma tajjñānaṃ tatpramāṇaṃ ca saprapañcaṃ nirūpyate.*

1.7 *Among the four human goals*[19] *called righteousness, wealth, desire, and liberation, liberation alone is the supreme human goal; śruti [texts] such as "he [who attains liberation] does not return here again" (CU 8.15.1) serve to determine the eternality of such goals, whereas of the remaining three, because of the understanding of their transitoriness by perception and śruti [texts as] "just as in this world, the merits acquired [in previous lives] through work become destroyed, even so the world which is won by merit becomes destroyed" (CU 8.1.6). And, because that [liberation] could be attained only by the knowledge of Brahman, the knowledge [of Brahman] and the means of that [knowledge] are described in detail.*

1.8 *tatra pramākaraṇaṃ pramāṇam. tatra smṛtivyāvṛttaṃ pramātvam anadhigatābādhitārthaviṣayakajñānatvam; smṛtisādhāraṇaṃ tv abādhitārthaviṣayakajñānatvam.*

1.8 *Of these, the unique cause (karaṇam) of a knowledge-event (pramā) is the means (pramāṇa) [of knowledge]. Here, the nature of such knowledge-event, which excludes retrocognition (smṛti), consists in being a cognition having for its content an entity that is not already known and [secondly] is not sublated; whereas, that [knowledge-event] which is common to retrocognition consists in being cognition, having for content an unsublated entity.*

1.8 *Pramāṇa* is the instrument that leads to a knowledge-event (*pramā*).[20] *VP* formulates the Advaitic account of *pramā* as what is not sublated (*abādhita*)[21] by any other knowledge and also as something that is not already known. A distinction is made between two types of *pramā:* the *pramā* that excludes *smṛti* (retrocognition), and the *pramā* that includes it. The former is regarded as the knowledge of an object that is neither sublated nor previously known, and the latter as the knowledge of an object that is not sublated by any other object of knowledge.

Nonsublatability is common to both definitions. In the erroneous perception 'this is silver', the knowledge of silver continues to be valid so long as the object of knowledge (i.e., the silver), is not sublated by any other object of knowledge (i.e., the shell). This implies that the knowledge of silver as silver must be taken to be valid as long as it is not known that it is a shell.

1.8.1 *Anadhigatatva* (previous unknownness or novelty) means the following: It is different from the content of knowledge, which is conditioned by the immediately preceding moments of the origination of knowledge. *PP*, in light of the standard requirement of a logically viable definition, anticipates a doubt with respect to retrocognition. Such a cognition is caused solely by the impressions of past experience. Therefore, technically, there is no basis for bringing it under cognition (*jñāna*), which is characterized by novelty.[22]

1.8.2 The discussion of *smṛti* and its resistance to assimilation under the category of *jñāna* found in *VP* is very much like that in other Indian philosophical systems. With the possible exception of the Jaina school, no Indian philosophical system concedes the status of *pramāṇa* to retrocognition. A significant point of discussion in the present context, and the one with unavoidable metaphysical overtones, is the issue of persistent cognition (*dhārāvāhika jñāna*). Persistent cognition is the name for a continuous stream of cognition of one and the same object, having a structure made of the elements of several cognitions within itself.

1.8.2.1 When *anadhigatatva* is explained as one of the two defining criteria of a *pramā*, implying the feature of novelty (literally, previous unknownness), the defining criterion excludes retrocognition from the ambit of knowledge. However, in the case of a persistent cognition, the cognition in the first moment surely has for its content an entity previously unknown, and hence qualifies as a case of a knowledge-event (*pramā*). The same, however, is not true with the cognitions of the second and subsequent moments, because these refer to the contents that are known already through the first cognition. Therefore the definition of a knowledge-event as one that has for its content an entity previously unknown does not apply to the phenomenon of persistent cognition, at least with respect to its second and subsequent moments.

The solution to this problem gives rise to the issue of the perceptibility of time. By admitting that time comes within the range of perception, an effort is made to demonstrate that cognitions in the second and subsequent moments, in the instance of a persistent cognition, undoubtedly refer to the same object, but as conditioned by the second and the subsequent moments. The object, although known previously, yet as conditioned by the second and the subsequent moments, remains 'previously unknown'. The solution of *VP* in this context displays rare discernment into experience: a persistent cognition of an object is still a unitary cognition so long as it lasts, because it is characterized by the feature of duration. There are no multiple cognitions within it. This also removes the objection that because cognitions in the second and the subsequent moments in a continuous stream of cognition cannot be considered to be valid, the definition of *pramā* is too narrow.

1.8.2.2 Elucidating the observations made by the author of *VP* about retrocognition and persistent cognition, *PP* observes that, in the analysis of a knowledge-event, the characteristic of being different from retrocognition should be included. This is simple enough. If one includes the condition, that is, the characteristic of being different from an object of knowledge that arises from latent impressions, then it ultimately results in saying that it is only different from an object of retrocognition. This cumbersome process does not serve any purpose.

1.8.3 The etymological meaning of the term *'anadhigata'* (unknown), *PP* observes, has something to do with *ajñāna* or *avidyā*. *Ajñāna* is admitted to be of a positive nature by the Advaitins, irrespective of whether one belongs to the camp of Vācaspati or Vivaraṇa. The term *'anadhigata'* simply means that which comes within the purview of what is characterized by *ajñāna*, and that which is positive in nature. To be more precise, *anadhigata* is of the nature of being characterized by the content of *ajñāna*, which exists in the moment before the functioning of the sense organ. To have the knowledge of an object, some preliminary conditions must be fulfilled. One such condition is the unknownness of the object before the means of knowledge turns its searchlight upon it. That is to say, before we can have the knowledge of the object, the self must have been aware incipiently of the object as unknown. When an object is known for the first time, there also is the recognition attendant upon such knowledge that the object was unknown before, but now it is known. In the language of Vedānta, it is a form of awareness of the object as qualified by *ajñāna*. Such a recognition will not take place if the person was not aware of the object as qualified by *ajñāna*. In the case of objects, such as a pitcher, at the moment of the rise of a mental modification (*vṛtti*) through the interaction of the sense organ and the object, there is effected the removal of *ajñāna*. In the moment immediately preceding the rise of a mental mode, the object, such as a pitcher, remains unknown. In the case of retrocognition, a mere revival of latent impressions itself is capable of removing the state of being the content of *ajñāna*. The author of *PP* draws the reader's attention in the present context to the insightful remark made by Brahmānanda in his commentary on *Advaitasiddhi*, in the Dvitīyamithyātva section,[23] in which he makes the point that in the case of retrocognition, the object is not concealed before the origination of the *vṛtti*. Therefore, it is not an object of *ajñāna*, and accordingly , the definition of *pramā* does not extend to retrocognition.

In summary, the content of retrocognition is not unknown at the moment of the experience, which is its instrument (*karaṇa*).[24] In the case of a valid knowledge-event, an object becomes the content of a cognition that is conditioned by the previous moment, and also the moment of its origination.

1.8.4 Parrying the argument of the Advaitin, the opponent may seek to reduce the observation made about *ajñāna*, in the context of defining a knowledge-event, to a case of absurdity. If what the Advaitins claim were the case, then they would have to face the contingency that the 'illusory objects', such as shell-silver, could not become the content of *ajñāna*. But they exist, and their existence is conditioned by being known. Avowedly they do not have any independent existence apart from their being known. Therefore, they are not the content of *ajñāna*. This will result in the following paradox: illusion will not exemplify ignorance, and illusory objects will not become the contents of ignorance. Moreover, paradox apart, this will also make the inclusion of the feature of unsublatability under the criterion of knowledge-event meaningless.

1.8.4.1 In reply to this objection, PP endorses the observations that Brahmānanda Sarasvatī makes in the section in which the world is proved to be false (*mithyā*) on the ground of its perceptibility.[25] A distinction is made between two functions of *ajñāna:* one which envelops the existence of an object, thereby causing the notion that the object does not exist (*asattāpādaka*); and the other prevents the revelation of the object, thereby causing the notion that the object is not manifest (*abhānāpādaka*). In the case of the erroneous perception of shell-silver, the *ajñāna* is present in the first of its functions. In an illusory cognition, before its occurrence, *ajñāna* exists, which causes the notion that the object does not exist. Unsublatability, therefore, is very much in place as the defining characteristic of a knowledge-event.

The term *'anadhigata'* is intended to convey the point that an object is conditioned by *ajñāna* of either of the two types distinguished earlier. *PP* prefers to describe it disjunctively to make it more inclusive and rejects the attempt to confine it simply to *ajñāna* of the first type; namely, the one that causes the notion that the object is not manifest. One may be tempted to do so to avoid the overlapping of the definition of *anadhigatatva* in the case of illusory cognitions. The point of *PP*, in interpreting it disjunctively, is to make room for the knowledge-event of states that belong, for example, to the category of happiness (*sukha*) and misery (*duḥkha*).[26] Subjective states, like happiness, are distinct from mental modes that take the form, say, of a pitcher, and other external objects. Both mental states and mental modes are objects of cognition, but the former exist only concurrently with the occurrence of a cognition and not as unknown. Such, however, is not the case with the cognition of external objects and mental modes.

1.8.4.2 The author of *PP* further analyzes the significance of the definition in terms of *anadhigata* and *abādhita*, demonstrating a more precise and inclusive understanding of validity than the standard interpretation of a knowledge-event in terms of correspondence. The Naiyāyikas discern two elements in the structure of a knowledge-event: the adjectival feature and the substantive feature. The cognition 'this is a pitcher' has 'pitcherness', for its adjectival feature and 'pitcher' ('this') for its substantive feature.[27] The cognition is said to be valid because it comprehends pitcherness as the adjectival feature with respect to the pitcher. One may contrast it to an instance of illusory cognition, such as 'this is silver', in which the adjectival feature silverness, normally present in the silver, is cognized in the shell. The cognition therefore is illusory.

1.8.4.2.1 According to the fundamental framework of Advaita, the Nyāya definition also will apply to cases of illusory cognition, because the extant object may or may not be the substratum of silverness. The Advaita explanation of illusory cognition, therefore, amounts to admitting that there is an illusory silver that exists as the object of our perceptual experience. The Nyāya definition of error or illusion, to the effect that it is a case of perceiving the adjectival feature in a substratum marked by the absence of such an adjectival feature, remains a purely ontic analysis and overlooks the phenomenologically significant aspect of illusion, namely, when the perceptual experience of illusion occurs, the object actually serves as the substratum of the adjectival feature. To say of an illusion that it is merely an instance of knowledge that comprehends an adjectival feature in a substratum where it does not exist is to overlook the perceptual-experiential basis of the occurrence of such a knowledge. The Advaitins consistently hold to a phenomenological orientation in analyzing and unraveling epistemological issues. They do not maintain that an object, for example, a piece of cloth, really exists in the substratum (the threads), where it is perceived. The expression 'floor is possessed of a pitcher' does not mean that the pitcher exists, but that a pitcher appears to exist thereon.

1.8.4.2.2 When the Advaitins say that the world is false (*mithyā*) or nonreal,[28] one must not lose sight of their explanation of falsity. If by falsity is meant that in the very substratum or locus of an object which is cognized there is the absence of that object in the three divisions of time—namely, past, present, and future—then even the ordinary perceptual valid cognitions of the Naiyāyikas, of the form 'cloth is in the threads' and 'the floor is characterized by the possession of a pitcher', will become instances of illusory cognitions. Consequently, the Advaitins define error or illusion with a simplicity that is of great phenomenological significance: Illusion is that which is sublated. Conversely, a knowledge-event is that which remains unsublated.

1.8.5 The deeper motivation that underlies the Advaitin interpretation of a knowledge-event in terms of previous unknownness and unsublatability is often ignored by writers who focus on these issues as logical resolutions of epistemological issues. The deeper motivation, in the present context, implies the soteriological interest that inspires the epistemological and logical analysis of knowledge. The object or the goal of Advaita, one must not forget, is realization of Brahman as pure consciousness, the implicate of all experience. Advaita as a hermeneutic is exercised to demonstrate that the Upaniṣadic texts, despite seeming inconsistencies in their statements, are coherent. *PP* strives to be faithful to the spirit of the tradition, as well as to the intentions of the author of *VP*. *VP* with its novel features reflects the true spirit of the tradition. *PP* connects the more immediate task of defining a knowledge-event (*pramā*), which the author of *VP* addresses, with the ultimate hermeneutical task of interpreting the Upaniṣads. The latter constitutes Vedānta in its original sense as a coherent exposition of the thesis of Brahman as pure consciousness.

1.8.5.1 To stress the point further, *PP* refers to *Advaitasiddhi*, which clearly states that the Upaniṣadic texts that speak of Brahman as endowed with attributes indeed do not convey the knowledge of the attributes, because these are already known.[29] However, these attributes are useful only in providing knowledge of the essential nature of nondual consciousness that is not known through any other *pramāṇa-s*.

1.8.5.2 In this connection it is useful to note that there are different marks (*liṅga*)[30] used by Mīmāṃsā to determine the purpose of such passages in the scripture: The beginning as well as the concluding portion of a scriptural text must point to one and the same subject matter. There should be a frequent repetition of the point one wishes to emphasize. *Apūrvatā* (novelty), in the sense of saying something new, is yet another condition. One immediately notices that *apūrvatā* is another word for *anadhigatatva*. Sarasvatī, in this context, reminds the readers of the inclusion of *apūrvatā* among the marks that are invoked to determine the import of the Upaniṣads. He further reminds us that if this condition is not included, then the invariable rule—the Vedas are authoritative as a source of knowledge-event (*pramā*) precisely because they convey that which is not hitherto unknown—will be broken.[31] The stipulation that a knowledge-event should have the virtue of previous unknownness may thus be seen to be an explication of the hermeneutical principle involved in the very acknowledgment of *śruti* as a valid source of knowledge.

1.8.6 The definition of *pramā* (*anadhigata abādhitārtha viṣyaka jñānam*) given in the *VP*—that it is of the nature of *jñāna* (knowledge) and has for its content something previously unknown and unsublated—is defended scholastically by the author of *PP*. In this context he also examines similar attempts made by other commentators. The author of *SM*,[32] for example, anticipates an objection to the definition of *pramā* given in the *VP*, particularly objecting to the aspect of the definition making it a case of *jñāna*, which has for its object mental activities that are cognate with it (e.g., desire, action, and so on). Such mental activities in a sense presuppose *jñāna*. One could have desires only with regard to something that is already known. The same is true of an activity in terms of its volitional effort. The very expression 'having as an object,' something whose content is previously unknown, is itself, *ipso facto*, indicative of *jñāna*. There is no need to mention it separately. The author of *SM* maintains that the inclusion of the term '*jñāna*' is necessary.[33] Otherwise having as content something not known before the functioning of *pramā* and not being contradicted also will apply to the function of sense organs (*indriyas*). Sense organs also have contents not previously known and apparently not contradicted. Therefore, to avoid the application of the definition in the case of sense organs, the term '*jñāna*' has been included in the definition.

1.8.6.1 The author of *PP* shows greater discernment in determining the more relevant use of the term '*jñāna*.' He maintains that the term under consideration has been used to avoid the application of the definition in the case of revived latent impressions. Here the object of *ajñāna* is not conditioned by the moment of each originating factor during the duration of an experience (*anubhava*). Experience gives rise to revived latent impressions, and, therefore, it is not necessary that it must be the content of knowledge that gives rise to it. Experience is the instrumental cause of revived latent impressions, which in turn gives rise to memory. Thus the term '*jñāna*' is used to avoid the inclusion of revived latent impressions and memory in the definition of *pramā*.

1.8.6.1.1 The author of *PP* likewise finds the comments of *Āśubodhinī* (hereafter cited as AB)[34] explaining the significance of the inclusion of the term 'content' (*artha*) in the definition of *pramā* questionable. *AB* maintains that such an inclusion is necessary to avoid the overextension of the definition to cases like universals (*jāti*), [35] which are non-contents. Universals, and the relation of inherence (*samavāya*)[36] through which universals stand related to particulars, are regarded by the Advaitins as 'unreal'. If they may be spoken of as substantive contents, they are unreal contents (*alīka padārtha*). Such *padārthas* cannot become contents of knowledge, and therefore they can never be cognized.

1.8.6.1.2 The observations of *PP* in this context, questioning the position of AB, are significant. The author reminds us that the nature of being an object (*viṣyatva*) lies in its identity with consciousness. Such an identity is not possible for something that either exists or is totally nonexistent. Unreal objects can never become objects of experience. Unreality is simply nonbeing. The totally nonexistent or unreal contents, although they satisfy the qualifications of previous unknownness and unsublatability, are still nonexistent (*asat*). Therefore, the question of their identity with consciousness does not even arise. Accordingly, the claim that the term '*artha*' is included in the definition to exclude false contents is meaningless.

1.8.6.2 At this juncture the author of *PP*, to show the relevance of the criteria of previous unknownness in the definition of *pramā*, returns to the issue of persistent cognition and throws further light on the solution of *VP* that a persistent stream of cognition is really a unitary cognition. One often tends to overlook an implicit sense of the term *'jñāna'*, namely, that which alone prompts one toward activity and which also performs the function of manifesting the object. When viewed in this light, it is not difficult to see that the second and subsequent moments of a persistent stream of cognition also have the activity of manifesting the object. Therefore it is not proper to hold that they are not valid, because they fail to qualify the criteria of previous unknownness.

In summary, the qualifying adjective *abādhita* excludes the application of the definition of *pramā* to erroneous cognitions, and the second qualifying adjective *anadhigata* rules out *smṛti* or retrocognition as an instance of *pramā*.

1.9 *nīrūpasyāpi kālasyendriyavedyatvābhyupagamena dhārāvāhikabuddher api pūrvapūrvajñānāviṣayatattatkṣaṇaviśeṣaviśiṣṭaviṣayakatvena na tatrāvyāptiḥ. kiṃ ca siddhānte dhārāvāhikabuddhisthale na jñānabhedaḥ; kiṃ tu yāvad ghaṭasphuraṇaṃ tāvad ghaṭākārāntaḥkaraṇavṛttir ekaiva, na tu nānā, vṛtteḥ svavirodhivṛttyutpattiparyantaṃ sthāyitvābhyupagamāt. tathā ca tatpratiphalitacaitanyarūpaṃ ghaṭādijñānam api tatra tāvatkālikam ekam eveti nāvyāptiśaṅkāpi.*

nanu siddhānte ghaṭāder mithyātvena bādhitatvāt tajjñānaṃ kathaṃ pramāṇam? ucyate, brahmasākṣātkārānantaraṃ hi ghaṭādīnāṃ bādhaḥ, "yatra tvasya sarvam ātmaivābhūt tat kena kaṃ paśyet" iti śruteḥ. na tu saṃsāradaśāyāṃ bādhaḥ, "yatra hi dvaitamiva bhavati tad itara itaraṃ paśyati" iti śruteḥ. tathā cābādhitapadena saṃsāradaśāyām abādhitatvaṃ vivakṣitam iti na ghaṭādipramāyām avyāptiḥ.

taduktam—

"dehātmapratyayo yadvat pramāṇatvena kalpitaḥ
laukikaṃ tadvad evedaṃ pramāṇaṃ tv ātmaniścayāt," iti.

"ā ātmaniścayāt" brahmasākṣātkāraparyantam ity arthaḥ. "laukikam" iti ghaṭādijñānam ity arthaḥ.

tāni pramāṇāni ṣaṭ, pratyakṣānumānopamānaśabdārthāpattyanupalabdhibhedāt.

1.9 *Because we have accepted that time, although colorless, could come within the range of perception, even a persistent cognition [for the second and subsequent moments] has for its content what is not the content of earlier cognitions, because the moments that serve as the adjectival feature of the object are different, so there is no [fallacy of] nonpervasion in that respect [in regard to the definition of persistent cognition]. Moreover, according to the principles [of Advaita], in the case of persistent cognitions, there is no variation in a persistent cognition. Rather as long as the pitcher exists, so long the mental mode in the shape of a pitcher is one and the same, and not many, because we admit the persistence of a mode till another mode contrary to that [initial mode] arises. And thus, because also in this case the knowledge of a pitcher, and so on, which takes the form of consciousness reflected in that [mode] is one only, lasting during that [intervening] time, there is no doubt [fallacy] regarding the narrowness of the definition [of pramā].*

[Objection]: But surely, in your view [the view of Advaita], pitcher, and so on, are sublated as illusory: how can their cognition be valid knowledge? The answer is: The empirical objects are sublated only when there arises the knowledge of Brahman because of śruti [text], "When, however, for him everything has become just one's own self, then whereby and whom would one see?" (BU 4.5.15). But there is no sublation in the state of phenomenal existence according to the śruti [text:] "Where there is a duality of some kind, there one sees another" (BU 4.5.15). Accordingly the word 'unsublated' means 'not being sublated during the state of phenomenal existence', there is no nonpervasion [in the definition of pramā] in the valid cognition of a pitcher, and so on.

So it has been said—

"Just as the belief that the body is the self is [falsely] imagined to be valid, exactly so is this worldly [knowledge] till the self is known."

'Till the self is known' means 'till the intuition of Brahman', and "ordinary [cognition]" refers to the knowledge of pitcher, and so on.

These means of knowledge are six, divided into perception, inference, comparison, verbal testimony, presumption, and non-apprehension.

1.9 The issue of the credibility of persistent cognition as a case of *pramā*, on the ground that its second and subsequent moments entail reference to time, and therefore the feature of previous unknownness is technically present, raises the phenomenologically significant question of the perceptibility of time. The Mīmāṃsakas[37] and the Naiyāyikas[38] are of the opinion that in ordinary experience there is no cognition where time is not manifested. The Advaitins, accept this position in a broad sense. The author of *PP*, however, introduces certain refinements which he believes to have a direct bearing on the issue. Those who object to the view that the second and subsequent cognitions have for their object contents associated with the second and the subsequent moments unwarrantedly assume that distinction in time is as clearly perceivable as the distinction between two objects. A moment is extremely subtle and cannot be comprehended with the naked eyes. Vācaspati himself, commenting on the Nyāya text, admits that it is impossible to comprehend differences in points of time with the naked eyes.[39] The Advaitins question it on the ground that an object must have a determinate shape to be distinguished from another object. Time obviously does not have any shape or form. The possession of color or shape is a possible criterion for visual perception only in cases that fall under a fixed sense organ. It does not apply to cases that are comprehended by all the sense organs.[40] The Advaitins, as well as the Mīmāṃsakas, maintain that time is comprehended by all the sense organs. The very mode of referring the different sense organs concurrently to the same referent rests on the presumption of the comprehension of time. It is in a similar strain that the Advaitins speak of *ātman* as free from any material, shape or form, and it therefore cannot be comprehended by any sense organ, while at the same time also admitting that it could undergo reflection. Although the latter idea, as will be explained later, appears odd from a logical perspective, it is phenomenologically meaningful.

1.9.1 In this context, the author of *PP* observes that even assuming that it is significant tọ speak of the possession of real color or shape as a criterion of perceptual cognition, the color or shape might be superimposed. And, as superimposed, it could serve as the cause of visual perception. Furthermore, the color that pertains to a reflecting medium and the color that is superimposed may be considered to be present in the case of time as well. Therefore there is no inherent implausibility in admitting visual cognition of time. Likewise, the etheric space becomes an object of perception, although it does not possess real color but only superimposed color.

1.9.1 In this context, the author of *SM* articulates an objection in the following words: Śaṃkara maintains that the etheric space does not fall under the ambit of visual perception. In other words, etheric space and similar objects are not perceived validly, even though they may serve as the substratum of superimposed color.[41] Do not then the teachings of Śaṃkara conflict with the position earlier maintained about time, namely, that time becomes perceptible through its adventitious possession of color, form, or shape? This is the objection the author of *SM* raises.

1.9.1.2 *PP* replies that when Śaṃkara states that ether, and so on, cannot come within the range of perception, he means to say that ether as such cannot be perceived. However, as associated with adventitious color it can be perceived. The same is true of the perception of time. The Advaitins accord perceptibility to time on the strength and validity of the experience, '*now*, there is a pitcher'. The Nyāya school, while defending the case of persistent cognition as involving reference to time, maintains that time could never fall within the range of perception, because it does not have the distinguishing mark of color or shape. When there arises the cognition of a pitcher '*now*, there is a pitcher', the contact may be accepted as the cause of the cognition and may itself be taken as also giving rise to the perceptibility of time. The 'pitcherness' that is related to the pitcher through the relation of inherence itself serves as a contact to comprehend the universal pitcherness in it. Time thus serves as the adjectival feature in the cognition '*now*, there is a pitcher'. This is the defense that the commentator of *AB* provides, making use of the Nyāya category.[42]

1.9.1.3 The author of *PP* does not find this defense convincing. Providing an account of its perceptibility on the basis of a particular contact will not suffice. *AB*'s explanation would hold if the objection had been that time is not validly perceived because there is no contact to perceive it. The point that *PP* wishes to make is that time, by merely serving as an adjectival feature of the pitcher, could be perceptual without requiring a contact. Furthermore, if it is maintained that such a contact is required, then *AB* must admit that in an inferential cognition of fire on the mountain, the fire is perceptual because sight is conjoined to the mountain to which fire is conjoined through the relation of *saṃyukta saṃyoga*.[43] This, however, is not the case. *PP* therefore finds the entire project of explaining the categories that are involved in the definition of *VP* through the help of Nyāya terms and concepts unacceptable and even contradictory.

1.9.2 *PP*, in this context, also refers to some of the internal varieties or interpretations of Advaita referred to in the *Siddhāntaleśa-saṃgraha* (hereafter cited as *SLS*),[44] and finds some of them throwing welcome light on the perspectives of *VP*. He refers to the distinction that some Advaitins make between primal nescience (*mūlāvidyā*) and the derivatives of primal nescience, termed 'modal nescience or ignorance' (*tūlāvidyā*). The former is one, whereas the latter are many. Primal nescience conceals pure consciousness while modal ignorances conceal the consciousness conditioned by the objects of the world, for example, the pitcher-consciousness. If this distinction is not maintained, then the *vṛtti* in the form of a pitcher would itself serve to remove primal nescience, and there would be instantaneous enlightenment for all. When there arises the *vṛtti* in the form of a pitcher, it only removes the modal ignorance concealing the pitcher while leaving other modes of ignorance functioning. Consciousness is reflected in the *vṛtti*. This is termed 'empirical cognition.' If the modal or the derivative nescience is admitted to be one only, then by the removal of it once, one would continue to have the knowledge of the pitcher until one attains the knowledge of Brahman. To avoid this it is admitted that modal ignorances are many. The question, however, still arises: When one modal ignorance is removed by the *vṛtti*, do all other modal ignorances continue to exist and conceal the object? In response, it is said that when a *vṛtti* arises, it only removes one modal ignorance but keeps other modal ignorances in check. It is like a medicine which, when administered, not only removes the particular form of illness but also keeps the other ailments under control.[45] It implies that when the *vṛtti* in the form of a pitcher ceases to exist, another modal ignorance, which is removed when a second mental mode arises, conceals the object. In this manner, we have the cognition as well as the noncognition of a pitcher.

Applying the above analysis to the case of a persistent stream of cognition, it is maintained that there are ignorances that conceal the object that are to be removed by the second and the subsequent mental modes. By the first mental mode, the modal ignorance concealing the object in the first moment is removed, and that object in turn becomes the content of the second modal ignorance. In other words, the same object is concealed by the second derivative nescience and the second mental mode removes this ignorance. The same object then would be the content of the third ignorance. The modal ignorances that are many conceal the consciousness conditioned by the object which is *indicated* by its respective moments. It is important to remember in this context that time is *indicated* and not constituted by these moments. It is only when it is maintained that the objects are actually constituted by the moments—that is, that objects literally are temporal—that the question regarding the difficulties pertaining to the perceptibility of time arise. Time, however, is only an indicating feature. It does not form a part of the object. This can be explained on the basis of an analogy. The sense of hearing is nothing but ether conditioned by the cavity of the ear. But the latter does not form part and parcel of the sense of hearing. It only serves as an indicating feature and helps distinguish the sense of hearing from other parts of the etheric space. In the present case, time also merely serves as an indicating feature. The object indicated by time may be spoken of as different in every moment. The mental mode in the form of a pitcher could thus remove ignorance, and the definition of valid knowledge thus could hold even without accepting the perceptibility of time.

1.9.3 The author of *PP*, while affirming the position outlined in *SLS*, also refers to another position cited therein.[46] In a persistent cognition, the modal ignorance associated with gross time is removed by the first mental mode, then in the second and the subsequent cognitions there is no manifestation of time previously unmanifest. Therefore, in a persistent stream of cognition, only one mental mode must be admitted. It does not consist of different mental modes. It is one only so long as it lasts. As long as there is the cognition of a pitcher, the mental mode in the form of a pitcher is one only and not multiple. The mental mode is admitted to be permanent till there arises a contrary mental mode. The contrary mental mode arises because of the rise of the mental mode assuming the form of another object.

It might be asked: If a mental mode is destroyed only when a contrary mental mode arises, how does one account for the mental mode in the form of impartite Brahman, because when such a mental mode arises, there is no other mental mode to remove it. It is said in response that such a terminal mental mode annihilates ignorance and also gets annihilated in the process. It is at once the annihilating factor and what is being annihilated.[47]

1.9.4 Instruments (*pramāṇa-s*) of valid cognition in Advaita Vedānta are six in number: perception (*pratyakṣa*), inference (*anumāna*), comparison (*upamāna*), verbal testimony (*śabda*), postulation, (*arthāpatti*), and noncognition (*anupalabdhi*).

Notes

1. Following the usual practice of orthodox Sanskrit writers, Anantakṛṣṇa Śāstrī begins his commentary with a discourse on appropriate *maṅgalam*. Such a benediction is necessary for the successful completion of a work because it is *siddha*, that is, an established procedure handed down by tradition. Tradition maintains that those who believe in a hereafter, those who believe in a self apart from the body, and so on, those who believe in God, perform some invocation at the time of the beginning of a particular work.

2. *ata eva mangalādīni mangalāmadhyāni maṅgalāntāni prayante śāstrāṇīti ma-*

hābhāṣyākārā vadanti. PP, 1. Also see *Kāvyaprakāśa* of Mammaṭa, ed. Raghunath Damodar Karmarkar (Poona: Bhandarkar Oriental Institute, 1933), 1–2.

3. *PP*, 2.

4. *PP* relies on *Yajñavalkya Smṛti* in this regard. By offering worship to Lord Ganeśa, by worshipping Tilakaswāmin, by worshipping the sun, one attains to perfection or fulfillment: *ādityasya sadā pūjāṃ tilakasvāminas athā mahāgaṇapateś caiva kurvan siddham avāprayāt*, *PP*, 1. If *Yajñavalkya Smṛti* is right, it is asked, how could the author of *VP* offer an invocation to a deity that is different from the ones mentioned in this text?

5. To support his position that reference to ultimate reality is a kind of *maṅgalam*, Śāstrī cites a passage from *BU*: *atha yo 'nyāṃ devatāsupāste 'nyo 'sāv anyo' ham asmīti na sa veda. BU* 1.4.10. It clearly states that one who worships God must worship it either as *sākṣin* or the individual soul. *Sākṣin* and the individual soul are one and the same, because *sākṣin* conditioned by the mind, is the individual soul, and when it transcends the mind, it is God. So even if one worships any God (e.g., Ganeśa, or the sun), it must be worshipped as the unconditioned reality, namely, Brahman. Keeping this in mind, the author of *VP* incorporates the following invocation: "I offer my salutation to that supreme self with which I am identical, and the world is the transformation of whose nescience." Therefore, *Yajñavalkya Smṛti* must be understood in light of *BU*. Irrespective of whether one worships the lord Ganeśa, or the sun, it must be worshipped as identical with oneself.

6. *Śruti*, etymologically means 'the hearing', knowledge acquired by listening to the instruction of a teacher. The term '*smṛti*' etymologically means 'recollection' or 'memory.' In its technical sense, *smṛti*-s refer to a vast body of texts and treatises. These are authored and therefore fallible. *Śruti*-s, on the other hand, are authorless and beginningless. Whenever there is a conflict between *śrutis* and *smṛti*-s, *śruti*-s prevail. *Śruti*-s are self-authenticating, while the *smṛti*-s are validated to the extent they are not in conflict with the *śruti*. *BSB* 2.1.1 reinforces this point when it states: "The authoritativeness of the Vedas in regard to the matters stated in them is independent and direct, just as the light of the sun is the direct means of our knowledge of form and colour; the authoritativeness of the personal views, on the other hand, is of an altogether different kind since it depends on the validity of *śruti* and should be consistent with it." S. Radhakrishnan, *The Brahma Sūtra: The Philosophy of Spiritual Life*, 19.

7. The first line of the introductory verse of *VP* gives the *taṭstha lakṣaṇa* and the second line the *svarūpa lakṣaṇa* of Brahman. The designation of Brahman as *saccidānanda*, that is, *sat* (existence), *cit* (consciousness), and *ānanda* (bliss), refers to *svarūpa lakṣaṇa*, that is ("the definition with reference to essence"). It is distinguished from *taṭstha lakṣaṇa*, that is ("the definition with reference to accidents"). The *taṭstha lakṣaṇa* is merely indicative of the existence of Brahman as the ground of phenomena. It gives no insight into the nature of Brahman. The latter is done by *svarūpa lakṣaṇa*, which is a nonrelational definition. This signifies that the so-called definition and what it defines are coincident: "*Sat, Cit* and *Ānanda*...all *denote, not connote*, one and the same entity, *Brahman*.... Each is *sui generis*, a self. Each is identical with Brahman, substantially, not conceptually." T. R. V. Murti, "The Two Definition of Brahman in the Advaita" in *Studies in Indian Thought*, ed. Harold G. Coward (Delhi: Motilal Banarsidass, 1983), 82–83. In other words, *sat*, *cit*, and *ānanda* are not qualifying attributes of Brahman, but rather expressions of its essence.

8. *yasyāvidyā yadāvidyā tasyā vilāsaḥ pariṇāmah. abhede tṛtīya. avidyā-pariṇāmarūpā ity arthah. PP*, 2. Śāstrī contends that '*yasyāvidyā*' is a compound word, which when split into '*yasya avidyā*' means 'whose *avidyā*.' Since *avidyā* is feminine, '*tasyā vilāsaḥ*' in the sixth case should be construed to mean that the world

is a transformation of *avidyā*. He further adds that the instrumental suffix in "*yad avidyāvilāsena*" conveys the sense of identity. If the literal meaning is taken into account, then it would imply that the creation of the elements as well as the elementals is the result of the transformation of *avidyā*. However, the creation of the elements and the elementals is not the result of the transformation, because they themselves *are* the transformations of *avidyā*. So in keeping with the general trend of Advaita, the instrumental suffix should be taken in the sense of identity.

9. In *NS*, Sureśvara favors the idea that Brahman is at once the content and the locus of ignorance and argues that ignorance cannot exist in a vacuum. Ignorance always refers to ignorance of something, and it must have a substratum in which to exist. The self and not-self are the only two categories that exist. The very nature of the not-self precludes its being the locus of ignorance, because the fact of ignorance implies a knower or at least knowledge. The not-self originates on account of ignorance: "It is absurd to suppose that that which is logically and causally prior can only exist supported by and dependent on its own effect. Nor, again, has the not-self any form independent of and different from ignorance whereby it could serves as its locus and support." *NS*, book 3, 111. Accordingly, because the not-self cannot serve as the support of ignorance, the only alternative remaining is that Brahman or the self is both the locus and the content of ignorance.

10. Sarvajñātman, like Sureśvara, maintains that Brahman is the locus as well as the content of *avidyā:* "Undifferentiated Consciousness is the locus as well as the object of *avidyā*. (The embodied soul and God) that come into being subsequent to *avidyā* can neither be the locus nor be the object of *avidyā* which exists prior to them" *SS* 1.319, 305–306. In other words, because ignorance presupposes *jīva*, *jīva* cannot serve as its locus. Sarvajñātman, in this context also discusses seven different views (2.132–138) of *ajñāna*, and then refutes them one by one.

11. Śamkara states that *avidyā* is *parameśvarāśrayā: avidyātmikā hi bījśaktiḥ avyaktaśabdanirdeśya māyāmayi mahāsuṣuptiḥ, yasyāṃ śerate svarūpapratibodha-rahitaḥ saṃsārino jīvaḥ*. The root cause of the world is *avidyā*, it is called *avyakta*, it depends on *parameśvara*; it is of the nature of māyā: the great sleep. And in it the *jīvas*, not aware of their identity with Brahman, rest. *BSB* 1.4.3.

12. Śāstrī's statement that *avidyā* exists prior to both the individual self and God should not be taken to mean that *avidyā* is temporally before the individual self and God. Such a relationship among these categories is not an issue here because temporally, these are beginningless. However, when viewed logically, we must have the conception of *avidyā* before we can have the conception of God and the individual self. It is useful to note in this context that the Advaita tradition accepts six categories to be beginningless: the individual self, God, pure consciousness, nescience, the relation between the individual self and God, and the relation between pure consciousness and nescience. See *SLS*, introduction, n. 44, 299.

13. Vācaspati interprets the word '*parameśvarāśrayā*' to mean that Brahman is the *āśraya* of *avidyā*, not in the sense of being its locus, but in the sense of its being the content. *Jīva* alone is the locus of *avidyā*. *jīvadhikaraṇāpyavidyā nimittatayā viṣayatayā vā īśvaramāśrayate iti īśvarāśrayā iti ucyate, na tu ādhāratayā, vidyāsvabhāve brahmaṇi tadanupapatteḥ. Bhāmatī*, 297.

14. In the context of articulating the theory of the erroneous cognition of shell-silver, Sarvajñānatman makes an illuminating distinction between the *ādhāra*, the 'this' that is connected with the illusory silver, and the *adhiṣṭhāna*, the real, that is, the 'shell', the knowledge of which cancels the illusion, but which never appears in the illusion. When we perceive the silver, we are ignorant of the shell, because the knowledge of the shell cancels the illusion. The *ādhāra* or the 'this' serves as the nexus

between the real and the illusory silver. The object of ignorance thus is identical with the real basis of illusion. "The designation of 'substrate' (*adhiṣṭhāna)* is well established not in the substance that serves as the locus (*ādhāra*) of the superimposed object, but in the substance that is the object of *avidyā* with its product.... In erroneous cognitions...only the superimposed object appears.... In no case does an object different from the one superimposed appear in the erroneous cognitions." *SS*, 1.31, 165; 1.36, 167.

15. *Smṛti* does not give us any new knowledge. At best, it is a reproduction of past experience. Even the most valid form of *smṛti* falls short of the self-evidential nature of direct cognition. For this reason, it seems more appropriate to translate *smṛti* as retrocognition rather than memory. See Krishna Sivaraman, *Śaivism in Philosophical Perspective* (Delhi: Motilal Banarsidass, 1973), 320–21.

16. In the introduction to *SS*, Veezhinathan explains what is entailed in the waking experience 'I am ignorant': "*Avidyā*, though present in pure consciousness is revealed in the form 'I am ignorant' by the intellect which is the limiting adjunct of *jīva*. It is well-known that the nature of revealing medium is such that what is revealed through it appears as though present in the medium itself.... The mirror which reflects the face appears to contain the face. The point that is of profound importance is that the revealing media reveals the things to be revealed as present in themselves. In the same way, the intellect which reveals *avidyā* reveals it as present in itself and consequently in the consciousness delimited by it, namely, *jīva*. Hence, there is the experience 'I am ignorant'" *SS*, 77–78.

17. Brahman, according to Śaṃkara, is both the efficient and the material cause of the world. The relationship between Brahman and the world has been articulated in terms of *vivarta* (appearance) and *pariṇāma* (transformation). Śaṃkara holds the *vivarta* view. He maintains that all objects, irrespective of whether they are physical and material, are apparent modifications (*vivarta*) of Brahman through the transformations of *māyā*. He uses the example of rope-snake to explain the dependence of the world on Brahman. Whereas the appearance of the snake depends on the existence of the rope, the existence of the rope in no way depends on the appearance of the snake. Similarly Brahman, although the cause of the world, is unaffected by the effect. The appearance of the world does not affect Brahman in any way. Change here is *vivarta*, transfiguration, and not transformation (*pariṇāma*).

The followers of Śaṃkara, although holding the *vivarta* view, explain the relationship between Brahman and the world differently. The author of *Padārthtatvanirṇaya* states that although both Brahman and *māyā* are the material cause, the world is the *vivarta* of Brahman but *pariṇāma* of *māyā*. *SS* contends that Brahman is the material cause, and the *māyā* is only a subsidiary cause. Vācaspati maintains that although *māyā* is an accessory it does not enter into the effect. For a discussion of different views, readers might wish to consult *SLS*, chap. 1, 2.23.

In *Hindu Theology: A Reader* (New York: Doubleday, 1976), José Pereira translates *vivarta* as *transmogrification*, contrasting it with *pariṇāma* (transfiguration), 201–206. I prefer the word 'transformation' for *pariṇāma* because the expression 'transformation' suggests a conjunction of an unchanging form with changing modes, the presence of 'form' in the mode of the expression pointing to it. This is precisely the sense in which *pariṇāma* is understood in the Indian context. *Pariṇāmā* is always *ekadeśa pariṇāma*, partial modification, and not a total one.

18. *PP*, 2.

19. The fact that *VP*'s introduction states that philosophy should be concerned with *parama puruṣārtha* should not be taken to mean that the book primarily discusses soteriological questions. Because *mokṣa* is *parama puruṣārtha*, which can be attained

only through the knowledge of Brahman, the means to the attaining of that knowledge become urgent and are elaborated in detail in *VP*. Hence the preoccupation of the text with epistemological issues.

20. In this book, *pramā* and *pramāṇa* are translated somewhat indifferently as knowledge-event and the means of knowledge-event, and again as valid knowledge and as the means of valid knowledge. The reason is obvious. It is the position of the author of this book that there is no ontic distinction between the two sets of ideas in the final analysis. Similarly, valid knowledge-event and the means of valid knowledge-event are the same.

21. Padmapāda gives the possible six meanings of sublation: "It may mean (i) the turning away of one from an object when in reality one is seeking another (say, silver) or (ii) the destruction of its (false object) *capacity* to provoke action; or (iii) the discrimination of what was not previously discriminated; or (iv) cognition of mutual negation, that is, cognition that this is not the 'silver' and *vice versa*; or (v) the cognition in the known-substratum (say the shell) that the silver is the counter-correlate of the negation; or (vi) eradication of ignorance (ajñāna). The first five are objections; the sixth is the siddhānta" *PPD*, 1st *Varṇaka* , 14.44, 33. Bhāratītīrtha explains sublation as "the removal of nescience, together with its own product present or past, by true knowledge; for sublation is well established in that kind of removal of non-knowledge." S. S. Suryanarayana Śāstrī and Saileswar Sen (tr.) *Vivaraṇaprameyasaṁgraha,* (Kumbakonam: Sri Vidya Press, 1941), 1st *Varṇaka*, 14.47, 83. Hereafter this work will be cited as *VPS*. In short, sublation signifies the eradication of ignorance and its effects for ever.

22. In the Indian systems of philosophy, *jñāna* (cognition) is a concrete occurrent, and truth is the predicate of a cognition. It is a *guṇa* or *kriyā* of the self, something that belongs to or occurs in relation to a self, that is, the knower. In the Nyāya school, *jñāna* is a quality of the self and is necessarily *of* an object. A cognition manifests only the object, and neither the cognizer nor the cognition. In short, a cognition or awareness cannot reveal itself. It is *parateḥ prakāśa*, that is, illumined by others. In Vedānta, on the other hand, it is a mode of the internal organ or *antaḥkaraṇa*, and accordingly has an *ākāra* or form. All objects are manifested by consciousness, and consciousness alone is self-manifesting. This is known as the theory of the self-validity of knowledge (*svataḥ pramāṇavāda*). A cognition is considered true until experience proves it to be false. It is a kind of psychology of belief. From the psychological perspective, the theory maintains that when a person perceives an object, he takes it to be true unless there is some reason to doubt. In other words, this theory provides us with a logical justification of the process of how we arrive at our beliefs.

23. Brahmānanda Sarasvatī, *Laghucandrikā* (Kumbakonam: Śrī Vidya Press, n.d.), 52–58.

24. *Tarka-Saṃgraha* defines *karaṇa* as an extraordinary or uncommon (*a-sādhāraṇa*) causal condition (*kāraṇam*). *Annaṃbhaṭṭa* clarifies what he intends to convey by the phrase uncommon causal conditions (*a-sādhāraṇa kāraṇam*). "An effect is dependent on two sets of conditions, one set comprising the condition that are necessary for effectuation as such and the other comprising those which are necessary for a specific effectuation. The members of the former set are known as 'common' or universal (sādhāraṇa) conditions and are exemplified by such entities as God, space, time, adṛṣṭa, and so on; the members of the other set are the uncommon or the specific (a-sādhāraṇa) conditions." *Tarka-Saṃgraha of Annaṃbhatta with Dīpika,* Gopinatha Bhattacharya (Calcutta: Progressive Publishers, 1976), 155. Hereafter this translation will be cited as *TSD*.

A *karaṇa* or instrumental cause, in other words, is a special or unique cause, which being operative produces the effect (*vyāpāravat asādhāraṇam kāraṇaṃ karaṇam*). In the perception of an object (e.g., the specific sense organ), the eyes, and not mind, are the *karaṇa or* the instrumental cause. Mind cannot be said to be the instrumental cause because it is operative in all cases of external perception. Again, space and time are general conditions of all sorts of effects and therefore should not be regarded as the instrumental cause of any particular effect. In short, an instrumental cause is the sum total of all the causal conditions unique to the effect produced.

25. In Advaita, the only inherent character of the illusoriness of the silver and so on, consists in its appearing as the 'given' (*dṛśyatva*). This also is true of the objects believed to be empirically real. They also are as false as the illusory object (*prātibhāsika*). Ultimately, therefore, the distinctions between 'illusory' and the 'empirically real' (*vyavahārika*) seem to be based on nothing more than purely practical considerations. The distinction that the illusory alone is false (*mithyā*) is itself false (*mithyātvamithyātva*). For a discussion of this and other related issues, see Brahmānanda Sarasvatī, *Laghucandrikā*, 72–89. Madhusūdana, in *Advaitasiddhi*, chap. 1, secs. 3–5, makes the same point when he says that "the object [world] under discussion is unreal...because it is perceptible." (*Indian Thought* 6, nos. 2 & 3 [1914]: 247). He further adds: "What is meant by the World being 'perceptible' is that it is the object of the 'Vritti' of cognitions not produced by Authoritative Word, or (b) that it is the object of qualified or limited cognition, or (c) that it forms the object of consciousness, or (d) that it is dependent upon a cognition which is different from itself, or (e) that it is not self-illumined" *Ibid.*, 281.

26. It should be noted here that one of the necessary conditions of internal perception, say of a pain, is the nondifference between the cognitive mode and the consciousness conditioned by the object of knowledge, say the mental state of pain. This nondifference is only possible when the means of knowledge become identical with the object of knowledge.

27. For the Naiyāyikas, sense contact with the object is the primary and indispensable condition of all knowledge. They further maintain that the senses can be in contact not only with their objects, qualities, and universals but also with their negation. All perceptual knowledge can be expressed in the form of a judgment, a subject with something predicated of it. A percept, such as a cow, really stands for a judgment. 'A cow', for example, 'means an object possessing the characteristic of cowness'. In the cases of perceptual illusions, the sense comes in contact with the real object; however, because of the presence of certain external factors, it is associated with the wrong characteristics, and the object is misapprehended. In other words, what is present in the mind appears as the object in front of us. For the Nyāya analysis, see *Tarka-Saṃgraha of Annaṃbhaṭṭa with Dīpīkā and Govardhana's Nyāya-Bodhinī*, trans. Yashwant Vasudev Athalye, Bombay Sanskrit and Prakrit Series, no. 55. (Bombay: R. N. Dandekar, 1963), 221–32. Hereafter this edition will be cited as *TSDNB*.

28. False (*mithyā*), for the Advaitins, is other than the real (*sadviviktatvam vā mithyātvam*); however, it is not unreal. Unreal is never an object of experience, true or false. In fact the concept of unreal is self-contradictory, for example, the son of a barren woman. False, on the other hand, is an object of experience, for example, rope-snake. One is at a disadvantage when attempting to translate the term *mithyā* into English, because there is no word in the language with the connotation of *mithyā*. No matter how one translates the term, one must not lose sight of the logical and ontological distinction between *mithyā* and unreal, so crucial to a proper understanding of the Advaita system.

Various attempts have been made in the system of Advaita to define falsity. *PPD* defines falsity as "not being the locus of either reality or unreality" (*sadasattvānadhi-*

karaṇatva). This means that falsity is distinct from both reality and unreality. Prakāśātman's definesfalsity as that "which is negated eternally in the same locus where it is cognized" (*pratipannopādhau traikālika niṣedha pratiyogitvam mithyātvam*). The false object does not exist even in the place where it appears to exist for the time being; it was not, it is not, and it will not be. Prakāśātman gives yet another definition: "Falsity is that which is cancelled by knowledge" (*jñāna nivartyatvam mithyātvam*). It seems that although falsity has been defined variously in the Advaita tradition, all the definitions point to one basic fact: the false is something that appears and is later negated or contradicted. For a detailed discussion of these definitions, readers might wish to consult A. K. Ray Chaudhuri , *Self and Falsity in Advaita Vedānta* (Calcutta: Progressive Publishers, 1955), 118–176. Madhusūdana in *Advaitasiddhi* gives five definitions of *mithyātva.* The thrust of all the definitions is that *mithyā* and its own absolute negation share the same locus. *AS*, chap. 1, secs. 3–4, *Indian Thought* 6, nos. 2 & 3 (1914): 249–81.

Śāstrī, in the context of clarifying the *VP* text '*ghaṭader mithyātvena bādhitatvāt*', clarifies the meaning of *mithyā*. This text, when translated, states that objects such as pitchers are sublatable because their being *mithyā* or indeterminable. It implies that indeterminabilty is the criterion for sublatability. The fundamental position of the Advaitins, however, is the opposite: sublatability is the criterion for the *mithyātva*. *Mithyātva*, Śāstrī points out, has the following three meanings: (1) that which does not exist in the three divisions of time, past, present, and future; (2) that which is removable by knowledge; and (3) that which is identical with the object of sublation. Therefore, *mithyātva* and sublatability are synonyms. Accordingly, when *VP* states that *mithyātva* causes sublatability, it should be taken to mean that *mithyātva* is identical with sublation, because the instrumental suffix in *mithyātvena bādhitatvāt* conveys the sense of identity. In short, *mithyātva* is identical with sublatability, that is, pitchers, and so on, are the objects of sublation, and that what is meant by indeterminability in the context of pitchers and so on. *PP*, 24.

29. Madhusūdana shows how the Upaniṣadic texts through the strategy of implied meaning succeed in speaking of pure, unspeakable Brahman: "The sentence 'the pure Brahman is self-manifest' is taken as expressing by *indirect indication*, the fact of the *impure (conditioned) Brahman not being self manifest.* And thus the *pure* Brahman is saved from being the object of verbal cognition; and this preclusion of the *self-manifest character* from the *impure Brahman* would naturally imply that it belongs to the *pure Brahman*; just as the preclusion of 'diversity' implies 'unity'." *AS*, chap. 1, sec. 5, *Indian Thought* 6, nos. 2 & 3 (1914): 284.

30. *upakramopasaṃhārau abhāyso'pūrvatā phalam*
arthavādopapattī ca lingaṃ tātparyanirṇaye iti.

The six marks that determine the purport of a particular text are the harmony of the initial and the concluding passages, repetition, novelty, fruitfulness, glorification by eulogistic passages or condemnation by deprecatory passages, and intelligibility in the light of reasoning. *PP*, 18.

31. Śāstrī maintains that the inclusion of *apūrvatā* in the six marks is significant. *Apūrvatā* and *andhigatatva* are synonyms. If *apūrvatā* is not included among the six marks, then the invariable rule—the scriptures always convey that which is not hitherto known—will be broken in light of the scriptural text "fire is the best medicine for the ice", which is well known in ordinary experience.

32. *PP*, 19.

33. *Ibid.*

34. *Ibid.*

35. For the Naiyāyikas, the universal is one of the seven categories that make up

the speakable world. A universal, for example, 'pitcherness', is eternal (*nitya*), and inheres in many particular instances (*aneka samveta*). Pitcherness, the Naiyāyikas contend, is present in all pitchers, and it would persist even if all pitchers were to be destroyed. When there is only one instance of a thing, its distinguishing feature is not a universal, for example, ether. The Advaitins reject the Nyāya category of universal. Pitcherness, for them, is the sumtotal of the characteristics of a pitcher, which distinguishes it from other objects. It is not eternal. Nothing except Brahman is eternal.

na hi gavādivyaktīnāmutpattimattve tadākṛtīnāmapyutpattimattvaṃ syāt, dravya-guṇakarmaṇāṃ hi vyaktaya evotpadyante nākṛtayaḥ. Śaṃkara, *BSB* 1.3.28. The universals of the cows etc, are not created afresh each time the cows and so on are born. Only individual substances, qualities, and actions are born, their universal essences, however, are not born.

The most devastating attack on the Naiyāyika category of universals comes from Śrī Harśa. To the Naiyāyikas' attempt to account for a common designation of certain objects possessing certain common characteristics by assuming the existence of a single feature residing in these objects, Śrī Harśa dialectically turns the table upon them. "Now, if the Naiyāyika were to accept an endless series of different existences and allow that we still call them all 'existence' and understand them to be the same, then he will have abandoned the principle that such common designation and cognition requires the presence of a single attribute, the universal. Thus he will fail to prove even the first *sattā*, in the absence of which nothing at all would exist, let alone causes!" Granoff, *Khaṇḍanakhaṇḍakhādya*, 95–96.

36. *Samavāya* etymologically means the act of coming together closely, and therefore is used to denote a kind of 'intimate union' between two things that are thereby rendered inseparable so that they cannot be separated without themselves being destroyed. Annaṃbhatta defines *samavāya* as 'a permanent connection existing between two things that are found inseparable'. *TSDNB*, sec. 8, 96. By virtue of this relation, two different things such as substance and attributes, substance and *karma*, substance and universal, cause and effect, appear unified and represent an inseparable whole (*ayutasiddha*). It is an eternal relation.

Śaṃkara rejects the relation of *samavāya.* He contends that if the relation of *samavāya* is needed to unite two different objects, then *samavāya* itself, being different from both of them, would need another *samavāya*, and so on *ad infinitum*. In the context of rejecting the Vaiśeṣika theory of atoms, Śaṃkara's historic refutation of *samavāya* is noted here: "Just as the dyad, though absolutely dissimilar to the two atoms, becomes connected with them through the relationship of inherence, so also inherence itself, which is absolutely different from the inhering things, should be connected with the inhering thing through a separate relationship of the nature of inherence, since the fact of similarity of absolute difference exists here as well. And from this it follows that for those successive relationships, other relationships of inherence have to be imagined. In this way the door is laid open for an infinite regress." Apte, *Brahma-Sūtra-Bhāṣya, BSB* 2.2.13, 390.

37. Mīmāṃsā, being a pluralist system, maintains that variety is at the root of the physical universe. The school of Kumārila accepts all nine *dravvyas* of the Nyāya school, and its conception of them is more or less the same as the Naiyāyikas. It adds two more to them, namely, *tamas* (darkness) and *śabda* (sound). Time is perceivable. All perceptual experience, irrespective of through what sense it is acquired, includes a reference to time. Time, however, cannot be apprehended by itself. It is always apprehended along with some other object.

38. *Kāla* (time), for the Naiyāyikas, is an all pervading, partless substance. It is only one and eternal. However, it appears as many because of the diversity of conditions presented by the production, persistence, and destruction of all produced

entities. It is not an object of visual perception, because an object of perception must have noninfinitesimal dimension and sensible color. Time cannot be perceived because it lacks visible form. It is inferred from our cognition of temporal modes, such as past, present, future, and now and then. Time therefore is the substratum of our temporal cognitions. The divisions and the distinctions that we make in time are purely conventional and do not signify real divisions and distinctions.

The Naiyāyikas distinguish between two kinds of time: absolute time, which is infinite and eternal, and the relative or empirical time arising from the association of absolute time with something else. Empirical time alone has practical value.

39. Vācaspati Miśra in *Nyāyavārtikatātparyaṭīkā* (henceforth this book will be referred as *NVTT*) maintains that in a persistent cognition, cognitions in the second and the subsequent moments comprehend objects as associated with different times. It is impossible to comprehend the differences among points of time, because these points are extremely subtle. He was first to suggest that time is inferred as the condition of our notions of priority and posterioty. Vācaspati Miśra, *NVTT*, 2.1.39.

40. Śaṃkara very clearly states that time, like space, is an effect of *avidyā* or *māyā*. *BSB* 2.3.7. Being an effect, it must have a beginning as well as an end. Time thus has the same level of objectivity as all the effects of *avidyā*, namely, it has an empirical reality. It is not a construction of human imagination. Time is comprehended by all the sense organs. Nobody can deny that time is immediately perceived. On seeing an object, say a pitcher, when I say, 'I see the pitcher now', the presentness of the pitcher is directly revealed through the sense perception of the pitcher itself. This experience not only tells us that time is an object of perception, but also that it becomes perceptible through the sense. Time is apprehended in every act of knowledge. Time, as a category of the phenomenal world, has no claims on eternal 'now', the state of *ātman* realization. *Āman* is timeless, it does not arise in time and is therefore not subject to a present or have an ending in time, because all these distinctions only apply to what is empirical and conditioned. *Kaṭha*, 1.2.10. Sureśvara makes the same point: "Time and space and so on, are the effects of delusion, and do not inhere in the Self. Once the Self is known, there is no more knowledge to gain and no ignorance left unconsumed." *NS*, 4.58, 223.

41. In the context of explaining superimposition of the self on the nonself, Śaṃkara, in *Adhyāsabhāṣya*, states: "The self is not absolutely beyond apprehension, because It is apprehended as the content of the concept 'I'; and because the Self, opposed to the non-Self, is well-known in the world as an immediately perceived (i.e., self-revealing) entity. Nor is there any rule that something has to be superimposed on something else that is directly perceived through the senses; for boys superimpose the ideas of surface (i.e., concavity) and dirt on space (i.e., sky) that is not an object of sense-perception. Hence there is nothing impossible in superimposing the non-Self on the self that is opposed to it." Swāmi Gambhirānanda, *Brahma-Sūtra-Bhāṣya of Śrī Saṅkarācārya*, 3.

42. *PP*, 21.

43. The entire discussion centers around the perceptibility of time. The Advaitins, like Pūrva Mīmāmsakas, maintain that time comes within the range of perception. The Naiyāyikas contend that time never comes within the range of perception because it does not posses any color or fixed material shape. The Advaitins, however, try to prove that the possession of fixed material shape is not a criterion with respect to the perceptibility of time. *AB*, keeping in mind the Nyāya perspective (that the universal pitcherness is related to the pitcher through the relation of inherence which serves to comprehend the universal pitcherness in it) maintains that when there arises the cognition of a pitcher in the form, 'now, there is a pitcher', the contact that is accepted

as the cause of this cognition will also give rise to the perceptibility of time.

To show the absurdity of *AB*'s position regarding the perceptibility of time, Śāstrī brings in the contact known as *saṃyukta saṃyoga* (contact with the object as well as with what the object is conjoined with). If *AB* is correct—that in the cognition 'now there is a pitcher' the contact with the pitcher gives rise to the perceptibility of time—then in the inferential cognition 'the hill is fiery,' the fire would have to be regarded as perceptual, through *saṃyukta saṃyoga*—which clearly is not the case. The relation of *saṃyoga* is intransitive in nature. If my eyes are in contact with the wig on a man's head, who is sitting on a couch conjoined with the floor of a room, I cannot argue that my eyes are in contact with either the couch or the floor.

44. *SLS*, chap. 1, 5.13, 191.

45. This is at least the case according to the holistic concept of medicine of the traditional Āyurvedic school.

46. The author of *SLS* refers to the various solutions and the difficulties posed by the phenomenon of the continuous stream of cognition within the fold of Advaita: "Some, however, (say thus): it is only the ignorance removable by the first cognition that obscures the bare existence (of the object); but what are removed by the second and subsequent cognitions are those whose objects are qualified by space, time and such attributes.... [It cannot be argued that] 'for the second and the subsequent cognitions of a continuous stream, there would not be the removal of ignorance, since ignorance as qualified by gross (that is, perceptible) time has been removed even by the first cognition, while, of the ignorance qualified by the subtle time other than those of the earlier and the later cognitions, the removal is impossible by the second and subsequent cognitions which do not have that (time) for content;' for in the case of a continuous stream, since it is possible even for the psychosis, that arises first, to last for that period [the entire duration of the cognition], no differences of psychosis are admitted... " (chap. 1, 5.132132, 197–198). All these difficulties arise when time is conceived as a bare instant. The Advaitins, however, recognize what in Western psychology is known as "specious present," which contains a residuum of the past and foreshadows the future. For a discussion of these and other related issues, see *SLS*, chap. 1, 5.13212–132133, 193–203.

47. *Akhaṇḍākāra vṛtti*, for the Advaitins, is the highest human achievement. It conforms to *brahma jñāna* or *svarūpa jñāna*: "The mahāvākya 'tat tvam asi' generates the final psychosis, 'vṛtti' of the form of the pure impartite Brahman ...which destroys the notion of difference between the individual self and Brahman, as wrongly held by the world. Brahman is self-luminous. The function of the Scriptures consists only in the removal of the obscuring nescience and not in manifesting Brahman." *PPD*, Fourth *Varṇaka*, 9.20, 307.

Indian philosophers generally maintain that the import of a proposition is relational, that is, the subject and the predicate constituting a sentence are mutually related as the substantive and the adjective. For example, 'the table is brown' means that the table is characterized by brownness. The Advaitins are the only exceptions in this regard. They maintain that propositions also convey a nonrelational meaning. In other words, the subject and the predicate are not two different things that denote a relation, but rather point to one and the same object. For example, *tat* and *tvam* in *tat tvam asi* point to one, nondual Brahman.

In this context, it is useful to note the distinction the Advaitins make between *vṛtti jñāna* and *akhaṇḍākāra vṛtti jñāna*. *Vṛtti jñāna* obtained through a mental mode is fragmented in form. *Akhaṇḍākāra vṛtti*, on the other hand, has no fragmented form, because Brahman has no form. The function of any *vṛtti* consists in removing the intervening veil, thereby facilitating in manifesting the ever-present identity between the consciousness and the content. Every such manifestation of identity by *vṛtti* is by its nature limited and contingent. When we know a pitcher, the consciousness or reality conditioned by the empirical pitcher also is known. It is not possible to approximate reality experientially by adding together several perceptions of empirical objects, like pitchers. Only a noetic experience, in which the empirical determinations do not appear, constitutes the experience of the infinite. Such is the nature of *akhaṇḍākāra vṛtti,* which alone sublates the world appearance. *Ajñāna*, 204–5.

2

Perception as a Criterion for Truth

2.10 *tatra pratyakṣapramākaraṇaṃ pratyakṣapramāṇam*

2.10 *Of these [the six means of knowledge], that which is the instrument of perceptual knowledge-event is the means known as perception.*

2.10 Of these (the six *pramāṇa-s* mentioned in the first chapter), perception refers to the instrument that leads to a perceptual knowledge-event (*pratyakṣa pramā*). The Naiyāyikas define a perceptual knowledge-event as that which arises from sense organs.[1] The Advaitins, however, reject this position. Their rejection is on the eminent ground that it fails to include a species of cognition, which for Advaita is perception *par excellence*, namely, the witness-cognition (*sākṣijñāna*). Witness-cognition is a case of knowledge that is perceptual but does not arise from any sense organs. *Sākṣin* is the consciousness 'associated' with *avidyā*, reflected or delimited by the mind. When immanent in mind it is technically the individual self (*jīva*); an agent, experiencer, and a subject; when it transcends the mind, it is *sākṣin*, a non-agent, a non-experiencer, a mere witness. For Advaita, the phenomeno-logical basis for the witness-consciousness is the commonplace experience 'I have the cognition of a pitcher'. What is given against such an experience, contends the Advaitin, does *not* arise from any sense organs.

2.10.1 The Nyāya understanding of 'I have the cognition of a pitcher' is that it is a cognition, although of a secondary type. To be precise, it is a cognition of cognition (*anuvyavasāya*).[2] For them, a cognition does not look at itself but beyond itself at an object. The primary act of cognition of an external object is followed by a secondary act with the primary act of cognition itself as its object. This is how the cognition of cognition takes place, although any cognition is self-transcendent and looks beyond itself (*viṣaya prakāśa svabhāva*). It is not self-luminous (*svaprakāśa*), as is held by the Advaitins.

But how can the secondary act of cognition of cognition validate the primary act without being itself validated? The second act of cognition of cognition would have to be known by a third cognition and so on *ad infinitum*. Keeping this in mind, the Advaitins reject such a cognition of cognition as a temporal mental event and maintain that it is a case of apprehension by the witness-consciousness. The nature of cognition for them is such that, although it is not an object either to itself or to any other numerically different act of cognition, it never remains unknown.

2.10.1.1 Furthermore, if perceptuality is defined in terms of origination caused by sense organs, then in the instance of a visual perception of 'fragrant sandalwood', the fragrance must be admitted to be perceptual, which clearly is not the case. The Naiyāyikas maintain that in the perception of fragrant sandalwood, although there is no normal contact of the eyes with the fragrance, the visual perception of sandalwood revives the memory of fragrance. With the help of this recollection there arises the visual perceptual cognition, 'the sandalwood is fragrant'. The Advaitins reject the notion of extra-empirical contact that the Naiyāyikas invoke to explain the case.[3]

2.10.1.2 Finally, if perception depends upon sense organs, then God's knowledge, since presumably it does not arise through the intervention of any sense organs, cannot be said to be perceptual. The knowledge that God has of the world created by him is admittedly of the nonmediate perceptual sort.

For these reasons, the Advaitins reject the Nyāya definition of perception as knowledge that results from sense object contact.

2.10.2 Perceptual knowledge, for the Advaitins, is that which has for its content an object that is perceptual. This definition involves a clear reference to the perceptibility of an object. The perceptibility of an object consists in being the content of knowledge that is perceptual. Perceptual knowledge is said to be of the object that is perceptible. So, their opponents contend, this definition involves the fallacy of self-dependence.[4]

The definition of the perceptuality of knowledge given above, the Advaitins maintain, does not involve self-dependence. For the Advaitins, an object does not have any independent existence apart from the reality of its underlying substratum. This will be elaborated at great length later on in the text. What is stated here, somewhat cryptically, is the overall thesis: immediacy of perceptuality is a generic attribute present in all cases of perceptual cognitions. Because of the factor of immediacy or 'oneness', the perceptibility of an object must be acknowledged as a necessary component of a knowledge that is perceptual.

2.11 *pratyakṣapramā tv atra caitanyam eva, "yat sākṣād aparokṣāt" iti śruteḥ. "aparokṣāt" ity asya aparokṣam ity arthaḥ.*

2.11 *Here [in the definition] valid perceptual knowledge-event is indeed only pure consciousness, because of the śruti: "That Brahman is direct and immediate" (BU 3.4.1). "aparokṣāt" [in the fifth case in the text] stands for "aparokṣam" (immediate) [which is in the first case].*

2.11 According to the fundamental tenets of Advaita, Brahman itself is immediacy. It does not depend on any *pramāṇa* for its manifestation.[5] *Pramāṇa* is needed to manifest an entity that is not manifest earlier. Brahman, being eternal, is ever-existent, and there is no need to bring it into existence.

2.11.1 Perceptual knowledge is pure consciousness. Consciousness is always perceptual. It is viewed, however, as mediate or immediate on the basis of the *vṛtti* element that conditions it. If *vṛtti* originates through the functioning of sense organs, then the consciousness is spoken of as perceptual. If, on the other hand, it originates through inference and other *pramāṇa-s*, the consciousness that is reflected therein is spoken of as mediate. In other words, it is *vṛtti* that is mediate or immediate. Depending on the perceptuality or the nonperceptuality of the *vṛtti* conditioning the consciousness, the consciousness is also spoken of figuratively as perceptual or nonperceptual.

2.11.2 It might be objected that although perceptual knowledge is identical with Brahman, it is manifested by the mental mode that arises in perception. Because such a mental mode has a beginning, pure consciousness must also be said to have a beginning.

The Advaitins answer this charge by reiterating the distinction between pure consciousness as knowledge and the mental mode inspired by the reflection of pure consciousness in it. The latter (i.e., the mental mode inspired by pure consciousness), is empirical cognition (*vṛtti jñāna*), which is neither a mere mental mode as such nor pure consciousness, but a complex of pure consciousness and *vṛtti*. Brahman is luminous, it manifests of its own, and does not require any manifesting factor. In order that it may be revealed, a mental mode assuming the form of Brahman is required. However, a mental mode assuming the form of Brahman is both impartite and terminal. It does not require a second mental mode as is the case with empirical cognitions. In other words, Brahman is only *vṛtti vyāpya* and not *phala vyāpya*.[6]

2.11.3 It might be asked: On what ground it is maintained that this consciousness is self-luminous and does not depend on any *pramāṇa* for its manifestation?

VP maintains that it is perceptual insofar as its own essence (*svāṃśe*) is concerned. Therefore, it does not depend on any *pramāṇa* (instrument of knowledge) for its manifestation. And it is only in its content aspect, the aspect in which it is different from consciousness, that one can legitimately speak of consciousness as an instrument of valid perceptual knowledge. In the latter sense, it is *pramāṇa par excellence*. The Upaniṣadic text *yat sākṣāt* means *'pramāṇā pekṣām vinā*', that is, without depending upon any other *pramāṇa*. *Aparokṣāt* means '*aparokṣam*', that is, it is 'im-mediate'.

2.12 *nanu caitanyam anādi; tat katham cakṣurādeḥ tatkaraṇatvena pramāṇatvam iti?*

ucyate, caitanyasyānāditve'pi tadabhivyañjakāntaḥkaraṇavṛttir indriyasannikarṣādinā jāyata iti vṛttiviśiṣṭaṃ caitanyam ādimad ity ucyate; jñānāvacchedakatvāc ca vṛttau jñānatvopacāraḥ. tad uktaṃ vivaraṇe 'antaḥkaraṇavṛttau jñānatvopacārāt' iti.

2.12 *[An objection is raised]: Now, consciousness is without a beginning; how, then, can the sense of sight, and so on, as the instrumental cause of that [consciousness], be the means of knowledge?*

It is said: Though pure consciousness is without a beginning, its manifesting factor, namely, the modification of the internal organ, is subject to origination because of sense-contact, hence consciousness conditioned by the mental mode is said to have a beginning, and because the mental mode conditions pure consciousness, the mental mode itself is metaphorically spoken of as 'knowledge'. Pañcapādikā of Vivaraṇa school states: "Because of the mental mode as being metaphorically spoken of as knowledge."

2.12 According to the Advaitins, perceptual *pramāṇa* is the instrument of perceptual knowledge-event. The question arises: Does perceptual *pramāṇa* pertain to the cases of perception in which pure consciousness allegedly is a knowledge-event (*pramā*) or does it pertain only to the perceptuality of the content aspect? In other words, is the perceptual *pramāṇa* a *pramāṇa*—that is, an instrument of knowledge with regard to the consciousness aspect which in itself is the knowledge-event, or is the perceptual *pramāṇa* a *pramāṇa* with respect to the content aspect, that is, the object presented to consciousness?

2.12.1 *PP* rejects both the alternatives. The first alternative does not hold. Consciousness is *pratyakṣa pramā*, and *pratyakṣa pramāṇa* is that which gives rise to *pratyakṣa pramā*, that is, consciousness. Consciousness cannot be said to have an origin because it is eternal. It also is self-luminous, because it does not depend upon any *pramāṇa* for its manifestation. Therefore, conceivably how could there be a *pramāṇa* or an instrument that gives rise to the knowledge of such consciousness?

2.12.2 If the second alternative, that *pratyakṣa* is *pramāṇa* only with respect to the content aspect, is accepted, then one will not be able to say that knowledge is perceptual while implying that only the object is perceptible. Consequently, the assertion itself, *VP* maintains, is contradictory. With this in view, doubt is raised in the text *nanu caitanyam anādi*. *PP* adds: *svaprakāśam ca*, that is, it is self-luminous. In other words, being *anādi*, it does not depend on any other *pramāṇa*,and being *svaprakāśam*, it does not depend on anything else for its manifestation.

2.12.2.1 *VP* elaborates on this point further. In any cognition of the form, 'this is a pitcher', there are two aspects: the consciousness aspect and the *vṛtti* aspect. The consciousness aspect is eternal, whereas the *vṛtti* aspect is occasional. Because of the interaction between the sense organ and a particular object, the mind functions through the sense of sight; it assumes, as it were, the form of the object. The *vṛtti* in the form of the pitcher thus originates because of the functioning of the sense organ. Accordingly, with reference to the content aspect (for example, the pitcher), the term 'instrument' can be used to explain its perceptibility. Sense organs themselves are not instruments, but they are 'instrumental' in the initiation of the *vṛtti* element. The *vṛtti* element is falsely attributed to consciousness and, as a result, consciousness associated with the *vṛtti* is metaphorically spoken of as being originated.

2.12.2.2 Brahmānanda Sarasvatī, in his commentary on *Siddhāntabindu*,[7] explains the above point in the following way: *pratyakṣa pramā* is *vṛtti* only in the form of the object inspired by the reflection of con-sciousness in it. It is neither pure consciousness nor pure *vṛtti* but a blend of the two. Therefore, it is said that consciousness as associated with *vṛtti* is originated, and the sense of sight which gives rise to such a *vṛtti* in this case is a *pramāṇa*.

2.12.2.3 The Advaitins anticipate an objection to the above position on the following ground: If consciousness alone comes under the category of perceptual cognition, and if the true nature of individual self (*jīva*) is consciousness, then, being all pervasive, a *jīva* will be in contact with all the objects of the world because of its essential nature. Experience, however, shows that a *jīva* attains knowledge of a particular object at a particular time and does not have knowledge of all objects at all times. How do we account for such variations?

2.12.2.4 The Advaitins respond that an apparent material world, which is phenomenally given, is the result of a superimposition on the principle of pure consciousness. A material object[8] of knowledge is called *viṣaya caitanya*, that is, consciousness falsely conditioned by the superimposed object. A material object then is nothing but a false projection of Brahman. Intellect or mind (*buddhi* or *antaḥkaraṇa*), to speak of it in the material mode, is an elastic and translucent substance that goes out to meet the object, gets modified into the shape of the object, and serves as the instrument manifesting the object in the form of a perceptual judgment. Thus, the cognizer, the instrument of knowledge, and the object, are basically the same consciousness differentiated into three different forms, given different limiting or extraneous conditions.

2.12.3 The function of *vṛtti* consists in effecting the removal of the modal ignorance that was concealing the object. Thus it brings about the identity between the consciousness conditioned by the mind and the consciousness conditioned by the object. When an object is manifested, the false projection of the material object is not removed by that empirical knowledge. It only removes modal or derivative nescience which has so long conditioned the consciousness of the material object. When the modal ignorance is removed, the object is manifested. Because such a removal occurs through the operation of the *antaḥkaraṇa vṛtti*, the latter serves as an instrument in the cognition of the object. Accordingly the *vṛtti* is considered to be a *pramāṇa* or the instrument of valid knowledge. In the case of Brahman knowledge, *vṛtti* in the form of Brahman is inspired by the reflection of consciousness in the *antaḥkaraṇa*. The consciousness reflected therein removes the primal nescience. Therefore, the instrumentation of *vṛtti* is not required to bring about the identity between the individual self and Brahman, because such an identity is eternally accomplished and self-evident.

To sum up, consciousness, as associated with *vṛtti*, although without a beginning, is considered to have a beginning. The Advaitins' use of the notion of the instrument of perceptual knowledge to describe perception refers only to the content aspect of valid perceptual knowledge. Furthermore, even in that respect, it must be understood in a specific sense, that is, perceptual knowledge with respect to a content, for example a pitcher, is due to the origination of *vṛtti* in the form of a pitcher *vis-à-vis* the contact of the sense of sight. The origination of *vṛtti*, is superimposed upon the consciousness reflected in the *vṛtti*,in the form of a pitcher. Consciousness thus conditioned by *vṛtti* is known as a perceptual knowledge-event (*pratyakṣa pramā*).

2.12.4 *PP* explains the operation of *vṛtti* as the revealing medium of consciousness in an original way. *Vṛtti* is invoked as the means for removing modal ignorance and the consequent manifestation of consciousness. *PP* borrows the analogy used by the Mīmāṃsakas and the Grammarians who consider 'sound' to be eternal. But the noneternal tone that manifests the sound arises because of its interaction with the throat and the palate. The noneternality present in the tone is adventitiously superimposed on the sound, which is eternal. The same is the case with *vṛtti*. Pure consciousness is eternal; its manifesting factor, namely *vṛtti*, however, is subject to origination, therefore consciousness conditioned by such a mental mode is also said to be originated.

2.12.4.1 The commentary *AB* uses the Nyāya example, 'the pitcher is made black or blue', to illustrate this point.[9] When the pitcher is colored black or blue, the pitcher is also spoken of as being originated. In other words, the pitcher is said to be originated because of the generation of its adjectival feature, namely, black or blue. Similarly, consciousness is eternal. But when associated with *vṛtti*, which is originated, it is also spoken of as being originated. *Vṛtti* arises because of sense-contact and it also serves as the delimiting factor of consciousness. What serves as the instrument of *vṛtti*, therefore, is spoken of as the instrument of perceptual knowledge.

2.12.4.2 *PP* questions the position of *AB* on the ground that it contradicts *VP*'s thesis that pure consciousness alone underlies a perceptual knowledge-event. *Vṛtti*, being the transformation of insentient mind, cannot be integral to the nature of a knowledge-event (*pramā*). Being insentient, it is of the nature of nescience.

2.12.4.3 Commenting on the notion of the determinant of knowledge used in apposition to consciousness, *PP* draws the attention of the reader to the fact previously stated that *vṛtti*, as such cannot be characterized as empirical cognition because it is always a blend of the *vṛtti* element and the element of consciousness. *Vṛtti* as the revealing medium of pure consciousness is spoken of as knowledge only by courtesy. Pure consciousness, simply a witness of ignorance or *avidyā* when reflected or delimited by *vṛtti*, effects the removal of modal ignorance.

2.12.5 The Advaitins make a distinction between the immediate and mediate mental modes to provide the rationale for a taxonomy of knowledge as immediate and mediate. A particular mental mode is said to be immediate when it is identical with the consciousness that is reflected or conditioned by the object. When, however, the consciousness is reflected or conditioned by *vṛtti* only (i.e., when it is not identical with the consciousness conditioned by the object), the mental mode is said to be mediate in character.

2.12.5.1 Opponents argue that the thesis of the identity of the consciousness conditioned by *vṛtti* and the consciousness conditioned by an object applies only to a sense such as sight, but not, say, to tactual perceptions. In the case of sight, there is a particular substratum, namely, the eyes.[10] The mind goes out through such a substratum, reaches the place of the object, and undergoes modification in the form of the object. That is *vṛtti*. The consciousness conditioned by the *vṛtti* is said to be identical with the consciousness conditioned by the object. However, in the tactual perception, there is no specific localized substratum for the sense of touch. Therefore, the question of *vṛtti* going out through the sense organ and reaching the place of the object does not make sense. Thus there is no need to admit, argues the opponent, a process of mind 'going out' and reaching the place of the object. We can simply say that where there is contact of the sense organ with the object, the mental mode is immediate. When such contact is absent, the mental mode is mediate. Furthermore, in the case of mental states such as desire and happiness, the question of *vṛtti* 'going out' of the body does not arise. For these reasons the Advaitins' position is untenable.

2.12.5.2 In response, *PP* reiterates the distinction that the Advaitins make between the noncognitive and the cognitive mental modes.[11] Mental states, such as desire, anger, and similar other events are noncognitive and immediate in nature; that is, they arise by being known to the self. They do not have any existence independent of their being perceived. Such, however, is not the case with the mental modes in the cognitive sphere, which are both immediate and mediate. In the perceptual cognition of a pitcher, the consciousness conditioned by the mental mode and the consciousness conditioned by the pitcher are identical. Consequently, in each instance the mental mode is said to be immediate. In the inferential cognition of fire on the mountain, on the other hand, because the sense of sight is not in contact with the fire, there is no possibility of the mind 'going out' through the sense organ. Therefore, consciousness conditioned by the mental mode remains, in a manner of speaking, inside the body; the consciousness conditioned by the object, namely, the fire, again in a manner of speaking, exists outside the body. There is no possibility of the two becoming identical. Therefore the mental mode is mediate in character. By emphasizing the consciousness element and not the *vṛtti* element, *PP* seeks to account for the distinction between immediacy and mediacy *contra* the Nyāya slanted interpretation of the commentators of *VP*, with their emphasis on *vṛtti*. In this context, one must not lose sight of the underlying thesis of *VP* that the essential nature of consciousness serves as the substratum in both the cases. Losing sight of this important fact might give the appearance that *VP* is discoursing from the Nyāya platform.

2.12.5.3 In elaborating the thesis that the *vṛtti* element as such is not knowledge, *PP* appeals to usages that involve a distinction of great phenomenological import. The experiences behind the two expressions 'I know the pitcher' or 'the pitcher manifests' are significantly different in that, in the first, the verb has an object, whereas the second simply refers to the subject. The two expressions will have to be treated alike if both of them are taken to be concerned only with the *vṛtti* element; the distinction between the two can be maintained only by admitting the consciousness element in *vṛtti*.

That *vṛtti* by itself cannot be called knowledge is further borne out by the fact that pure consciousness as such does not remove *ajñāna* but instead is a 'witness' of *ajñāna*. And when the *vṛtti* element is (as it were), added to it, it removes the ignorance present in consciousness. In other words, when *vṛtti* is absent, consciousness serves to manifest ignorance instead of removing it.

2.12.6 Mind is only a transformation of *ajñāna*. Because of the predominance of *sattva guṇa*,[12] mind is compared to the light of the sun, subject to contraction and expansion and existing intermittently between the body and the object. Inside the body, it is termed the 'ego-sense' and the 'agent.' Existing between the object and the body, it is known as *vṛtti jñāna*.

2.12.6.1 The quality of expansion associated with the specific parts of the mind is described as the transformation of mind (*pariṇāma*).[13] But, when going out through the sense organ and undergoing modification in the form of the object are involved, it is known as *antaḥkaraṇa vṛtti* or simply *vṛtti*. When consciousness is associated with the *vṛtti* that is in contact with the object, the consciousness is known as a knowledge-event (*pramā*). The same consciousness is called *pramāṇa* when it is associated with the *vṛtti* that is in contact with the object as well as the body, and it is known as *pramātā* when it is associated with the *vṛtti* that is in contact with the body.

2.12.6.2 One of the most refreshing insights for a phenomenology of perception provided by *PP* in this context is its investigation into the nature of similarity between the mind and the form that it takes, similar to the form of the object, for example, the pitcher. Is the relation between the one that undergoes transformation (mind) and the one that is the result of the transformation (*vṛtti*), the same as the relation that exists between a lump of clay and the pitcher? If we accept the *pariṇāma pariṇāmībhāva* between the *vṛtti* and the mind, as in the case of clay and the pitcher, then the question arises: Does the mind transform or change after coming into contact with the pitcher or before the contact? The former alternative does not hold, because our purpose will be served by merely admitting the contact between the mind and the object. Accordingly, no change in the form of *vṛtti* will be needed. The second alternative is also untenable, because in that case there will not be any identity between the consciousness conditioned by the object and the consciousness conditioned by the mind.

2.13 *nanu niravayavasyāntaḥkaraṇasya pariṇāmātmikā vṛttiḥ katham?*

ittham. na tāvad antaḥkaraṇaṃ niravayavam, sādidravyatvena sāvayavatvāt. sāditvaṃ ca 'tan mano'sṛjata' ityādiśruteḥ

2.13 *[An objection is raised]: Now, the internal organ being partless, how can there be a mental mode of the nature of modification?*

It is said: The internal organ is not partless, [and] being a substance with a beginning, it has parts. And that it has a beginning is [known] by śruti: "It created the mind" (BU 1.2.1).

2.13 Mind, according to the Naiyāyikas, plays a crucial role in any perceptual process. They regard mind as an instrument that the self uses in internal perceptions. They adduce many reasons for regarding mind as an organ. Without the mind there would be nothing that could serve as a medium for the contact between the object and the self in external perceptions; there will be no basis for regarding internal perceptions as instances of perceptions; and finally, knowledge, determination—the qualities of the self—require mind as an instrument so that they may be perceived.

2.13.1 They maintain that mind is atomic, partless, and eternal. Because it is atomic and partless, it is associated with one organ at a time. Accordingly, a person is not able to perceive more than one thing at a time. The Naiyāyikas further maintain that when the five sense organs are associated with their respective objects, the mind perceives only one object at a given time. The mind, however, moves so rapidly from one object to another that it creates the appearance of perceiving all the objects simultaneously. Accordingly, they maintain that the internal organ, being partless, cannot assume modification in the form of the object. This is the objection.

2.13.2 In response *VP* says that mind is finite and it is of medium magnitude. Supporting the *VP* thesis, Śāstrī explains that mind cannot be of infinite magnitude, because in that case it would be all pervasive and would be in contact with everything at a given time. It is, however, a light-like substance (*taijasa padārtha*), and like the rays of the sun, has the capacity to function quickly. Furthermore, *śruti* texts describe mind as an effect and, being an effect, it is subject to origination. In other words, the mind is created and is composed of parts. It can be connected with more than one organ at a time, therefore a person is able to perceive different objects simultaneously. They adduce the counterbalancing (*satpratipakṣa*) reasoning of the form: 'Mind is composed of parts, because it is originated'. The opponents, on the other hand, say that mind is a partless entity because it is not originated. In this context we must remember that according to the Advaitins, unlike the Naiyāikas , the mind is not a substance and does not possess any independent reality. It is one of the several modes of the *antahkaraṇa* and is the product of beginningless nescience.

2.14 *vṛttirūpajñānasya manodharmatve ca "kāmaḥ saṅkalpo vicikitsā śraddhāśraddhā dhṛtir adhṛtir hrīr dhīr bhīr ity etat sarvaṃ mana eva" iti śrutir mānam. dhīśabdena vṛttirūpajñānābhidhānam. ata eva kāmāder api manodharmatvam.*

nanu kāmāder antaḥkaraṇadharmatve "aham icchāmi, ahaṃ jānāmi, ahaṃ bibhemi" ityādyanubhava ātmadharmatvam avagāhamānaḥ katham upapadyate?

ucyate. ayaḥpiṇḍasya dagdhṛtvābhāve api dagdhṛtvāśrayavahnitādātmyādhyāsād yathā "ayo dahati" iti vyavahāraḥ, tathā sukhādyākāraparināmyantaḥkaraṇaikyādhyāsāt "ahaṃ sukhī" "ahaṃ dukhī" ityādivyavahāro jāyate.

2.14 *That the knowledge conditioned by the mental mode is an attribute of the mind is ascertained by śruti: "desire, certitude, doubt, faith, absence of faith, firmness, absence of firmness, shyness, fear, and knowledge—all this is truly mind" (BU 1.5.3). The word "cognition" (dhīḥ) denotes cognition conditioned by the mental mode [empirical cognition]. Accordingly, desire, and so on, also are the attributes of the mind.*

[Objection]: Now, if desire, and so on, are of the nature of being the attributes of the internal organ, how could experiences such as 'I desire, I know, I fear', which apprehend [them] as attributes of the self, be explained?

It is said: Just as though an iron-rod does not have the capacity to burn, [yet], because of the superimposition of identity with fire which has the capacity to burn, we use the expression, 'the iron-rod burns' in the same way we have the empirical usage such as 'I am happy' and 'I am sad', because of the superimposition of the identity [of the self] with the internal organ which undergoes modification in the form of happiness, and so on.

2.14 The significance of the Upaniṣadic texts cited above in *VP*, as *PP* explains, is that mental states such as desire, certitude, and doubt are of the nature of the mind, not the qualities of the mind. It notes that the identity between the mental states and the mind outlined above is underscored in *VP*. The identity between the parts and the whole is a part of the general doctrine that is accepted by Mīmāṃsakas and the Advaitins.[14] Even according to the Naiyāyikas, observes *PP*, desire and mind fall under the range of the cognition of identity through the relation of inherence. However, they differ in a very important respect. For the Naiyāyikas, the whole exists but in the parts. Cloth comes into existence over and above the parts, namely, the threads. This is held to be logically correct even though phenomenologically the reverse seems to be the case. The Advaita perspective in this context is precisely to affirm an identity on experiential grounds between the parts and the whole. It is only in the cloth that the threads exist. The mind is admitted to be the agent of mental modes but only in the sense of identity. *Vṛtti* is the transformation of mind, and therefore the latter cannot be considered to be its agent or the efficient cause. The identity that is spoken of in this context is the identity that exists between a material cause and its effect.

2.14.1 *PP* emphasizes this point to refute any suggestion or insinuation of a distinction between the mind and the *vṛtti*-s. *SM*, for example, seems to underplay the identity when, while commenting on the Upaniṣadic texts, it states that there is a coordinate relation between the mind and the mental modes.[15] *AB* likewise scouts the idea of transformation in the present context, because a transformation or change is impossible in a partless entity.[16] The Nyāya point of view, incidentally, must be kept in mind in this context, because for them, 'mental' states such as happiness and pain are not attributes of mind but rather attributes of the self. The Advaita point of view, however, is that the mental states are simply transformations of the mind. These mental states, cited in the Upaniṣadic texts, include the expression '*dhīḥ*', which stands for knowledge (*vṛtti jñāna*). It must be noted here that *vṛtti* is inspired by the reflection of consciousness in it, because the knowledge which is of the nature of pure consciousness cannot be said to be the transformation of mind. The *vṛtti* therefore, is spoken of as knowledge by courtesy.

2.14.2 While the Advaitins seem to appeal to experiential validation for their thesis here, they are at the same time careful to subject the experience to a rigorous evaluation, applying the criterion of unsublatability. In the hierarchy of *pramāṇa-s*, it is true that perception comes first and foremost and testimony comes later.[17] Therefore, it is argued that perception is the sustaining feature. Auditory perception, if only in a trivial sense, is the sustaining factor of *śruti*. The Mīmāṃsakas, with their penchant for *śruti*, are still very empirically minded when they imply that perception is more powerful than testimony. *Śruti* texts are often reinterpreted in such a way so that there is no contradiction between *śruti* and perception.

Applying the above criterion, the *śruti* claim that mental states are of the nature of mind and may be subjected to a different interpretation. Perception, one may argue, in experiences such as 'I desire' and 'I know', proves that mental states are only attributes of the self and not of the mind. Without reference to the 'I', the self cannot be experienced at all at any time. On the basis of the recollection 'I slept happily', when one comes back to the waking state from the state of deep sleep, we assume the manifestation of the 'I' even in the state of deep sleep, although the 'I' was not introspectively available in that state. This accounts for the fact that mental states such as happiness and desire are qualities of the self and not of the mind. Therefore, to avoid contradiction with perceptual experiences, such as 'I know' and 'I desire', the mind should be spoken of as the efficient cause and not the material cause of such mental states.

2.14.3 There is no doubt that perception as a means of knowledge is first and foremost among the *pramāṇa-s*. But does it mean that it is the most powerful? If it is maintained that what is given first in the order of enumeration is most powerful, then what comes first, for example, in an erroneous cognition will be entitled to greater credence than the sublating cognition. One might even reduce it to absurdity, stretching the meaning of the rule by showing that an erroneous perception of shell as silver will sublate the subsequent cognition 'this is not silver'. The Advaitins do not subscribe to the view that *śruti* contradicts perception. Rather they claim perception, when properly analyzed, favors the verdict of *śruti*. The Upaniṣadic texts do not contradict the empirical validity of perception.

2.14.3.1 The point stated above is highly controversial and deserves serious examination, if only to appreciate the way the Advaitins integrate transcendental insights of *śruti* within the ambit of experience, and the precise sense in which a phenomenology of experience becomes assimilable to saving knowledge. When it is stated that *śruti* does not contradict the empirical validity of perception, the objection that can arise may be anticipated immediately. *Śruti* proclaims the nonreality of the world: 'this world of plurality is not real'.[18] Perception, however, shows that the world of objects is real. Considering that perception is more powerful than *śruti*, *śruti* texts must be reinterpreted to suit perception. This essentially is the standard objection raised by non-Advaitins, including the Mīmāṃsakas.[19] Perception is the sustaining factor, and verbal testimony is that which is sustained. It is only when the sustained factor totally contradicts the sustaining factor that there arises a conflict.

2.14.3.2 The Advaitin response to this objection, implied in *VP*, is elicited in unambiguous language by the author of *PP*. The sustaining factor, in the present context, is not perception as such but rather the empirical validity of perception. *Śruti* texts, although they convey the nonreality of the world, do not sublate or annihilate empirical validity with respect to perceptual cognitions, but rather support it. When these texts emphasize the nonreality of the world, they take 'real' in the technical sense of what is real in the three temporal divisions of time—past, present, and future. Strictly speaking, only that which has *always been* and will *forever be* deserves to be termed 'real'. The perception simply shows that the world is real in the present. Perception indeed supports *śruti* in the aspect of empirical validity. Likewise, *śruti* does not annihilate the empirical validity of perception, but only sublates absolute reality with respect to perception.

2.14.4 The opponents contend that the Upaniṣadic texts dealing with desire and determination[20] contradict the verdict of perception and should be reinterpreted. The entire controversy between *śruti* and *pramāṇa* it seems, gives rise to two important issues: Is there entailed a contradiction with perception in the present case? And, does the statement, as interpreted by opponents with a view to achieving consistency with the sustaining factor of perception, amount to being a significant revelation?

2.14.4.1 I will discuss these two issues in reverse order. If the Upaniṣadic statements intend to convey that mind is the efficient cause of mental states like desire and determination, then this fact can be known through other *pramāṇa-s* as well. Therefore, if the Upaniṣads convey the same sense that is disclosed by other avenues of knowledge— for example, inference or reason—then it merely will be a restatement and not a valid assertion in its own right. As for the first issue, perception can conceivably contradict the apparent sense of *śruti* texts, and therefore, call for a reinterpretation of the latter in its own light.

2.14.4.2 The content of the cognition 'I', for the Advaitins, is not simply pure consciousness. Because there is the superimposition of the mind on the self, the self is spoken of as an agent, enjoyer, and the experiencer in expressions such as, 'I know' and 'I desire'. When the mind is falsely superimposed upon the self, we have the cognition of 'I'. Thus pure consciousness conditioned by the mind alone is considered to be *ahaṃ padārtha*, or the content of the notion 'I'.[21] It is of the same species as the erroneous cognition 'this is silver'. Opponents, in this context, point to the structural differences between the two cognitions. In the case of the erroneous perception of shell as silver, there is the superimposed entity 'silver' and the substratal principle verbalized as 'this'. Both of these are manifest when one has the cognition 'this is silver'. In the cognition of 'I' in 'I desire', on the other hand, a similar manifestation of these two elements is not there. The alleged substratal principle is the self and the superimposed element is the mind—and the two are not manifested distinctly. In the absence of their distinct manifestation, therefore, it is questioned, how one can maintain that the cognition 'I' refers to a blend of the self and mind and that it is similar to an illusory cognition?

2.14.5 *VP*'s response to the abovementioned objection is an emphatic 'no'. The analysis that *PP* provides of this response elucidates the Advaita perspective with proper focus. Even the experience of 'I' in 'I know' and 'I desire', like erroneous cognitions, has two elements as its content: the substratal principle and the superimposed element. These two elements, however, are not manifested distinctly. Only one is manifest, although both are present in that cognition. This may be explained on the model of the experience 'the iron-ball burns'. Burning is in reality the property of fire. However, because of the false identification of fire with the iron-ball, one uses the expression 'the iron-ball burns'. Likewise, in the experience 'I know', because the expression 'know' is used and because knowledge is the essential nature of the substratum, it can be said that the substratal element, the self, is implicitly present.

2.14.5.1 To gain a proper and precise perspective on the error of superimposition entailed in the experience, 'the iron-ball burns' used in *VP*, *PP* directs the reader to two kinds of superimpositions referred to by Śaṃkara in the Preamble to his commentary on *Brahmasūtrabhāṣya:* Superimposition not caused or conditioned by any limiting adjunct (*nirupādhika adhyāsa*), and the superimposition caused by a limiting adjunct (*sopādhika adhyāsa*).[22] The standard examples of rope-snake and shell-silver fall under the first kind, and 'iron-ball burns' and 'I desire' are examples of the second kind. In superimpositions not conditioned by some limiting adjunct, there is always the necessity of the manifestation of the substratal principle and the superimposed entity in a distinct manner. In the other kind, which is occasioned by the determinate presence of some limiting adjunct, there is no such necessity.

2.14.5.1.1 This distinction further clarifies the Advaitin view that in experiences such as 'I know' and 'I desire', distinct manifestation of the substratal principle is not necessary, because in such cases the mind is superimposed distinctly not upon the self but upon the self conditioned by ignorance. This has been termed the "subsequent superimposition," because it is based upon the initial superimposition of the self or consciousness upon ignorance. In *ātman*, ignorance is identified, and in the self associated with ignorance, there is the superimposition of another entity, the mind, which is followed by the superimposition of the qualities of the mind upon the self.

The distinction that is made here between the different orders of superimposition is significant. There is superimposition between two *dharmīs* (i.e., substantives or that which possess the qualities and the attributes) and superimposition between *dharmas* (i.e., qualities and attributes that inhere in *dharmīs*).[23] The point of *PP* in referring to these details is to show that the example under consideration—'the iron-ball burns'—is not a case of the kind of superimposition that is not conditioned by any limiting adjunct, and that it is not a case of superimposition of things that have qualities. The analogy then, according to the analysis intended in *VP*, is of the kind that may be described as a superimposition of qualities and also of the kind that is conditioned by the presence of an external limiting adjunct. Defining the nature of the superimposition, in the example cited as an analogy, has the virtue of demonstrating the precise analysis of the nature of the cognition 'I desire' and similar such cognitions.

2.14.5.1.2 The case of iron-ball burns cannot be described as similar to the erroneous cognition of shell as silver or rope as snake. If we have the clear cognition that this is simply an iron-ball, then there is no possibility of mistaking it as identical with the fire. One may contrast it with the situation of cognizing shell as silver, in which the experience and the verbal usage takes the form 'this is not silver but shell only'. Nor again can we describe this analogy as a case of superimposition of things that have qualities (leaving the door open for *dharma adhyāsa* for the reasons that will follow).

An example illustrative of the kind of superimposition that exists between the qualities or attributes of two things is cited in the misperception of conch as yellow, when one suffering from jaundice or some other disorder perceives the white conch as yellow. The question in this context arises whether the substratal principle, namely, the conch, is cognized before mistaking it as yellow. If we say that it was cognized before mistaking it as yellow, then it must have been cognized only as white in color. If it is maintained that it was cognized as yellow initially, then it will simply be a case of the modification of the mind. To say that it is cognized as a mere conch without its color being cognized is inadmissible. What comes within the range of perception must have some color or quality, thus the conch must possess some color so that it may be perceived.

2.14.5.1.3 *PP*, at this point, cites the solution of Vācaspati,[24] that because of some conceivable defect in the conch itself, it is perceived in the first instance as yellow when its inherent whiteness is being suppressed for the time being. So the substratum is mistaken as yellow in color. Thus, it may be seen as a case of superimposition of two entities followed by the superimposition of qualities upon it. In the initial stage, a quality is superimposed upon a particular substance. There is the superimposition of yellow color even when we have the cognition that it is a conch. Similarly, in the example 'the iron-ball burns', one can have the cognition that it is an iron-ball and there is the superimposition of the qualities of burning, and so on, with respect to it.

In the case of superimposition caused by some limiting adjunct, the cognition of difference is not at all a counteracting factor. The 'iron-ball burns' clearly is an example of this sort. The cognition of the distinction between the substratal principle and the superimposed entity is not the counteracting factor for viewing one thing as the other.[25]

When we apply this analysis to the case of 'I desire' and 'I know', we note that the superimposition of agency and other similar things on the part of the self is also caused by some limiting adjunct, namely, the mind. The noncomprehension of the distinction between the substratum and the superimposed entity is not the criterion here.

In this context, the author of *PP*, seeks support for his analysis from the writings of Śaṃkara. After explaining the cognition of false identification of two entities like the self and the mind, Śaṃkara proceeds to say that the cognition 'I desire' is a case of superimposition of the qualities upon the 'I', which is a *dharmī* (i.e., that which has the attributes). The 'I' is a case of *dharmī adhyāsa*, and 'I desire' is a case of *dharma adhyāsa*.

2.14.5.2 When there is a false identification of the mind caused by modification, say in the form of happiness, the quality of happiness in turn is superimposed upon the self, and accordingly we have the cognition 'I am happy." The superimposition is caused by the superimposition of the identity of the mind with the self. Similarly, in 'the iron-ball burns', the superimposition is caused by the superimposition of the identity of the iron-ball with the fire.

2.14.5.3 In ordinary experience, we have the clear cognition of fire as distinct from the iron. It may be asked: Do we ever have the cognition of mind as distinct from the self before their alleged superimposition? In response, *PP* appeals to *śruti* and *smṛti.* The Upaniṣadic statement, 'first there is the instruction regarding the nature of the mind'[26] proves that the mind and the self are distinct. Under the heading of *smṛti*, *PP* appeals to the Yoga system. In their system, "*mahat tattva,* prompted by the power of God, undergoes transformation and produces the ego-sense (*ahaṃkāra*). From that *ahaṃkāra* predominated by the power of action, it [mind] comes into existence."[27] It implies the use of the 'I' (*ahaṃ*) as distinct from the mind. It is true that the texts embodying the transcendent experience assume the distinction between the mind and the self, but one wonders how it is relevant for establishing the distinction between the 'I' and the self. In response it has been pointed out that 'I' cannot be viewed as distinct from the self. The mind as inspired by the reflection of pure consciousness in it is identical with the cognition of 'I'. One could not have the cognition 'I' anywhere else except in the mind.

2.15 *nanu aṇtahkaraṇasya indriyatayātīndriyatvāt kathaṃ pratyakṣaviṣayateti?*

ucyate. na tāvad antaḥkaraṇam indriyam ity atra mānam asti.

'manaḥṣaṣṭhānīndriyāṇi" iti bhagavadgītāvacanaṃ pramāṇam iti cet, na; anindriyeṇāpi manasā ṣaṭtvasaṃkhyāpūraṇavirodhāt. na hīndriyagatasaṃkhyāpūraṇam indriyeṇaiveti niyamaḥ; "yajamānapañcamā iḍāṃ bhakṣayanti" ity atra ṛtviggatapañcatvasaṃkhyāyā anṛtvijāpi yajamānena pūraṇadarśanāt; "vedānadhyāpayāmāsa mahābhāratapañcamān" ityādau vedagatapañcatvasaṃkhyāyā avedenāpi bhāratena pūraṇadarśanāt; "indriyebhyaḥ parāhy arthā arthebhyaś ca paraṃ manaḥ" iti śrutyā manaso 'nindriyatvāvagamāc ca.

2.15 *[Another objection]: Now, the internal organ being a sense organ is [itself] imperceptible, how could it be an object of perception?*

It is said [in reply]: There is no proof that the internal organ is a sense organ.

If it is maintained that the evidence is the statement of the

Bhagavadgītā: "The sense organs with the mind as the sixth one" (15.7), the answer is 'no', because there is no contradiction in filling mind as number six, though it is not a sense organ. There is no hard and fast rule that the completion of a number [in the list of organs] must be done by an organ alone; for in 'those with yajamāna (sacrificer) as the fifth, eat the iḍā', we see that the number five relating to the priests is completed by the sacrificer who is not a priest. In the same way, in 'he taught all the Vedas by rote with the Mahābhārata as the fifth (Mbh. I. lxiv. 131, xii. ccil. 20), the number five is completed by the Mahābhārata which is not a Veda; furthermore, śruti [text] such as: 'Objects are superior to the sense organs, the mind is superior to objects' (Kaṭha 3.10), proves that the mind is not a sense organ.

2.15 The position outlined thus far is that the 'I' (*ahaṃ padārtha*) is a blend of two factors, namely, the mind and the self, and that it is a case of illusory perception—an illusory superimposition of a kind different from that of the superimposition of the rope on the snake and similar such perceptual illusions. The objection that is voiced in this context is articulated by the author of *VP* as providing the context for the meaning of the passage under consideration.

2.15.1 Opponents raise the following objection: If the 'I' is a blend of the mind and the self, then mind will come within the range of perception. This, however, is not the case, because mind is a sense organ and, as a sense organ, it transcends sense perception. A sense organ, in itself unperceivable, cannot come within the range of perception. The point that *PP* is trying to make is as follows: The sense of sight, though involved in perception, does not itself fall within the scope of visual perception. What we perceive are only the eyeballs, which serve as the abode of the sense of sight. From this it follows that mind cannot be the content of the notion of 'I'.

2.15.1.1 It is asked: What reason is there to think that the mind is a sense organ? The *Gītā* text, which speaks of mind as the sixth sense organ, appeals to a potential experiential basis for conceiving mind analogously with other sense organs. There also is what may be called a presumptive proof in further support of conceding the status of sense organ to the mind. It is a fact of perceptual experience that happiness, sorrow, and other such states are cognized. These objects of experience obviously do not fall within the ken of the well-known five senses of knowledge. And, because they could be cognized only by some sense, mind plays such a role. Therefore, mind must be a sense organ.

The Vivaraṇa point of view to which the author of *PP* refers, is relevant here. According to them, perceptuality of knowledge does not depend upon the instrument of cognition but on the object. It is important to remember from a phenomenological point of view that if the object is perceptual, *knowledge also is perceptual*, irrespective of how such knowledge arises. The Nyāya position, which favors an ontic analysis, maintains that perceptual cognition entails a sense organ.

2.15.1.2 *PP* asks whether, in the experience 'my mind', there is a perceptual cognition of the mind or not. If such a cognition exists, then how will the Naiyāyikas account for the perceptuality of mind, which admittedly is a sense organ? The Nyāya reply to this is simple: Mind comes within the sweep of inferential cognition, not of perceptual cognition. The perceptual experience "my mind" does not arise from an ordinary sense-contact, but rather through an extra-empirical contact. *PP*, on the strength of the Upaniṣadic text cited in *VP*, "objects are superior to sense organs while mind is superior even to objects,"[28] finds the Nyāya analysis unacceptable. The only experiential basis for viewing mind as a sense organ, for the Naiyāyikas, is that it is similar to other sense organs in some features. The sense organs serve as causative factors and so does the mind. The Nyāya analysis of the perceptuality of mind arising through the extra-empirical contact is unacceptable to the Advaitins.[29] Keeping this in mind, Śāstrī says: *na tāvad iti.*

2.15.2 The author of *AB*, whom *PP* cites, throws further light on the plausibility of explaining mind as a sense organ on the ground of similarity of function.[30] Invoking the very general rule that the opponent uses in support of his thesis—that the mind can be classified as a sense organ—*AB* elicits the sense of similarity. The rule is that if B fills the number in the series A, then B belongs to the category A. Belonging to the category in this context need not be through the presence of a particular feature that is adjectival to the category; it may be through other features as well. The similarity on the basis of a common feature of 'thisness' (i.e., presentedness), which is present in the mind as well as in the sense organs may be taken into consideration. Thisness is a common feature present in all objects, as attested to by the experience of counting such as, 'this is one' and 'this is second'. Taking this into consideration, mind can plausibly be grouped with sense organs.

2.16 *na caivaṃ manaso'nindriyatve sukhādipratyakṣasya sākṣātkāratvaṃ na syāt, indriyājanyatvād iti vācyam. na hīndriyajanyatvena jñānasya sākṣāttvam, anumityāder api manojanyatayā sākṣāttvāpatteḥ; īśvarajñānasya anindriyajanyasya sākṣāttvānāpatteś ca.*

2.16 *It cannot be argued that if mind is not considered to be a sense organ, there would be no immediate perceptual knowledge of happiness, or misery, because they are not generated by a sense organ. The criterion for the immediacy of knowledge is not origination from a sense organ, because in that case inferential cognition being mind generated [which is the same as being sense generated for the Naiyāyikas] would be immediate; and God's knowledge, which is not sense generated [being eternal], would be nonimmediate.*

2.16 The above *VP* passage raises an objection from the Naiyāyika perspective. The Naiyāyikas maintain that if mind is not considered to be a sense organ, then one will not be able to account for the perceptual cognition of happiness, misery, and similar other cognitions, which conceivably cannot arise from a sense organ, because the criterion for the perceptuality of knowledge rests in its being originated from a sense organ. In this context, we must not lose sight of the fact that they regard mind as an instrument used by the self in internal perception. Imagination, knowledge, and so on, are the qualities of the self, and can only be produced by the mind.

2.16.1 VP rejects the position outlined above, and the author of PP explains what this rejection entails. The Nyāya school indeed cannot defend their position that knowledge is perceptual only if it arises through a sense organ. In their system mind is a sense organ and inferential knowledge arises from the mind. If whatever arises through a sense organ is considered to be perceptual in nature, then the inferential knowledge of fire on the hill being a product of the mind (sense organ) must be viewed as perceptual, which, however, is not the case.

2.16.1.1 The Naiyāyikas' reply in this context is very subtle. They say that only if mind as a sense organ is taken to give rise to an inferential cognition, only then will there be force in the Advaitin objection. Mind *qua* mind gives rise to the inferential cognition and not mind as a sense organ. When they define perceptuality of knowledge as arising from a sense organ, what is meant is that it arises from the contact of a sense organ. Inferential cognition, although it arises from the mind, does not arise from the mind in its capacity as a sense organ with its sense contact. There is a difference between the empirical cognition of fire and the inferential cognition of fire.

2.16.1.2 The author of *PP*, rejecting the Nyāya view, cites the conflicting case of God's knowledge, which is avowed as not sense generated and yet is perceptual in character. The point to note here, *PP* maintains, is that while there are different views of the nature of God's omniscience, what is commonly accepted both by the Naiyāyikas and the Advaitins is that our knowledge of God is not sensory. While conceding that it is not sense generated, the Advaitins go a step further and contend that it is unoriginated, their theory being that it arises from *māyā*.

2.16.1.3 The author of *PP* brings to the reader's notice the difference in the perspective on the question of the status of mind as a sense organ within the fold of the Advaita tradition itself. Vācaspati accepts the discourse of mind as a sense organ. Religious texts, for example, *smṛti* texts do at times speak of mind as a sense organ distinct from other sense organs. Vācaspati Miśra cites the maxim of 'cow and bull' as helpful in understanding the textual ambiguity in respect of discourses about the mind.[31] The term 'go' is common to both cow and bull. But the expression *balīvarda* only means bull. So the hyphenated expression '*go-balīvarda*' signifies that it belongs to the bovine category. The expression for bull (*balīvarda*) belongs to the bovine category, and it is also used to distinguish it from a cow. If mind is a sense organ, on what basis can it be distinguished from other sense organs? Vācaspati says in response that sense organs, in general, comprehend only those objects that are present before us, while mind can comprehend objects that would come in the future as well. When it is argued that a sense organ does not come within the range of perception, what is intended is that a mere sense of action or a mere sense of knowledge cannot come within the range of perception. However, as *Manusmṛti* states: "Mind comes under the sense of action as well as the sense of knowledge."[32] This peculiar status occupied by the mind enables the mind to be known perceptually. In his commentary on *Adyhyāsabhāṣya,*[33] Vācaspati explains that consciousness comes within the range of perception because of its association with the mind.

In the considered judgment of the author of *PP* there are subtle differences within the fold of Advaita in this context. However, all of them agree that mental states such as happiness and misery are merely the attributes of the mind that are superimposed upon the self. One may contrast here the ecclecticism of *PP* with a commentary like *AB* that seeks to reconcile or draw support from the internal traditions of Advaita.

2.16.2 The more significant difference, however, between the schools of Bhāmatī and Vivaraṇa, which also accounts for the difference in their attitudes toward the question of the status of mind, must be kept in view. *PP* draws the attention of the reader to this significant point. The Vivaraṇa school maintains that verbal testimony itself could give rise to perceptual cognition. As a result, they believe that mind is not a sense organ. Vācaspati, however, holds that verbal testimony itself could not give rise to the perceptual cognition of an object. Verbal testimony initiates the process by which the mind mediates and accomplishes the experience initiated by the hearing of verbal testimony. Therefore, mind has to be acknowledged as a sense organ so that mind when initiated by the hearing of testimony and perfected by *yoga* can give rise to immediate knowledge.

While not joining the issue in favor of one or the other, *PP* agrees with the perspective of *VP*, which rejects the view that mind is a sense organ. Experiences such as 'I am deaf' and 'I am blind' exemplify superimposition, not as between the sense organs and the self, but as between the qualities of the sense organs and the self. Insofar as these experiences do not take the form 'I am the ear' or ' I am the eye' it is only the qualities of the sense organs; namely, the deafness or the blindness and not the sense organs themselves that are superimposed upon the self. Superimposition of quality *(dharma adhyāsa)* is what experience directly attests. It is not necessary to posit mind as a sense organ to explain the immediate experiences of happiness or pain.

2.16.3 The author of *PP*, in support of the position outlined above, draws our attention to a passage from Śaṃkara's commentary: 'He who does not have the false notion of identity with the body, sense organs in the form 'I', 'mine', etc., the false identification with respect to sense organs is not one of 'I' but of 'mine'." In this instance *dharmī adhyāsa,* or superimposition of the 'substance', is not necessary.[34] Just as merits and demerits, being mediate in nature, are not perceived, neither are the sense organs. Analyzing the sense of 'mine', the author translates it to mean 'I possess', and then asks how one can explain the experience 'I possess sight', especially if the eye or the sense of sight is not itself perceivable.

2.16.4 It is said that 'I possess sight' in this context refers to the body, which is in contact with the sense organs. Perceptual knowledge arises on the basis of the functioning of the sense organs with reference to the body in which the sense of sight operates. Similarly, the experience 'I am deaf' is a case of superimposition of qualities.

2.16.5 The position of the Bhamatī school is that it is necessary to recognize mind as a sense organ for the reasons already explained. Accordingly the followers of Bhamatī construe the text of Śaṃkara quoted above as referring to one who is devoid of the false cognition of identity with respect to both the physical body and the sense organs, so that he could make room for including the sense organs within the scope of superimposition. To be a sense organ is not necessarily to be in conflict with being perceptual, because there can be perceptual illusory cognitions of sense organs. This is what seems to be conceded by Śaṃkara in that passage. The author of *PP*, however, sides with *VP* and supports the Vivaraṇa position. The Vivaraṇa explanation of the above cited passage of Śaṃkara is given in support of it. The explanation is that Śaṃkara, in the aforementioned passage, refers to one who does not have any false notion of the 'I' with respect to physical body, or the false notion of the mind with respect to the sense organs, thus relegating sense organs to a position of the function or quality superimposed on the self, instead of construing it to refer to the sense organ, which has a sensory quality.

Notes

1. For the Naiyāyikas, perception is cognition that arises from the contact of a sense organ with an object, is not itself linguistic, is not erroneous, and is well ascertained (*indriyārthasannikarṣotpannaṃ jñānaṃ avy apdeśyaṃ avybhicāri vyavasā yatmakaṃ pratyakṣa) Nyāya-Sūtras*, 1.1.4. The self, the mind, sense organs, objects, and particular kinds of contact between them are necessary conditions for perception. In other words, unless the self is in contact with the *manas*, *manas* with the sense organs, and the sense organ with the object, no perception can arise. All knowledge is revelation of objects, and the contact of the senses with an object is not metaphorical but literal.

2. Ontologically, a cognition for the Naiyāyikas is a quality of the self. This quality, a product of various causal factors, originates under special conditions and from an epistemological perspective, refers beyond itself to an object. A cognition does not cognize itself—it reveals its object (*viṣaya*). Accordingly, a cognition is related to the *viṣaya* by the relation of *viṣayatā*, that is, by making it an object. In response to the question of how a cognition cognizes itself, the Naiyāyikas maintain that a cognition is cognized in a secondary act of retrospection. The primary act does not cognize itself but only the external object; for example, a pitcher, in "here is a pitcher" (*ayaṃ ghaṭaḥ*). However, the cognition 'I know that here is a pitcher' is different. It succeeds the first cognition and is called 'after (*anu*) cognition (*vyavasāya*)'. The Naiyāyikas further maintain that the *anu-vyavasāya* of the primary act of cognition is infallible and intrinsically true, a position that when viewed phenomenologically makes sense. Both *Vācaspati* and Udayana reiterate this point: "No one who does not have a knowledge introspects 'I am knowing'; no one who has the introspection 'I am knowing a silver' when in fact he has knowledge of a shell." Udayanācārya, *Tātparya Pariśuddhi*, quoted in J. N. Mohanty', *Gangeśa' Theory of Truth* (Shantiniketan: Centre of Advanced Study in Philosophy, 1966), 54.

Whether *anuvyavasāya* is intrinsically true is debatable. However, nobody can deny that *anuvyavasāya* does not err and is therefore beyond any doubt: "The fact that one never introspects 'I know a jar' when in fact one is knowing a cloth is sufficient to show that here there is no reasonable probability of doubt. Even if the primary knowledge be erroneous, its *anuvyavasāya* is not, for it accurately describes its object which is the primary knowledge. The knowledge 'This is silver' may be false, but that the knowledge has 'silverness' for its qualifier is true." *Ibid.*, 230.

3. Annambhaṭṭa explains *jñānalakṣaṇa* as that "in which one percept gives rise to another, as when one perceives a piece of sandal-wood at a distance, one at once knows that it is fragrant. Here the fragrance could be perceived neither by the eye, nor by the nose as the sandal piece was at a distance, it is therefore apprehended by a kind of extraordinary perception." *TSDNB*, sec. 42, 214. This process corresponds to what has been articulated as perception through complex association in western psychology.

The Advaitins reject *jñānlakṣaṇa*. They maintain that the process is one of inference that which can easily be subsumed under the category of normal perception. There is no need to postulate any sort of extra-empirical contact to explain such perceptions. To explain the perceiving of a piece of sandalwood from a distance, it is not necessary to have recourse to a category of *jñānlakṣaṇa* perception, because such a category is riddled with contradictions. Is such an extraordinary perception, presentative or nonpresentative? It cannot be the first because of the absence of the apprehending mental mode assuming the form of fragrance, nor can it be the second because of the absence of the conditions that account for the nonpresentative knowledge, like inference. In other words, there is no knowledge of an invariable relation between sandalwood and fragrance such that the latter may be inferred on perceiving the former. For the Advaitins, therefore, the visual fragrant sandalwood is a mixed mode of consciousness made of the elements of presentative and representative knowledge; that is, it is a case of compound perception. For a detailed account, see Jadunath Sinha, *Indian Psychology*, vol. 1 (Calcutta: Sinha Publishing House, 1958), 88.

4. *PP*, 27.

5. Śaṃkara clearly states that Brahman, although known by intuition, is not an object of the senses. *BSB* 1.1.2. He further contends, as stated earlier, that Brahman is self-luminous. Self is not an object, yet it has fitness to be immediately aware of itself. Brahman is not an object of *pramāṇa-s*, because the function of *pramāṇa-s* is to make, what is unknown, known. Brahman indeed is known. He is the self of everything. However, it is difficult for finite individuals to comprehend its nature completely. Therefore, an inquiry into the nature of Brahman is essential (*athāto Brahmajijñāsa*). *BSB* 1.1.1. *Pramāṇa-s* do not cognize Brahman like any finite material object. In ordinary knowledge, when ignorance is destroyed about an object, the object becomes manifest. However, in Brahman-knowledge, *pramāṇa-s* only destroy ignorance about Brahman; they cannot manifest it. In other words, when nescience obscuring Brahman is lifted, Brahman is revealed; not manifested, because Brahman is never nonmanifest.

6. The Advaita distinction between *vṛtti vyāpya* and *phala vyāpya* signifies that a thing may be referred to in thought but need not be objectified as *this* or *that*. The Naiyāyikas maintain that any usage of words implies objectifying a thing or making it an object. The Advaitins, however, do not subscribe to such a view. Something that is not known as an object still can be referred to and validly known. The final *vṛtti* that results from the study of texts, such as *tat tvam asi*, refers not to a remote object, but to something that is immediately present, because the immediacy of experience is not caused by any of the means of knowledge.

The following account by A. K. Ray Chaudhuri explains the difference between *vṛtti vyāpya* and *phala vyāpya*: "A *vṛtti* about a pot, being illumined by the reflection of *cit*, destroys *ajñāna* about the pot and manifests it. There is a two-fold effect with regard to the pitcher. The *ajñāna* about it is destroyed by the *vṛtti* (*vṛtti-vyāpya*) and it is manifested by the *caitanya* reflected in the *vṛtti* (*phala-vyāpya*). But, in the present case, the undifferentiated (*akhaṇḍakāra*) *vṛtti*only cancels the *ajñāna* about Brahman; the reflected *caitanya* cannot manifest the self-luminous Brahman which shines by itself. In other words, Brahman is *vṛtti-vyāpya* only and not *phala-vyāpya*." *The Doctrine of Māyā* (Calcutta: Dasgupta & Co., 1950), 162–163.

7. *PP*, 28.

8. *Viṣaya* is the intentional object of thought, which is different from the actual object (i.e., *vastu).* In other words, from an epistemological perspective, the object is what is meant, the content actually present in it. The content is neither true nor false. Rather, it is the act of judging in which we either affirm or deny the actuality of an object corresponding to the content that is said to be true or false. Thus knowledge is a mode of consciousness to be determined by its object.

The central position of the Advaita theory of knowledge, as defined by Śaṃkara, is that the object of knowledge should exist before knowledge. However far back we may trace our knowledge, it always will presuppose the priority of the object, a priority that is not temporal but points to the eternally accomplished character of the object, a *siddha vastu*. In simple terms, it signifies that an object is not brought into being through knowing itself. This is the distinction of knowledge as distinguished from, say, volition. The following passages from Śaṃkara explain this point clearly: "*jñānaṃ tu pramāṇa-janyam, pramāṇaṃ ca yathābhūtavastuviṣayam, ato jñānaṃ kartum akartum anyathā vā kartum aśakyam, kevalaṃ vastutantram eva tat, na codanātantraṃ nāpi puruṣatantraṃ.*" *BSB* 1.1.4; and "*na vastu-yāthāt-myajñānaṃ puruṣabuddhyapekṣaṃ, kiṃ tarhi, vastutantram eva tat.*" *Ibid*., 1.1.2. In short, whereas with knowledge the object is the content present in it, in illusion the real object never appears, and what appears as the content is later cancelled by right knowledge. As long as one keeps in mind this distinction, no harm is done by using object and content interchangeably, as I have done. Also see T. R. V. Murti, "Knowledge and Truth," *Studies in Indian Thought*, ed. Harold G. Coward (Delhi: Motilal Banarsidass, 1985), 114.

9. *PP*, 29.

10. Whether mind is a sense organ or not has given rise to a great deal of controversy. Vācaspati, following *śruti*-s and *smṛti*-s, considers mind to be a sense organ. The Vivaraṇa tradition, on the other hand, maintains that mind is not a sense organ. The function of mind is to go out to grasp the object and make it manifest. In other words, the mind is active in perceiving an object and not a passive instrument that simply records the impressions. It is important to note in this context the unique Vedāntin conception of sense organs, which is different from the generally accepted notion of sense organs. In Vedānta , the term '*indriya*' does not refer to the outer organs of the eyes, ears, nose, and so on located in the physical body, rather, their subtle counterparts constitutive of the subtle body and composed of the same type of subtle subtance as mind *antaḥkaraṇa,* the main constituent of the subtle body. Sense organs thus can expand and contract as freely as mind. See Swami Satprakashananda, *Methods of Knowledge*, 44–45.

11. *Vṛtti* in this book is used specifically to refer to *antaḥkaraṇa vṛtti,* which is entailed in any cognitive endeavor. This is distinguished from mental 'modes' that operate in the case of noncognitive states of mind like the experience of happiness and pain. This is consistent with the use of the term *vṛtti* in the Advaita tradition. However, for the sake of clarity, the latter kind, when used for example in their noncognitive context, are indicated by substituting the term 'state' for 'mode.' In the tradition of Advaita writings, however, the term '*vṛtti*' has sometimes been used by analogous extension, to refer to *sukha vṛtti*, and so on, which, at times, have been articulated as *avidyā vṛtti.*

12. The *sattva guṇa* is one of the three *guṇas* recognized in Indian thought. *Sattva* is the principle of knowledge, purity, and joy; the *rajas* is the principle of motion leading to activity, restlessness; and the *tamas* is the principle of inertia. All objects consisting of these three *guṇas* in different proportions account for the variety that we see in this world.

According to the Vedānta tradition, sense organs are composed of the same subtle and pure substance of which the mind is composed. The *sattva* aspect of these subtle elements (i.e., ether, earth, water, fire and air), join to produce the mind. Being constituted of the finest essence of matter, mind has the quality to expand and contract and assume the form of the object of knowledge, irrespective of whether it is large or small, fine or gross.

13. *evañcantaḥkaraṇa pariṇāmo vṛttir iti granthasya na mṛtpariṇāmo ghaṭa ity ādāv iva rūpāntarāpattir ity arthaḥ, kintu vikāsāvasthāprayuktāntaḥkaraṇāvayava-viśeṣāṇāṃ deśaviśeṣe daṇḍāyamānānām avasthānam evātra pariṇāma-padārthaḥ.* Śāstrī explains the meaning of the term "*pariṇāma*" that occurs in text *VP*. When it is said that *vṛtti* is a transformation of the mind, it is not implied that it is a transformation in the same sense in which a pitcher is a transformation of the clay. On the other hand, the presence of the specific parts of the *antaḥkaraṇa* , the parts with the quality of expansion, in a specific place is known as *pariṇāma* . The relationship between the mind and its object is the same as the relationship that exists between a pitcher that has been coated with the paint inside out. Similarly, the mind goes out, reaches the place of the object, undergoes transformation in the form of the object, and coats it, as it were, with the object, namely, the pitcher. *PP*, 31.

14. The identity between parts and the whole is a part of the general doctrine accepted by Advaitins that the effect exists before its origination and is nondifferent from its cause. The relation between substance and attribute, action and substance, universal and particular is one of identity (*tādātmya*). See *BSB* 2.1.28; 2.2.38.

15. *PP*, 34.

16. *Ibid.*

17. The question generally are asked: Which is more powerful, *śruti* or *pratyakṣa*? Do they conflict with each other? In response, it is said that there is no conflict between the two, because they operate in two separate spheres. Perception operates where the plurality of names and forms, brought about by nescience, is manifested. *Śruti* texts repeatedly assert that reality is nondual; hence, there is no conflict.

The author of *Iṣṭsiddhi* reinforces the very same point by demonstrating the relative superiority of scriptures as a means of knowledge when compared to perception: "Since *pramāṇas* only dispel the ignorance and since ignorance or knowledge can be spoken of only with reference to Self and not not-self, the ignorance of the true nature of the Self can be dispelled by the *śruti* alone. Pratyakṣa and so on, therefore, deal with the world of difference and ignorance. Scripture declares the truth. Thus there is no conflict between perception and other *pramāṇas* on the one hand and scripture on the other. *ataḥ na tadvirodhāśaṅkā śrutyarthe, tadviruddhārthatvābhāvātteṣām.*" P. K. Sundaram, *Advaita Epistemology* (Madras: University of Madras, 1984), 189.

18. *vācārambhaṇaṃ vikāro nāmadheyam, mṛttikety eva satyam*. *eva* shows that effects have no reality. The world, being an effect, is not real, only the cause is real; the modification being only a name arising from speech, and clay is simply the truth. *CU* 6.1.4. Other texts, for example, *Kaṭha,* 4.11, "*neha nānāsti kiñcana*," and BU 2.4.14, "*yatra hi dvaitam iva bhavati*," also show that the world of duality does not really exist in Brahman.

19. *PP*, 35.

20. *BU* 1.5.3.

21. *PP*, 36.

22. There is no clear reference to the distinction between *nirupādhika adhyāsa* and *sopādhika adhyāsa* in the *Adhyāsabhāṣya* of Śaṃkara. One may even wonder whether according to his rigorous formulation of consciousness as nondual (i.e., indeterminate and unrelated), one can admit of *nirupādhika adhyāsa* in the strictest sense of the term. Śaṃkara's definition of *adhyāsa,* however, covers the twofold aspects of perceptual error: cognizing a thing as something different from what it is (e.g., perceiving a rope as a snake); and cognizing a thing as different from what it actually is, for example, perceiving a white conch as yellow. In the first type of

adhyāsa, one falsely ascribes one thing to another; in the second type, one ascribes the attributes of one thing on another. The first one is generally known as *artha adhyāsa* (superimposition of object) and the second one as *jñāna adhyāsa* (superimposition of cognition). Mistaking a tree for a person and apprehending Brahman as manifold are examples of the first kind. A crystal appearing red because of its proximity to the red rose, and a white conch appearing yellow to jaundiced eyes are examples of the second kind. It is important to remember here that on the Advaitin contention the nonreal is intelligible only as dependent on the real for its existence. There is thus no illusion without the external substratum. In short, a superimposition without a substratum is neither experienced nor conceivable. "The 'silver' that appeared is false by its very nature; it has not even a semblance of existence apart from the shell where it appeared. What it is in itself apart from this connection cannot be determined. Its intrinsic nature is indescribable. The 'thisness' (*idaṃatā*) of the shell is also false, for it appeared not independently in its own right, but as identified with the 'silver'." *Ajñāna*, 141.

The followers of Śaṃkara, however, make a clear distinction between *nirupādhika adhyāsa* (superimposition with limiting adjunct) and the *sopādhika adhyāsa* (superimposition without limiting adjunct). Padmāpada, for example, states: " The shell-silver illusion is known as 'nirupādhikādhyāsa ' and the double moon illusion as 'sopādhikādhyasa'. The first disappears the moment the right knowledge comes; but the second, inspite of knowledge to the contrary persists as long as the adventitious cause (upādhi) lasts. The superimposition of the ego on cit is an instance of nirupādhikādhyāsa and the superimposition of duality on cit is sopādhikādhyasa." *PPD*, Ist *Varṇaka*, 21.67, 46.

23. Padmapāda explains the significance of using *dharma* as follows: "The use of the word dharma is to indicate that the superimposition is of the body, only as associated with attributes 'manhood' being a man and so on, and not to denote (association with others as illustrated in 'I am body." *PPD*, Ist *Varṇaka*, 42.160, 120.

24. The words of Vācaspati deserve to be quoted here: "The yellow, which resides in the bile that is in contrast with the exceedingly pure rays going forth from the eye, is experienced in dissociation from the bile; the shell too is experienced (but) with the whiteness concealed by a defect (in the sense organ); the non-relation of the yellow-colour to the shell is not experienced; because of similarity in respect of nonapprehension of non-relationship, the appositional relation previously seen in (experiences) like 'yellow mass of gold, yellow *bilva* fruit' is imposed on yellow-ness and shell-ness and one speaks of the yellow shell." Vācaspati offers many similar arguments to explain *sopādhika adhyāsa*. Such an explanation assumes that there are two mental modes: one in the form of 'this', and the other which apprehends the 'yellowness' present somewhere else. It might be asked then, that because the function of a mental mode is to remove ignorance, which of these two mental modes performs that function? *Catussūtrī*, *Adhyāsābhāṣya*, 18–19.

Several attempts have been made to preserve the view that there are two modes. Sarvajñātmuni contends that in shell-silver, the ignorance about 'this' element is definitely removed, but not about the shellness, because that is the material cause of the illusion. To support his thesis he makes a distinction between *adhiṣṭhāna* and the *ādhāra* of an illusion. See chap. 1 n. 14 above for the distinction between the two.

25. Vācaspati further notes: "Let there be no reciprocal identity between different substrates (that is, the self and the not-self); there may occur yet the reciprocal superimposition of their attributes, such as inertness and intelligence, eternality and noneternality, and so on Even where substrates are distinguished, there is indeed seen to occur superimposition of their attributes, for example, in the crystal though apprehended as different from the flower, yet because of its absolute transparency, there arises the illusion of redness, in the experience 'red crystal' generated by the reflection of hibiscus flower.... It is indeed a substance with colour, which, on account of its

absolute transparency takes on the reflection of another substance with colour, though apprehended as different from itself; the intelligent self, however, is the colourless subject and cannot take on the reflection of the object.... Superimposition is pervaded by non-apprehension of difference; the opposite therefore, that is, the apprehension of difference, is present here, which getting rid of that non-apprehension of difference, gets rid also of the superimposition pervaded thereby." *Ibid.*, 6–7. Accordingly, it is said that in the case of *sopādhika adhyāsa*, the cognition of difference is not at all a counteracting condition.

26. *athāto '"hankārādeśaḥ" ity anantaram "athāta ātmādeśa" iti śrutau*. *PP*, 37.

27. *mahat tattvād vikurvāṇāt bhagavadvīryacoditāt*
kriyāśaktir ahankārastrividhaḥ sampaydyate. Ibid.

In the context of discussing the notion of *ahaṃkāra*, Professor Larson notes: "It is important to separate what the principle becomes from what it is in itself. From the point of view of what it becomes, *ahaṃkāra* pervades all of experience including the function of mind, senses, and so on In itself, however, it precedes all of these manifestations or functions, although it contains in itself the potentiality of such functions. In itself, the *ahaṃkāra* is simply the sense of 'I' or 'mine'. It is simply the fact of self awareness, apart from all the functioning in the realm of mind, senses, and so on It is, thus, a kind of general self awareness dissociated from ordinary experience." *Classical Sāṃkhya* (Delhi: Motilal Banarsidass, 1969), 203.

28. *Kaṭha*, 3.10.

29. Nyāyakośa defines *alaukika pratyṣaka* as: *alaukikasannikarṣajanyaṃ pratyakṣam, atra sannikarṣe alalukikatvaṃ ca sāmānyalakṣaṇa jñanālakṣaṇa yogaja etad anyatamatvam* (Poona: The Bhandarkar Oriental Research Institute, 1978), 82. Cases of perception that cannot be explained in terms of ordinary contact between the object and any of the sense organs are termed *alaukika pratyṣaka* (extra-empirical perception) by the Naiyāyikas. Such perceptions are three: *sāmānyalakṣaṇa*, *jñanalakṣaṇā*, and *yogaja*. The Naiyāyikas maintain that when we perceive a particular object, we not only perceive the object presented to the sense but also the universal that inheres in it. For example, when I perceive a pitcher, I not only perceive the pitcher, but also the universal 'pitcherness' that determines the particular pitcher. In this instance the contact between the sense organ and the pitcherness is not direct. The pitcherness is apprehended mediately, through the perception of at least one pitcher, by recollection. Such a contact is called *sāmānyalakṣaṇapratyāsatti*. *Yogaja* refers to the concentration of mind in which a *yogī* sees things that are beyond the scope of ordinary senses. For a discussion of *jñānalakṣaṇa*, see n. 3 of this chapter. For a discussion of extra-empirical contacts, readers might wish to consult Viśvanath Nyāya-Pañcānana's *Bhāṣā Pariccheda with Siddhānta-Muktavalī*, trans. Swāmi Mādhavānanda (Delhi: Advaita Ashrama, 1977), 99–104. Henceforth this work will be cited as *BP*.

30. *PP*, 40.

31. "*ta indriyāṇi tad avyapadeśād" ity atra manasa tv indriyatve smṛter avagate kvacid indriyebhyo bhedenopādānaṃgobalīvardanyāyena*. *PP*, 41.

32. *ekādaśendriyāṇy āhur yāni pūrve manīṣaṇaḥ*
tāni samyak pravakṣyāmi yathāvad anupūrvaśaḥ
śrotraṃ tvak cakṣuṣī jihvā nāsikā cava [caiva] pañcamī.
pāyūpasthaṃ hastapādaṃ vāk caiva daśamī smṛtā
ekādaśaṃ mano jñeyaṃ svaguṇenobhayātmakam ity uktam. Manusmṛti, 2.90–92; *PP*, 42.

33. In his commentary on *Adhyāsabhāṣya*, Vācaspati states: "When one devoid of the conceit of 'I' and 'mine' in one's body, senses, and so on, cannot intelligibly be a knower, the functioning of the means of valid knowledge is unintelligible. Indeed, empirical usage relating to perception, and so on, is not possible without the employment of the senses, and the functioning of the senses is not possible without control,

nor by a body on which is not superimposed the nature of the self can anything be operated. And when none of these is present, the unattached self cannot intelligibly be a knower. And without a knower, there can be no functioning of the means of valid knowledge." *Catussūtrī, Adhyāsabhāṣya*, 47. In short, the means of valid knowledge (e.g., perception), refer to or are located in the person suffering from ignorance.

34. *dehendriyādiṣv ahaṃ mamābhimānarahistasyeti bhāṣye indriyeṣu mamatābhimānasyairoktatvena tatra dharmyadhyāsasyānāvaśyakatvāt dharmādīnām iva parokṣatvam evendriyāṇām yuktam*. *PP*, 42. Śaṃkara maintains that all empirical usage is characterized by nescience. Because of the reciprocal superimposition of the self and the not-self and the attributes of one on the other, an individual is subject to bondage. T. M. P. Mahadevan brings out the nature of superimposition, taking into account not only the superimposition of the form I', but also of the form mine'. The first is the superimposition of the substance (*dharmī*) and the second that of the attribute (*dharma*): "In empirical usages such as 'I am lean', 'I am dark in colour', and so on, there is the superimposition of the features of the body on the Self. In expressions such as 'I am blind', 'I am one-eyed', 'I am deaf', and so on, the superimposition on the Self is of the qualities of the sense organs. Similarly desire, anger, and so on, are the modes of the mind or the internal organs which are superimposed on the Self when one says 'I desire this', 'I am angry at this', and so on" *Superimposition in Advaita Vedānta* (New Delhi: Sterling Publishers, 1985), 7–8.

3

Three Kinds of Consciousness

3.17 *siddhānte pratyakṣatvaprayojakaṁ kim iti cet, kiṃ jñānagatasya pratyakṣatvasya prayojakaṃ pṛcchasi, kiṃ vā viṣaya-gatasya? ādye pramāṇacaitanyasya viṣayāvacchinnacaitanyābheda iti brūmaḥ. tathā hi. trividhaṃ caitanyam: viṣayacaitanyaṃ pramāṇa-caitanyaṃ pramatṛcaitanyaṃ ceti. tatra ghaṭādyavacchinnacaitanyaṃ viṣayacaitanyam. antaḥkaraṇavṛttyavacchinnaṃ caitanyaṃ pramāṇa-caitanyam. antaḥkaraṇāvacchinnaṃ pramātṛcaitanyam.*

tatra yathā taḍāgodakaṃ chidrān nirgatya kulyātmanā kedārān praviśya tadvad eva catuṣkoṇādyākāraṃ bhavati tathā taijasam antaḥ-karaṇam api cakṣurādidvārā nirgatya ghaṭādiviṣayadeśaṃ gatvā ghaṭā-diviṣayākāreṇa pariṇamate. sa eva pariṇāmo vṛttir ity ucyate. anumi-tyādisthale tu nāntaḥkaraṇasya vahnyādideśagamanam, vahnyādeś cakṣurādyasannikarṣāt.

tathā ca "ayaṃ ghaṭaḥ" ityādipratayakṣasthale ghaṭādes tad-ākāravṛtteś ca bahir ekatra deśe samavadhānāt, tadubhayāvacchinnaṃ caitanyam ekam eva; vibhājakayor apy antaḥkaraṇavṛttighaṭādiviṣa-yayor ekadeśasthatvena bhedājanakatvāt. ata eva maṭhāntarvartighaṭā-vacchinnākāśo na maṭhāvacchinnākāśād bhidyate.

3.17 *[Objection]: What determines the condition of percept-uality, according to your [Vedāntins] principles? [It is replied]: Do you ask about the condition of the perceptuality of knowledge or the content? With respect to the first, we say that it is the nondifference of the consciousness conditioned by the means of knowledge [cognitive consciousness] from the consciousness conditioned by the content. Accordingly, consciousness is threefold: the consciousness conditioned by the content, the consciousness conditioned by the means of knowledge, and the consciousness conditioned by the cognizer. To speak of them individually, the consciousness conditioned by the pitcher is the consciousness conditioned by the content, the consciousness conditioned by a mode of the internal organ is the consciousness conditioned be the means of knowledge, and that conditioned by the internal organ is the consciousness conditioned by the cognizer.*

Just as the water of a tank, having come out of an aperture, enters a number of fields through channels assuming like those [fields] a quadrangular or any other form, so also the internal organ, which is characterized by light, goes out [of the body] through the door [sense] of sight, and so on, and [after] reaching the location of the object, say a pitcher, it is modified in the form of the objects like a pitcher. This modification [of the internal organ] is called a mental mode (vṛtti). In the case of inferential cognition, and so on, however, there is no going out of the internal organ to the location of fire, because fire, and so on [other inferred objects], are not in contact with the sense of sight, and so on [other sense organs].

Thus in the case of the perceptual cognitions such as 'this is a pit-her', because the consciousness conditioned by the pitcher and the consciousness conditioned by the mental mode in the form of a pitcher are located in one and the same place [outside the body], the consciousness conditioned by both [the object perceived and the vṛtti] is one. This is because the modification of the internal organ and the objects like pitchers, although having the capacity of differentiation [between the consciousness conditioned by the vṛtti and the consciousness conditioned by the object], do not give rise to any difference on account of their being located in one and the same place [where the object exists]. For this very reason, ether conditioned by a pitcher in a monastery is not different from the ether conditioned by a hall in the monastery [inspite of being two distinct limiting adjuncts].

3.17 Having explained the criterion of knowledge, *VP* first proceeds to analyze the criteria with respect to the perceptuality of knowledge, and then discusses the perceptibility of object. *PP* reminds us that the term 'knowledge' in this context stands for the consciousness conditioned by the *vṛtti*. Because pure consciousness alone is perceptual in the true sense of the term, the criterion for the perceptuality of knowledge is the absence of any essential differencebetween the consciousness conditioned by the mental mode and the consciousness conditioned by the object. *PP*'s insightful reminder in this context is that consciousness is the very essence of a perceptual cognition.

3.17.1 The criteria for the perceptuality of knowledge is first stated in the text in a clear and an unambiguous language: It is non-difference of the cognitive consciousness; that is, the consciousness conditioned by the means of cognition and the consciousness conditioned by the object. Consciousness, although one, becomes many because of different limiting conditions. Consciousness conditioned by the means of knowledge is the cognitive-consciousness (*pramāṇa caitanya*), consciousness conditioned by the object is the content-consciousness (*viṣaya caitanya*), and the consciousness conditioned by the internal organ is the cognizer-consciousness (*pramātṛ caitanya*). This threefold stratification of consciousness in a cognitive relation is spelled out in great detail in *VP*. However, in the pages that immediately follow, *VP* focuses on the epistemological role of *pramāṇa caitanya.* The most important aspect of *pramāṇa caitanya* is its comprehensive nature, which becomes obvious when one contrasts this classification with the one given by Madhusūdana Sarasvatī.[1]

3.17.1.1 It will be useful here to outline the views of Madhusūdana in *Siddhāntabindu* (*SB*), frequently referred to and commented upon by *PP*. To explain the role of a mental mode in the perceptual process, *SB* introduces the internal sense as the modification of nescience residing in and pervading the body. Because of its translucent constitution (*sattva guṇa*), however, the internal sense is extremely clear. It goes out through the eyes, and so on, and assumes the form of the appropriate object. Like molten copper and solar light, it is capable of expanding and contracting. The important point to note here is that it becomes transformed and pervades the body and functions between the body and the object. The portion of the internal organ conditioned by the body, termed 'ego,' is spoken of as the doer. The portion which, like a rod, extends between the body and the object is called the *modal knowledge* (*vṛtti jñāna*), and it is spoken of as the operation or the activity of the internal sense. The portion of the internal sense that pervades the object is spoken of as the object's quality of being rendered fit for manifestation, which confers upon it the quality of being the object of knowledge. This is the tripartite division of the internal sense.[2]

3.17.1.2 Thus while *VP* classifies consciousness into *pramāṇa caitanya, pramātṛ caitanya*, and *viṣaya caitanya* and identifies the first one with the *pramiti caitanya*, Madhusūdana maintains that *pramiti* and *pramāṇa caitanya* are distinct. *PP*, at this juncture, enters into a critique of the narrower understanding of the *pramāṇa caitanya* given by Madhusūdana. The narrower interpretation of *pramāṇa caitanya* refers to the consciousness conditioned by the *vṛtti,* which is the name for that part of the internal organ that pertains to the body. *PP*'s criticism of it is with a view to defending the more comprehensive and epistemologically significant interpretation of *pramāṇa caitanya* given in *VP*.

3.17.1.3 Such a narrow interpretation gives rise to difficulties. One of the difficulties will be the ineptness of the example that the author of *VP* adduces to explain the function of *vṛtti.* The example of water issuing forth from a reservoir, on the face of it, contradicts the view that *vṛtti* is only a partial modification of the internal organ. According to the view that *vṛtti* is only a modification of the part of the internal organ, it must be admitted either that the *vṛtti* issues out of the body already modified, or, alternately, it may be said that the mind or the internal organ itself directly contacts the object, and then undergoes modification in the form of the object. Neither of these positions hold. On the first view, it will amount to saying that perception results from a mere contact of the sense of sight with the object, without any involvement on the part of mind. The Advaitins, however, maintain that a mere contact of the sense organ with the object is not the cause of perception, but that the contact of mind with the object is also essential. They affirm the identity between the consciousness conditioned by the object and the consciousness conditioned by the mind. Such an identity will be impossible on the view that *vṛtti* undergoes modification before it contacts the object. The other alternative—that the mind first contacts the object and then a part of it undergoes modification—also cannot be maintained, because that will amount to saying that we cannot clearly ascertain the perceptibility of the object without contacting the object. Perception of mental states (i.e., introspection), is an example of perception without sense contact. Mental states, such as happiness and misery, are directly manifested by the *sākṣin*. It is true that the author of *VP* admits that the objects that are directly manifested by the *sākṣin* also are manifested by *vṛtti*. However, in this context it must be kept in mind that these *vṛtti-s* do not originate by the functioning of a *pramāṇa*, for example, the sense of sight. *Vṛtti-s* in the form of happiness and misery are not like the *vṛtti-s* admitted in the context of the functioning of a *pramāṇa*-like sensory perception.

3.17.2 The description of the threefold division of consciousness given in the *VP* carries the significance that the three are identical because they are located in one and the same place. This admission will not be intelligible if it is maintained that only a part of the mind 'goes out' and gets transformed. According to the view of the partial modification of the mind as representing the meaning of *pramāṇa caitanya*, location of *vṛtti* in one and the same place is conceivable, but location in one and the same place of all the three factors—the *vṛtti*, the object, and the mind—will not be possible. According to the position maintained in *VP*, however, the location of the three in one and the same place is intelligible. Just as the space conditioned by a particular hall and the space conditioned by the pitcher located inside the hall may alike be referred to as conditioned by the hall—both being located in one and the same place—similarly the consciousness conditioned by mind (i.e., *vṛtti*), and the consciousness conditioned by a part of the mind when located in one and the same place may be treated as identical.

3.17.3 Further discussion about the consciousness conditioned by the *antaḥkaraṇa* being nondifferent from the consciousness conditioned by the mental mode in the form of the object and the contradictions involved in such an explanation, and elaboration of the analogy of non-distinction between the space conditioned by the pitcher located in a hall and the space conditioned by the hall on the one hand and the analogy of nonidentity between the space conditioned by the pitcher located in the hall and some other space, say, the space conditioned by a granary are discussed in great detail in *VP*. Śāstrī interprets *VP* text '*bhedājana-katvāt*' as '*bhedapratītyajanaktvāt*'. It is not a question of not causing the distinction but rather of not causing the cognition of the distinction.

3.18 *tathā ca "ayaṃ ghataḥ" iti pratyakṣasthale ghaṭākāravṛtter ghaṭasaṁyogitayā, ghaṭāvacchinnacaitanyasya tadvṛittyavacchinna-caitanyasya cābhinnatayā, tatra ghaṭajñānasya ghaṭākārāṁśe pratyakṣa-tvam.*

sukhaduḥkhādyavacchinnacaitanyasya, tadvṛittyavacchinnacaita-nyasya ca, niyamenaikadeśasthitopādhidvayāvacchinnatvān niyamena "ahaṃ sukhī, dukhī" ityādijñānasya pratyakṣatvam.

3.18 *Similarly, in the perception 'this is a pitcher', the mental mode in the form of a pitcher being in contact with the pitcher, the consciousness conditioned by the pitcher and the consciousness conditioned by the mental mode in the form of the pitcher are nondifferent, so for the cognition of the pitcher there is perceptual character with respect to its form as the pitcher.*

Because consciousness conditioned by happiness, pain, and so on, and the consciousness conditioned by the mental mode in the form of happiness, and so on, are invariably conditioned by two limiting adjuncts [happiness and the mental mode in the form of happiness] which are located in the same place, the cognitions 'I am happy, sad', and so on, are perceptual.

3.18 In this passage, *VP* discusses the use of the term 'contact' to explain how there accrues a perceptual character for the pitcher-cognition in relation to the form of the pitcher. In this context, the author of *PP* observes that the contact in question is unique, because the mode of the mind possessing the form of the pitcher (*ghaṭākāravṛtti*) is said to be in contact with the actual pitcher.

3.18.1 The Nyāya explanation of contact is well known.[3] It is given in terms of the two factors both necessary and sufficient to explain this concept; namely, the substratum (*anuyogin*), where the contact obtains and that which is in contact therewith, which is its counter-correlate *(pratiyogin)*. When we say the 'ground possesses the pitcher', (*bhūtalam ghaṭavad*), the ground is the substratum and the pitcher that characterizes the ground as being in relation to it is the counter-correlate.

When *VP* speaks of a transformation or modification of the mind, what is simply meant is that there is contact of the mind with the object. The contact is similar to that between the pitcher and the lime *(chunnam)* that is used in coloring the pitcher. The contact of the mind with the pitcher is unique or specific, similar to the contact between, for example, a pitcher and the floor, yet significantly different from it.

By thus explaining 'contact' as an aspect of the transformation of the mind, *PP* seeks to answer the objection often raised against the notion of contact as an external relation. Contact, in the very nature of the case, so the criticism runs, has to be nonpervasive, because contact between two finite objects cannot be pervasive. For example, when one describes a monkey sitting on a tree as being in contact with the tree, what one is claiming is that the monkey is only in contact with a portion of the tree. This amounts to saying that two things are in contact and yet not in contact with each other. This criticism is anticipated and rejected when such a contact is explained as being of a specific kind, such as the illustration of the contact between the *chunnam* and the pitcher. Mind pervades the entire object; there is no question of its not coming in contact with all the parts of the object.

3.18.2 In this context, *PP* explains the text that affirms an identity between the consciousness conditioned by the pitcher and the consciousness conditioned by the mental mode in the form of the pitcher. Such an identity is required to explain the perceptual character of the cognition of a pitcher. In the cognition of the pitcher, technically speaking, it is pure consciousness that serves as the substratum which becomes perceptual when it is conditioned by the pitcher.

The statement 'the pure consciousness becomes perceptual' must be analyzed carefully. By its very nature, pure consciousness is nonmediate and consequently does not require the instrument of mind to become immediate. This being the case, the alleged perceptuality of pure consciousness insofar as it relates to the object that is superimposed upon it must be understood properly. It must be kept in mind that when a pitcher is viewed as perceptual in nature, what becomes perceptual is only the consciousness conditioned by the superimposed entity; namely, the pitcher and the consciousness conditioned by that aspect or the mode of the mind that assumes the form of the pitcher.

3.18.3 The criterion for perceptuality thus articulated (i.e., in terms of consciousness) is common to the perceptuality of mental states like pleasure and pain, and the perceptibility of objects, for example, a pitcher or a table. Additionally, such an explanation demonstrates that perceptuality holds good even without mind being viewed as a sense organ.

PP illustrates the application of the definition of perceptuality in the case of introspection of mental states like pleasure and pain. The consciousness is always perceptual and one's introspective cognition of one's state of happiness is always perceptual. What does it mean? When it is said that the cognition of happiness is a case of perception, what is implied is that happiness is the content of a cognition that is perceptual. It is similar to the pitcher-cognition when that is spoken of as perceptual. A common definition of the perceptibility of objects is applied to objects like pitchers as well as to objects like the modes or the modifications of mind. Happiness and pain, like pitcher and other objects, serve as the limiting conditions of consciousness (i.e., as *vṛtti*), and may therefore be spoken of as knowledge (*jñāna)*. Knowledge or cognition may be used in a particular sense that may serve as the ground for its use. In other words, the term may be used more generally to refer to anything that is opposed to nonknowledge (*ajñāna*). Stated differently, *PP* observes that use of the term 'knowledge' with reference to mental states like happiness is justified, because these mental states serve as the limiting condition of consciousness. Therefore it is not surprising that the delimiting factor of consciousness itself is metaphorically spoken of as *jñāna*.

3.19 *nanv evaṃ svavṛttisukhādismaraṇasyāpi, sukhādyaṁśe pratyakṣatvāpattiḥ.*

iti cet, na. tatra smaryamāṇasukhasyātītatvena smṛtirūpāntaḥkaraṇavṛtter vartamānatvena tatropādhyor bhinnakālīnatayā tattadavacchinnacaitanyor bhedāt; upādhyor ekadeśasthatve saty ekakālīnatvasyaivopādheyābhedaprayojakatvāt.

yadi caikadeśasthatvamātram upādheyābhedaprayojakam, tadā

"pūrvam ahaṃ sukhī" ityādismṛtāv ativyāptivāraṇāya vartamānatvaṃ viṣayaviśeṣaṇaṃ deyam.

3.19 *[Objection]: Now, if this is the case [happiness, misery, and so on, are perceptual in nature],*[4] *the [experience of] retro-cognition of happiness in oneself would also be perceptual with respect to the aspect of happiness.*

It is said [in reply] "no." For there [in the instance under consideration], the recollected happiness, and so on, being past, and the mental mode in the form of retro-cognition being present, the limiting adjuncts belong to two different times. As a result, consciousness conditioned by them [two limiting adjuncts] is different, because the criterion for nondifference of the substratum having two limiting adjuncts is that they must be located in the same place at the same time.

If, however, being located in itself alone be the criterion for nondifference of that which is conditioned [consciousness] in one and the same place, then in order to avoid overpervasion in cases of retro-cognition such as 'I was happy before', the qualification 'presentness' [existence in the present] must be added to the content [in the definition of perception].[5]

3.19 *VP* next considers an objection stated earlier relative to the perceptual character of cognitions such as 'I am happy' or 'I am miserable'. If two limiting adjuncts are located literally in one and the same place, they cannot be distinguished from one another. What applies in the instance of two things in the name of the principle of the identity of indiscernibles also applies to the case of two limiting adjuncts. The objection to this formulation has been articulated in the context of one's recollection of one's happiness. Like happiness, recollection of one's past happiness also takes place in the same location, that is, in one's own mind. If this is admitted, then memory or retro-cognition would also become a case of perceptual cognition which, however, is not true.

3.19.1 *VP* answers the objection by saying it is true that in the example under consideration the two limiting conditions belong to the same substratum. That in itself, however, is not sufficient. They also must belong to the same time. If they happen to exist in one and the same substratum at different points of time, then what is conditioned by each one of them will be different. Extending this stipulation to include concurrence in time as well as coincidence in the same location, *PP* applies it to the example of the retro-cognition, 'I was happy before'. In the same location, two things are coincidental: the modification of the mind in the form of happiness, and the 'object' happiness that existed therein. That is to say, the two limiting conditions in this context are the mental mode in the form of happiness and the object happiness. There is no doubt that the two refer to one and the same place, but are they also concurrent in time? Happiness as an object must exist before the mode of assuming its form, that is, in the past in relation to the mode. The two limiting conditions, namely, the consciousness conditioned by the mental mode and the consciousness conditioned by the object, strictly speaking, refer to different times.

The point of raising this question by the author of *PP* seems to be as follows: The objection raised in *VP* about the memory experience of 'I am happy' as a qualification for being considered as a case of recollection must not be overstated. In the perceptual experience 'I am happy', one may insinuate a similar discrepancy of a lack of coincidence in time. It is true, ordinary objects and mental states are not objects in the same sense. In the latter, the objects do not pass through the two modes of previous unknownness and the present knownness. 'Objects' of introspective cognitions exist, but as manifested by consciousness, without the mediation of any mental mode whatsoever. True, these mental occurrences are also known by the witness-consciousness by the mediation of a mental mode, but these mental modes are qualitatively different from the modes that assume the form of objects such as pitchers in the perception of an external object. The author of *PP* is quite aware of this, yet he maintains that in the introspection of mental occurrences it is permissible to discern a distinction in terms of prior and posterior, that is, between what exists *qua* the mental mode and what exists before it.

3.19.2 The extended discussion into which the author of *PP* enters in this context, justifying the propriety of the stipulation of concurrence in time, may be understood as attempting to provide an exegetical answer to the question as to why the author of *VP* offers two different explanations in defense of the charge of overpervasion. First, the two limiting conditions should not only occupy the same location but also must be simultaneous. Secondly, instead of extending the stipulation of coexistence in space to also include concurrence in time, one may stick to the first condition, namely, the two occupying the same locus while adding the proviso that they exist in the present. This will avoid the overpervasion entailed in the experience of the recollection 'I was happy previously'.

3.19.2.1 The answer of the author of *PP* to the above exegetical issue is briefly as follows: *VP* seems to be aware of the fragile character of the objection raised, and so his explanation also shares the same character. Thus *PP*'s explanation of this is humorous: the explanation offered by the text is intentionally facetious, keeping in view the not very smart nature of the objector.

3.19.2.2 *AB* maintains that *VP* introduces the qualification of 'being present at a given point in time' to explain the identity between the consciousness conditioned by the mental mode and the consciousness conditioned by the object.[6] What this implies, says *AB*, is that the consciousness conditioned by the mental mode must be present at the time when there is the absence of consciousness that is conditioned by an object that is different from the object of the mental mode. The statement, presented in the manner of the Indian neological tradition of reinforcing an assertion through the mode of double negation, surely appears opaque. But the following may be said to explain it. In the cognitive experience 'this is a pitcher', the consciousness conditioned by the pitcher is identical with the consciousness conditioned by the mental mode assuming the form of the pitcher. By their identity is meant that the two are not at all different; that is to say, there is the absence of the consciousness that is conditioned by an object that is different from the object of the mental mode. In the case of the experience of recollection 'I was happy', the consciousness conditioned by the object itself is impossible because happiness, which is only recollected now, does not exist now. The consciousness conditioned by the mental mode in the form of happiness exists at a time when there is the absence of the consciousness conditioned by the object that is different from the mental mode in the form of the recollection of happiness. Therefore, it is appropriate that the description of 'presentness' as an adjectival feature to the object be made in the text.

3.19.2.3 The author of *PP* observes that even if we include the adjectival feature 'presentness', the problem will still remain. The assumption of difference between the consciousness conditioned by the mental mode and the same in the form of recollected happiness is arbitrary. The Advaita perspective in this context must be maintained. Every object apart from Brahman exists in the cause until there arises the direct knowledge of Brahman. In Brahman there is negation of the world, not only of the world in the past but also of the world in the present. In the immediate experience of Brahman, it is intelligible that the world as such does not exist now. But how can it be similarly maintained with respect to the world that was present earlier, and the world that will be present in the future? In other words, how could Brahman-knowledge negate the world in the three divisions of time? *PP* maintains that although the world existed in the past, the consciousness conditioned by the world exists even now. *AB* contends that when an object like a pitcher is recollected, there is the presence of the mental mode in the form of the pitcher as well as the consciousness conditioned by the mental mode.[7] However, this consciousness exists at a time when there is the absence of the consciousness conditioned by an object, the object that is different from the object of the mental mode. When one recollects a pitcher, the pitcher surely does not exist; if it did, it would be a case of perception and not retro-cognition. If the pitcher that is recollected does not exist now, then the consciousness conditioned by the pitcher also does not exist, although the consciousness conditioned by the mental mode in the form of the pitcher exists. *PP* objects to this interpretation because the very mention of the expression 'the consciousness conditioned by the mental mode' in itself implies that the object must be there. Therefore, the inclusion of the feature of 'presentness' does not seem to be necessary. The fact that *VP* articulates the definition of the perceptuality of knowledge in terms of the identity of object-defined consciousness with the mode-defined consciousness implies the presence of the object. Any answer to such a question is based on the assumption that the object exists now or existed earlier. *PP* further observes that if the author of *VP* had thought along the lines of *AB*, there would have been no need to bring in the experience of the recollection of happiness as a counter instance to the definition of the perceptuality of knowledge. Any recollective experience, such as the recollection of a pitcher, would have served the purpose.

3.20 *nanv evaṃ svakīyadharmādharmau vartamānau yadā śabdādinā jñāyete tadā tādṛśaśābdajñānādāv ativyāptiḥ, tatra dharmādyavacchinnacaitanyatadvṛttyavacchinnacaitanyayorekatvāt.*

iti cen na; yogyatvasyāpi viṣayaviśeṣaṇatvāt. antaḥkaraṇadharmatvāviśeṣe 'pi kiñ cid yogyaṃ kiñ cid ayogyam ity atra phalabalakalpyaḥ svabhāva eva śaraṇam; anyathā nyāyamate 'py ātmadharmatvāviśeṣe 'pi sukhādivad dharmādeḥ pratyakṣatvāpattir durvārā.

3.20 *[Objection]: Now, even then [granting the qualification of 'existing in the present time', when merits and demerits as belonging to oneself, [and] as existing in the present time are cognized by verbal testimony, and so on [other pramāṇa-s], then there is overpervasion in such cognition acquired through verbal testimony and so forth, because then the consciousness conditioned by merit, and so on [demerit], and the consciousness conditioned by the mental mode in the form of those [merit, demerit, and so on], are one.*

It is said [in reply] "no," for 'competency' (or fitness) also is a qualification of the content. Although being equally the attributes of the internal organ, some [attributes] have the competency while others do not; the only resort is the intrinsic nature [of the attributes] assumed on the strength of the [ensuing results]. If this is not accepted, then even on the Nyāya view, merit, and so on, like happiness, and so on, both alike being the attributes of the self, the contingency of perceptuality [for both] would be difficult to get over.

3.20 The definition of perceptuality that the author of *VP* seeks to vindicate is as follows: the consciousness conditioned by the mental mode must be identical with the consciousness conditioned by the actual object, and the two as thus indicative of their identity must exist in their essential nature at the present time. A person's merit and demerit are not perceived quite in the same manner as the perception of the mental occurrences of pleasure and pain. They are cognized solely on the strength of verbal testimony which is a valid means of knowledge. Verbal testimony, it may be recalled, is indicated as a *pramāṇa* with respect to cognizing things that do not fall within the range of perception and inference. And when a person's merit and demerit are cognized in this special sense, they still exhibit the feature of concurrence in time and coincidence in space, which explains perceptuality. Then, does not the definition become too wide and extend beyond the range of one's introspection?

3.20.1 *VP* further maintains that the definition of perceptuality does not unduly extend to verbal testimony. The explanation that the author of *PP* provides in this respect is very instructive. Experiences, such as 'one is meritorious', or 'one is sinful', are indeed similar to experiences such as 'I am happy' or 'I am miserable'. All of these are modes of the mind with one significant difference. Unlike happiness or pain, the experience of merit and demerit is mediate and not perceptual. Lest it might be thought arbitrary that some modes of mind be characterized as perceptual and others not, the author of *VP* provides the necessary stipulation that perceptibility depends on the essential nature of the object. In other words, perceptibility entails the ability of an object to be perceptible.

3.20.2 *PP* reflects on the case under consideration to show how plausible it is to consider verbal cognition on a par with perception. The verbal cognition of the form 'I am meritorious' is very similar in structure to the cognition 'I am happy'. Merit or demerit, it may be noted, exist in the mind as does happiness, and through the verbal statement 'I am meritorious', there arises a mental mode in the form of merit. Consciousness conditioned by the merit and the consciousness conditioned by the mental mode in this form of merit are present in the same locality, the locus being the mind belonging to the body. *PP* observes that to make the definition of perceptuality consistent with our understanding of perceptuality as entailing the identity of consciousness, the cognition of one's own merit should be deemed perceptual in nature as long as one bears in mind that it is only a verbal cognition.

3.20.2.1 In the cognition of an internal object such as happiness, it may be recalled that the explanation in terms of modification of the mind-stuff was accepted, provided it is understood to mean a specific contact of the mind with the object, the contact being understood as a case of pervasion. Is a similar explanation viable in the case of merit or demerit?

3.20.2.2 Some commentators of *VP* demur from applying the explanation of the mind-stuff 'going out' and assuming the form of the object. Although this explanation applies in the case of the cognition of a pitcher, for example, it fails in the case of the cognition, say, of primal atoms. Likewise, with reference to internal objects, the case of coming into contact will have to be redefined as an instance of modification. The same is true of one's perception of one's merit and demerit, in which apparently there is neither a mental mode assuming the form of merit nor any modification of mind. Even in the absence of a mental mode in the form of merit, consciousness conditioned by such transcendent objects surely exists. There is, however, no identity between the two. Consequently, the cognition 'I have merit', arising on the strength of verbal testimony, is impossible.

3.20.2.3 *PP* finds the above explanation unsatisfactory. The explanation of specific contact understood as modification does not apply to the instance of primal atoms, because atoms admittedly do not come within the range of sense perception. In the case of merit and demerit, however, mind is always in contact with them because they are located in the mind. Therefore, the cognition of merit is not different in structure from a case of perceptual cognition. What makes it a class by itself, however, is that it is not strictly perceptual but a case of verbal cognition.

3.20.3 The reference to the cognition of a person's merit and demerit is not without significance. *PP* reveals it while commenting on the expression 'one's own merit and demerit' as cognized by verbal testimony. The cognition of another person's merit and demerit would not qualify as having parity with a perceptual cognition. In such cases the mental mode assuming the form of the merit and demerit of others would exist in one location, and the object, namely, merit and demerit, would exist in another. There will be no possibility of the two limiting conditions being located in the same place. Consequently the question raised with reference to the cognition of *others*' merit would become inappropriate.

3.20.4 The conditions so far stipulated about perceptuality are two: consciousness conditioned by the mode of the mind-stuff must be identical with the consciousness conditioned by the object (i.e., the coincidence of the two in the same location, like the coincidence of the pitcher-defined ether and the hall-defined ether); and the object must possess a particular nature that befits it to fall within the range of perception. The notion of befittedness or competency stipulated herein precludes verbal cognitions in the form of one's own merit and demerit from coming within the scope of perception. *PP* rejects the interpretation of *AB* that fitness means what is fit enough to come within the range of the respective sense organ.[8] The reasons for this are obvious. Such a definition will not apply to the cognition of one's happiness, in which the consciousness conditioned by a mode of the mind exists but not the consciousness conditioned by the object, namely, happiness in its objective mode. The latter never comes within the range of any sense organ. Therefore, *AB*'s interpretation of the term '*yogya*' as 'fitness to come within the range of respective sense organ' is not sound and must be given up. Merit and demerit, although they may be present, are not fit enough to come under the range of perception.

3.20.5 Merit and demerit possess a particular counteracting feature that accounts for their mediacy. *VP* articulates it in terms of its own intrinsic nature presumed on the strength of the consequences. The author of *PP* argues that: one does not attempt to bring in an effect simply because the cause exists—because a lump of clay exists one does not wish that it become a pitcher.[9] If the effect exists, one searches for the cause. Based on this adage, no school of thought suggests that merit and demerit should come under the range of perception. Merit, demerit, and latent impressions possess an intrinsic nature of their own which make them a class by themselves, different from the class of mental 'objects' such as happiness or pain. Merit, demerit, and latent impressions do not possess manifestedness, whereas pleasure and pain do. Except for this difference, merit and demerit are like the cognitions of pleasure and pain. Just as a cognition of happiness or pain is superimposed upon the witness-consciousness, merit or demerit also are superimposed upon the witness-consciousness. But because of their nonmanifest nature, they do not come under perception.

The Nyāya school maintains that merit and demerit, like happiness or pain, are attributes of the soul and not of the mind. In this context, we must not lose sight of the fact that a cognition for them is not a mode of the mind. Pleasures and pains, like cognitions, are not self-revealing. These originate because of certain conditions and are manifested in association with other objects either directly (e.g., in perception), or indirectly, in memory. Merit and demerit are the concomitant causes of their (pleasures and pains) production. In internal perception the mediation of mind is necessary because mind as a sense organ generates the perception of happiness or pain as well as of merit or demerit.

3.20.5.1 *VP*, at this juncture, asks the Naiyāyika, how can you maintain that only cognitions of happiness and pain and not of merit and demerit come under the range of perception, when all alike are the attributes of the self? Commenting on this issue, the author of *PP* claims that the Naiyāyikas do not have any alternative but to argue that it is because of the very nature of merit and demerit that they do not come under the range of perception. When both parties have the same defect (*ubhāyoḥ samo dosaḥ*), one cannot point a finger at the other.

3.20.5.2 Elucidating the Advaitin ground for maintaining that merits and demerits are attributes of the mind, *PP* cites the Upaniṣadic text, which lists mental 'objects' beginning with desire, resolution, and so on, and concludes "all these are of mind only."[10] In this list, however, merit and demerit do not find any place. Therefore, opponents ask, on what basis do the Advaitins conclude that merit and demerit are invariably present in the mind? *PP*'s response to this question exhibits a rare exegetical discernment. *PP* maintains that the term used for merit (*dharma*) is the same as that used for a duty, such as the performing of a sacrifice. When a sacrifice is performed there arises an extra-empirical merit that is only the continuance of the act in its subtle form. Therefore merit actually refers to the presence of such subtle states as accrue upon the performance of optional and obligatory duties enjoined as meritorious.

3.20.6 *AB* questions the propriety of considering experiences arising from verbal testimony as possible candidates for being considered as perceptual.[11] Because the cognition of merit and demerit conceivably cannot be perceptual, arising as they do from verbal testimony, there is no question of the overpervasion of the definition of perceptuality of knowledge in such cases. *AB* therefore does not understand why the author of *VP* goes to the extent of answering it.

3.21 *na caivam api sukhasya vartamānatādaśāyāṃ "tvaṃ sukhī" ityādivākyajanyajñānasya pratyakṣatā syād iti vācyam. iṣṭatvāt, "daśamas tvam asi" ityādau sannikṛṣṭaviṣaye śabdād apy aparokṣajñānābhyupagamāt.*

3.21 *Even then [granting the stipulation of yogyatva], it cannot be argued that although happiness is present now, the cognition arising from statements such as "you are happy," and so on, would be perceptual, for this [view] is acceptable to us, because sentences like, 'you are the tenth man' and the like refer to contents in [sense] contact [with the organ]. [In these cases] immediate cognition is admitted even from the verbal testimony.*

3.21 According to Bhāmatī as well as Nyāya, any cognition that arises from verbal testimony is bound to be mediate or nonperceptual only. Sentences composed of words can only give rise to mediate knowledge.[12] Immediate knowledge can arise only through the instrumentation of sense organs. Therefore, sentences cannot give rise to immediate knowledge. Through the statement 'you are happy' there arises a cognition in me that 'I am happy'. Here the consciousness conditioned by the mental mode in the form of happiness is present as well as the consciousness conditioned by the actual happiness. Thus the criterion of the perceptuality of knowledge exists in this verbal cognition because the two conditions—the object must be fit to be perceived and it must be concurrent in time—for anything to fall under the scope of perception are present. Hence Bhāmatī 's followers contend that the stipulated definition of perceptual cognition overlaps with respect to verbal cognition.

3.21.1 According to the Vivaraṇa school of Vedānta, knowledge arising from verbal testimony is perceptual or immediate.[13] Because the knowledge arising from the statement 'you are happy' also is perceptual, the objection raised by the followers of Bhāmatī does not pose any threat. According to the Vivaraṇa tradition, which *VP* represents, the defining characteristic of perception—immediacy—can arise from verbal test-imony. The knowledge that arises from the great Upaniṣadic statement 'thou art that' is immediate, because it has for its content a perceptual object like any visual perceptual cognition. That verbal statement 'thou art that' can generate an immediate cognition and should be understood on the model of 'you are the tenth man', which will be discussed shortly.

3.21.2 To test the strength of the Vivaraṇa perspective in this regard, the counter view as represented by the Bhāmatī school must be appreciated properly. The knowledge that arises from 'thou art that' is similar to the knowledge that arises from the statement 'he who desires heaven may perform Vedic sacrifices'. How can knowledge arising from such statements be perceptual in nature? The point of view of Bhāmatī can be formally presented as an inference: The cognition generated from 'thou art that' is mediate because it arises from sentences. The counter-balancing argument of the Vivaraṇa school, which in effect tries to demonstrate the absence of 'what is sought to be proved' (*sādhya*)[14] through another reasoning, is a rebuff to the above inference. A cognition arising from 'thou art that' is immediate because it has for its content an object that is immediate.

3.21.3 Elaborating the points of criticism that are implied in this counterbalancing argument, *PP* vindicates the position adopted by *VP* by exposing the fallacies involved in the position of the opponent. *PP* maintains that the inference of the Bhāmatī school is vitiated by three fallacies:[15] *sopādhika hetu* (*hetu* vitiated by a limiting adjunct), *vyabhicara* (lack of correspondence between the *hetu* and the *sādhya*), and *svarūpāsiddhi* (nonestablishment of the *hetu* in the *pakṣa*).

1. *Sopādhika hetu*. According to the Vivaraṇa tradition, the inference of the Bhāmatī school entails the contradiction known as the *sopādhika hetu*, that is, it is vitiated by an upādhi or a limiting adjunct. When the *hetu* in the form in which it is given is not accompanied by *sādhya* (what is sought to be proved), the defect is known as *sopādhika hetu*. Such a *hetu* is true only conditionally. In these cases the *hetu* and the *sādhya* are not necessarily related to each other. The inference of the Bhāmatī school, namely, 'the knowledge arising from "thou art that" is mediate because it arises from a sentence', has as its *upādhi* an object having an immediately given content. This objection is from the Vivaraṇa tradition, because for them 'wherever there is sentence-generatedness, there is the immediacy of knowledge'. So they argue that in the Bhāmatī inference, the *hetu*, (the sentence-generatedness) is

present, but the *sādhya* (the mediacy of knowledge) is not present. In other words, the sentence-generatedness is not copresent with the mediacy of knowledge, therefore the *sādhya* cannot be established.

2. *Vyabhicāra.* If the *hetu* is present in the absence of *sādhya*, then such an argument is vitiated by the fallacy of *vyabhicāra*. It involves a discrepancy between the *hetu* and the *sādhya*. If the *hetu* is present in a substratum in the absence of *sādhya*, then there is *vyabhicāra* or the lack of correspondence between the *hetu* and the *sādhya*. There is such a lack of correspondence in the present argument of Bhāmatī. In the example under consideration what is sought to be proved is the presence of mediacy. Experiences such as 'you are the tenth man' lack mediacy. In such cases, the 'reason', namely, the sentence-generatedness, is present, but along with it is the absence of mediacy (from the standpoint of the Vivaraṇa school). There is the fallacy of *vyabhicāra*.

3. *Svarūpāsiddhi.* A *hetu* is *svarūpāsiddha* when it is nonexistent in the *pakṣa*. In *svarūpāsiddhi* the *hetu* and *āśraya* are real things; however, the connection between them is absent because the *hetu* does not reside in the *pakṣa*. Such a *hetu* indirectly impedes the emergence of right inferential cognition. To have a successful inferential cognition, the *pakṣa* must possess the *hetu* which has invariable con-comitance with the *sādhya*. One cannot have the inferential cognition of fire in the mountain if the *hetu* smoke does not exist in the *pakṣa* mountain. The argument of Bhāmatī, *PP* maintains, suffers from this fallacy because the *hetu* (i.e., 'the sentence-generatedness') does not exist in the *pakṣa*, namely, the cognition arising from 'thou art that'.

To clarify his thesis further, Śāstrī next proceeds to discuss how the cognition of a sentence arises.

3.21.4 How the cognition of a sentence arises has been answered differently by philosophers. Broadly speaking, there are two views in Indian philosophy: *anvitābhidānavāda* and *abhihitānvayavāda.* [16] The first one holds that the relation among the word meanings is the sense of a sentence, and such a relation is conveyed by the words themselves. According to the second, the words convey individual meanings but when joined together, because of congruity, they convey the meaning of a sentence. Thus, for the second view the knowledge of the sense of a sentence arises from the meaning of the individual words and not from the sentence itself. Accordingly, sentence-generatedness does not exist in 'thou art that': the knowledge simply arises from the individual word meaning. In other words, word meanings, not a sentence, cause a verbal cognition. Therefore, the cognition arising from 'thou art that' cannot be explained as mediate in nature. The analogue offered for this mode of interpretation of the Upaniṣadic text provides one with the phenomenological clue for understanding the sense of immediacy attached to a cognition arising through language. The analogue 'you are the tenth man' gives rise to a cognition that is perceptual in nature.

3.21.4.1 A case, however, can be made to the contrary (as has been done) by the followers of the Bhāmatī school. The statement 'you are the tenth man' partakes of the character of ordinary sentences and can only give rise to mediate knowledge. But the mediate knowledge generated by the sentence becomes transformed into immediate knowledge because of its association with a sense organ.[17] *PP* again rejects this view by appealing to introspection. Is it correct that the knowledge that arises from the statement 'you are the tenth man' arises from a sense organ? Even before the auditory perception of such a statement, sense contact with the object was there, but the cognition 'you are the tenth man' had not arisen. How can such a knowledge be considered to have arisen from sense organs supported by language? The implied argument of the opponent that a sense organ may give rise to immediate knowledge as duly supported by the auxiliary cause, lacks in experiential verification. If the knowledge arising from 'you are the tenth man' is mediate only, as is the case with any ordinary sentence, it would be impossible for the statement to remove the superimposed cognition of oneself not being the actual tenth man, which is perceptual in nature. The perceptual knowledge of the object is necessary to remove the superimposed cognition. The argument of the opponent, that the sense organ itself gives rise to the knowledge of the object associated with 'you are the tenth man', is unconvincing. Nowhere in experience is it seen that the sense organ, to give rise to the perceptual knowledge of an object, requires the help of language (*śabda*).

3.21.4.2 The exact nature of the Vivaraṇa position requires careful analysis. *PP* in this context refers to the view of Sureśvarācārya, who maintains that on the mere rise of correct knowledge from 'thou art that', there ensues the immediacy of Brahman realization.[18] It means that knowledge is perceptual even when it arises from *śabda,* provided that the object is immediate.

3.21.4.3 In this context, *PP* elaborates the anecdote surrounding the statement, 'you are the tenth man', as stated in the *Pañcadaśī* of Vidyāraṇya.[19] Ten friends stopped in a midway village and, afraid of thieves, decided to take different routes, agreeing to meet at a certain place. When they reached their destination, they each counted everybody, leaving himself out. A passerby came to their rescue and informed them that the tenth man was the person who was counting. So he says, 'You are the tenth man'. Consequently, the tenth man has a cognition of himself as the tenth man. The statements of the Upaniṣads to the effect that Brahman is existence, consciousness, and bliss likewise give rise to the mediate knowledge of Brahman. In all cases, however, where there is an inquiry into the meaning of the great sayings of the Upaniṣads, such as 'thou art that', there arises perceptual knowledge. In other words, for an immediate knowledge of Brahman to arise, an appeal is made to such great sayings like 'thou art that'. Thus they conclude that for knowledge to be perceptual, the object must be in proximity to the person who comprehends it.

3.22 *ata eva "parvato vahnimān" ityādijñānam api vahnyaṁśe parokṣam, parvatāṁśe 'parokṣam. parvatādyavacchinnacaitanyasya bahirniḥsṛtāntaḥkaraṇavṛttyavacchinnacaitanyasya ca parasparaṃ bhedābhāvat; vahnyaṁśe tv antaḥkaraṇavṛttir nirgamanābhāvena vahnyavacchinnacaitanyasya pramāṇacaitanyasya ca parasparaṃ bhedāt. tathā cānubhavaḥ "parvataṃ pasyāmi, vahnim anuminomi" iti. nyāyamate "parvatam anuminomi" ity anuvyavasāyāpattiḥ. asannikṛṣṭa pakṣakānumitau tu sarvāṁse 'pi jñānaṃ paroksaṃ. "surabhi candanam" ityādijñānam api candanakhaṇḍāṁśe 'parokṣam, saurabhāṁśe parokṣam; saurabhasya cakṣurindriyāyogyatayā yogyatvaghaṭitasya niruktalakṣaṇasyābhāvāt.*

3.22 *Now, even such a cognition as 'mountain is fiery', is mediate with respect to the fire-aspect, [but] immediate with respect to the mountain-aspect, because [in the latter case] the consciousness conditioned by the mountain, and so on, is not different from the consciousness conditioned by the mental mode in the form of fire. But with respect to fire, however, because there is no outgoing of the mental mode in the form of fire, the consciousness conditioned by the fire and the consciousness conditioned by the mental mode in the form of fire are mutually different. Thus there is the experience 'I see the mountain, I infer the fire'. On the Nyāya view, there would result a cognition of cognition of the form, 'I infer the hill'.*[20] *However, in the case of inferential cognition whose subject is not in [sense] contact,*[21] *the cognition is mediate in all respects. Even a cognition such as 'the sandal is fragrant' is immediate with respect to the sandal aspect [but] mediate with respect to the fragrance aspect, because fragrance is not competent with respect to [to be comprehended by] the sense of sight, and so on; the given definition [of perceptuality] articulated in terms of competency is not applicable [here].*

3.22 Elaborating on the *VP* text, which speaks of inferential cognitions such as 'the mountain is fiery' as being partially perceptual and partially inferential, *PP* observes that for the knowledge to be perceptual, it is not necessary that it arise from a sense organ; it could arise from verbal testimony. What is necessary is that the object must be in proximity to the person who comprehends it.

3.22.1 Opponents contend that if this is the case, then the inferential cognition 'the mountain is fiery' will be perceptual, at least admittedly insofar as the aspect of 'mountain' is concerned. The defining characteristic of perceptuality thus will overlap in the case of inference. *VP* welcomes such an objection. It maintains that it is indeed true that in the inferential cognition under consideration, the cognition relating to the mountain aspect is perceptual and the cognition relating to the fire aspect is mediate. The consciousness underlying the inferential cognition, 'the mountain is fiery' is conditioned by two aspects—the mountain-aspect and the fire-aspect and the mental mode comprehends both. Insofar as the fire aspect is concerned, it is not perceptual. The mountain is perceptual, but only in a specific sense.[22] The consciousness conditioned by the mental mode assuming the form of the mountain is identical with the consciousness conditioned by the actual mountain. The condition is not at all impeded so far as the mountain is concerned. But with respect to the fire, the consciousness conditioned by the fire and the consciousness conditioned by the mental mode in the form of fire are different, because mind has not assumed modification in the form of the fire. In this context, we must remember that modification (*pariṇāma*) of the mind-stuff is only a species of what, in the language of Nyāya, has been termed the 'contact' of the mind with the object. This specific contact or the modification does not obtain between the fire and the mode of the mind. Therefore such a cognition has been considered, and rightly so, as inferential. However, it is inferential only insofar as the consciousness conditioned by the mental mode in the form of the fire is concerned, because the consciousness conditioned by the mental mode in the form of the mountain is perceptual. This is substantiated by the experience, 'I see the mountain and infer the fire', which is implicit in the structure of the inferential experience 'the mountain is fiery'.

3.22.2 The author of *PP* reiterates further that even the Naiyāyikas will have to concede that an inferential cognition is not mediate in all its aspects. They will have to accept in principle the distinction made by the author of *VP*, that the consciousness conditioned by the mountain is perceptual and the consciousness conditioned by the fire is nonperceptual. That is why the reflective experience takes the form, 'I see the hill and infer the fire'. If it is maintained that an inferential cognition is mediate in all respects, then the cognition of cognition will take the form 'I infer the mountain', which, however, is not the case.

3.22.3 In one and the same cognition, there are two features: mediacy and immediacy. Furthermore, this does not entail any contradiction because it is not with reference to one and the same object. *VP* illustrates this point with the help of an example of the cognition of a perceptual variety which, in the language of modern psychology, has been termed 'perception by complication.' 'The sandalwood is fragrant' is a perceptual experience that is immediate with respect to the sandal aspect, but mediate with respect to the fragrance aspect. Fragrance, being at a distance, is not fit enough to come within the range of olfactory perception. Technically speaking, there is no modification of the mind-stuff in the sense of a unique kind of relation of the mind to its object in the perception of fragrance. It must not be forgotten that mind-stuff as a modification of mind issues forth through the sense organ. So far as the sandalwood is concerned, there is contact with the sense organ. The consciousness conditioned by the sandalwood and the consciousness conditioned by the mental mode assuming its form, being coexistent in one and the same place, are nondifferent. Therefore the sandalwood element is perceptual. But there is no similar perceptuality regarding the element of fragrance. Just as the fire-element in the cognition 'the mountain is fiery' is not perceptual, similarly, in the cognition 'sandalwood is fragrant', fragrance is not perceptual; that is to say, the consciousness conditioned by the mental mode in the form of fragrance is not identical with the consciousness conditioned by the fragrance as an object. Thus immediacy and mediacy can coexist in the same cognition. The Nyāya school also makes a similar distinction. However, as noted earlier, they articulate it in terms of ordinary and extraordinary perception. Perception of sandalwood is ordinary, and perception of fragrance is extraordinary. Two elements can be present in one and the same cognition. Mediacy and immediacy can likewise exist in one and the same cognition. Therefore, there is no defect.

3.22.4 The author of *SM* raises an objection here.[23] The fragrance-aspect in the 'sandalwood is fragrant' is not perceptual.

However, it must not be overlooked that it has competence or fitness to come within the range of perception. Therefore when the term 'competence' is used, what is meant is that it must be fit enough to come within the range of the *appropriate* sense organ. In the example under consideration, only the sense of sight is in contact with the sandalwood; the sense of smell is not operative there.

PP finds this objection untenable. Because there is no identity between the consciousness conditioned by the object and the consciousness conditioned by the mental mode in the form of fragrance, there is no possibility of the fragrance-element coming within the range of perception in any conceivable sense. Therefore, there is no need to add that the object must be fit enough to come within the range of the appropriate sense organ. Although *VP* reiterates that the fragrance-element is not fit enough to come within the range of the sense of sight, but this is done simply for the purpose of indicating that, even according to the Nyāya school, the perception of fragrance arises through extraordinary and not ordinary empirical means.

3.22.5 A clear understanding of the term 'fitness' is very crucial in this context. *PP* takes the term to imply 'a *manifested* entity', that is, the entity must be nonconcealed.[24] It is maintained that the sense of unconcealment is entailed in the stipulation that there be identity between the consciousness conditioned by the object and the consciousness conditioned by the mental mode in the form of the object. This accounts for variability in the manifestation of the different aspects pertaining to an object. When one perceives the color of a pitcher, one has the mental mode in the form of the color of the pitcher, and not in the form, say, of the size of the pitcher. Therefore, it is only the color of the pitcher that becomes perceptual, and not its size. Likewise, in the case of the cognition 'sandalwood is fragrant', fragrance is not perceptual because, although there exists a mental mode in the form of fragrance, there is no 'going out' through the functioning of the senses. Therefore there is no possibility of the consciousness conditioned by the fragrance element and the consciousness conditioned by the mental mode in the form of fragrance becoming identical.

An object falls within the sphere of being perceived if it is directly manifested by the witness-consciousness or if it is identical with the consciousness conditioned by the mind. In the cognition 'I am happy', 'happiness' is directly manifested by the witness-consciousness. So there is no need of pressing that it must fall within the ambit of the respective sense organs. The author of *PP* thus defends the use of the expression 'fitness' to include reference to the witness-consciousness and avoids explaining it with reference to the sense organs. Here it may be observed in a quick review of this interesting debate that while *SM*'s objection has a clear merit in terms of empirical adequacy, by bringing into the discussion the issue of the appropriateness of the sense organ, one cannot fail to see the greater justification, from an experiential perspective, of *PP*'s position. The condition of competence, interpreted merely in terms of the appropriateness of the sense, seems trivial. *PP* further maintains that the issue at stake, in the name of competence, is really that of the manifestation by the witness-consciousness. *PP*'s suggestion at least has the virtue of relating it to the vantage point of experience and what is disclosed therein as unconcealed. It must be observed, however, that *PP* is not very original in this regard, and, as he himself concedes, draws from *SBT*, which interprets *yogyatā* to mean the unconcealment of the object.

3.22.5.1 In the case of the inferential cognition of merit and demerit, there arises the cognition 'I have merit' or 'I am meritorious'. This cognition is also directly manifested by the witness-consciousness. However, merit and demerit are not fit enough to be manifested by the witness-consciousness, because they are not fit to be perceived. According to the Advaitins, the idea of the witness-consciousness itself as transcending mind and its modes is of two kinds: as appositional to the individual self and as appositional to God.[25] Even without drawing on the theological aspect of the distinction between God and the individual self, one can contemplate the significance of this distinction on experiential grounds. Perception in its ideally realized form, as in the case of God, involves immediate comprehension. Every individual self, as well as his merit and demerit, falls under the purview of the witness-consciousness in its ideal form. However, they are not fit enough to be manifested by the witness-consciousness in their existential form as appositional to the individual self.

3.22.5.2 There is another sense in which merit and demerit can be thought to fall under perception. It is stated that every object is manifested by the witness-consciousness either as known or unknown. Merit and demerit are manifested by the witness-consciousness as being known, but their essential nature is not manifested by it. This exploration, however, observes *PP*, overlooks the contention of *VP* that merit and demerit are manifested by the witness-consciousness through a valid means of knowledge.

3.23 *na caivam ekatra jñāne parokṣatvāparokṣatvayor abhyupagame tayor jātitvaṃ na syād iti vācyam. iṣṭatvāt, jātitvopādhitvaparibhāṣāyāḥ sakalapramāṇa gocaratayāprāmāṇikatvāt. "ghaṭo 'yam" ityādipratyakṣaṃ hi ghaṭatvādisadbhāve mānam, na tu tasya jātitve 'pi. jātitvarūpasādhyāprasiddhau tatsādhakānumānasyāpy anavakāśāt. samavāyāsiddhyā brahmabhinnasakalaprapañcasyānityatayā ca nityatvasamavetatvaghaṭitajātitvasya ghaṭatvādāvasiddheś ca. evam evopādhitvaṃ nirasanīyam.*

"parvato vahnimān" ityādau parvatāṁśe vahnyaṁśe cāntaḥkāraṇavṛttibhedāṅgikareṇa tattadavacchedakabhedena parokṣatvāparokṣatvayor ekatra caitanye vṛttau na kaś cid virodhaḥ.

3.23 *It cannot be argued that if in the one and the same cognition both mediacy and immediacy are present, there would not be generic nature (universal) for either of them, because we agree that the technical language of such as generic natureness (jātitatva) or limiting adjunctness (upādhitva) is not justified by any valid means of knowledge and cannot therefore be accepted. Perceptions such as 'this is a pitcher' are a proof regarding the [attribute] reality of pitcherness, but not with respect to its being a generic attribute. For [additionally] the thing to be proved, namely the generic nature, not being established, there is no room for an inference that seeks to establish it. And because the inherence [as a category] is not proved and the entire world other than Brahman is noneternal, the definition of generic nature as being eternal and inherent in many things cannot apply to pitcherness, and so on. The [notion of a] limiting adjunct (upādhitva) is to be refuted in the same manner.*

In cases like 'the mountain is fiery', because the mental modes are admitted to be different with respect to the mountain-aspect [immediate] and the fire-aspect [mediate], their distinguishing characteristic being different notwithstanding, there is no contradiction whatsoever in accepting mediacy and immediacy in the same consciousness.

3.23 The admission of two mutually exclusive characteristics of mediacy and immediacy in one and the same knowledge gives rise to the objection that neither mediacy nor immediacy can be a generic essence or universal (*jāti*).

3.23.1 *PP* explains the objection made from the perspective of Nyāya and refers to Udayana's *Kiraṇāvalī*.[26] The Naiyāyikas define universal as a character that is one and inheres in many. When there is only one instance of a thing (e.g., the ether), its distinguishing feature is not a universal. Etherness, therefore, is merely a distinguishing characteristic (*upādhi*) and not a logical universal.

3.23.1.1 Of the various defects discussed in this context in Udayana's *Kiraṇāvalī*, *VP* discusses the one known as *sāṅkarya.* Such a defect exists when two mutually exclusive characteristics are present in one and the same substratum. For example, the characteristic of being an element is common to the five elements—earth, water, fire, air and ether; and the characteristic of being of a limited size is present in earth, water, fire, air and mind. Thus both these characters have earth, water, fire, and air in common. Although the character of being an element applies only to ether and not to the mind, the characteristic of being of limited size applies to mind and not to ether. Therefore, if the 'elementness' is taken to be a universal, it will apply to the four elements earth, water, fire, and air which are of limited size as well. Similarly, 'limited sizeness' will apply to ether, which is not limited in size. That is why characteristics with partially overlapping denotations are not logical universals. Likewise, mediacy does not exist in a cognition such as 'this is a pitcher' in which immediacy exists, and immediacy does not obtain in the case of an inferential cognition which has for its object something that is remote. If it is maintained that both mediacy and immediacy exist in an inferential cognition, the presumption can only be that neither mediacy nor immediacy is a universal.

3.23.1.2 *PP* refers to the view of the Nyāya thinkers who demur using the label universal to refer to cross-dividing characters that merely coexist in a given instance and sometimes exclude each other. They would restrict it to refer to the feature exclusive to the instance, wherein such cross-dividing characters coexist. A universal cannot be partially coincident and partially coexclusive. There are, however, other Nyāya thinkers, says *PP*, who would apply the notion of universal to neither of the two, the general feature coexisting with other similar features or the feature which is unique to an instance. The position of *VP* that neither mediacy nor immediacy can be a universal conforms to the second of the aforementioned positions. Neither of them can be universals, however, not because a universal needs a more stringent rule of application, as some Naiyāyikas argue, but because for the Advaitins universals in themselves as well as those of the quasi-kind called *upādhi* -s, from which a universal is sought to be distinguished,[28] are alike unintelligible.

3.23.2 The position of Advaita with regard to universals has been clarified in *PP*. The Advaitins do not reject outright the existence of a universal. Usages like 'this is a pitcher' do require a persistent form or feature, but the Advaitins would be averse to establishing a universal 'pitcherness' on that basis. There is no valid proof either of a perceptual or an inferential kind that such a feature should be called a universal. 'Cowness' and 'jarness' are merely the sum total of the characteristics of cows and jars, respectively; they, however, are not eternal.

3.23.3 The Naiyāyikas maintain that when a particular object is comprehended by a sense organ, then the universal is present in it. According to them absence is as much real as any presence. Both the presence of an object when it is present as well as its absence when it is absent are comprehended by the sense organs. When viewed in this light, it is the sense of sight that comprehends the pitcher as well as the universal 'pitcherness'. Hence they invoke perception as the means of establishing the universal pitcherness. To counter this objection, the author of *VP* states that the perceptual experience "there is a pitcher" is a proof with respect to the existence of pitcherness as a persistent form, but is no proof of its being a universal.

3.23.3.1 The Naiyāyikas contend that to account for the continuity of cognition (*anugata pratīti*), we require a *jāti*. For example, when one says, 'This is one jar' or 'this is another jar', what pervades all the instances of jar is the content called universal. The Naiyāyikas make such a claim in support of continuous cognitions that comprehend 'jarness' as a continuous feature (*anugata dharma*). The Advaitins reply that the fact that jarness is a *dharma* does not prove that it is also a universal. Additionally, even without so accepting it, we can account for enumerating cognition by simply maintaining it (jarness) as a *dharma*—a *sat viśeṣa* (i.e., a species or kind of what may be said to be).

3.23.3.2 The Naiyāyikas hold that objects (e.g., tables, chairs, and so forth), are a mosaic of many independent entities (substances, attributes, universals) held together through a special kind of relation known as 'inherence', which in itself is a discrete entity. The Advaitins reject such a relation. If a relation is as independent of an entity as the terms related, then there arises the necessity of a second relation to connect the first relation with each of the terms, and the second relation requiring a third, and so on *ad infinitum*. Accordingly, because inherence cannot be accepted, and because a universal is related to a substance through the relation of inherence, universals cannot be accepted either.

3.23.4 The author concludes that there is no need to admit

mediacy and immediacy as universals. In the example, 'the mountain is fiery', there is mediacy and immediacy for one and the same consciousness. Consciousness conditioned by the mental mode in the form of fire is mediate. The same consciousness conditioned by the mental mode in the form of the mountain is immediate. In short, the distinction is made on the basis of the distinction between the *vṛtti*-s. Such is the considered view of the author of *VP*.

3.24 *tathā ca tattadindriyayogyavartamānaviṣayāvacchinnacaitanyābhinnatvaṃ tattadākāravṛttyavacchinnajñānasya tattadaṁśe pratyakṣatvam.*

3.24 *And, so, the nondifference from the consciousness conditioned by a content, competent for any particular sense, and present for the consciousness conditioned by the mental mode in the form of that object, constitutes perceptuality with respect to that particular aspect.*

3.24 The concluding statement of the text of *VP* about the perceptuality of knowledge explained in terms of nondifference between the consciousness defined by a content and the consciousness defined by a mental mode assuming the form of the content provides the occasion for *PP* to give a conclusive interpretation of the terms involved and to exclude the Nyāya overtones that are either implicitly or explicitly avowed in the earlier commentaries. For example, *VP* maintains that the constitutive condition of perceptuality of consciousness defined by a content must be nondifferent from the consciousness defined by the mental mode in the form of the content. The content, as the text qualifies it, is that which is competent for any particular sense and is, temporally speaking, present in the consciousness. *PP* interprets these qualifications and in so doing summarizes his own position. For example, in his opinion, 'competence for any particular sense' should not be interpreted literally in the sense of fitness to come within the range of a particular sense organ; it should be taken rather to mean 'not concealed'. If the literal meaning is admitted, as some commentators of *VP* have done, then there would arise the impression that the text has also proved the perceptuality of cognitions such as happiness and pain in relation to mind as a sense organ, which contravenes the Vivaraṇa view that mind is not a sense organ. The author of *PP*, on this issue, sides with *SBT* that *yogyatā* means that the object must not be veiled or concealed.[29]

This meaning, he believes, renders the statement of the condition of perceptuality more plausible and also simpler than the elaborate discussion regarding the fitness to be manifested by a sense organ or the witness-consciousness. This also keeps the general tenor of the Advaitin doctrine.

3.24.1 *PP* provides the above construction of the text in the context of rejecting *AB*'s thesis that, with respect to the perceptual knowledge of mental occurrences such as pleasure and pain, mind is a sense organ because *smṛti* texts speak of the mind as an instrument.

3.24.2 Similarly, interpreting the term *'vṛtti'* which defines consciousness, *PP* writes that *vṛtti* means modification either of the internal organ or of ignorance. In the Upaniṣadic texts dealing with *"kāmaḥ sankalpah,"* 30 and others, *vṛtti* is understood in the sense of the transformation of the mind, and not in the sense of the transformation of *avidyā*. This description of consciousness in terms of the modification of the internal organ or ignorance, it may be noted, is common both to erroneous and valid cognitions. The actual objects are the contents of ignorance, which account for the usage that the objects do not exist, because they are not manifested at that time. When manifested, they are not the content of ignorance, and accordingly possess competence, that is, the state of being not concealed. For objects that are eternally mediate, there is absolutely no possibility of their being the content of ignorance. Therefore, they do not possess the characteristic of competency. The term 'unconcealed' (*anāvṛta*) in the text means the characteristic of being the content of the usage manifest; because a hare's horn, for example, does not satisfying the condition, it is not competent to be perceived.

Finally, *PP* observes that to make the definition not apply to an erroneous cognition, the adjectival feature (i.e., unsublatability), must be added or included as qualifying the object, to make it consistent with the earlier stipulation of the text of *VP* about the truth as being unsublatable as well as previously unknown.

Notes

1. *SB*, 234–238.
2. Madhusūdana states: "Though the Self which has become manifest is one (only), it is given three (different) designations owing to the difference between the portions of the inner organ which are the media of its manifestation. (Thus) the portion

of the Self circumscribed by the doer portion (of the inner organ) is (spoken of as) the knower, the portion thereof circumscribed by the operation portion (of that organ) as the means of knowledge, and the portion thereof circumscribed by the fitness-for-manifestation-portion (of that organ) residing in object as the act of knowledge. As for the thing to be known, it is the Brahma-chaitanya (that is, the Supreme Soul) residing in the object, in the state of being unknown. That itself when known (becomes) the fruit (of knowledge)." *Ibid.*, 236.

3. Annaṁbhaṭṭa defines *saṁyoga* as a contact between two things that were apart initially. Accordingly, no contact exists between entities that are all-pervasive and have never been apart from each other. *TSDNB*, 164–65. *Bhāṣā-Parricched*a explains contact as follows: "The meeting of two things that are removed from each other is called conjunction. It is described as being of three kinds: The first is due to action in either of them.... Similarly it may be due to action in both; and the third is due to contact. The conjunction of a falcon and a hill and so on is described as being of the first kind.... The encounter of two rams is said to be of the second kind. The conjunction of a jar and a tree owing to the conjunction of one-half of the jar and the tree is of the third kind." *BP*, 115–18, 207–08.

4. The preceding passage from *VP* seemed to suggest that the only necessary condition for the perception of pleasure and pain is that the two limiting conditions of consciousness should be located in one and the same place. If this is the case then, opponents contend, Advaitins must accept that we can perceive past pleasures, because there is a mental mode in the form of the past pleasure, which, in the present instance, has become the content, and the internal organ has assumed modification in its form.

5. It is argued that the content must be qualified by *vartmānatva*, that is, it must be qualified as existing in the present time. The definition of perceptuality, so qualified, cannot include *smṛti* or retrocognition in its purview, and therefore will be free from the charge of overpervasion.

6. *PP*, 50.

7. *Ibid.*, 51.

8. *tattad indriyayogyatva*. *Ibid.*, 52.

9. *naimittke sati nimittānusaraṇam, na tu nimittam astīti naimittkāropaḥ*. It signifies the cause that occasions the rise of something as an effect, and the effect that is occasioned by a cause. *Ibid.*, 52.

10. *BU* I.5.3.

11. *PP*, 54.

12. Vācaspati maintains that after *śravaṇa*, we have *manana* and *nididhyāsana*. With the help of intense contemplation (i.e., constant meditation), the mediate knowledge obtained by *śravaṇa* is changed into immediate knowledge. Vācaspati clearly follows Maṇḍana on this issue: "Vācaspati adopts Maṇḍana 's view regarding the relation between *Prasaṁkhyāna* and *Brahmasākṣātkāra* and Amalānanda specifically ascribes this view to Vācaspati, and says that Vācaspati understands the expression *Scriptural* realisation (*Śāstradṛṣṭi*), as used by Bādarāyaṇa , to mean exactly what Maṇḍana understands to be *Brahman-realisation* springing from *Prasaṁkhyāna*—the true knowledge which arises from meditation on the true import of the *mahāvākyas* (*śāstrārthadhyānajā pramā*) and that this view is supported by Bādarāyaṇa in the *Brahmasūtra—Api ca saṃrādhane pratyakṣānumānābhyām*." Maṇḍanamiśra, *Brahmasiddhi*, ed. S. Kuppuswami Śāstrī (Madras: Madras Government Press, 1937), xxix.

13. Notice that for the Vivaraṇa tradition, the contact of the senses with the object does not determine the perceptual character of sensory knowledge. Followers of the tradition hold that "the principal texts of the Vedānta, such as 'That thou art', are themselves directly the cause of intuition, and that, though they work through the mind, the latter is not a sense organ or the direct cause of immediateapprehension. According

to this view, *verbal knowledge may of itself be immediate, though its content be not sensed* [emphasis supplied]." *SLS*, part 1, introduction, 60.

14. Similarities between the use of the terms of Indian logic, particularly with regard to the fallacies of an argument, and Aristotelian logic are striking. However, in this context, we must not lose sight of the fact that, unlike Aristotelian logic, Indian logic deals with entities rather than with terms. In classical or Aristotelian logic, the validity of a syllogism depends on the extension of the minor term. The extension of the minor term 'he' (in the example, all human beings are mortal, he is a man, therefore, he is mortal) is subsumed by the middle term 'human being' and the extension of the middle term by that of the major term 'mortal.' For Indian logicians to say 'he is mortal' amounts to saying that 'he' (*pakṣa*) has the property of mortality (*sādhya*). The point here is that the Indian *sādhya* , *pakṣa* , and the *hetu* (reason, or *liṅga*) are not equivalents of Aristotelian major, minor, and middle terms respectively. In Indian logic, *sādhya* or *dharma* is the property, which the *pakṣa*, the *dharmīn* , possesses, and the *hetu* or *liṅga* is the mark, by means of which the *sādhya* is inferred in the *pakṣa*. "The Indian syllogism has neither Mood nor Figure. It has what can be recognised as *corresponding* to the three terms of the Aristotelian syllogism. The 'major term' is denominated the Probandum, and the 'Subject' (or 'minor term') is defined as 'that which has the Probandum doubtful. What corresponds to our middle term is called by various names signifying Probans, Mark, Reason.... The appellations major, minor, and middle term, are also misleading, at any rate in speaking of the earlier logic. The earlier Indian logician never considers the distribution and quantification of the terms in the syllogism, and the way of regarding subsumptions which is exemplified in Euler's circles, and which is second nature to us trained in the formalism of Western school logic, does not seem to have entered into his account of syllogism." H. N. Randle, "A Note on the Indian Syllogism," *Mind* 33 (1924): 398–99.

15. A fallacy is an invalid or incorrect type of argument. In Western logic, generally a distinction has been made between formal fallacies and material fallacies. Formal fallacies are exclusively concerned with the structure or form of an argument. They are the results of the violation of some formal rule and they do not deal with the soundness of an argument. Informal or material fallacies are either fallacies in the content of an argument or occur because of some confusion in or misunderstanding of the meaning of the phrases, words, or sentences of an argument.

Fallacies in an inferential process, in the Indian context, do not bear so much upon the form or structure of the inference as upon the possibility of the resulting cognitions, which once obtained will make the inferential process complete. For example, from the Nyāya *hetvābhāsas* (fallacies of the *hetu*): 'The hill has smoke because it has fire'. This inference is fallacious because the relationship between the *hetu* and the *sādhya* is not invariable. That is, though the *hetu* fire is present wherever smoke (*sādhya*) is present, it is also present where smoke is absent. In other words, the *hetu* fire is present both in a similar and a contrary instance, for there is fire on the hill which possesses smoke (a similar instance); and it is also present in a red-hot iron, which, since it lacks smoke is a contrary instance. That is why this fallacy is designated 'common' (*sādhāraṇa*) *hetu* in the sense that it is common to both a similar and a contrary instance. Now, because of its presence in a contrary instance, it is obvious that it lacks invariable concomitance with the *sādhya* fire. The *hetu* impedes the emergence of the right cognition of *vyāpti*." For a comprehensive discussion of this issue, see Bina Gupta, "Are *Hetvābhāsas* Formal Fallacies?" *Journal of Indian Philosophy* 8 (1980): 141–42.

When one translates the above fallacious inference into the form of the three-membered Aristotelian syllogism, one gets the following result:

All fiery things are smoky (major)

The hill is fiery (minor)

Therefore, the hill is smoky (conclusion)

This is a formally valid syllogism in the Aristotelian logic of the form *BARBARA*. In short, the fallacies of inference in Indian logic are not formal fallacies and are not errors of inference. These are factors which, if present and recognized, will stop an inferential cognition from emerging. In other words, in Indian logic, at least in its early stages, what is at issue is not the formal validity, but the soundness of an inferential cognition. For a detailed discussion of these fallacies, see *TSDNB*, 293–26.

16. In response to the question, how is the meaning of a sentence known, generally a distinction is made between *anvitābhidānavāda* and *abhihitānvayavāda*. These theories are associated with the Prābhākara and Bhāṭṭa schools of Mīmāṁsā, respectively.

According to the Prābhākara theory, words themselves have the inherent capacity to convey their individual meanings, that is, the construed sense of a sentence. Thus the words themselves make the sense of the sentence known. Upon hearing someone utter words in sequence, one immediately understands the meaning of the sentence that the words express. According to the Bhāṭṭa theory the words have the inherent capacity to signify their senses alone, which in turn give rise to the sense of the sentence. In other words, the words cease to function after indicating their senses. Because the relation of the sense of the words is based on the words, Bhāṭṭas contend that the words have the capacity to connote the knowledge of their senses. In short, the word initially signifies its own meaning, then the words in a sentence are put together to construe the sentence sense. Professor Karl Potter succinctly explains the distinction between these two theories: "The two Mīmāṁsā theories are primarily theories about the process by which we come to understand the meaning of a sentence.... Prābhākara's principle is: understanding of sentence meaning first, word-meanings later; Kumārila's is: understanding of word meanings first, sentence-meaning later." "Some Thoughts on the Nyāya Conception of Meaning," *Journal of Indian Philosophy* 3 (1975): 210.

The difference between these theories accounts for the differing interpretations of the terms '*tat*' and '*tvam*' in '*tat tvam asi*.' In *abhihitānvaya vāda*, the terms 'tat' and 'tvam' would convey the cognitions of their primary meanings, similar to retro-cognition. In *anvitābhidāna vāda*, these words would convey the cognitions of their primary meanings—the cognition whose nature is retro-cognition. Sarvajñātman takes this line of interpretation a step further: "The primary meanings of the words cannot be mutually related, in view of their inherent opposition. So the two words through exclusive-non-exclusive secondary signification refer to Brahman and Ātman respectively. It follows from this that, if *abhihitānvaya vāda* is adopted, then the words *tat* and *tvam* through exclusive-non-exclusive secondary signification give rise to the cognition of Brahman and Ātman—the cognitions which are similar to recollection. If *abhihitānvaya vāda* is adopted, then the cognitions arising from the words are of the nature of recollection." *SS*, introduction, 45.

17. Explaining the position defended by the Bhāmatī school, the author of *SLS* further clarifies the point: "Deep meditation, however, is of service as an auxiliary to the mind.... 'The internal organ, aided by maturity of contemplation of the sense of the text, manifests in the case of the immediately experienced denotation of the 'thou' its being the denotation of the 'that,' through the negation of the respective adjuncts'. Even in the text '(Becoming) pure of intellect through clarity of knowledge, thereupon he perceives that partless one by contemplation', contemplation is accepted only as the cause of mental concentration signified by 'clarity of knowledge'. " *SLS*, chap. 3, 4.2, 362–63.

18. Sureśvara in *NS* severely criticizes the position that Bhāmatī represents. He maintains that Brahman realization results only from hearing the great scriptural texts (e.g., tat tvam asi). The *mahāvākyas* and the meditation, no matter how useful, cannot bring forth the actual realization. "If an objector says 'man knows (reality) through symbolic meditation (*prasaṇkhyāna*)'—then how can the word be teaching the truth? We hold that knowledge derived from words is mediate and indirect (*parokṣa*).... " *NS*, 3.123, 196–97.

19. Swami Vidyāraṇya, *Pañcadaśī*, 8.22–27. The Vivaraṇa school maintains that verbal testimony can give us immediate knowledge. However, all verbal testimony does not give rise to immediate knowledge. Statements about objects that are immediate are capable of generating immediate knowledge, for example, 'thou art the tenth man'. In this well-known story, according to Vivaraṇa, there is the immediate realization of everybody's being fine and relieved upon hearing 'thou art the tenth'. Words have the capacity to produce immediate knowledge. Sarvajñātman argues that whether a sentence "gives rise to mediate knowledge or immediate knowledge depends upon the nature of the object concerned. If the object is mediate, then the sentence would give rise to only a mediate knowledge of the object. If the object is immediate, then, knowledge could be immediate. Here Brahman-Ātman is always immediate and hence the Upaniṣadic texts give rise to the immediate knowledge of it." *SS*, introduction, 49. The Bhāmatī tradition, on the other hand, maintains that 'thou art the tenth' does not generate any immediate intuition except with the help of mind. Mind has the capacity to produce such an intuition because it is a sense organ. Words have an inherent capacity to produce mediate knowledge.

20. Advaitins maintain that an inferential cognition such as 'the mountain is fiery' is partly mediate and partly immediate—it is mediate with respect to the fire-aspect and immediate with respect to the mountain-aspect. The Naiyāyikas , on the other hand, maintain that an inferential cognition is mediate in all its aspects. If an inferential cognition is entirely mediate, maintain the Advaitins, the Naiyāyikas cognition of cognition, which results from this primary cognition, also must be mediate. Therefore, rather than saying, 'I infer the fire', the Naiyāyikas ought to say, 'I infer the hill'. This is the objection that the Advaitins raise.

21. The Advaitins maintain that there is only one instance of an inferential cognition being mediate in all its aspects, 'an atom of earth possesses smell because it is earth, like a pitcher'. In this instance, because the ultimate atom of earth is imperceptible, it can never come in contact with the eyes, which can only perceive substances. Therefore, the cognition is mediate in both of its aspects—the thing to be inferred, the smell, and the subject, the atom.

22. *bahir niḥsṛtaṃ yad antaḥkaraṇaṃ tat sambandhaviśeṣarūpā yā vṛttiḥ tad avacchinnasyety arthaḥ. vahna tv iti vahnyākārety arthaḥ. vahner bahir niḥsṛtāntāḥkaraṇasambandhaviśeṣābhāvād ity arthaḥ. PP*, 56. Again: *cakṣur indriyadvāraka-nirgamavad antaḥkaraṇaparimāṇa [read: pariṇāma] śūnyatayety arthaḥ yogyatvaghaṭi-tasyetiyogyavartamānaviṣayāvacchinnacaitanyābhinnatvaghaṭitasyety arthaḥ. Ibid.*, 57.

23. *Ibid.*, 58.

24. *Ibid. PP* follows *SBT* and *SLS* on this issue.

25. For a detailed discussion of these concepts, see chap. 5.

26. *PP*, 60.

27. *vyakter abhedeḥ tulyatvaṃ saṇkaro ' thānavasthitīḥ rūpahānir sambandho jāti-bādhakasaṁgrahaḥ.* Udayana, *Kirṇāvalī*, trans. and edit. Śrī Gaurinath Śāstrī (Banaras: Research Institute, 1980), 321. Of the six defects mentioned above, the first three defects—*vyakter abhedeḥ, tulyatvam* , and *sāṇkarya*—occur when particular attri-

butes which are not universals are admitted as universals; and the remaining three—*anavasthā*, *rūpahāni*, and *asaṁbandha*—occur when certain categories that are not universals are regarded as universals.

28. Of the six *jātibādhaka* mentioned in Udayana's *Kiraṇāvalī*, *sāṅkarya* is rejected by the neo-Naiyāyikas. The neo-Naiyāyikas make a distinction among three classes of universals: (1) two universals may be mutually exclusive; that is, they do not have any members in common, for example, cowness and horseness; (2) two universals may be such that the extension of one is subsumed by the extension of the other, for example, substancehood and earthhood; and (3) two universals might be such that they partially overlap, e.g. *bhūtatva* (the character of being an element), and *mūrtatva* (the character of moving). The traditional Naiyāyikas accept only the first two as universals. They regard the third one as a *upādhi* (a limiting condition). That is why characters with partially overlapping denotations are not accepted by the traditional Naiyāyikas as genuine universals.

The distinction between *jāti* and *upādhi* is very significant. It clearly brings out the Naiyāyika conception of universals as real, eternal, natural class essences existing in the objective world. A universal is a simple *padārtha*, and cannot be analyzed into other attributes, properties, or property components. That is why a general term, for example, 'horse' would stand for a universal, but a term like 'black horse' would not. 'A black horse" according to the Naiyāyikas, represents a complex of properties and does not imply the existence of an additional ontologically distinct entity over and above blackness. In other words, the property of being a black horse is not over and above blackness and is not reducible to it. For a detailed account, see Raja Ram Dravid, *The Problem of Universals in Indian Philosophy* (Delhi: Motilal Banarsidass, 1972), 32.

29. *atra ca vṛttipadenāntaḥakaraṇapariṇāmo vidyāpariṇāmo vā vivakṣyate*. *PP*, 62.

30. *Ibid.*

4

The Perceptibility of Objects

4.25 *dvitīye ghaṭāder viṣayasya pratyakṣatvaṃ tu pramātṛ-abhinnatvam.*

4.25 *With regard to the second [question],[1] however, the perceptibility of the content, pitcher, and so on, consists in its non-difference from the cognizer (i.e., the perceiving subject).*

4.25 So far *VP* has discussed the process through which one arrives at the perceptual knowledge of an object. The author of *VP* now discusses what determines the perceptibility of the object that is immediately cognized.

4.25.1 What constitutes perceptibility in regard to the content or the object? The author of *PP* exegetes the answer given in *VP* by bringing it into a dialectical relation with the Nyāya perspective. *VP* articulates the perceptibility of the content, the object perceived, in terms of its identity with, for example, nondifference from, the perceiver. Such an explanation rejects the Nyāya contention that an object is perceptible if it is the content of perceptual knowledge.[2] The Nyāya contention, the circular nature of the definition apart, does not accord with the verbal usage that objects, like pitchers, are perceptible. The evidence that is implicit in the common place verbal usage of the form (e.g., 'I know the pitcher') lends support to the Advaitin contention that the perception of an object cannot be defined except in terms of the object's identity with the witness-consciousness. The Vivaraṇa thesis about the witness-consciousness has been invoked in this context; namely, that every object is manifested by the witness-consciousness either as known or unknown.[3] Manifestation of objects, therefore, such as pitchers, will not be possible without being related to the witness-consciousness. This is what *VP* terms the identity of the content with the cognizer-consciousness.

4.25.1 Pure consciousness is perceptual in its essential nature. Its perceptuality does not require the aid of any instruments. In relation to a content, say a pitcher, however, consciousness is perceptual by being conditioned by the mental mode and also by the internal organ or the mind. The witness-consciousness, appositional to the individual self, is the consciousness that transcends the internal organ. The latter exists and functions but as superimposed on the former. Similarly, the witness-consciousness, appositional to God, is the consciousness that transcends *māyā*. *PP* reiterates the point that consciousness as conditioned by the mental mode is invariably related to the witness-consciousness, and on this ground accounts for the usages such as 'I know the pitcher', precluding usages such as 'I know the cloth'. If this is not maintained, there would arise a conflict with the conclusive view of Vedānta that every object is manifested by the witness-consciousness either as known or unknown. It therefore follows that what accounts for the verbal usage that an object is perceptible is not its being the content of perceptual knowledge but identity of the object with the witness-consciousness.

4.25.2 The author of *AB* explains the significance of rejecting the Nyāya position differently.[4] *AB* contends that the Nyāya thesis (an object is perceptible if it is the content of perceptual knowledge) would lend support to the claim that fragrance also is perceptual in the cognition 'sandalwood is fragrant'. *PP* finds such an interpretation unnecessary, because in the perceptual cognition under consideration there is no modification of the mind assuming the form of the object, that is, fragrance. As a result, there is absence of identity between the consciousness conditioned by the object and the consciousness conditioned by the mental mode in the form of the object.

4.25.3 The author of *AB* seems inclined to accept the Nyāya description of perceptibility as the content of perceptual knowledge except for the need to qualify it with the adjectival feature of 'fitness'. This qualification is proposed to deny perceptibility to 'fire' in the inferential cognition 'the mountain is fiery'. AB himself concedes that because of the absence of identity between the consciousness conditioned by the mental mode in the form of fire and the consciousness conditioned by the fire, the cognition of fire is not perceptual. The situation regarding the example of the fragrant sandalwood is not any different from the cognition 'the mountain is fiery'. Therefore, there is no need to add 'fitness' as an additional qualification. Additionally, the precise sense of the text of *VP*, namely, the identity of the object with the witness-consciousness, calls for a rejection of the Nyāya perspective.

4.26 *nanu katham ghaṭāder antaḥkaraṇāvacchinnacaitanyābhedaḥ, "aham idaṃ paśyāmi" iti bhedānubhavavirodhāt?*

iti cet, ucyate; pramātṛbhedo nāma na tāvad aikyam, kintu pramātṛsattātiriktasattākatvābhāvaḥ. tathā ca ghaṭādeḥ svāvacchinna-caitanyādhyastatayā viṣayacaitanyasattaiva ghaṭādisattā; adhiṣṭhānasa-

ttātiriktāyā āropitasattāyā anaṅgīkārāt. viṣayacaitanyañ ca pūrvoktaprakāreṇa pramātṛcaitanyam eveti pramātṛcaitanyasyaiva ghaṭādyadhiṣṭhānatayā pramātṛsattaiva ghaṭādisattā nānyeti siddhaṃ ghaṭāder aparokṣatvam.

4.26 *[Objection]: Now, how can a pitcher, and the like, be nondifferent from the consciousness conditioned by the internal organ, because it contradicts the experience of difference in 'I see this'?*

The answer is: What is termed nondifference from the cognizer does not mean [a literal] oneness or identity [with it], but rather not having any existence apart from that of the cognizer. Accordingly, because pitcher and the like are superimposed on the consciousness conditioned by them [pitcher and the like objects], the existence of the pitcher is the existence of the consciousness conditioned by the pitcher, because the superimposed objects do not have any independent existence apart from the reality of their substratum. And because the consciousness conditioned by the content is the content-consciousness in the manner described above, and because the cognizer-consciousness alone is the substratum of the pitcher and the like, the existence of cognizer is itself the existence of pitcher, and so on, and not any other, hence the immediacy of pitcher, and so on, is as proved.

4.26 Identity of the object with the witness-consciousness is the main focus of the chapter on perception in *VP*. The author of *PP* interprets the issues involved here in such a way that they are consistent with the basic principles of Advaita. In so doing, he calls into question those facets of the commentaries *AB* and *SM*, which are inconsistent with the basic principles of Advaita.

4.26.1 *AB* maintains that the mental mode, the cognizing consciousness, and the consciousness as defined by the cognizing object, really constitute the content of a cognition.[5] Because all alike are the contents of a cognition, one must necessarily define the perceptibility of an object as that which is identical with the cognizer-consciousness. *PP* rejects such an explanation because such a position would amount to accepting a mental mode with respect to the cognizer, another mental mode with respect to the object, and still another mental mode with respect to the mental mode itself. The mental modes in these three cases will be perceptual. And then to explain perceptuality, *AB* would have to say that the perceptuality of knowledge is only the identity of the consciousness conditioned by the object and the consciousness conditioned by the mental mode. Hence, he might very well say that that which is the content of such a perceptual knowledge is perceptual. There is no need to say that in a cognition there are three elements, *vṛtti*, *pramātā*, and *prameya*, and that their perceptuality consists in their being identical with the consciousness conditioned by the cognizer.

4.26.1.1 *PP* also rejects the view articulated in *SM*.[6] *SM* maintains that 'fitness', which the author of *VP* invokes to exclude merit and demerit, should be accepted as the criterion of the perceptibility of an object. The ground for its rejection on the part of *PP* exhibits a great sensitivity and attention to the datum of experience and the linguistic usage attesting to it. Mere nonconcealment—that which fitness amounts to in the final analysis—cannot account for verbal usages, such as 'I know the pitcher'. The verbal usage implies that an object is perceptible only in the sense that the object is identical with the consciousness that manifests it. If this position is not admitted, then objects such as 'hare's horns' would be considered as perceptual.

4.26.1.2 Identity with the witness-consciousness (*sākṣyabhinnatvaṁ*), observes the author of *PP*, is what is imported by the expression 'being nondifferent from the cognizer', used in *VP*. Such an identity must be functionally distinguished from identity with the consciousness conditioned by the mental mode. The witness-consciousness must be associated with the mental mode in the form of an object with which its identity takes place, resulting in the perceptibility of an object. If the identity of the consciousness conditioned by the mental mode were in itself a sufficient criterion for the perceptibility of an object, then the mental mode would be associated with another mental mode. Although it is possible for the witness-consciousness to be associated with a mental mode, it is not possible, however, for the consciousness defined by a mental mode to be associated with another mental mode. If this is not acknowledged, then the mental mode will not become perceptual.

4.26.2 The objection verbalized in *VP* to the thesis of an object's identity with the witness-consciousness, although seemingly trivial, calls for the exercise of an imaginative inspection of experience and the usage based thereon. The objection takes the form that the object cannot become identical with the consciousness, because objects are insentient and consciousness sentient. Therefore there is no possibility of the two becoming identical. *VP* formulates the objection in terms of conflict with the experience such as 'I see this'. In the words of *PP*, this implies that the perceptual evidence assumes the existence of the difference between the witness-consciousness and the object.

PP argues that the difference between an object, for example, a pitcher, and the witness-consciousness is legitimately comprehended because of the defining features of being a pitcher and being the witness-consciousness, respectively. However, when both are viewed as existent, the superimposition of the identity between the two would hold. *PP* finds this explanation an instance of intrusion of unwarranted realism. According to the fundamental position of Advaita, objects, such as pitchers, when viewed ontologically, do not exist in their own right.

4.26.3 It might be argued that it is true that the object does not have an independent existence, yet the existence present in the consciousness conditioned by the pitcher is superimposed upon the pitcher. Consequently, there results a false identity between the pitcher and the existence. Even this position, although offered from within the perspective of Advaita, does not find favor with *PP*. Objects, observes *PP*, are the transformation of ignorance. As a result, there is an identity between the pitcher and the consciousness conditioned by the pitcher.

The important point to be noticed here is that the object (the pitcher) is not a superimposition upon the witness-consciousness. Therefore there cannot be any identity between the object and the witness-consciousness. Pitcher, on the other hand, is viewed as the object of knowledge in the experience 'I know the pitcher'. To claim that there is a superimposed and not a real identity between the two is to miss the point. The expression of *VP*, 'nondifference from the consciousness conditioned by the internal organ' (*antaḥkaraṇa avachinna caitanya abheda*) does not mean identity with consciousness that is immanent in the mind. It implies identity with the consciousness that transcends the mind. This is precisely the conception of the witness-consciousness (*sākṣin*).

4.26.4 The Advaitins maintain that the consciousness conditioned by the object is the substratum of the object. However, in the case of immediate cognition (i.e., perception), the consciousness conditioned by the object, the mental mode, and the mind become one. The object, it is important to note, is not superimposed upon the cognizer-consciousness, and so there cannot be any identity between the two. *VP* reiterates that the identity—of not having any independent existence apart from the cognizer-consciousness—however, exists in the object, namely, the pitcher. Thus in the cognition 'I know the pitcher', one and the same consciousness manifests the pitcher, its mental mode, and the mind. The identity of the pitcher with the witness-consciousness implies nothing more than the pitcher having no independent existence apart from the witness-consciousness. *PP*, in light of the clarity that is accorded for discerning the true sense of the identity of the object with the witness-consciousness, finds the Vivaraṇa position intelligible. The Vivaraṇa school maintains that Brahman is the substratum of ignorance. On the face of it, this seems to conflict with the cognitive experience 'I am ignorant'. If Brahman is the substratum of ignorance, then the appropriate experience and usage should be 'it is ignorant' or something to that effect. *PP* maintains that there is no conflict here because both ignorance and the internal organ are superimposed upon one and the same consciousness.

4.26.5 Opponents raise the following objection. According to Advaita there are three levels of reality. The objects belonging to the lowest one, for example, the shell-silver, are sublated during the time of phenomenal existence. The objects of the second level, like the appearance of the world, are sublated only by the direct knowledge of Brahman. The highest level of reality belongs only to Brahman. When viewed in light of the three levels of reality, the Advaitin thesis of the identity of the object with the witness-consciousness, and an object not having any independent existence apart from the witness-consciousness, would give rise to an unwelcome position, that is, on this thesis the illusory objects, like shell-silver, would never come within the range of perception.

In response it is said that *VP*'s thesis—that objects do not have any independent existence apart from the witness-consciousness—must be understood against the background that, in the final analysis, according to Advaita, there is only one kind of being, 'reality', which in the system of Advaita has been articulated in terms of the aforementioned triple modes. From the perspective of reason and empirical experience, these three levels are incommensurable; they are different qualitatively.[7] The identity of an object with the witness-consciousness only implies that the objects do not have any independent existence apart from the witness-consciousness. The reality of existence that pertains to the substratum is manifested in the superimposed objects as well. It is similar to the manifestation of 'thisness' of 'this is silver' in the silver itself. At the time of the immediate cognition, the consciousness conditioned by the object, the mind, and the mental mode are one, so the existence that pertains to the consciousness conditioned by the object is one with the consciousness conditioned by the mind. Therefore, objects such as pitchers do not have any independent existence apart from the consciousness that is conditioned by the mind, that is, they do not have any independent existence apart from the existence that is the essential nature of the witness-consciousness. Accordingly, the verbal usage, that is, 'pitcher is perceptual', is intelligible. Similarly, the shell-silver has for its substratum the consciousness that is conditioned by the 'this' element. The consciousness conditioned by the 'this' element becomes identical with the witness-consciousness through the mental mode in the form of 'this'. Therefore, shell-silver does not have any independent existence apart from the witness-consciousness, and hence it is perceptual.

4.27 *anumityādisthale tv antaḥkaraṇasya vahnyādideśanirgamanābhāvena vahnyavacchinnacaitanyasya pramātṛcaitanyānātmakatayā vahnyādisattā pramātṛsattāto bhinneti nātivyāptiḥ.*

4.27 *In the sphere of inferential cognitions and the like [other pramāṇa-s], because the internal organ does not go out to the location of fire, and so on, there is no identity between the consciousness conditioned by the fire and the consciousness conditioned by the individual self; therefore, the consciousness conditioned by fire is different from the cognizer-consciousness. The reality of fire being different from the reality of the cognizer, there is no overpervasion [of the definition with respect to the inferred objects].*

4.27 The same, however, is not the case with an inferential cognition such as 'I infer fire on the mountain'. In this instance, fire does not have any existence apart from that constituted by the essential nature of consciousness conditioned by it. Such a consciousness, it may be noted, is not identical with the witness-consciousness. Therefore, its existence is different from that pertaining to the witness-consciousness. This is what is implied in saying that the fire is not perceptual.

In the case of the perceptual experience of shell-silver, the definition of perceptuality entailing identity of the object with the witness-consciousness is applicable because it (shell-silver) has for its substratum consciousness conditioned by the 'this' element. The consciousness conditioned by the 'this' element becomes identical with the witness-consciousness through the interposition of the mental mode in the form of 'this'. Thus it may be seen that shell-silver does not have any independent existence apart from the witness-consciousness, and hence, it is perceptual.

4.27.1 *VP*'s statement 'nonexistence of the object apart from the witness-consciousness' must be understood in light of the three levels of reality recognized earlier. It means superimposition upon the witness-consciousness. The witness-consciousness is consciousness that transcends ignorance, and the internal organ is an offshoot of ignorance. When a pitcher is perceived, the consciousness conditioned by the pitcher is identical with the witness-consciousness which, in turn, implies that the pitcher is superimposed upon the witness-consciousness.

The same explanation must be extended to illusory objects such as shell-silver or dream objects. Ignorance and the internal organ, being superimposed upon the witness-consciousness, are identical with it.

4.27.2 The question is raised as to whether the explanation of the perceptibility of an object in terms of its identity with the witness-consciousness will be applicable in the case of the immediate experience of Brahman. In response it is said that Brahman does not fall under the category of the object to be defined. When it is said that Brahman is not an object of cognition, a distinction is made between Brahman as an object of comprehension, in the sense in which any object is cognized, and Brahman as comprehended. To appreciate this distinction, one has to recall the dynamics and the mechanics that are involved in the perception of an object as explained earlier. When the sense of sight comes into contact with the object, the mind also comes out, reaches the place of the object, and comes into contact with it. This contact is technically known as a mental mode. Consciousness gets reflected in the mental mode, and the object is superimposed upon the consciousness conditioned by it. The mental mode, in other words, serves as the bearer of the reflection of consciousness. Thus inspired by consciousness, the mental mode removes the modal ignorance and the object thus unveiled comes into contact with the consciousness that is reflected in the mental mode. The element of consciousness underlying the mode is technically known as the result (*phala*).[8] This signifies that the manifestation of an object from its concealment by modal ignorance is the final outcome of the process. In the perception of a pitcher, for example, unconcealment of the content (i.e., the pitcher), is the result of the perceptual process.

The perception of Brahman, however, is different. When the Vedāntic texts are studied, it is true, there arises a mental mode, that is to say, there is a 'contact' between mind and Brahman. This consciousness is reflected in the mental mode and it removes primal ignorance, which is generically different from modal ignorance with respect to objects superimposed upon the consciousness conditioned by the object. The important distinction that must be borne in mind is that the consciousness element in the mental mode manifests Brahman, because when primal ignorance is removed, Brahman the selfmanifest consciousness shines of its own accord. Brahman, in other words, is not literally the result of the process of cognition. This is another way of saying that Brahman does not fall under the category of the thing to be defined. Thus there is no defect of underpervasion, because such a charge will be applicable to contents that come under the class of definable objects.

4.27.2.1 The expression 'the identity of the object with the witness-consciousness' can itself be understood in either of two senses. It may mean that the object is not the content of ignorance, which accounts for the empirical usage that the object *does* not manifest; or, it may mean that the object is identical with the consciousness that is not the content of ignorance, which gives rise to the empirical usage that the object *is* not manifest.

4.27.2.2 The significance of the distinction that *PP* makes between the two senses emerges when it proceeds to review the statement of *SM* made in this context.[9] *SM* maintains that the identity of consciousness with the cognizer does not mean that the object is superimposed upon the cognizer-consciousness. If the term 'cognizer' is taken to mean the consciousness that is implied by the mental mode, then in the case of the cognition 'the mountain has fire', the fire will have to be viewed as perceptual. If, on the other hand, it is taken to mean the consciousness that is conditioned by the mind, then there will be the defect of underpervasion, because the perceptibility of objects, such as the pitcher, will remain unaccounted for. Identity of the object with the cognizer then would mean that the object must be the content of knowledge that is identical with the cognizer, and it must be fit enough to come within the range of perception.

4.27.3 *PP* maintains that *SM*'s thesis requires further analysis, because the objects, such as pitchers, are not the content of the knowledge that they are identical with the consciousness conditioned by the internal organ. One might argue that a cognition such as 'I know the pitcher' points to the cognition of difference between the pitcher and the cognizer-consciousness, and the cognition such as 'a pitcher is existent' proves the perceptibility of a pitcher, because in this cognition existence is simply the consciousness conditioned by the mind. Śāstrī maintains that such arguments do not take us very far. This amounts to arguing that because there is no cognition in the world where existence is not manifested, every cognition has for its content the identity of the object with the consciousness conditioned by the mind, which is absurd.

It might be argued that for objects, such as pitchers, the consciousness conditioned by the object serves as the substratum. If the existence of the substratum is but the substratum of the superimposed entity, then how could a pitcher be viewed as having no independent existence apart from the existence of a cognizer?

The gloss of the author of *PP* in this regard is very useful and persuasive. He consistently defends the thesis that the cognizer-consciousness is not the substratum of the object, namely, the pitcher. The term '*eva*' in the text eliminates the nonassociation of identity between the cognizer-consciousness and the consciousness conditioned by the pitcher. By rejecting the difference caused by the different limiting adjuncts, the word *'iti'* conveys the sense of cause. The text *anumityādi sthale iti* shows that the criterion of perceptibility of an object excludes the perceptibility of fire in 'the mountain is fiery'. *SM* himself concedes that by the word 'cognizer'. we should understand the witness-consciousness that transcends the mind. The perceptibility of an object depends on several factors: the object must be superimposed upon the witness-consciousness, the witness-consciousness must be associated with the mental mode assuming the form of the respective object, and the object must be fit enough to come within the range of perception.[10] Accordingly, the author of *PP* concludes that the perceptibility of an object consists in its identity with the witness-consciousness.

4.28 *nanv evam api dharmādharmādigocarānumityādisthale dharmādharmayoḥ pratyakṣatvāpattiḥ, dharmādyavacchinnacaitanyasya pramātṛcaitanyābhinnatayā dharmādisattāyāḥ pramātṛsattānatirekāt. iti cen na; yogyatvasyāpi viṣayaviśeṣaṇatvāt.*

nanv evam api "rupī ghaṭaḥ" iti pratyakṣasthale ghaṭagata-parimāṇādeḥ pratyakṣatvāpattiḥ; rūpāvacchinnacaitanyasyaparimāṇā-dyavacchinnacaitanyasya caikatayā rūpāvacchinnacaitanyasya pramā-tṛcaitanyābhede parimāṇādyavacchinnacaitanyasyāpi pramātṛabhinna-tayā parimāṇādisattāyāḥ pramātṛsattātiriktatvābhāvāt.

iti cen na; tattadākāravṛttyupahitatvasyāpi pramātṛviśeṣaṇatvāt. rūpākāravṛttidaśāyāṃ parimāṇādyākāravṛttyabhāvena parimāṇādyākā-ravṛttyupahitapramātṛcaitanyābhinnasattākatvābhāvenātivyāptyabhāvāt.

4.28 *[Objection]: Even then, in the case of inferential cognition of merit, demerit and the like, there would be the contingence of perceptibility for merit and demerit, because consciousness conditioned by merit and demerit is nondifferent from the cognizer consciousness, the existence of merit, and so on, is not apart from the reality of the cognizer. It is said [in reply]: "no," for fitness or competency is an important qualifying attribute.*

[Objection]: Even then [even if we accept what is given above], in the case of the perception of 'a colored pitcher', the size, and so on, of the pitcher would become the object of perception; for the consciousness conditioned by the color and the consciousness conditioned by the size are one, and because the consciousness conditioned by the color is not different from the consciousness conditioned by the cognizer, the consciousness conditioned by the size is also not different

from the cognizer-consciousness. Hence, the existence of size, and so on, is not over and above the reality of the cognizer.

It is answered, "no," because having limiting adjuncts the mental modes in the form of those objects [the objects immediately cognized], is also a qualification of the cognizer. At the time of a mental mode in the form of color, there is no mental mode in the form of size. The consciousness associated with the mental mode in the form of size is different from the existence of the cognizer-consciousness [the cognizer-consciousness associated with the mental mode in the form of color], and there is no overpervasion of the definition [with respect to the size].

4.28 It is objected that in the case of inferential cognition of merit and demerit, the consciousness conditioned by them is not different from the consciousness underlying the cognizer; therefore they must be viewed as perceptual. Thus there is the defect of overpervasion. Opponents argue that although in an inferential cognition the consciousness conditioned by fire is not identical with the consciousness conditioned by the cognizer, the same answer cannot be given in the case of merit and demerit, because they are nondifferent from the cognizer-conditioned consciousness and do not have any existence independent of the witness-consciousness.

It is answered by saying that the 'fitness' of the content also is a part of the criterion of perceptibility, and when the adjectival feature 'fitness' is added to the content, there is no overapplicability of the definition in the case of merit and demerit. *PP* further notes that 'fitness' means the state of being nonconcealed. However, the object is said to be concealed because it serves as the limiting adjunct of the consciousness. Mere identity with the witness-consciousness does not constitute the criterion of the perceptibility of an object. One can only say that it is necessary but not sufficient.

4.28.1 If 'fitness' is interpreted to mean 'occasional nonconcealment', then there will arise the unwelcome position of the size of the pitcher being perceived at the time of the perception of the color of the pitcher, even in the absence of the mental mode in the form of size. Size has fitness to be indicated by the verbal expression of the form 'it is manifest occasionally'. Because color and size are superimposed on the same consciousness, and because the consciousness conditioned by color is nondifferent from the consciousness conditioned by the cognizer, the consciousness conditioned by the size also will not be different from the consciousness conditioned by the cognizer. Consequently, size either would be superimposed upon the cognizer-consciousness or would have no independent existence apart from it.

4.28.2 To the above objection—namely, how could there be identity of the cognizer-consciousness with the size in the absence of a mental mode assuming the form of size—*VP* answers, "no." The cognizer-consciousness must be qualified by the feature with which it is associated, namely, the mental mode in the form of respective objects. Thus size does not possess any independent existence apart from the cognizer-consciousness qualified by the above attribute. When *PP* stipulates that the object become unconcealed at the time of its manifestation, it implies manifestation by the witness-consciousness without the mediation of any mental mode. Thus understood, the verbal usage that supports perceptuality of mental states like happiness or pain becomes intelligible. *VP*, on the other hand, adds the qualifying attribute 'fitness' to the object or content, meaning that an object is manifested by the witness-consciousness only through a mental mode.

4.29 *nanv evaṃ vṛttavyāptiḥ, anavasthābhiyā vṛttigocaravṛttyanaṅgīkāreṇa tatra svākāravṛttyupahitatvaghaṭitoktalakṣaṇābhāvāt.*

iti cen na; anavasthābhiyā vṛtter vṛttyantarāviṣayatve 'pi svaviṣayatvābhyupagamena svaviṣayavṛttyupahitapramātṛcaitanyasattābhinnasattākatvasya tatrāpi sambhavāt.

4.29 *[Objection]: Even then [accepting the above qualification], there will be nonpervasion [in the definition] with regard to mental mode, because for the fear of infinite regress you [the Advaitins] do not admit that a mental mode can have another mental mode as its content. In that case, the definition stated above, which is qualified by the condition that the mental mode be in the form of its own (sva) object, does [would] not apply.*

The answer is "no," for although because of the fear of infinite regress, a mental mode is not admitted to be the content of another mental mode, [yet] because we admit that it is its own content, and because here [in the example given] also, the consciousness conditioned by the object has an existence not different from that of the consciousness conditioned by the mental mode of its own content, it [the definition] applies here as well.[11]

4.29 So far the identity between the cognizer-consciousness and the object has been explained. Similarly, the identity between the cognizer-consciousness and mental mode must be explained. The not very difficult to explain, because we admit a mental mode in the form of the object and another mental mode in the form of the cognizer. But how does one account for the perceptibility of the mental mode itself? Opponents argue that comprehension of one mental mode will require another mental mode and so on *ad infinitum*.

4.29.1 The Advaitins maintain that a mental mode does not itself become an object of another mental mode: a mental mode comprehends itself.[12] Therefore, to comprehend one mental mode, another mental mode is not needed. A mental mode only comprehends the object that is associated with it; for example, the mental mode in the form of pure Brahman comprehends the latter as associated with it.[13]

4.29.2 In the context of explaining why most Advaitins concur that a second mental mode in the form of the first mental mode is not needed, the author of *PP* reminds the reader that the purpose of admitting a mental mode with respect to objects, such as pitchers, is to avail of the reflection of the light of consciousness in it. The Advaitins, it may be recalled, conclude that mental states, such as happiness and pain, are manifested by the witness-consciousness without the requirement of a mental mode. The witness-consciousness gets reflected of its own accord, but the perceptibility of external objects, such as pitchers, requires the help of a mental mode. This distinction that the Advaitins make consistently, between the perception of external objects and introspection of mental states is not a theory-laden construction in support of some preconceived ideas. On the contrary, it rests on sound phenomenological grounding. Experience attests to such a distinction. In the perceptual cognition 'I am happy', there is no warrant for positing a mental mode with respect to experience. In 'I experience happiness', happiness is the immediate object of knowledge because it receives the reflection of the witness-consciousness. In the experience 'I am happy', happiness pertains to the subject. Similarly, in the experience 'I know the mental mode', the mental mode is the object. And in the experience 'I know the pitcher', the mental mode is a form of activity. Thus one and the same object can be viewed as a subject, or as an object, or as a kind of activity when viewed from different perspectives. When it is observed that the mental mode assumes its own form, a unique kind of contact of mental mode with itself is implied.

4.29.3 Commenting on the expression of *VP* that a 'mental mode is its own content', *PP* further explains it as implying that a mental mode falls within the range of perception without requiring another mental mode. It is a kind of self-relation.[14] Self-relation means the identity of generic essence with being itself. Similarly, a mental mode can be viewed as identical with itself. At this point, *PP* reminds the readers of the stipulation that was made earlier about the cognizer-consciousness, namely, that it must be associated with the mental mode assuming the form of the respective object and that it is applicable with respect to external perceptions only. However, in the introspection of mental states, the criterion is simply the identity with the witness-consciousness. Because this is the case, the question whether one mental mode requires another mental mode does not even arise. The mental mode itself is pressed into service because of its ability to be manifested by the witness-consciousness. As a result, it is not perceived as an objective content but apperceived by the witnessing consciousness, whose light it reflects and consequently becomes manifest.

4.30 *evañ cāntaḥkaraṇataddharmādīnāṃ kevalasākṣiviṣayatve'pi tattadākāravṛttyabhyupagamenoktalakṣaṇasya tatrāpi sattvāt nāvyāptiḥ.*

na cāntaḥkaraṇataddharmādīnāṃ vṛttiviṣayatvābhyupagame kevalasākṣivedyatvābhyupagamavirodha iti vācyam. na hi vṛttiṃ vinā sākṣiviṣayatvam kevalasākṣivedyatvam; kintv indriyānumānādipramāṇavyāparamantareṇa sākṣiviṣayatvam.

ata evāhaṅkāraṭīkāyām ācāryair ahamākārāntaḥkaraṇavṛttir aṅgīkṛtā. ata eva ca prātibhāsikarajatasthale rajatākārāvidyāvṛttiḥ sāmpradāyikair aṅgīkṛtā. tathā ca antaḥkaraṇataddharmādiṣu kevalasākṣivedyeṣu vṛttyupahitatvaghaṭitalakṣaṇasya sattvāt nāvyāptiḥ.

4.30 *In the same way, although the internal organ and its attributes are contents of pure witness-consciousness alone, because of the admission of mental modes in the form of those [e.g., happiness, misery], the preceding definition applies here as well, and so there is no nonpervasion [in the definition].*

It cannot be argued that if the internal organ and its attributes are admitted to be the contents of mental modes, there would be contradiction with the admission of their being known by the pure witness-consciousness. That is because being cognized by the pure witness-consciousness alone does not consist in being the content of witness-consciousness without [the aid of corresponding] mental modes; rather it consists in being the contents of the witness-consciousness without [the functioning of] the well-accepted means of valid knowledge, like sense organs, inference, and so on [other pramāṇa-s].

Hence the Ācārya, in his commentary on the passage on egoism, has accepted a mental mode in the form of 'I' or the 'ego'. In the case of illusory silver also, traditional Advaitins accept a mode of nescience in the form of silver. Thus because the definition involving qualification of being associated with the mental modes applies in the case of the internal organ and its attributes, which can be cognized by the pure witness-consciousness alone, there is no nonpervasion.

4.30 It is objected that the definition of the perceptibility of an object as entailing a mental mode fails to apply to the case of introspective perception of mental states such as happiness and pain. The latter are the attributes of the mind that are manifested by the witness-consciousness without a mental mode assuming the form of those respective mental states. Thus we cannot have the identity of the cognizer-consciousness as associated with mental mode in the form of happiness and pain, and the definition of the perceptibility of an object does not apply here.

4.30.1 It is said in reply that, even if we do not admit a mental mode assuming the form of another mental mode, a mental mode definitionally translucent receives the reflection of the witness-consciousness in it. The opponent here might parry the same reply with respect to mental states such as happiness and pain. *PP* maintains that it cannot be done. A mental mode is translucent, whereas mental states, like happiness and pain, are not. Therefore, a state such as happiness cannot directly reflect the light of the witness-consciousness without the mediation of a translucent mental mode.

VP shows that the identity of the cognizer-consciousness and the witness-consciousness, associated with the mental mode assuming the form 'I', exists. This implies, according to *PP*, that even in the case of objects that are alleged to be directly manifested by the witness-consciousness, such as happiness and other mental states, we admit mental modes.

4.30.2 It might be objected that in the case of illusory objects, like shell-silver, there is no identity of the witness-consciousness with the mental mode in the form of shell-silver. If such an association were present, it would no longer be an illusory object. The Advaitins admit a mode of primal ignorance in illusory cognitions. Consequently, an association between the witness-consciousness and the mental mode of ignorance of the form of silver is not possible in illusory cognitions. Such might be the objection of the *pūrvapakṣins.* The answer to the above question, as elaborated by *PP*, is as follows: It is true that in this instance a mode of ignorance in the form of silver is admitted, but *only* as conditioned by the mental mode assuming the form 'this', as in the illusory cognition 'this is silver'. Therefore, similar to the mental mode of the form 'this', the mode of ignorance in the form of this also serves as a limiting consciousness for the witness-consciousness. Thus the definition of the perceptibility of an object in terms of its identity with the witness-consciousness applies to the case of illusory perceptions. The verbal usage, that the illusory objects are manifested by the *sākṣin*, is based upon the acceptance of the mode of *avidyā*. With this in view, the author states *ata eveti*. The word *'svākāra'* in the text means 'of the form of the object'; the expression *pramātṛ satteti* means 'the existence that constitutes the nature of *sākṣin*', and the expression *viṣayasya pratyakṣatvam* means 'perceptibility that is in the object'.[15]

4.31 *tad ayaṃ nirgalito'rthaḥ. svākāravṛttyupahitapramātṛcaitanyasattātiriktasattākatvaśūnyatve sati, yogyatvaṃ viṣayasya pratyakṣatvam. tatra saṁyogasaṁyuktatādātmyādīnām. sannikarṣāṇāṃ caitanyābhivyañjakavṛttijanane viniyogaḥ.*

4.31 *Therefore, the following sense emerges: The perceptibility of an object consists in its competency, having no existence other than the existence of the consciousness conditioned by the cognizer ,which is associated with the mental mode in the form of that object [its own content]. This being the case, the application of the modes of sense contact, namely, contact, identity with what is in contact,[16] and the like is with respect to generating the mental mode that manifests consciousness [underlying the object].*

4.31 The essence of the discussion of the perceptibility of the content of perception given earlier is summarized in this passage.

4.31.1 The perceptibility of a content consists in its being devoid of reality other than the reality of the cognizer-consciousness associated with the mental mode assuming the form of that content, which must have competency to be perceived. Among the conditions laid down in the text is that the content should be devoid of reality other than the reality of cognizer-consciousness, but as qualified by or associated with a mental mode assuming the form of the object or the content itself. The exegesis that *PP* provides of the mental mode assuming the form of the content means 'perceptibility that is present in the object'. *PP* uses this expression to refute the position of Sautrāntika Buddhism that an object is inferable only,[17] and explains their position as follows. In the illustrative example, 'like the reflected image of a face in the mirror', 'the reflected image of the object' is the *pakṣa* or the subject; 'what is based upon the original' is the *sādhya* or the thing that is sought to be proved, and 'it is because it is a reflected image', that is the *hetu* or the ground of the inference. This view cannot be maintained, reiterates the author of *PP*, because the method of agreement and difference can be used to prove that the contact of the sense organ with an object (e.g., a pitcher) is the cause of the specific cognition of a pitcher. The instrumentality in the case of the contact of the sense organ that is ascertained would be contradicted on the hypothesis of the Sautrāntika school.

One must remember that the Advaita position, that pure consciousness alone is perceptual, is in principle different from the Sautrāntika position. Opponents argue that if pure consciousness alone is perceptual without being caused by a sense organ, then the Advaita position is more or less similar to the Sautrāntika position that objects are inferrable and not perceived. *PP* observes that such an argument is wrong. For the Advaitins the sense contact serves the function of giving rise to a mental mode which reveals consciousness, and this is different from the function of sense-contact in the Sautrāntika school of Buddhism. Mental mode, *PP* observes, always means the specific contact of the mind. Such a specific contact of the mind, which has been termed the modification of the mind-stuff, reveals the consciousness.

4.31.2 The expression *tatra saṁyogeti* explains the nature of sense contact, according to *PP*. The term '*tatra'*, means 'that which is involved in the concept of perceptibility'. This sense of the term must be construed with the sense of the word *'vṛtti'*. What it means, reiterates *VP*, is that the contacts, such as conjunction, are helpful in giving rise to the mental modes that are involved in the perceptibility of an object.

This concludes the discussion regarding the perceptibility of an object or the content. The author of *PP*, at this juncture, provides an elaborate summary of the points made so far.

4.31.3 He begins with the notion of *pramāṇa* as the instrument of valid knowledge, and reminds readers that the Advaitins define valid knowledge as 'the state of being consciousness'. Valid knowledge, in the wide sense of being consciousness, underlies perception, inference, testimony, and all other means of knowledge. Valid knowledge that arises from the sense organs (i.e., the perceptual means of knowledge in the technical sense) is again only the consciousness conditioned by the mental mode which is identical with the consciousness conditioned by the object. In this context, the author of *PP*, reiterates that it does not consist in the identity of the cognizer-consciousness with the consciousness conditioned by the mental mode. *PP* reiterates this point throughout to distinguish the Advaita perspective from other idealistic positions such as Vijñānavādins.

4.31.4 According to the Advaitins, senses indeed cause the modification of the mind technically known as a mental mode. They are referred to as instruments with respect to the conditioned consciousness. The Advaitins' notion of the mental mode as a modification of the mind is based upon the Upaniṣadic texts that discuss desire, resolution, and the other similar mental states. The interesting observation that the author of *PP* makes in this context is that while it certainly looks as though the Advaitins rely on scriptural testimony for such a key notion as the mental mode, they also maintain that it is not contradicted by perception.

The opponent, however, might say that it is contradicted because in experiences such as 'I desire', the reference is to desire directly as the attribute of the self, indicated by the term 'I'. *PP* here reminds us that the Advaitin analysis of the 'I' must be kept in mind. The sense of the term 'I' is only the blend of pure consciousness and mind. Mental states, like desire, when referred to as the attributes of the mind, are transferred to the soul. And so the above experience is not contradictory.

4.31.5 *PP* next discusses how the internal organ (i.e., the mind) gets itself involved in the perceptual experience and manifests itself. *PP* maintains that there is no valid proof that mind is a sense organ. The declaration of the Upaniṣadic texts—objects are external to senses and the mind is inward when compared to objects—does not amount to saying that mind is a sense organ. It simply implies that the mind is distinct from the sense organs. Similarly, the text of the *smṛti*, which states that mind is the sixth sense organ, on a par with the other five sense organs does not refer to mind as a sense organ at all. The rule that the number of a particular series has the same characteristics as the objects in the series is only a general one and not an invariable one.

4.31.6 *PP* further points out that the criteria of the perceptuality of knowledge does not lie in the knowledge being created by a sense organ, because such a definition will not apply to the genuine case of God's knowledge. God perceives things without the instrumentality of sense organs, and therefore represents, in its operation of mechanism, knowledge in its ideal form. One may argue, as do the Naiyāyikas, that mind is a sense organ based on the presumption that the perceptual knowledge of happiness and pain would be unintelligible otherwise. But *PP* informs us that if the knowledge arising from a sense organ is considered perceptual, then it would be inapplicable in the case of God's knowledge. So he maintains that we must abandon the view that knowledge, to be direct, must arise from a sense organ. In this respect, *PP* sides with the Vivaraṇa tradition and argues against the Bhāmatī school, which accords the status of sense organ to mind and also assigns a role for it in the generation of knowledge. It might be asked: If sense-generatedness is not the criterion, then what exactly is the criterion of the perceptuality of knowledge? Consciousness, although one, attains a threefold designation as *viṣaya caitanya, pramāṇa caitanya,* and *pramātṛ caitanya* when it is conditioned by the object, the mental mode, and the mind, respectively. The nondifference from consciousness conditioned by an object, fit for any particular sense and present for the consciousness conditioned by the mental mode in the form of that object, constitutes perceptibility with reference to that particular aspect.

4.31.7 When the mind envelopes the object by reaching the place of the object, then the object and the mental mode serve as the limiting adjunct of one and the same consciousness. So the consciousness conditioned by the object and the consciousness conditioned by the mental mode become one. The criterion of the perceptuality of knowledge then lies in the identity of the consciousness conditioned by the object and the consciousness conditioned by the mental mode. In the case of mediate cognition, such as 'the mountain has fire', the object and the mental mode are located at different places and so there is no perceptibility insofar as it relates to the element of fire. To exclude from the definition the cases of recollection of happiness, merit, and demerit, the adjectival features, namely, 'it must be present at a given time' and 'fitness', are added. *PP* maintains that the cognition that arises from the statement 'you are happy' is perceptual in nature. It is very much like the immediate cognition 'I am the tenth man,' which arises from the statement 'you are the tenth man' when the state of being the tenth man is not known. *PP* further adds that this also explains the capacity of the text 'you are Brahman' to generate the perceptual knowledge of Brahman.

4.31.8 *PP* also discusses the Nyāya contention that in one and the same knowledge (namely, 'the sandalwood is fragrant'), there exists perceptuality caused by the empirical as well as the extraempirical contact. The Advaitins similarly maintain that in the case of the cognition "the mountain has fire', there is both mediacy (fire-element) and immediacy (mountain-element). The experience 'I perceive the mountain and infer the fire' becomes intelligible on this ground. If, however, the mountain is not in proximity to the perceiver then the cognition 'the mountain has fire' is mediate in all its aspects.

4.31.8.1 Opponents argue that mediacy and immediacy are mutually exclusive characteristics. If they exist in one and the same substratum, there will be the defect known as *sāṅkarya*, that is, a fusion of the illegitimate bringing together of two things that should not be brought together. Thus neither of these two could be said to have a defining characteristic of a universal. 'Pitcherness' is the defining characteristic of a pitcher. In the same way, mediacy is the defining characteristic of mediate object and immediacy of immediate object.

4.31.8.2 The Advaitins welcome such an objection. They maintain that everything apart from Brahman is noneternal. The concept of 'universal' entailing eternality cannot be accepted.

The perceptibility of an object consists in its being identical with the witness-consciousness. This implies that the object does not have any independent existence apart from such a consciousness. If we maintain that there is only one kind of reality, then the absence of independent existence can be achieved at the time of the perception of the pitcher when the consciousness conditioned by the pitcher and the consciousness conditioned by the mind become identical. If one believes in the three levels of reality, then the absence of independent existence is accounted in terms of the object's superimposition upon the witness-consciousness. According to both views, however, there is no perceptibility regarding the fire-element in the cognition 'the mountain has fire'.

4.31.9 As one and the same internal organ is spoken of as the mind, the intellect, the ego, and the internal sense in view of the fourfold modification it undergoes, similarly, one and the same consciousness is viewed both as produced and as many in view of the distinctive mental modes it assumes. The sense contacts are useful in generating *vṛtti*. With this in view, our author states, *sa ca vṛttir iti*. The term *'icchā'* conveys the sense of *hrī*. The sense of sight is referred to as a *pramāṇa* by giving rise to the perceptual cognition, which is only the consciousness conditioned by the mental mode.

Notes

1. At the outset of Chapter 3, two questions were raised: What determines the condition of the perceptuality of knowledge, and what determines the perceptibility of an object or content immediately cognized? In response to the first question, *VP* maintains that the criterion is the nondifference of the consciousness conditioned by the means of knowledge, that is, the cognitive consciousness from the consciousness conditioned by the content. Chapter 4 provides an answer to the second question. The perceptibility of an immediately cognized content consists in its nondifference from the cognizer-consciousness. In other words, immediately perceived objects do not have any existence apart from the existence of the cognizer.

2. The Naiyāyikas articulate the definition of perception in terms of sense object contact. This implies that perception as a form of valid knowledge originates and is caused by sense stimulation. This definition follows the etymological meaning of the term '*pratyakṣa*'. Etymologically, it is said, *pratyakṣa* is a combination of *prati* (to, near, before) and *akṣa* (sense organ). So *pratyakṣa* means 'present before eyes or any

other sense organ', signifying direct or immediate knowledge. Gautama takes the term 'object' to signify three kinds of objects: the physical objects (e.g., table, chair, pitcher; 3.1.1); specific objects (e.g. color, hard, soft; 1.1.14; 3.1.2.; 3.1.58); and internal objects (e.g. pleasure and pain; 1.1.10). In short, perception is a cognition that is always of an object. The cognition of substances like tables and chairs, is known as an external perception; of pleasure and pain as internal perceptions.

Gautama further adds that perception is *avyapadeśa* (not impregnated by words) and *vyavasāyātmaka* (definite). Śāstrī points out that such a definition of perception involves arguing in a circle. It amounts to explaining a sense organ or its stimulation in terms of perception, and perception in terms of sense stimulation. *PP*, 63.

3. The importance and significance of '*ajñātatayā*', 'unknown', by the *sākṣin* was recognized very early in Vedānta. It is the conclusive view of Vedānta that everything is illumined by the *sākṣin* either as 'known' or 'unknown'. Knownness or unknownness are not objective characteristics, as if they were labels or tags that every object invariably carried with it. If such were the case, they should be known with the knowing of the things and by all persons indifferently. Knownness or unknownness therefore entails a contrast between two states: "We shall not be wrong if we take 'knownness' or 'unknownness' as relational properties or relations born out of a contrast between two states. If this is conceded, we should further grant that the two termini of a relation must be known before the relation is known. The 'unknown' therefore has to be apprehended in some way before the rise of the specific source of knowledge—Perception, Inference, and so on None of these sources of knowledge is in a position to give us an apprehension of the prior 'unknownness' of its object; each is confined to the actually present. A conscious experience before the rise of any specific knowledge (*pramāṇavṛtti*) has to be accepted." *Ajñāna*, 152–153. Ignorance, in other words, is a necessary presupposition of all knowing. Empirical knowing is always the knowing of the unknown. As a matter of fact, it is only the unknown that really can be known. There can be disclosure in knowledge (*jñāpana*) but only of what has remained concealed (*ajñāta*). *PP*, 64. Also see Introduction, sec. 7.

4. *Ibid.*, 64.

5. *Ibid.*

6. *Ibid.*

7. In his writings, Śaṁkara clearly recognizes three levels: *paramārthika*, the level of reality; *vyavahārika*, the level of appearance; and *pratibhāsika*, the level of illusory existents. Reality is that which cannot be sublated by any other experience. Appearance is sublated only by direct knowledge of Brahman. Illusory existents can be sublated by all other types of experience.

Professor Deutsch articulates Śaṁkara's three levels of being in terms of reality, appearance, and unreality. Reality is the same in both the classifications. In Deutsch's classification, illusory existents are included as the lowest existent within the domain of appearance. Unreality is that which cannot be sublated by any existence. An 'object' is unreal when it is not a datum of any experience. Unreal objects are self-contradictory, like 'a hare's horn', or 'a son of a barren woman'. In his writings, Śaṁkara never clearly formulates the level of unreality as a 'level of being' as such. It is accepted only implicitly. However, I believe, Professor Deutsch's classification makes Śaṁkara's writings more understandable. Eliot Deutsch, *Advaita Vedānta: A Philosophical Reconstruction*, chap. 2.

The term 'level' in this context should not be construed in its spatial connotations. These levels differ qualitatively and in kind; they are different because reason cannot establish any causal relation among them. Deutsch, in the work referred to above, brings out the ontological, epistemological, and logical characteristics pertaining to a level of being: "The term 'level' seems to function in discourse primarily as a spatial metaphor: in common language it connotes 'aboves' and 'belows'—one forms an image of 'levels' by thinking of one thing as being above or below another thing or of one thing as being 'deeper' than another thing, as in the expression 'levels of meaning'. The term 'level', however, for purposes of ontology, can be given a more precise conceptual meaning. Two orders of being can be said to be on different levels: (1) when, epistemologically, because of differences in kind between them (temporal, qualitative, and so on), relations cannot be established rationally between them; (2) when, logically, assertions made about one of the orders from the standpoint of the other may legitimately violate the formal requirements that govern the thought of the one order when confined to itself (for example, assertions about the Godhead or Absolute in religious literature made from the empirical standpoint may legitimately violate and they frequently do the law of contradiction); and (3) when, axiologically, different grades of value are ascribed to the orders." *Ibid*, 25–26, n. 9.

8. Śāstrī explains what is involved in the assertion that Brahman is not the content of *phala*. When the sense of sight comes into contact with the pitcher, mind also 'comes out', reaches the place of the object and comes into contact with it. This contact is known as *vṛtti*. The object is superimposed upon the consciousness conditioned by it. Therein modal ignorance exists. The mental mode, inspired by the reflection of consciousness in it, removes the modal ignorance, and the object comes into contact with the consciousness reflected in the mental mode. Consciousness element in the mental mode is known as *phala*. The object, namely, the pitcher, comes into contact with the consciousness, and the object is manifested. Accordingly, it is said that the pitcher is the content of *phala*.

The case of Brahman, however, is different. When the Vedāntic texts are studied, there arises the *vṛtti* and the mind comes into contact with Brahman. The consciousness is reflected in the *vṛtti* and it removes the primal nescience. The consciousness element in the mental mode is not needed to manifest Brahman, because when ignorance is removed, Brahman manifests of its own accord. Therefore, Brahman is not the content of *phala*.

9. *PP*, 67.

10. *pramātṛpadenāntaḥkaraṇopahitacaitanyavivakṣaṇena "yogyatve sati svākāra-vṛttyupahitasākṣicaitanyādhyas tattvaṃ viṣayasya pratyakṣatvam" iti uktam. Ibid.*

11. *VP* maintains that one of the conditions of perception is that the mental mode must be modified in the form of the object, and that the cognizer-consciousness must be associated with that mental mode. Opponents maintain that if this is accepted, then the first mental mode would require another mental mode, which in turn would require still another mental mode and so on *ad infinitum*. And because the infinite regress of mental modes cannot be accepted, the definition given in *VP* is defective. In response, it is said that the first mental mode is its own object, and the second mental mode is not needed. Therefore, a mental mode does not require another mental mode to be cognized.

12. Although all Advaitins agree that the function of *vṛtti* is to manifest objects, they differ regarding the way in which an object becomes manifest to a subject. These differences are primarily a function of their views of the knowing self and its relation to the world. Professor Sundaram reveals the precise nature of the distinction between the Vivaraṇa and the Bhāmatī tradition on this issue: "According to the Vivaraṇa school of thought the function of the *vṛtti* is to remove the obscuration of Brahman which is the material cause of the world, by first establishing a connection with it. So the function of the *vṛtti* is twofold here; connecting and enlightening. The obscuration of Brahman means being the object of the individual's ignorance. According to *avacchedavādins* of the Bhāmatī persuasion, as the individual soul itself is the material cause of the world, only the obscuration is removed and nothing more, because the soul as the material cause is always connected with the object. So here the function is only one." Sundaram, *Advaita Epistemology*, 4.

In general, there are three different views as to how the mental mode meets the object and leads to the perception of it: For the sake of association with consciousness (*ciduparāga*); for the sake of the removal of the veil that hides the object (*āvaraṇa-bhibhava*); and for the manifestation of nondifference of the consciousness conditioned by the object and the consciousness conditioned by the subject (*abhedābhivyakti*). *SLS*, chap. 1, 51, 187. *PP*, as we shall see, favors the third view. Most Advaitins recognize the first two functions of the mental mode in the perception of an object. They agree that a mental mode that shines with the reflected light of consciousness meets the object, and the veil of consciousness that hides the object from the cognizer is withdrawn. The consciousness that conditions the object becomes manifest through the transparent mental mode and the object is illuminated.

VP, however, accepts the third theory of the functioning of a mental mode. *VP* maintains that in the perceptual process the consciousness conditioned by the mind and the consciousness conditioned by the object become nondifferent (see chap. 3). On the first two theories, the mental modification leading to perception only connects the consciousness underlying the object and the consciousness conditioned by the subject. However, they do not become nondifferent. Nondifference in this context must not be construed to mean total identity; it is rather 'unity' or 'coincidence', because the limiting adjunct of each consciousness endures.

13. Anything that is perceived is perceived by the cognizer-consciousness. He perceives that aspect or form of the object with which the mental mode coincides. A mental mode comprehends itself; a second mental mode is not needed to comprehend the first mental mode. Even the mental mode of the impartite is not itself impartite. "It is admitted by all schools of advaita, that the final psychosis [mental mode], called intuition of Brahman, has the capacity to annul not merely the rest of the world of appearance, but itself as well.... (F) or the destruction of the final psychosis, something over and above that psychosis is [not] needed; this other is undoubtedly required when a pot, and so on, is destroyed, but to insist on that here would be to argue from illegitimate analogy...." *SLS*, Śastri, introduction, 61.

14. *svaviṣayatvābhyupagamena svasaṁbandhābhyupagamena, vṛttyantarānape-kṣasvavyavahārābhyupagamena. sattādātmye sattādātmyavat vṛttāv api svasaṁbandho na doṣāyeti bhāvaḥ*. *PP*, 71.

15. *svākāreti. viṣayākārety arthaḥ. pramātṛsatteti. sākṣisattety arthaḥ. viṣaya-sya viṣayagatam. Ibid.*, 73.

16. According to Advaitins, there are six types of contacts. (1) *Saṁyoga* is contact of an object with the sense organ; for example, the visual perception of a pitcher results from its contact with the sense of sight. This is a direct contact. (2) *Saṁyukta tādātmya* is contact with an object that is in contact with the sense organ; for example, the perception of the color of the pitcher that is in contact with the sense of sight. In this context, we must remember that for the Advaitins the substratum and the attributes are nondifferent. (3) *Saṁyukta abhinna tādātmya* is the identity of the generic nature of color with the color itself; for example, the perception of the generic nature of the color of the pitcher that exists in the color of the pitcher in contact with the sense of sight. This follows from the principle accepted in the second contact. (4) *Tādātmya* is identity, e.g. in the perception of sound, it having a quality like ether makes it identical with it. (5) *Tādātmya abhinnatva* is identity with what is the same; for example, the perception of the generic essence of the sound, being identical with the sound, is the same as ether. (6) *Viśeṣya viśeṣaṇa bhāva* is the relationship that exists between the thing qualified and the attribute qualifying it; for example, the perception of the absence of pitcher on the floor is caused by the absence qualifying the floor which, therefore, possesses the qualification, namely, the absence of the jar. The absence of jar in the system of Vedānta is cognized by means of a special *pramāṇa* known as *anupalabdhi*. *TSDNB*, sec. 43, 221-32.

17. Sautrāntika Buddhist maintain that the external objects are not perceived directly but are inferred from our perceptions, because "the objective constituents of perceptual situations are particular existents of a particular kind; they are not literally parts of the perceived object, although they resemble physical objects as ordinarily conceived. They are more like mental states in their privacy and dependence on the mind of the observer." Herbert V. Guenther, *Buddhist Philosophy in Theory and Practice* (Maryland: Penguin Books, 1972), 73.

This should not mislead one into believing that for Sautrāntika the universe consists only of the subjective world of mental states. They maintain that cognitions cognize external objects as well as internal mental states. The subject imposes its own form of consciousness on the cognitions that are caused by external objects, and the object is inferred from these forms. The consciousness of the cognition can never be the object of cognition, and it is evidenced by the fact that consciousness is the same everywhere. So the external object must be admitted, otherwise one will not be able to explain the difference between different conscious states; for example, between the consciousness of green and the consciousness of blue. In other words, the existence of objects is inferred through the presentations of mental states. Objects must exist because perception without an object of perception is impossible. The varieties of the forms of consciousness testify to the existence of external objects. As Guenther explains it: "An object such as a jug is never actually observed. The appearance of a jug, and the place where this appearance is believed to exist, are indistinguishably hypothetical. We speak in common parlance of a cognition experiencing an object, because we are made aware of a likeness when, in the first instance, the three causal factors of object, sensory capacity, and cognition combine, and when subsequently a sensum (believed to be) an object is sensed, (which is the process) similar to the reflection in a mirror." *Ibid.*, 85.

5

Forms of Perception

5.32 *sā ca vṛttiś caturvidhā—saṁśayaḥ, niścayaḥ, garvaḥ, smaraṇam iti. evaṃ sati vṛttibhedena ekam api antaḥkaraṇaṃ mana iti buddhir iti ahaṁkāra iti cittam iti cākhyāyate.*

taduktam—

mano buddhir ahaṁkāraś cittaṃ karaṇam āntaram.
saṁśayo niścayo garvaḥ smaraṇaṃ viṣayā ime.

5.32 *Mental modes are of four kinds: doubt, certitude, egoism, and retro-cognition. Considering this division of the mental mode, the internal organ, although one, receives different appellations, namely, mind (manas), intellect (buddhi), ego-sense (ahaṁkāra), and retro-cognition (citta).*

[Accordingly], it has been said:

"the internal instruments are manas, buddhi, ahaṁkāra, and citta, and the [their] contents [functions] respectively are: doubt, certitude, egoism, and retro-cognition."

Four Functions of the Internal Organ

5.32 This section of *VP* makes a functional differentiation within the internal organ, which, although one, because of its different aspects or functions, comes to be known by different appellations such as mind (*manas*), intellect (*buddhi*), the ego-sense (*ahaṁkāra*), and recollection (*citta*). At this juncture, *PP* invokes the textual canon to vindicate the general Advaita epistemological standpoint thus far stated: Only pure consciousness is perceptual knowledge. The sense of sight, for example, is deemed a means of perception insofar as it provides the occasion for generating a mental mode in the form of an object, say, a pitcher. The mental mode causes or constitutes the validity of a cognition in its relation to the object and not with reference to the element of consciousness, because the latter is always perceptual in a trivial sense. The internal organ thus becomes central in the epistemological situation, serving, as it does, as the instrument or the means through which the percipient acquires perceptual knowledge.

Thus there are different functions of the internal organ.[1] When it has for its limiting adjunct the mental mode in the form of doubt, it is called mind; when it has for its limiting adjunct a mental mode in the form of certitude, it is termed 'intellect'; when the mental mode takes the form of egoity, it is called 'I-ness'; and when it has a mental mode in the form of memory, it is termed 'recollection'.

5.33 *tac ca pratyakṣaṃ dvividham, savikalpakanirvikalpakabhedāt. tatra savikalpakaṃ vaiśiṣṭyāvagāhi jñānaṁ, yathā ghaṭam ahaṃ jānāmi' ityādijñānam. nirvikalpakaṃ tu saṁsargānavagāhi jñānam, yathā "so'yaṃ Devadattaḥ," "tat tvam asi" ityādivākyajanyaṃ jñānam.*

5.33 *The perception is twofold because of the difference as determinate and indeterminate. Of these, the determinate [perception] apprehends the relatedness [of the substantive feature and the adjectival feature], for example, the cognition 'I know the pitcher'. The indeterminate [perception], on the other hand, does not comprehend the relation in a cognition; for example, the cognition generated by the sentences such as, 'this is that Devadatta' or 'thou art that'.*

Determinate and Indeterminate Perception

5.33 The determination of the perceptual character to the extent that it relates to the object is twofold: determinate and indeterminate. It is important to underscore the point made by *PP* in this context: the aforementioned enumeration pertains to the perceptual character insofar as it relates to the element of content (e.g., a pitcher), thereby rejecting the view that this division relates to the element of consciousness as such.

5.33.1 Even though the author of *VP* does not identify the opponent when he explains or elucidates the twofold nature of the perceptuality of cognitions, *PP* maintains, and justifiably so, that the position that *VP* criticizes can be identified with the point of view represented in the epistemological treatise of *Yatīndramatadīpikā*, belonging to the tradition of Viśiṣṭadvaita[2] of Rāmānuja. One of the points at issue between Advaita and Viśiṣṭadvaita is the nature of indeterminate perception. Rāmānuja severely criticizes the Advaitin concept of consciousness as pure immediacy. He maintains that the distinction between perception as indeterminate and determinate is one of degree and not of kind. Some scholars argue that in the so-called indeterminate perception, there is a manifestation of the universal, the attribute, and the substratum without their internal relation being apprehended, whereas in the determinate perception, there is a manifestation of these associations as well, and the cognition of the qualifying attributes causes a complex cognition. Rāmānuja, however, contends that this is not true. In indeterminate perception, the specific disposition of the parts of the object is what is initially manifested as 'this'. In the second and the subsequent cognition, the specific disposition of the parts and configurations is manifested as related to many objects of the same kind.[3] The configuration serving as the adjectival feature is manifested in relation to other objects as well, and it is in this aspect that it becomes the content of the second and the subsequent cognitions, technically termed 'determinate perception.'

5.33.2 *PP* holds that the text of *VP* entails a repudiation of the view outlined above. If the distinction between the two perceptions is one of degree only, one would not be able to distinguish between the two in a perceptual experience. There will be no phenomenological warrant for enumerating them as two kinds. The second and subsequent cognitions also, on Rāmānuja's view, refer to the configuration as 'this' so that they may be viewed as indeterminate. *PP* questions whether there can arise the knowledge of the persistence of a configuration without the knowledge of many objects of the same kind. In the first instance of the perception, there is the persistence of the configuration with respect to one object. In the second and subsequent perceptions, the configuration is comprehended in another object, which would amount to the knowledge that every object is similar to the first one, thereby making a recognition of the determinate perception pointless. In short, such a theory cannot draw a line of demarcation between the indeterminate and determinate perception, the distinction Rāmānuja himself recognizes. The Advaitin position that the author of *VP* sets forth, therefore, is the only tenable solution; that is, the indeterminate aspect of the perceptuality of a cognition is that which comprehends the object as unrelated to anything.

5.33.3 Opponents may ask whether it is possible to have a valid cognition devoid of any relation whatsoever. It is true that perception as experience involves a relation among several elements. However, we must keep in mind that the Advaitins here, as *PP* rightly observes, are not referring to a perception of the ordinary discursively experientiable sort, but to a kind of knowledge that does not involve any relation and has for its content only the object in itself without reference to the relation of the percipient in whose context it is given. The Advaita text, for example, *Laghucandrikā*, makes a distinction between statements like 'bring a pitcher' and 'truth, knowledge, and infinitude is Brahman'.[4] The latter has no relation whatsoever with its content. Indeterminate perception belongs to the latter category. It does not refer to the relation that exists among the several factors of the content of a cognition. Keeping this in view, *VP* states, *nirvikalpakaṃ tu saṁsargānavagāhi iti.*

5.33.4 It is of exegetical interest to note that the text of *VP* does not merely cite the Upaniṣadic statement 'thou art that', as an example of the relationless character of indeterminate perception but also the instance of recognitive cognition 'this is that Devadatta' to clinch the point. The decisive phenomenological slant of approach of the text of *VP* is indicated by the second example.

5.33.5 Opponents at this point might argue that a complex cognition is caused by the cognition of its adjectival feature.[5] This causality would not be intelligible unless we have the cognition of the adjectival feature, that is, indeterminate perception. This means that knowledge arising from statements such as 'thou art that' does not possess the characteristic of being the cognition of an adjectival feature. How, then, can such Upaniṣadic statements be viewed as conveying the relationless ultimate?

In response *PP* argues that the example illustrative of the indeterminate character of perception does not have to rely solely on the scriptures. Ordinary life also provides basis for such an experience. The statement embodying the recognitive experience 'this is that Devadatta' is a case in point. In such an experience, Devadatta is manifested as conditioned by spatio-temporal relations, indicated by the terms this and that. These terms here serve as an indicating factor (*uplakṣaṇa*).[6] The statement in this respect is different from the verbal cognition 'thou art that', in which spatio-temporal relation is not the import and therefore is not manifested. The statement 'this is that Devadatta' is intent on conveying the object in itself (i.e., Devadatta) to know the person. This statement derives its meaning from its opposition to the contrary cognitions in the form of a doubt, 'whether this is the same Devadatta or not'. The person in himself is manifested because it alone has the semantic fitness. It is not manifested because of the manifestation of the adjectival feature.

5.33.6 It might be asked: What, then, is the nature of the

cognition of the sense of identity imported by the sentence 'this is that Devadatta'? Is it the identity of the particular place and the specific time with a different place and a different time? Or, does it signify the identity between the present time and place with a past time and a place? Additionally, it might be asked that if the statement signifies the person in himself, does that not make the use of the two words with two sets of sense as well as reference insignificant?

5.33.6.1 In answer to these queries, *PP* says that the perceptual experience that this statement imports is the identity of the person in himself. In a perceptual cognition, *bādha* or the absence of the identity of one thing with another acts as the counteracting factor. A perceptual cognition does not refer to the identity of the complex factors, because the cognition that the two cannot become identical—the two experiences indicated by 'this' and 'that' being nonidentifiable—acts as the counteracting factor. Hence perceptual experience refers to the identity of the person in himself.[7]

5.33.6.2 *PP* maintains that the illustration of the recognitive experience provided to exemplify indeterminate perception is very appropriate. A recognitive experience like 'this is that Devadatta' alone has for its content the identity of the knowledge arising from two words that imply a seeming duality. Recognitive experience itself typifies a feature present in all ordinary experiences where, however, it tends to remain obscured. The content of ordinary experience indeed stands for a complex whole, while that of recognitive experience is more typically the object in itself. The latter is cited as an example to demonstrate the possibility of the arising of the knowledge of the object in itself from texts like 'thou art that'.

5.33.6.3 The point stressed above, *PP* continues to observe, also provides an answer to the objection that on the basis of the cognition arising from the statement 'this is that Devadatta', one cannot establish that the scriptural text 'thou art that' refers to a nonrelational object. The statement 'this is that Devadatta' undoubtedly conveys identity between Devadatta associated with the past in a different place and Devadatta associated with the present in a given place. If this is not maintained regarding the example, then the person in himself would already be known, and the sentence becomes futile. Furthermore, if the person in himself alone was the import, then one word alone should suffice, and the second will become superfluous.

5.33.6.4 In the expression 'the blue pitcher', the adjectival features of each word are different, yet because of an appositional or co-ordinate relation between the two, the unity of the senses of the two words is imported. Similarly, a recognitive experience also must be interpreted as importing a complex unity while at the same time retaining the duality of the adjectival features. Thus the recognitive experiences must not be treated as different from the expressions such as 'the blue pitcher'.

Such is the objection raised by Dvaita Vedānta. Dvaita Vedānta is Vedānta in the sense that it upholds the identity of soul and Brahman in the sense of similarity of consciousness. They reject the Advaitin contention that the two are identical *per se*. If, as the Advaitins claim, the two are identical, then Brahman being self-luminous will always be manifested, and there will be no need of any instructions regarding it. Moreover, Dvaita Vedānta continues, Brahman is known by statements such as 'Brahman is existence, consciousness, and bliss', so there is no need to take a special recourse to a text like 'thou art that' as central and then seek to explain it on the basis of a recognitive cognition, and then further seek to distinguish it from expressions like 'the blue pitcher' on experiential grounds.

5.33.6.5 In reply to these objections, *PP* demonstrates the need for according a special status to the identity statements of the Upaniṣads.[8] The major texts of the Upaniṣads convey the identity of consciousness indicated by the seemingly opposed description of omniscience and limited knowledge, and such identity is not known through any other *pramāṇa*-s.[9] *PP* notes that the definition of Brahman as *satyaṃ* (truth), *jñānam* (knowledge), and *anantam* (infinite) differentiates Brahman from those who possess the opposite of those qualities. 'Brahman is truth' negates the quality of untruth, 'Brahman is knowledge' negates the quality of nonknowledge, and 'Brahman is infinite' negates the quality of being finite. Each of these three words removes a specific ignorance and therefore is useful and necessary. Similarly, the instruction regarding the fact of identity is not futile.[10] The illustration provided by the recognitive experience 'this is that Devadatta' does not have for its content anything more than the content of the ordinary experience of 'this Devadatta' and 'that Devadatta'. Yet such an experience is not considered to be futile. Nor is it a mere repetition in a context in which the words alone will be sufficient. Additionally, because it cannot be maintained that Devadatta in himself is already known, it is pointless to say 'this is that Devadatta'. In the same way, the expression 'thou art that' is neither futile nor a simple tautology.[11] The three terms in the statement are significant for understanding the identity of the individual aspect of Brahman and the cosmic aspects of Brahman.[12] The major texts of the Upaniṣads give rise to the cognition of the supra-relational Brahman which removes the erroneous cognition about its manifestation in a complex manner.

5.34 *nanu śābdaṃ idaṃ jñānaṃ na pratyakṣam, indriyājanyatvāt.*

iti cen na; na hīndriyajanyatvaṃ pratyakṣatve tantram, dūṣitatvāt; kintu yogyavartamānaviṣayakatve sati pramāṇacaitanyasya viṣaya-caitanyābhinnatvam ity uktam. tathā ca "so 'yaṃ devadattaḥ" iti vākyajanyajñānasya sannikṛṣṭaviṣayatayā bahirniḥsṛtāntaḥkaraṇavṛtty-abhyupagamena devadattāvacchinnacaitanyasya vṛttyavacchinnacaitan-yābhedena "so'yaṃ devadattaḥ" iti vākyajanyajñānasya pratyakṣatvam. evaṃ "tat tvam asi" ityādivākyajanyajñānasyāpi; tatra pramātur eva viṣayatayā, tadubhayābhedasya sattvāt.

5.34 *[Objection]: This cognition obtained through words is not perception because it is not sense-generated.*

[To this, we the Advaitins say]: "no," because the sense-generatedness is not the criterion of perceptibility as it has [already] been rejected. It [criterion] has been stated [rather] as the nondifference of the consciousness conditioned by the means of the knowledge from the consciousness conditioned by the content, and when there is the content [in the consciousness conditioned by the means of knowledge] that is appropriate and present. Because the cognition generated by the sentence 'this is that Devadatta' has a proximate object [the object in contact with the senses], the mind goes out, assumes modification in the form of Devadatta, and the consciousness conditioned by Devadatta becomes nondifferent from that conditioned by the mental mode [in the form of the object]. So the knowledge generated by the sentence 'this is that Devadatta' is perceptual. Similarly, even in the case of cognition generated by sentences such as 'thou art that', because the cognizer himself is the content, the nondifference between the two [the consciousness conditioned by the vṛtti in the form of the cognizer, and the cognizer himself] exists.

5.34 The text of *VP* encounters an objection to the illustration 'this is that Devadatta' as a model for indeterminate perception on the ground that indeterminate perception of the kind spoken of in the Upaniṣads does not arise from a sense organ. *PP* draws out the implication underlying the answer that *VP* gives to the objection, thereby providing a favorable framework for the reader to approach the text:

There is no invariable relation between generation from a sense organ and the knowledge of a nonrelational object.[13] Perceptuality of the nature of identity conditioned by the mental mode and consciousness conditioned by mind also is applicable in the case of knowledge arising from a sentence. It is true that in the case of the knowledge of Brahman, we do not have the identity of the consciousness conditioned by the object and the consciousness conditioned by the mental mode. Brahman-cognition is not, for example, like pitcher-cognition, in which the pitcher itself serves as the limiting adjunct of consciousness. To the extent that the identity of consciousness conditioned by the mental mode with the consciousness conditioned by the essential nature of the object is constitutive of the perceptuality of knowledge, Brahman-knowledge is perceptual. If, however, the expression 'the identity of the consciousness conditioned by the object and the consciousness conditioned by the mental mode' is taken to signify the removal of the characteristic of being an object of ignorance in general, then such a removal would not be possible without the mental mode reaching the place of the object, and therefore there would be no contradiction in the definition of the perceptuality of knowledge in relation to the knowledge of Brahman.

Attending to the objection that 'this is that Devadatta' is not an instance of indeterminate perception because it has not arisen from a sense organ, *PP* takes great pains to show the applicability of the definition of the perceptuality of knowledge in the example under consideration on the ground that sense organ is indeed involved in recognitive cognitions. The general theory outlined earlier was that the internal organ that goes out has a specific contact known as modification (*pariṇāma*). It is possible to refer to this instance of recognitive cognition as a case of visual perception, because there is a contact of the sense of sight with the object Devadatta. But the knowledge of Devadatta in himself, as indicated by the spatio-temporal relation, should be admitted as arising from the respective words, because what is arrived at from these indicating features, it must be noted, can only be verbal in nature. Such a cognition does not have a complex object as its content, because 'thisness' and 'thatness' being the countercorrelate of identity that is manifested are not adjectival features.[14]

5.35 *nanu vākyajanyajñānasya padārthasaṁsargāvagāhitayā, kathaṃ nirvikalpakatvam? ucyate; vākyajanyajñānviṣayatve hi na padārthasaṁsargatvaṃ tantram; anabhimatasaṁsargasyāpi vākyajanyajñā-*

naviṣayatvāpatteḥ. kiṇtu tātparyaviṣayatvam.

prakṛte ca "sad eva somyedam agra āsit" ity upakramya "tat satyaṃ sa ātmā tat tvam asi śvetaketo" ity upasaṁhāreṇa viśuddhe brahmaṇi vedāntānām tātparyam avasitam iti kathaṃ tātparyāviṣayam saṁsargam avabodhayet?

5.35 *[Objection]: Now, because the sentences-generated cognition is apprehended by the word meanings, how can it be [called] indeterminate? [In reply]: It is said that with respect to being the content of sentence-generated cognition, the relation among the word meanings is not the criterion [for being such], because of the contingence that even an unintended relation might become the content of sentence-generated cognition. Rather, it [criterion] is the purport [intention] of the content.*

And in the passage under consideration beginning with "my dear, this [world] was alone in the beginning" (CU 6.3.1) and ending with "that is reality, that is ātman, 'thou art that', Śvetaketu," the intention of the Vedāntic texts is ascertained to be pure Brahman. How, then, can it [such text] make known a relation which has a different object from its intention [intended object]?

5.35 Opponents argue that a statement like 'thou art that' cannot have for its import a nonrelational entity. It is said in response that the importing of the indeterminateness of a cognition should be understood analogously to the import of the statement 'this is that Devadatta'. The criterion of the identity of a verbal cognition is that a sentence represents expectancy, fitness, and other features. Expectancy is not merely the feature that is responsible for the experience of relation among the word meanings. Because a relation that is not intended also may be the content of a verbal cognition, it must be maintained that expectancy is that which gives rise to the experience of the relation among the meaning of the words. The relation, in such instances, is the chief import. It might sound too simplistic, however, to assume that expectancy is of the nature outlined above. That which is the primary import is relational at certain places but supra-relational at other places. Expectancy may stand for the mere cognition of a word meaning that is conducive to the verbal cognition, in which the concept of relation is not involved. Similarly, the criterion 'fitness' does not involve reference to a relation. It consists rather in the nonsublatability of the import. The validity of verbal cognitions arising from text like 'that thou art' thus stands vindicated. Its import is nonrelational, and it at the same time fulfills the criteria of expectancy and fitness. The statement 'thou art that' conveys an impartite or nonrelational sense, because it is an answer to the question regarding the nature of the object itself.

5.35.1 On another ground, namely, the ground of hermeneutical reasoning applied in support of interpreting Vedic sentences, one may argue that a sentence necessarily comprehends a relation. Such is the viewpoint of Mīmāṁsā, dualistic Vedānta, and other non-Advaitins. They maintain that a sentence which gives rise to the knowledge of an object that is unknown hitherto and not sublated subsequently can only be relational. As examples, Vedic texts may be cited that speak of a particular rite as a means to heaven, the sentence in that case signifying a causal relation between the performance of a sacrifice and heaven. Such a relation was unknown previously. The major texts of the Upaniṣads, if they signify only the object in itself, do not signify anything new. Therefore the scriptural texts are valid, and they are relational in their import.

In reply to the above objection, *PP* concedes the relational nature of a verbal cognition like that of the texts which speak of rites. He, however, denies that the import of a valid verbal testimony should necessarily be relational. The content of ' thou art that' is Brahman and its identity with the *ātman* that is indicated by the cognizer-consciousness. Such an identity was unknown previously through any *pramāṇa*-s. Non-association with any feature is only a description of the object in itself, which leads to the removal of erroneous cognitions. The important thing to note, therefore, is that it is not the relation but the intention that constitutes the true import of word senses in conjunction in a statement.[15]

5.35.2 The dualists maintain that 'thou art that' does not convey an impartite sense, because the identity between *jīva* and Brahman is not the import of the scripture. In addition, the perceptual experience 'I am not an omniscient being' points to the difference between the soul and Brahman. In the text *brahma veda brahmaiva bhavati* (he, who knows Brahman, becomes Brahman) *eva* in *brahmaiva* does not convey the sense of identity but similarity. Likewise, the sentence 'this is that Devadatta' does not convey an impartite or nonrelational sense. All these texts point to Brahman endowed with attributes. The real import is *viśuddhe brahmaṇi vedantānāṃ tātparyam avasitam iti.*[16]

PP rejects this contention and demonstrates that according to *VP* the Upaniṣadic sentences convey an impartite sense. The difference between *jīva* and Brahman is not absolutely real, claims the Advaitin; it is only superimposed. Applying the six marks that determine the import of the Upaniṣads,[17] the Advaitin takes the inculcation of nondifference to be the overall intention of the Upaniṣads. The perceptual experience 'I am not an omniscient entity' does not point to the difference between the *jīva* and Brahman, thus it may be used as an argument against texts like 'thou art that' conveying an impartite sense. The perceptual experience underlying the statement 'I am not an omniscient entity', observes *PP*, rather comprehends the difference between consciousness conditioned by the mind and consciousness conditioned by ignorance. It does not comprehend the difference in consciousness that is free from all limiting adjuncts, such as mind, ignorance, and the like. The Advaitins do not negate the difference as such but rather their absolute reality. The validity of the texts that convey the nonimpartite sense will not be intelligible unless what is given in perception is taken to be nonreal. The individual self and Brahman, when divested of all limiting adjuncts, are only pure consciousness. They are not really the substrata of contradictory features. Difference between self and Brahman is admitted by the Advaitins during phenomenal existence. Therefore it is futile to argue that the two must be different because they possess contradictory features.

The essence of the entire discussion given in *PP* is that statements such as 'thou art that' convey an impartite sense. It is only in this sense, *PP* shows, that the expressions (namely, 'that is real' and 'such is *ātman*') that precede the text 'thou art that' become meaningful and satisfactorily answer questions regarding the nature of Brahman.

5.36 *idam eva "tat tvam asi" ityādivākyānām akhaṇḍārthatvaṃ yat saṁsargānavagāhi yathārthajñānajanakatvam iti.*

taduktam—

saṁsargāsaṅgisamyagdhīhetutā yā girām iyam
uktākhaṇḍārthatā yad vā tatprātipadikārthatā.

prātipadikārthamātraparatvaṃ akhaṇḍārthatvam iti caturtha pādārthaḥ.

5.36 *That sentences like "thou art that' convey a simple sense of non division [posses an impartite sense] only means that they generate a valid cognition that does not comprehend any relation [among the word-meanings constituting a sentence]. So it has been said: "The capacity of the words to produce a valid cognition without reference to the relation of their [word] meanings, is what has been termed as possessing an impartite sense, or it conveys the stem-sense alone [which is devoid of any reference to relations]. The fourth quarter [in the above couplet] means the sense of non-division [between words]."*

5.36 The purport of a sentence like 'thou art that' is to convey an impartite sense. In other words, the object of statements expressive of identity is to generate a valid cognition that is nonapprehensive of any relation. *PP* further observes that in Upaniṣadic statements such as 'the one who realizes Brahman attains the highest', it is Brahman who is to be realized.[18] Accordingly, Upaniṣadic statements like 'truth, consciousness, infinitude is Brahman'[19] provide an answer to the question regarding the nature of the object as such. The primary meaning of the term 'truth' (*satya*) is Brahman as associated with the characteristic of *satyatva*, the sense that admits of a relation. However, even in this context, the *lakṣyam* (that is the secondary sense) is *akhaṇḍameva*, the impartite one.

The reason the author of *PP* has drawn attention to this text is to show that even statements that appear relational in their primary sense signify an impartite sense in their implied sense (secondary or non-direct).[20] *PP* further observes that the words 'truth, consciousness, infinitude' are not synonyms and so it cannot be said that they are redundant. On the contrary, these three words are absolutely essential, although alike in importing the impartite sense. The term 'truth', on the one hand, conveys the principle of the nature of reality; on the other hand, it eliminates the opposite principle of nonreality. Therefore, although conveying one and the same principle, they eliminate the opposites of their primary sense.

Further explaining the sense of the impartite, *PP* observes that in some contexts the chief characteristic may serve as a definition, while in other contexts it may serve as the essential nature of the object, or the object as such may serve as the definition. When the attributes serve as the definition, the sense surely will be partite (a sense that admits of relation). But when the object as such serves as its definition, the sense will be impartite (nonrelational).[21] *PP*'s important insight here is that one and the same object may serve as the object to be defined and as the definition itself, an insight that might seem logically odd but phenomenologically meaningful. Just as in one and the same Brahman, which is identical with bliss as well as consciousness, the bliss aspect may be concealed while the consciousness aspect is manifested, in the same way, if the object as such serves as the definition only in a specific aspect, in another aspect, which is assumed, it may serve as an object to be defined. In short, one and the same object can serve as a *lakṣya* (the object to be defined) and the *lakṣaṇa* (the definition itself) without involving any kind of contradiction. Brahman is the only reality, the world is nonreal, yet it can serve as the basis for the empirical usages, like the implied and the implication.

Jīvasākṣin and *Īśvarasākṣin*

5.37 *tac ca pratyakṣaṃ punar dvividham—jīvasākṣin, īśvarasākṣin ceti.*

5.37 *And this perception is again twofold: Individual-defining witness-consciousness and the God-defining witness-consciousness.*

5.37 Introducing the topic of the distinction of individual-defining witness-consciousness and the God-defining witness-consciousness, which the text of *VP* next undertakes, *PP* makes an observation. In the perceptual cognition 'this is a pitcher', the consciousness conditioned by the mental mode assuming the form of the pitcher is admitted to be at once perceptual as well as originated. As consciousness it is perceptual, and as related to the object pitcher it is originated. In the perceptual cognition of an object, there are three factors manifested: the cognizer, the cognized content, and the cognition itself. The term 'witness' refers to consciousness on which the internal organ is superimposed. The internal organ plays the role of the cognizer-consciousness in a cognitive relation. The perceptuality of knowledge consists in the state of being the consciousness conditioned by the mental mode associated with the consciousness conditioned by the object. Perceptuality relating to the witness-consciousness lies in its identity with the content-consciousness. And perceptibility of the content lies in its identity with the cognizer-consciousness. This clarification that *PP* provides is very useful as a preamble to the Advaita thesis that every object is manifested by the witness-consciousness either as being known or unknown. The point of the clarification is that the manifestation of objects, such as pitchers, will not be possible without being related to the witness-consciousness. The ultimate criterion for the perceptibility of an object then lies in its identity with the cognizer-consciousness, of which another name is the witness-consciousness. The witness-consciousness and consciousness are ontologically the same, although they are not synonymous. Thus is introduced the relevance of the notion of consciousness as witness to perception, whether in apposition to the individual self or God.

5.37.1 Pure consciousness is perceptual and does not depend on any aid insofar as its essential nature is concerned. In relation to an object, say a pitcher, however, it is perceptual by being conditioned by the mental mode and also either by the internal organ or by cosmic force or power, described in Advaita in a unique fashion as *māyā*. Individual-defining witness is the consciousness that transcends the internal organ. God-defining witness is the consciousness that likewise transcends *māyā*.

5.37.2 At this point, *PP* enters into a discussion about the nature of the individual and God in the different writings of Advaita thinkers.[22] It is not our goal to analyze here the different theories, because they do not bear on the issue of perceiving as a datum for phenomenological analysis. Important, however, is the distinction and the similarity between *māyā* as a cosmological idea and *ajñāna* or *avidyā* as a notion of immediate existential significance directly relating to the idea of knowledge as the soteriological means. With this distinction is tied up the distinction between the individual and God.

One particular way of distinguishing between the individual and God deserves attention as underscoring an experiential basis. The latter tends to become obscured when such issues are treated as theological. In the case of the individual, the internal organ serves as the limiting adjunct, whereas in the case of God it is the absence of such an internal organ. The individual is the consciousness conditioned either by the internal organ or nescience, whereas God is consciousness conditioned by the absence of either of the two. Problems arise with this otherwise lucid distinction, which *PP* is not slow to point out. If God is explained as consciousness defined by the absence of the limiting adjuncts, then it will be difficult to account for God's omniscience. As a solution, it is proposed therefore that consciousness conditioned by the internal organ is the individual and the consciousness conditioned by *māyā* is God.

5.38 *tatra jīvo nāma antaḥkaraṇāvacchinnacaitanyam; tatsākṣin tv antaḥkaraṇopahitacaitanyam. antaḥkaraṇasya viśeṣaṇatvopādhitvābhyām anayor bhedaḥ.*

viśeṣaṇaṃ ca kāryānvayi vyāvartakam; upādhiś ca kāryānanvayī vyāvartako vartamānaś ca; yathā "rūpaviśiṣṭo ghaṭo 'nityaḥ" ity atra rūpaṃ viśeṣaṇam; "karṇaśaṣkulyavacchinnaṃ nabhaḥ śrotram" ity atra karṇaśaṣkulyupādhiḥ. ayam evopādhir naiyāyikaiḥ paricāyaka ity ucyate. prakṛte cāntaḥkaraṇasya jaḍatayā, viṣayabhāsakatvāyogena viṣayabhāsakacaitanyopādhitvam.

5.38 *Of these, what is known as the individual self is the consciousness conditioned by the internal organ, and the witness-consciousness is the consciousness that is 'qualified' by the internal organ. The difference between these two is through [caused by thinking of] the internal organ being a qualifying attribute or a limiting adjunct.*

A qualifying attribute is inherent in a product. A limiting adjunct, though a present distinguishing feature, is not inherent in it. For example, in the sentence 'the colored pitcher is noneternal', the color is a qualifying attribute; and in the sentence 'ether as conditioned by the ear-cavity is the sense of hearing', the ear-cavity is a limiting adjunct. The Naiyāyikas call this limiting adjunct an 'indicator.' In the present case, because the internal organ is insentient, it cannot manifest objects [of its own]; it [the internal organ] is a limiting adjunct for the consciousness that manifests the content.

5.38 It is in the face of the alternatives outlined above that the author of *PP* proposes the following distinction: *Jīva* is the internal organ-defining consciousness and the *sākṣin* is the consciousness qualified peripherally by the internal organ.

The distinction between the state of being an individual and the state of being a witness is made by the author of *VP* with the help of the ideas of a qualifying attribute (*viśeṣaṇa*) and a delimiting mark (*upādhi*). A qualifying attribute is the one that is related to the defining entity, is present, and also distinguishes it from all other objects. It is a distinguishing mark that is syntactically related to the predicate and serves to distinguish it from other objects. Such a stipulation is added, says *PP*, to ward off the unwelcome position that a cloth may be viewed as the qualifying attribute of a pitcher in the expression 'he sees both a pitcher and a piece of cloth'. Being in syntactical relation to the predicate, which more simply stated is 'being related to the delimited entity', is to avoid the overlapping of the definition in the case of what is technically termed 'a delimiting mark.' Ether, which is all-pervasive, cannot be limited. In the sentence 'ether as qualified by the ear-cavity is the sense of hearing', the ear-cavity is a limiting adjunct. It has no syntactical relation with the predicate, although the limitation or the qualification is not separable from the predicate in question. Separable or not, the qualification serves to mark out the object defined.

5.39 *ayañ ca jīvasākṣin pratyātmaṃ nānā; ekatve caitrāvagate maitrasyāpy anusandhānaprasaṅgaḥ.*

5.39 *Now, this individual-defining consciousness is different in each individual; for if it were one, then what is cognized by Caitra would also be recollected by Maitra.*

5.39 The individual-defining consciousness is different for each individual, maintains the author of *VP*. Otherwise, what is cognized by A would be recollected by B. Explaining this, *PP* observes that, for *VP*, *sākṣin* is identical with Brahman. Yet it falls under the category of *jīva* because it is 'the consciousness that transcends the internal organ'. This may be explained with the help of an example from an epistemological situation. In the case of the erroneous cognition of a shell as 'this is silver', the silver is superimposed upon a specific aspect of the shell that is unknown, but is manifested as identical with the 'this' element of the shell. Similarly, the witness-consciousness, although identical with Brahman, is manifested as related to the individual. As the limiting adjunct, the internal organ is manifold, and 'what transcends each internal organ' also appears to be manifold.

5.40 *īśvarasākṣin tu māyopahitaṃ caitanyam. tac caikam; tadupādhibhūtamāyāyā ekatvāt.*

"Indro māyābhiḥ pururūpa īyate" ityādiśrutau "māyābhiḥ" iti bahuvacanasya māyāgataśaktiviśeṣābhiprāyatayā māyāgatasattvarajas-tamorūpaguṇābhiprāyatayā vopapatteḥ.

"māyān tu prakṛtiṃ vidyān māyinaṃ tu maheśvaram."

"taraty avidyāṃ vitatāṃ hṛdi yasmin niveśite."

"yogī māyām ameyāya tasmai vidyātmane namaḥ."

"ajām ekām lohitaśuklakṛṣṇām bahvīḥ prajāḥ sṛjamānāṃ sarūpāḥ. ajo hy eko juṣamāṇo' nuśete jahāty enāṃ bhuktabhogām ajo'nyaḥ."

ityādiśrutismṛtiṣu ekavacanabalena lāghavānugṛhītena māyāyā ekatvaṃ niścīyate.

tataś ca tadupahitaṃ caitanyam īśvarasākṣin, tac cānādi, tad-upādher māyāyā anāditvāt.

māyāvacchinnaṃ caitanyam parameśvaraḥ; māyāyā viśeṣaṇatve īśvaratvam, upādhitve sākṣitvam; iti īśvaratvasākṣitvayor bhedaḥ; na tu dharmiṇor īśvarasākṣiṇor bhedaḥ.

sa ca parameśvara eko 'pi svopādhibhūtamāyāniṣṭhasattvarajas-

tamoguṇabhedenabrahmaviṣṇumaheśvarādiśabdavācyatām bhajate.

5.40 *But the God-defining witness-consciousness is the consciousness qualified by nescience (māyā). It is one because of the oneness of māyā, its limiting adjunct.*

In śruti [texts] such as, "Indra manifests himself in different forms through māyā-s," the plural form māyā-s" either conveys the different powers of māyā or [refers] to the constituents (guṇa-s), [namely], purity (sattva), activity (rajas), and inertia (tamas) present in māyā.

[Śruti texts such as]: "Know māyā to be Nature and the wielder of nescience to be the supreme lord" (Śvet., 4.10); "On whose, having entered his heart, a yogīn crosses the vast nescience, to that immeasurable soul of knowledge [I offer] obeisance" (Vis., 5.17. 15); and "the one, unborn, red, white, and black, who produces off springs like herself, with her lies the one unborn male taking his delight, another unborn male leaves her with whom he had his enjoyment" (Śvet., 4.8); ascertain the oneness of māyā, by the force of the singular in the śruti and smṛti [texts as those above] supported by the law of parsimony.

Thus consciousness qualified by the limiting adjunct of that (māyā) is the God-defining witness-consciousness. Such is beginningless, because its limiting adjunct, māyā, is beginningless.

Consciousness conditioned by māyā is the supreme lord. When māyā is a qualifying attribute, it is the state of being a God (Īśvaratva); when it is a limiting adjunct, it is the state of being a witness (sākṣitva). Such is the difference between the state of being a God (Īśvaratva) and the state of being a witness (sākṣitva), and not between God and the witness-consciousness possessing these attributes.

The supreme lord, although one, has been designated by such names as Brahmā, Viṣṇu, and Maheśvara, because of the difference in purity, activity, and inertia, the three constituents grounded in māyā, which is its limiting adjunct.

5.40 *PP* next discusses why God-defining witness-consciousness is described with reference to *māyā* and thereby sets the stage for what is to follow. It suggests that it is desirable to distinguish *māyā* from illusory cognitions or the latent impressions that arise from them or from *karma*. All these have a beginning and cannot serve as the limiting condition for God, who is beginningless. *Māyā*, on the other hand, is positive as well as beginningless, but it nevertheless is removable by the knowledge of Brahman. There is no unintelligibility in maintaining this position unless one believes dogmatically that a beginningless entity cannot be removed. The author of *PP* cites the case of antecedent negation accepted by the opponent as a category.[23] Antecedent negation is beginningless; however, it is not without an end. Regarding the positive nature of *māyā*, *PP* adverts to the perceptual and inferential evidences adduced in its support. The perception, phenomenologically speaking, which is of great import, is of the form 'I do not know'. The object referred to in such commonplace experiences is 'not knowing', which although is negative linguistically speaking, points to 'non-knowing as a positive content.[24] Inference also, as given in the Vivaraṇa text, proceeds in effect as a similar reconstruction of any perceptual experience.[25] A perceptual knowledge manifests an object not manifested earlier. All knowledge is preceded by concealment and knowledge simply unconceals it. The important thing to note here is that the proofs offered in support of the positive nature of nescience are treated by the author of *PP* as also being the proofs for the positive nature of *māyā*. *Māyā* and *avidyā* denote the same thing, although importing different connotations. At this juncture, opponents might say that the text 'Brahman assumed many forms owing to *māyā*-s' conveys the sense of the plurality of *māyā*-s, and so it cannot be said to be one. In response to this objection, *PP* states: *Indro māyābhiḥ māyāgataśaktiriti. avasthājñāneti*, there are many modes of the *māyā* that are known as *avasthājñāna-s.* In other words, the plural '*māyābhiḥ*' should be taken to signify modal ignorances.[26]

5.41 *nanv īśvarasākṣiṇo 'nāditve "tad aikṣata bahu syāṃ prajāyeya" ityādinā sṛṣṭipūrvasamaye parameśvarasyāgantukam īkṣaṇam ucyamānam katham upapadyate?*

ucyate; yathā viṣayendriyasannikarṣādikāraṇavaśena jīvopādhy-antaḥkaraṇasya vṛttibhedā jāyante, tathā sṛjyamānaprāṇikarmavaśena parameśvaropādhibhūtamāyāyā vṛttiviśeṣaḥ "idam idānīṃ sraṣṭavyam, idam idānīṃ pālayitavyam, idam idānīṃ saṁhartavyam" ityādyākārā jāyante; tāsāñ ca vṛttīnāṃ sāditvāt tatpratibimbitacaitanyam api sādīty ucyate.

5.41 *Now, if God-defining consciousness is beginningless, how to make sense of the supreme lord's thought [to create] prior to the creation of the universe as declared in the following and other texts: "then he thought, I would be many, I would," (CU 6.2.3)?*

We reply that just as different modes arise in the internal organ, the limiting adjunct of the individual self, because of sense-object contact and other such causes, similarly, because of the past deeds of human beings that are to be created [because of their actions, the human beings are destined to be reborn], different modes in the form 'now, this is to be created', 'now, this is to be nurtured', and 'now this is to be destroyed', arise in māyā, the limiting adjunct of the supreme lord. And because these modes have a beginning, the consciousness reflected in them also is said to have a beginning.

5.41 In response to the objection that if God-defining witness-consciousness is to be considered without any beginning then certain texts of the Upaniṣads would not be intelligible, *VP* provides an answer which the author of *PP* elucidates. The individual-defining witness-consciousness may be described as perceptual and, accordingly, can be explained in terms of genesis or origin. The God-defining witness-consciousness, however, is not perceptual in relation to created objects, and any discourse about its origination, therefore, can only be symbolic and not literal. The individual-defining witness-consciousness comprehends not only the objects but also the individual self. The internal organ affects the relation between the witness-consciousness and the object as well as the individual knowing self. Therefore, the individual-defining witness-consciousness, which is perceptual in relation to an object, say a pitcher, and the perceiving self may be said to be produced. The God-defining witness-consciousness, on the other hand, has *māyā* as its limiting adjunct at the time of the first creation, and this *māyā* does not have any relation to objects. At the time of creation there arises a specific mode of *māyā* in the form 'this must be created now', owing to the merits and the demerits of the individual self. This has been termed "symbolic" and is necessary in make sense of the Upaniṣadic statement to the effect, 'Brahman thought, may I become many'.[27]

Notes

1. The Advaitin classification of the four states or functions of the internal organ—*manas, buddhi*, *ahaṁkāra* and *citta*—stresses the cognitive aspect of the mind. Of the three aspects, the cognitive, the affective, and the conative, the cognitive is fundamental because feeling and willing always presuppose some sort of a cognition. Most Vedāntins, however, recognize only two functions of the internal organ: the function of deliberation, which is performed by *manas*, and determination by *buddhi*. Sadānanda includes *ahaṁkāra* in *manas* and *citta* in *buddhi*. Sadānanda Yogīndra,

Vedāntasāra, trans. Swami Nikhilananda (Calcutta: Advaita Ashrama, 1978), 46.

Datta draws our attention to the pertinent point that in Western psychology mind has been articulated both as a subject and as an object. In Vedāntic philosophy, however, subject and object are different qualitatively, therefore, one common term cannot be used to signify both. The two are distinct entities, mind as a subject is the self and the mind as an object is the *manas* or *antaḥkaraṇa*. Again, in Western psychology, the mind, in perception, only receives sense stimulation, but in Advaita the mind assumes the form of the object upon meeting it. Finally, in the Western view the mind, is stationary and does not come into direct contact with the object, because it simply reacts to the light stimuli that it receives from the object.

Thus in Western psychology the visual perception is a physiological function. For Advaitins, problems of perception have a metaphysical basis. Neither sense organs nor *manas* nor their contact can give rise to a cognition in the absence of the light of consciousness. See D. M. Datta, *Six Ways of Knowing* (Calcutta: University of Calcutta, 1972), 65–66.

2. Viśiṣṭadvaita is the label for the rival school of Vedānta, that originated with the commentary of Rāmānuja on *Brahmasūtras,* in which the author joins issue with the Advaitins over the question of the nature of consciousness and the viability of recognizing a veil for consciousness. The label 'Viśiṣṭadvaita' used to refer to this school means qualified (as theistic) nondualism. For an exhaustive account of the tradition, see S. N. Dasgupta, *A History of Indian Philosophy*, vol. 3 (Delhi: Motilal Banarsidass, 1975).

3. The author of *Yatīndramatadipīkā* explains the distinction between *nirvikalpaka* and *savikalpaka* perception as follows: "What is called nirvikalpaka is the cognition of the first individual qualified by its attributes, configurations, and so on The savikalpaka is the cognition of the second (third and so on) individual qualified by its attributes, configurations, and so on grasped with retrospection. In both cases this (perception) has for its object only what is qualified (by attributes, and so on). Since it is not possible to possess knowledge which apprehends unqualified (objects), (the perception of nondifferenced objects) is inadmissible." Srinivasa, *Yatīndramatadipīkā*, trans. Swāmī Ādidevānanda (Madras: Sri Ramakrishna Math, 1949), 13. Henceforth this work will be cited as *YMD*.

According to Rāmānuja, knowledge is invariably of a complex object. It is not possible for the mind to cognize anything in isolation without apprehending some qualities or characteristic at the same time. What is cognized is necessarily cognized as qualified, its *jāti* or universal being inseparable from it. When an object is known for the first time, it is called *nirvikalpaka* perception. At this point previous impressions are not recalled. When a child sees a cat, for the first time, for example, he undoubtedly sees it as qualified in some manner. When the child sees a cat again, the former impressions of the cat are revived, and this and the subsequent apprehensions are *savikalpaka* perception, according to Rāmānuja. In short, 'this is a cat' gives us the perceptual experience at the *nirvikalpaka* level, and this is *also* a cat', at the *savikalpaka* level. The development in perception, in other words, is not from simple to complex, but in the complex perception itself, from less familiar to becoming more familiar. Therefore, Rāmānuja rejects the Advaitin contention that in perception the object in itself can be cognized. Knowledge implies a subject and also an object that serves as its referent. See M. Hiriyanna, *Outlines of Indian Philosophy* (Bombay: George Allen & Unwin (India) Pvt. Ltd., 1973), 386–87.

For Rāmānuja, all perceptual experience involves judgment. Accordingly, it is always of the form 'this is so' and thus involves a manifestation of some character or other. Even in the *nirvikalpaka* perception the entity perceived is characterized, and in the absence of such a perception it will not be possible to have a *savikalpaka* perception of the form 'this is that'. In such a cognition 'this', points to an object perceived in the past, and 'that' points to some distinguishing feature that allowed it to be cognized again as 'this'. Rāmānuja argues: "Indeterminate perception must apprehend an object with some distinguishing feature: *for if the indeterminate perception is to be followed by a determinate one*—when the dimly perceived object draws near and is perceived for what it is with all its peculiarities—we *recognize* it as such: 'this is that same object'. So we must originally have perceived a differentiating feature to *recognize* it by. The identification 'this is that' presupposes a common feature to both terms sufficiently peculiar to warrant an identification [emphasis supplied]." Rāmānuja, *Vedārthasaṁgraha,* trans. J. A. B. van Buitenen (Poona: Deccan College Postgraduate and Research Institute, 1956), 203.

4. *satyādivākyajanyapramā, saṁsargāgocarā, lakṣaṇavākyajanyajñānatvāt, vyatirekeṇa ghaṭamānayeti vākyavad iti saṁsargāgocarajñānam eva nirvikalpajñānam iti sādhitam. sarvathā ca vaiśiṣṭyānavagāhijñānam eva nivikalpakam ity aṅgīkaraṇīyam ity āśayenāha—nivikalpakam tu saṁsargānavagāhīti*, 78. Also see *Laghucandrikā*, chap. on *akhaṇḍārthvādaḥ. PP*, 390–416.

5. *BP*, passage 58, 89–90.

6. Madhusūdana explains *upalakṣaṇa* as follows: "[W]hen the idea of the Object being different from other things is brought about by a character (not by itself directly, but) through the indicating of a distinguishing property of the Object,—and the connection of the character itself is put aside (as not being of much consequence)—such a character comes to be called the 'accident' of that object; an example of this we have in the shape of the *crows* (seated on a house and serving for the time being to mark the location of the house, which distinguishes it from other houses)...." *AS*, chap. 1, sec. 24, *Indian Thought* 9, no. 1 (1916): 26.

Upalakṣaṇa, in other words, is an ascribed or an indicative characteristic. The crow on the roof of Devadatta's house serves as an indicative characteristic to single out the house from among several houses. Although the crow is not an attribute of the house, it still identifies the house: the identification is the significance here, it is never lost although the crow may fly away. It is to be distinguished from *viśeṣaṇa* or *lakṣaṇa* , which enters into the very being of an object and distinguishes the object from other objects. According to the Advaitins, it is not necessary that a real property must serve as the mark to distinguish one object from the other. An ascribed or assumed property might well serve the purpose.

This distinction between *Upalakṣaṇa* and *viśeṣaṇa* or *lakṣaṇa* is very important to an adequate understanding of Advaita literature, and they make use of it throughout to substantiate their theses; for example, the relationship between Brahman and the world. The implied, nonconstitutive relation between the definition and the definiendum has been articulated with great precision by T. R. V. Murti: "It is commonly held that the differentia alone can be the definition (*lakṣaṇa*); and only by *belonging* to the *definiendum* does it serve to distinguish it from the rest. How can the world which is not integral to Brahman, yet define and distinguish it from others? It is not, however, necessary that the definition must be a real property of the definiendum to serve as a mark of distinction. Even an assumed mark will do equally well.... Likewise, the world may be *indicative* of Brahman *without being constitutive of it*. There is distinction without differentia." "The Two Definitions of Brahman in Advaita," *Studies in Indian Thought,* ed. Harold Coward (Delhi: Motilal Banarsidass, 1983), 77.

It is of interest to note here briefly the observation that Murti makes in the above article cautioning his readers against over-emphasizing this distinction: "We may even assert the converse: all *lakṣaṇa* is *upalakṣaṇa*, all definition is ascription. The reason is that the difference between the mark and the marked will not obtain if the marking characteristic were integral to the latter.... A correct analysis of the relation between the definition and the definiendum leads us to the conclusion that like the true subject of a proposition which is never a predicate, nor the sum-total of all possible predicates, the definition is non-constitutive of the definiendum. *Brahman* is transcendent to thought (*nirdharmaka*), and we can define it only by ascribing features to it." *Ibid.*, 77–78.

7. *pratyakṣasya viśiṣṭābhedaviṣaye bādhasya pratibandhakatayā svarūpamātrā-bhedaviṣayatvāditi*. *PP*, 79.

8. Advaitins reject the Dvaita contention that the expression 'the blue pitcher' is similar to identity statements such as 'thou art that' and 'this is that Devadatta'. Such identity statements, Advaitins hold, should be construed in their secondary sense (*jahatajahatlakṣaṇa*). For a discussion of implied meanings, see n. 17. Accordingly, Advaitins maintain that the statement 'the blue pitcher' is not like 'thou art that'. In the phrase 'the blue pitcher', the words 'blue' and 'pitcher' qualify each other and express a common idea. The statement refers to that pitcher which is blue, and the blue color is associated with a pitcher, that is, the two words together signify what we generally understand by a blue pitcher. This is known as mutual qualification or connection (*saṁsarga*). In 'thou art that', the words 'that' and 'thou' do not have the relation of qualifier and the qualified, because both terms refer to contradictory ideas: 'thou' refers to consciousness characterized by immediacy, and so on, and 'that' refers to consciousness characterized by remoteness and so on. In short, 'thou art that' is different in import: 'thou' does not qualify 'that', nor 'that', 'thou'. For a clear and philosophically persuasive statement of the Dvaita position, see Dasgupta, *A History of Indian Philosophy*, vol. 4.

9. Neither sense perception nor any other means of knowledge dependent on sense perception can give rise to the knowledge of Brahman-Ātman identity. Such an identity can only be known through the Upaniṣads. Śaṁkara himself states that the self is different from objects of perception and cannot be proved by perception. Śaṁkara, *BSB* 2.3.1. Sense perception operates in the phenomenal realm in which the plurality of names and forms is manifested. Regarding supersensuous truths, *śruti*-s are the sole authority. Sarvajñātmuni makes the same point: "the criterion for an object to be cognized by other proofs is its possession of the qualities of colour, and so on As Brahman-Ātman is without qualities, it cannot be cognized by any proof other than the scripture." *SS*, introduction, 47.

Śaṁkara holds that even reason, independently of scriptures, cannot ascertain the nature of Brahman. His critique of *tarka* demonstrates that reasoning which may hold good in certain cases is inept with regard to ultimate questions on the nature of reality and release when it is not sanctioned by *śruti*. A mere inference may take different forms and may leave us in doubt about the nature of what *is*. It is not universal and constant like the perception of heat in fire. *Śruti*, being self-evident and eternally the same, cannot be challenged by reasoning. Śaṁkara, *BSB* 2.1.11.

In short, the purpose of scriptures is to give us knowledge that otherwise cannot be had. Reason, however, is accepted as an important tool that helps us understand and explain the phenomenal world of experiences. However, it cannot give us immediate knowledge of Brahman.

10. When Śaṁkara maintains that '*tat tvam asi*' asserts the identity between Brahman and the individual self, he is not talking of identity, meaning tautology, in either of the senses explained in the next note. "It does not involve the unnecessary repetition of the same idea in different words nor is it a tautology in virtue of its formal structure. What is asserted is that the underlying self of the individual is Brahman or ultimate reality. Each individual *qua* individual is locked into subject/object distinctions. Through an understanding of scriptures, and proper discipline, an

individual comes to realize that there is something changeless, permanent behind all that appears in the world, and that is Brahman. '*Tat tvam asi*' asserts that *Ātman* is Brahman. But it must not be expressed as x=x because what is meant by *Ātman* for the individual is different from what is meant by Brahman for the individual.

Thus, it is not surprising that Advaita maintains that identity statements are indeed highly significant. In the statement under consideration, 'art' is the 'is' of identity, not of predication. It does not designate an action enjoined, as there is no expected result. As the statement does not speak of any relation between the two, no further question is logically possible." Bina Gupta and William C. Wilcox, " '*Tat tvam asi*': An Important Identity Statement or a Mere Tautology?" *Philosophy East and West* 34, no. 1 (January 1984): 89–90.

11. I clarifiy the logical status of statements like 'thou art thou' elsewhere: "In one sense, an earlier sense, a tautology involves the unnecessary repetition of the same idea in different words; it is sometimes called a 'pleonasm'. In the more modern sense in which the word is used by most contemporary philosophers, a tautology is a sentence that is true solely by virtue of its formal structure. Some people reserve the word tautology simply for logical truths or, possibly, for the subset of logical truths of propositional logic. Others use the word in a broader sense, such that not only logical truth but analytic propositions, that is to say, propositions which are reducible to logical truths by the use of definition, would be considered tautologies. One must be very careful to understand the sense in which the word is being used. A tautology in the first sense given above, one which involves the unnecessary repetition of words, need not, as in our example, even be true, let alone necessarily true. 'He is writing his own autobiography' could very well be false because he is not writing an autobiography, not because the autobiography that he is 'is not writing' is not his. Or, perhaps, after years of writing autobiographies for other people he may finally get around to writing his own, in which case the repetition may be necessary and quite informative. The second sense of tautology also does not appear to be one under consideration here, since, '*tat tvam asi*' is not an instance of a structurally redundant sentence. It may be, however, that the sense of tautology which we have indicated above means the same thing as 'analytic'. 'Thou art thou' would be a tautology in the first sense, but 'thou art that' would be a tautology only if 'thou' and 'that' were interdefinable, or if the concept of one of these was contained in the other. This may very well be the case, but it is not obviously so, and the claim that the proposition in question is a tautology ought not to be accepted lightly." *Ibid.*, 85–86.

Thus, according to Advaita, the text 'thou art that' does not express a mere tautology. It is very similar to statements such as 'this is that Devadatta'. When I perceive Devadatta for the second time and report to my friend 'this is that Devadatta' I saw yesterday, I do not mean to suggest that the two places and the times are identical. When I saw Devadatta yesterday he was in a supermarket, and today I see him in a hospital. He was happy yesterday, and he is in pain today. The identity is the identity of 'person' devoid of all accidental qualifications. The same is true of 'thou art that' where the individual self as pure consciousness is said to be identical with Brahman, the pure consciousness.

12. *PP* adds that the three words in 'thou art that' are not futile. They are significant for the purpose of comprehending the identity of *viśva, taijasa*, and *prājña*, the individual aspects of Brahman with *virāt*, *Hiraṇyagarbha*, and God, the cosmic aspects of the self. *PP*, 80–81. Sadānanda explains it as follows: "The *jīva* or embodied soul has three kinds of limitations, namely that of ignorance, the subtle body, and the gross and the subtle body... The embodied soul identifying itself with each of these limitations is known as *Prājña* , *Taijasa* , and *Viśva* respectively.... Consciousness associated with this [this vast universe], from *Vaiśvānara* to *Īśvara* [*Vaiśvānara* ,

Hiranyagarbha, and *Īśvara*] is also one and the same.... Consciousness unassociated with any adjuncts (*Upādhis*) whatsoever, when not discriminated—like the red-hot iron ball—from the vast universe and the consciousness associated with it, becomes the direct thought of the (great) Vedic dictum, 'All this is Verily Brahman' (*Ch. UP*. 3.14.1), and when discriminated from them it becomes the implied meaning of that text." Sadānanda, *Vedāntasāra*, passages 113–20, 64–68.

13. *nahīndriyeti yogyavartamāneti*. *PP*, 81.

14. *attedantayor api na prakāratā bhāsamānavaiśiṣṭyapratiyogitvābhāvāt ity*. *Ibid*., 81.

15. The Naiyāyikas maintain that the intention of the speaker is called *tātparya*. *Bhāṣā-Parricheda*, verse 84, 170. To know the desire of the speaker is crucial to an understanding of the import of a sentence. Vedāntins, on the other hand, define *tātparya* "as the competency to generate that cognition" (*tatpratītijananayogyatvam tātparyam*), S. S. Suryanarayana Śāstrī, *VP*, chap. 4, verse 39. The sentence 'there is a pitcher in the house' has the capacity to produce a cognition of the relation between the pitcher and the house, and not of the relation between the the house and a piece of cloth. Hence 'that' in the definition signifies the relation between the pitcher and the house and not between, say, the cloth and the house.

Purport is the capacity of a sentence to convey a particular meaning. The same word can have different meanings in different contexts. When a sentence is spoken, if the word has more than one meaning, doubt may arise with reference to the purport, and only from the context can a person know the intention of the speaker: "A stock example is that of a father asking his beloved son to 'drink poison'. The word-senses can come together to make a sense, but that is not the sense of the statement, as no father would wish his son to act upon the statement and die. The context is one where the son desires to do something detrimental to himself, like making friends with an enemy or eating in his house; the father's counsel to drink poison is only intended to indicate the harmful nature of the course the son proposes to pursue; this is the purport of the father's words, not the actual consumption of poison, though the latter is what is conveyed by the word-senses in conjunction." S. S. Suryanarayan Śāstrī, *VP*, 180. It may be noted here that *VP* adds an additional qualification that the sentence must not be uttered with the desire to produce any other cognition than that which is actually desired. *Ibid*., verse 41, 81–82. In all identity texts the content is the capacity of a sentence to convey a particular meaning and not simply the word senses. If this is not accepted, then there would be the danger that the word senses might be construed as the sense of the sentence-generated cognition, and if that happens, unintended relations would become the content of such a cognition.

16. *PP*, 85.

17. See chap. 1, n. 30.

18. *brahmavid āpnoti param*. *TU* 2.1.1.

19. *satyaṃ jñānam anantam Brahman*. *Ibid*.

20. According to Śaṁkara, the statement 'thou art that' asserts the absolute identity between Brahman and *jīva*. The individual self, he holds, is nothing but pure consciousness conditioned by the *antaḥkaraṇa* because of *avidyā* or ignorance. If 'that' is taken to refer to pure consciousness (or Brahman) and 'thou' to refer to pure consciousness in association with the mind-body complex, then the two cannot be said to be identical. Śaṁkara says that 'thou' refers to pure consciousness apart from the mind-body complex whose substratum is pure consciousness, and 'that' refers to direct, immediate pure consciousness. Accordingly, the sentence under consideration expresses *samānādhikarnya*, that is, the relation between words having the same locus, because both of them are pure consciousness.

It is maintained that when the primary sense of the terms does not suit the context, the secondary or the implied sense (*lakṣyārtha*) should be accepted. According to one classification, the implied sense is of three kinds: *jahat* (exclusive), *ajahat* (non-exclusive), and *jahatajahat* (exclusive non-exclusive). In the first, primary meaning is entirely given up. In the second one the implied meaning also includes the primary meaning. In the third, the primary meanings are partly excluded and partly included. In the statement 'thou art that' part of the meaning is left out and part of it is retained. When the 'thou', the individual self, is said to be identical with Brahman, the self conditioned by ignorance—egoism—is not said to be identical. It is self, the pure consciousness, that is said to be identical. Similarly 'that' should be construed to refer to pure consciousness only and not to the other part of its meaning, which refers to 'omniscience', 'remoteness', and so forth. In short, both 'this' and 'that' refer to their substratum, Brahman. Sarvajñātman makes the Advaita position very clear when he states: "The exclusive-non-exclusive secondary signification is well-known in the case of the sentence 'This is that Devadatta', wherein the words discarding a part of their primary sense, namely, the place, and so on, convey the other part, namely, the person-in-himself." *SS*, 1.156, 224.

21. *akhaṇḍārthatvasyoktarūpatve pramāṇam āha—tad uktam iti. saṁsargā-saṅgīti.saṁsargāgocarā yā samyagdhīḥ tad dhvetutā taj janakatā, girām aparyāya-śabdānām, akhaṇḍārthatā ukteti yojanā. tatprātipadikārthateti*. *PP*, 91.

22. In this context, Śāstrī mentions the following views of the relation between the individual soul and God.

(1) *Prakaṭārtha* view: The reflection of pure consciousness in *māyā* is God. This *māyā* possesses innumerable parts. The reflection of consciousness in *ajñāna* or *avidyā* is the individual soul.

(2) *Tattvaviveka* view: *Māyā* and *avidyā* are responsible for the reflected images of the individual soul and God. *Prakṛti* is composed of three *guṇa-s*: when the *sattva guṇa* predominates; it is *māyā*; and when *sattva* is defiled, it is *avidyā*. Reflection in *māyā* is God, and that in *avidyā* is the individual soul.

(3) *SS* view: *Prakṛti* in its aspect of projection is *māyā*, and in its aspect of concealment, is *avidyā*. The consciousness reflected in *māyā* is God and, when reflected in *avidyā*, it is the individual soul.

(4) Vivaraṇa view: Following *smṛti* text that one and the same *ajñāna* is responsible for the distinction between God and the individual soul, Vivaraṇa holds that God is the prototype, the individual soul is the reflection.

(5) Vācaspati's view: The individual is not a reflection of ignorance but rather a limitation. Like a pitcher conditioned by the space, the individual soul is the consciousness conditioned by the mind, and the consciousness not conditioned by the mind is God.

(6) *SLS* view: Consciousness conditioned by the internal organ is the individual self, and the consciousness that is not so conditioned is God. Śāstrī, however, as he himself concedes, favors the view that consciousness conditioned by the mind is jīva and the consciousness conditioned by *avidyā*is *Īśvara* or God. He holds that a distinction between the two must be admitted to make intelligible Śaṁkara's statement: "that which has *māyā* as its limiting adjunct is the cause of the world defined by omniscience, and *śruti* statement, God has *māyā* as its limiting adjunct." He further adds that such an interpretation is necessary to make sense of the Upaniṣadic text, which states that *māyā* and *avidyā*, are responsible for the appearances of *Īśvara* and *jīva*, respectively. *PP*, 94–97.

23. Because all knowledge points to an object outside it—the object that is necessarily real and independent—the knowledge of negation also implies its existence apart from such knowledge. In other words, the absence of an object is different from

the knowledge of its absence. The Naiyāyikas maintain that negation (*abhāva*) is always of a real negation from a real locus. There is no such thing as pure or bare negation. Both presence and absence are objective facts. They accept four kinds of nonexistence or negation. Of these four, *prāgabhāva* is antecedent nonexistence or prior negation. Annaṁbhaṭṭa defines *prāgabhāva* as that "which is 'without any beginning' (*anādi*) but 'with an end' (*santa*) is 'prior absence' (*prāgabhāva*), [e. g., the absence] of an effect before its emergence." TSD, 374.

When one says, before the production of a pitcher, that there is no pitcher in the lump of clay, there is antecedent nonexistence or absence of the pitcher in the lump of clay. Such an absence is without any beginning but it has an end. It might be observed that an instance of antecedent negation is cited by *PP* as an argument against the objection that a beginningless entity cannot be removed. The Advaitins, however, do not recognize antecedent negation, or negation of any other kind for that matter, either as a category or even as a logically viable notion.

24. *Ajñāna* has been defined as "*sadasadbhyām anirvacanīyam triguṇātmakam jñānavirodhi bhāvarūpam yat kiñcit iti*." Sadānanda, *Vedāntasāra*, 21. *Ajñāna* is neither real nor unreal, and it cannot both be real and unreal, so it is indeterminate. It is a composite of three *guṇa*-s, *sattva*, *rajas*, and *tamas*. It does not possess these three *guṇa*-s as its attribute, but it itself is the three *guṇa*-s. It is destroyed by knowledge. *Ajñāna*, however, is not the negation of knowledge; it is *bhāvrūpa*; that is, it is a positive entity. The positivity of *ajñāna* should not be taken to mean that it is absolutely real, because it is destroyed by right knowledge. In short, although *ajñāna* is not positive like Brahman, it is not unreal like 'a hare's horn' either. It is the matrix of the manifold world of names and forms, and it is a fact of experience. Following Śaṁkara (*BSB* 1.4.3), *PP* uses *avidyā* or *ajñāna* and *māyā* interchangeably, although in theological discourse and debates a distinction is generally implied between *māyā* and *avidyā*.

25. Various arguments have been given to prove the positive nature of *ajñāna*. The distinction of Vivaraṇa lies in giving an inferential proof for demonstrating the viability of nescience as a category, as standing for something positive and beginningless: *vivādagocarāpannam pramāṇajñānam svaprāgabhāva vyatirikta svaviṣayāvaraṇa svanivartya svadeśagata vastvantara pūrvakam bhavitumarhati aprakāśita arthaprakāśakatvāt andhakāre prathamotpanna pradīpa prabhāvat iti*.

The argument, in a nutshell, states that a valid act of knowing is preceded by something else that is terminated by it. The reason adduced is that it is an instance of knowledge or knowing. All knowing manifests a thing that was not manifested earlier. A pitcher, previous to its being perceived, was unmanifest, was covered by a veil which perception rends or removes before manifesting it. The example given in which one may see the co-existence of the reason and what is sought to be demonstrated by that reason is that the initial rays of a lamp, when lit , remove the darkness in a room and cause the manifestation of the objects out of the shroud of darkness. *PPDV*, 1st *Varṇaka*, 84. *PP* points out how the inference rests its case on a reconstruction of the structure of perceptual experience entailing manifesting of what previously was unmanifest. See also section 6, of the introduction.

26. *PP*, 98.

27. *CU* 6.2.3.

6

The Nature of Error

6.42 *evam sākṣidvaividhyena pratyakṣajñānadvaividhyam. pratyakṣatvañ ca jñeyagataṃ jñaptigatañ ca nirūpitam. tatra jñaptigatapratyakṣatvasya sāmānyalakṣaṇaṃ cittvam eva; "parvato vahnimān" ityādāv api vahnyādyākāravṛttyupahitacaitanyasya svātmāṁśe svaprakāśatayā pratyakṣatvāt.*

tattadviṣayāṁśe pratyakṣatvan tu pūrvoktam eva. tasya ca bhrāntirūpapratyakṣe nātivyāpitḥ; bhramapramāsādhāraṇapratyakṣatvasāmānyanirvacanena tasyāpi lakṣyatvāt.

yadā tu pratyakṣapramāyā eva lakṣaṇaṃ vaktavyam, tadā pūrvoktalakṣaṇe 'bādhitatvaṃ viṣayaviśeṣaṇaṃ deyam. śuktirūpyādibhramasya saṁsārakālīnabādhaviṣayaprātibhāsikarajatādiviṣayakatvenoktalakṣaṇābhāvāt nātivyāptiḥ.

6.42 *Because of the two kinds of witness-consciousness, two kinds of perceptual cognition have been described. Perceptuality has been explained both as pertaining to the object cognized and to the cognition [itself]. Of these, the perceptuality pertaining to cognition, the general definition [of knowledge] is that it is consciousness only; for even in the examples; 'the mountain is fiery' and the like, there is perceptuality, because the consciousness qualified by the mental mode in the form of fire, and so on, is directly perceived; for it [consciousness] is self-revealing with respect to its own nature.*

Perceptuality of their respective contents, however, is as explained earlier.[1] *This definition does not go too far [in including] erroneous perception, for that [erroneous perception] too is included in the general definition of perception, common to both the valid and the erroneous cognition.*

When, however, the definition of perceptual knowledge-event alone is to be given, then in the definition given above, 'unsublatedness' must be added as a qualification of the object. Because erroneous cognitions, like shell-silver, have empirical silver, and so on, for their objects that are sublated during phenomenal existence, the above definition does not apply in those cases, and so there is no over-pervasion.

6.42 As stated previously, the author of *VP* offers the general definition of the perceptuality of cognition as consciousness itself and raises a doubt whether it goes too far in including the erroneous cognitions. He concedes that the definition offered is intended to be common to both valid and erroneous perceptual cognitions, because erroneous cognitions also fall under what is sought to be defined. However, to ensure that the criterion of valid perceptual knowledge does not include erroneous cognitions within its scope, Śāstrī (*PP*) states that when the criterion for valid perceptual knowledge is set forth, the qualification unsublatedness must be introduced to demarcate it from the erroneous cognitions.

6.42.1 In this context, he observes further, that one may argue that the stated stipulation regarding the illusory objects also might extend to the introspective knowledge of mental states, such as happiness and pain. The latter, like the illusory objects, are manifested by the witness-consciousness. *PP* accordingly amends the amendment to the definition of perceptual criterion given in *VP*. He maintains that the illusory objects must be qualified with the adjectival feature "that which is the content of sublating cognition during the time of phenomenal existence."[2] He adds further that an object that is the content of sublating cognition during the time of phenomenal existence must either be modal nescience or its effect. The knowledge of these illusory objects is excluded from the scope of the definition of valid perceptual knowledge given in the text of *VP*.

6.42.2 The brief but incisive account of the different theories of error that the author of *PP* interpolates serves as a useful backdrop for understanding the particular theory of erroneous cognition that the author of *VP* singles out to criticize in order to vindicate the Advaitin theory of erroneous cognition.[3]

6.42.3 The point of view that may be described as representing the radical right is the view that there is no such thing as an erroneous cognition.[4] Every knowledge is *ipso facto* valid. In the case of an erroneous cognition, such as 'this is silver', two cognitions different in nature are dovetailed: one in the form of this, which is perceptual; the other in the form of silver, which is a recollection. The difference between the two is not comprehended. The former cognition claims to be valid and such a claim is justified; the latter, however, does not make that claim.

6.42.3.1 Opponents maintain that failure to comprehend the

distinction between the two is inadequate to account for erroneous cognitions.[5] Error is not a simple absence of knowledge.[6] It is not merely failure to comprehend the distinction between the two, because if that were the case, errors would occur even in the dreamless sleep.

6.42.3.2 *PP* also subjects this view to an acute phenomenological analysis, drawing its material from such general Advaita literature as Bhāmatī. The main thrust of the author's objection is to ask whether actual experience testifies to the correctness of the theory, that equates error with the noncomprehension of difference. Actual experience, the author of *PP* observes, testifies that in an erroneous cognition we have two experiences and not one. Furthermore, if error was simply negative (i.e., noncomprehension of difference between the two), it would not bring about a positive practical reaction, such as withdrawing in fear, for example, in the snake-rope illusion, or proceeding to seize it in the case of the shell-silver illusion. Those who articulate erroneous cognition in terms of the lack of comprehension of the difference maintain that error consists in a failure to distinguish between the 'this' and 'silver'. This, however, is not the case. The experience neither shows that illusion is simply negative nondistinguishing, nor that in an illusory cognition we have two experiences rather than the one. Positive identification, as well as nonknowledge of difference, can account for a positive activity. Never, indeed, does there arise activity on the basis of the mere noncomprehension of difference. In fact, as the author of Bhāmatī states, both verbal usage and activity are premised upon the comprehension and not on the noncomprehension of difference.[7] If it is insisted, however, that there could be activity by the mere noncomprehension of difference, then at the time of the cognition of the pitcher, for example, if there is noncomprehension of the difference from the gem, then there would exist the possibility of activity with a desire to obtain gem. The silver in the shell-silver example is perceptual. It is not a simple case of recollection. Without the identity of the silver with the 'this' element before us, there would not be any activity toward it by merely recalling silver. Therefore, Mīmāṁasā view of error cannot be accepted.

6.42.4 The theory that does not deny the content-character of the erroneous cognition, but rejects its objectivity, its extramentality, is next taken up by the author of *PP*.[8] He maintains that the 'false' is not a mere nothing, but that it is a cognitive fact mistaken for an extra-mental reality. The knowledge of silver appears as if it exists outside. What is cognized is simply a subjective state of consciousness, but it is erroneously taken to be the cognition of an external object. External objects in reality do not exist.

The problem here again is how plausibly, on experiential grounds, can one maintain that the silver is of the nature of cognition. Is the identification of silver with cognition an instance of identification determined on the basis of the experience 'this is silver'? Or is it a case of identification on the basis of the sublating cognition 'this is not silver'? If the first alternative is accepted, then it will follow that the perceiver would know the silver in a far off place, and the silver would not be of the form of immediate knowledge. If the latter is accepted, the problem would be how to account for the genesis of knowledge in the form of silver. The point of view of the theory is that consciousness, and what is related to it in the form 'this is a pitcher', arise with the help of the auxiliary causes, namely, the sense organs, subsequent cognition, and the 'I' cognition. *PP* maintains that the explanation given in terms of these factors, however, does not render the account intelligible, because of the underlying thesis of momentariness.[9] Nor can the theory be vindicated on the hypothesis of earlier latent impressions that give rise to mental modes in the form of, for example, silver. Latent impressions cannot serve the role of subsequent cognition nor will they exist, according to the general theory of momentariness, at the moment when the effect exists. The explanation is thus inefficacious in accounting for the rise of knowledge-events, whether of the valid or the invalid sort.[10]

6.42.5 At the extreme left of the spectrum stands the theory that erroneous cognition is a cognition of 'what is not'.[11] In illusory cognition something nonexistent is apprehended. It is a cognition without any content. A snake is or may be, but a snake that is also a rope is a pure figment of imagination.

The Advaitin's critique of this position, as *PP* recalls it to us, is that an absolute nothing can never be manifested. Cognition without a content is not attested to by experience. The absolute nonexistent, like a hare's horn, is never manifested.

6.42.6 All knowledge is of the given and is of nothing but the given, but it need not be of the whole of what is given. This is the viewpoint of the theorists of error who seek to explain the distinction between truth and error as only a practical issue and never, from a theoretical point of view, as posing a problem. When the mirage and the shell-silver are described as false, what one must keep in mind is that the water and silver are not present there and also that they cannot be put to practical use.

6.42.6.1 Rāmānuja uses the doctrine of quintuplication to substantiate his theory.[12] The followers of this doctrine maintain that, metaphysically, everything is present everywhere. Some particles of silver, it is conceivable, are present in the shell. When the shell is mistaken for silver, silver, one may say, is there in a miniscular form. Furthermore, scriptures themselves maintain that the substance that possesses a part similar to that of another substance is considered to be similar to that substance. If a *somā* creeper is not available, then the scriptures prescribe the use of *pūtika* in its place, because the *pūtika* consists of the parts of the *somā*. Not all illusions, however, can be explained in this manner.[13] A person's perception of a white conch as yellow requires a different explanation. How do we account for the yellowness of the conch in such cases? Rāmānuja maintains that a person with a jaundiced eye, perceiving a white conch as yellow, actually transmits to the conch the yellowness of the bile through the rays of the eyes, and as a result the new color is imposed on the conch and its natural whiteness is obscured. This can be extrapolated to the concept that the objects in a dream are created by God to make the dreamer reap the fruits of his actions. Hence there is no subjective element in error; it is only partial knowledge.

6.42.6.2 *PP*'s critique of this theory of error does not appeal to an inspection of immediate experience, but rather calls into question the understanding of the principle of quintuplication of the element underlying the thesis that everything is everywhere. The constituent elements of the shell and the silver thus are never stated to be originally different and later on mixed up with one another. Although the subtle elements are mixed up with one another, it cannot be said that the gross elements or other evolutes are mixed up with one another. Even when admitting the existence of the formative elements of one object in another, that might account for one being mistaken as the other, one cannot maintain that one really exists in the other. It is true that the adoption of the *pūtika* is prescribed when the *somā* creeper is not available. This, however, by no means implies that *pūtika* possesses the part of the *somā* creeper. *Pūtika* as a substitute for *somā* is based upon the similarity between the two and not on identity. Similarity does not imply partial-identity. The experience of a conch as yellow, or of dream objects as facts of dream experience, are private to the person with a jaundiced eye and the dreamer.

6.43 *nanu visaṁvādipravṛttyā bhrāntijñānasiddhāv api, tasya prātibhāsikatatkālotpannarajatādiviṣayakatve na pramāṇam, deśāntarīyarajatasya klṛptasyaiva tadviṣayatvasaṁbhavāt.*

iti cen na; tasyāsannikṛṣṭatayā pratyakṣaviṣayatvāyogāt. na ca jñānaṃ tatra pratyāsattiḥ; jñānasya pratyāsattitve tata eva vahnyādeḥ pratyakṣatvāpattau, anumānādyucchedāpatteḥ.

6.43 *[Objection]: Although erroneous cognition may be established by one's unfruitful effort [of the person trying to possess such an object], yet there is no proof that it has for its content an illusory silver and the like, produced at that time, because it is possible even for the silver present in some other place to be taken as the content of that [cognition].*

If such is said [the answer is] "no," because that [silver] not being in sense-contact cannot be the content of perception. Nor is the cognition in that instance a sense-contact [extra-empirical], for if that were the case, that alone would make fire and the like the content of perception and thus would make inference, and so on [other means of valid knowledge], unnecessary.

6.43 *VP* introduces the theory of error which holds that the content appearing in error is a remote object that becomes identified with the object immediately present. The Naiyāyika theory is introduced apparently in rejection of the Advaitin thesis of the presence of illusory objects: "The silver present in some other place is the cause in prior experience of cognition with the form of silver, that is the content of that cognition." The author of *PP* sums up the essence of the argument in a manner that brings it close to the Advaita perspective and at the same time renders it vulnerable to criticism.[14] The label of the theory itself, as he points out, means the knowledge of the one thing in another, for example, shell as silver. Here the two objects are absolutely distinct and so there cannot be any identity between the two. Yet a superimposed identity is admitted between the them.

6.43.1 According to the Naiyāikas, each experience is complex and single. They maintain that in the erroneous cognition, say of shell as silver, we are not aware of two experiences but of a single complex experience of a perceived 'this' (shell) appearing to be silver. The silver character perceived in it inheres in silver 'elsewhere'; not in the 'this' that is presented to the eyes through the natural contact but in the silver that exists 'elsewhere' (e.g., in a jewelry shop). The silver character in the erroneous cognition is perceived through an extra-empirical contact.

6.43.2 The Advaitins, as *PP* points out, have good reasons to reject the above contention. The silver in the shop is not in contact with the eyes, and it is contact that serves as the cause of the origination of a perceptual cognition. That is why the opponent takes recourse in the notion of extra-empirical contact. Reinterpreting the observation made in *PP* in experiential terms, it may be said that an experience of erroneous cognition does not attest to the appearance of a remote silver. Experience only shows that 'this' appears as silver. The shell is perceived as 'this', and silver is known as identified with the 'this'. The sublating experience also only proves that the yonder object is not silver; it does not establish the remoteness of silver. Alhough cognition always refers to an object, the manifestation of silver in the erroneous cognition can be explained, in terms of greater fidelity to experience, by postulating an illusory silver existing in the very locus of 'this'. This is the contention of the Advaitins.

6.43.2.1 To state the same in terms of the terminology used in *VP*, the Advaitins maintain that consciousness conditioned by the object, and 'this consciousness' as conditioned by the 'this' element, is the substratum of silver. This explains the perceptuality of silver. The consciousness conditioned by the mode of *avidyā* (i.e., the knowledge of silver) is not a case of consciousness conditioned by the means of cognition as would be the case with the knowledge of actual silver. The Advaitin thesis of the witness-consciousness and its role has already been explained. According to it, an object is manifested by the witness-consciousness when it is associated with the mental mode assuming the form of the object. The important ingredient here, as pointed out by the author of *PP*, is the admission of a mode of *avidyā* that is entailed in the process. Only by such an admission would the definition of the perceptibility of an object hold good, because perceptibility is nothing but the superimposition of the object with the witness-consciousness that is associated with the mental mode assuming the form of the object.

6.43.2.2 The opponent explains his case by resorting to extra-empirical contact of the sense with the remote object. *VP* rejects such a contact, because its acceptance would make all inferential cognitions impossible. If the opponent's thesis of extra-empirical contact is viable, then, in the inferential cognition 'the mountain is fiery', the fire instead of being inferred should be extraordinarily perceived. Therefore, observes *PP*, the notion of extra-empirical contact is not tenable. In the case of the cognition 'the sandalwood is fragrant', insofar as the fragrance-element is concerned, the knowledge is inferential and not perceptual. All cases of inferential cognitions, in other words, would be cases of knowledge through extra-empirical contact. Furthermore, if the opponent is right in holding that the fragrant sandalwood is perceived with the help of extra-empirical contact, then by the same token the inference of fire in the hill should also be deemed not as an instance of inference but of extra-ordinary perception.

6.43.3 The Advaitin theory of erroneous cognition postulates the existence of illusory objects in the context of error. This is done to justify the appearance as well as the sublation of the error content. The nonreal is different from the real as well as the unreal. If it were real, it would not be sublated. Shell-silver, however, is sublated when one experiences 'this is not silver'. Therefore, shell-silver is not real. It cannot also be unreal, because shell-silver does not have an objective counterpart, and unreal objects, according to the Advaitin thesis, can never become objects of experience. For them, the indeterminability lies in being different from the real as well as from the absolute nothing. On the basis of presumption, from the very circumstances of manifestation and sublation, the concept of being different from the real and the absolute nothing is established. Shell-silver is neither real nor an absolute nothing, so it is termed *'anirvacanīya'*.[15]

6.44 *nanu rajatotpādakānāṃ rajatāvayavādīnām abhāve śuktau kathaṃ tavāpi rajatam utpadyate.*

iti ced ucyate. na hi lokasiddhasāmagrī prātibhāsikarajatotpādikā, kintu vilakṣaṇaiva. tathā hi, kācādidoṣadūṣitalocanasya purovartidravyasaṁyogāt, idamākārā cākacakyākārā ca kācid antaḥkaraṇavṛttir udeti. tasyāñ ca vṛttau idamaṁśāvacchinnaṃ caitanyaṃ pratibimbate. tatra pūrvoktarītyā vṛtter bahirnirgamanena idamaṁśāvacchinnacaitanyaṃ vṛttyavacchinnacaitanyam pramātṛcaitanyaṃ cābhinnaṃ bhavati. tataś ca pramātṛcaitanyābhinnaviṣayacaitanyaniṣṭhā śuktitvaprakārikāvidyā cākacikyādisādṛśyasandarśanasamudbodhitarajatasaṁskārasadhrīcīnā kācādidoṣa samavahitā rajatarūpārthākāreṇa rajatajñānābhāsākāreṇa ca pariṇamate.

6.44 *[Objection]: It is asked in the absence of silver particles, and so on, which produce the silver, how, even according to your system, is silver created in the shell?*

If such is said, it is replied that the causal apparatus established in ordinary experience does not produce the illusory silver but something quite distinct. It is as follows: To the one, whose eyes have the defect cataract or the like, when the [his] eyes come in contact with the object in front, there arises a mental mode in the form of 'this' and [another one] in the form of [its] glitter. And, in that mental mode, the consciousness conditioned by the 'this' [content] is reflected. That being the case, in the manner described earlier, because of the outgoing mental mode, the consciousness conditioned by 'this', the consciousness conditioned by the mental mode, and the consciousness associated with the cognizer become nondifferent. And then the nescience in the form of shell, which is present in consciousness conditioned by the content, that is nondifferent from the cognizer-consciousness, aided by the residual impression of silver, revived by the sign of similarity with respect to glitter, and so on [of the presented content to the silver already cognized], and that is associated with defects like cataract, undergoes transformation in the form of silver and into an illusory cognition of silver.

6.44 *PP* responds to the objection that arises with respect to the thesis that the illusory silver in an erroneous cognition is not real. The objection takes the following form: activity arises on the part of the one who desires silver by the knowledge 'this is silver'. This is based on the contention that such knowledge must have for its content real silver. Indeterminable silver cannot be adopted to the practical needs of life and so there cannot be any activity in the form of drawing near to the silver.

6.44.1 It might be said that in an indeterminable silver, silverness is assumed to be common to both the illusory silver and the actual silver. To account for activity toward the silver, what is needed is a mere perception of silverness as common to both. Even then, argues the opponent, in the absence of the material cause of silver, the origination of indeterminable silver is not possible. The indeterminable silver surely could not have come into existence in the absence of silver and the particles producing silver. That which is manifested as associated with a particular feature of the object may be held to be the material cause of that object. Silver is not manifested as associated with ignorance but appears as silver only. Therefore only the parts of silver are described as the material cause of the silver. In the shell-silver, however, because the parts of silver are not present, how can the cognition of the silver take place?

It is said in response that the indeterminable silver is neither absolute nothing nor actual silver that one finds in the shop. By the process of elimination, then, it must be admitted that it is a transformation of nescience that exists in the consciousness conditioned by the shell. The sublating cognition in the form 'this is not silver' removes nescience. This proves that when the material cause is destroyed, the effect is destroyed also. Therefore the requirement of the parts of silver is intelligible for the actual silver and not for the illusory silver. For the latter, there is the origination by mere nescience without its depending upon the parts of silver.

6.44.2 The illusory silver thus does not originate from silver particles in the way the latter produces actual silver. It is asked: Is the non-origination of silver attributed on the ground that there is the absence of causal aggregates well known in ordinary experience, or on the ground that there is no such aggregate at all? *PP* holds that the causal aggregate is well known in ordinary experience. When considering the illusory silver, although it appears to be caused, its appearance is more like a dream perception, in which one perceives, for example, a chariot. With this in view, the author says "no" (*nahīti*) for the first alternative and 'sometimes' (*kintviti*) for the second.

6.44.3 *PP* next anticipates a question from the *pūrvapakṣins*: Is nescience, the material cause of the illusory silver, originated or beginningless? It cannot be the former, because it will force one to admit another material cause, and so on *ad infinitum*. Nor can it be explained based of the maxim of the seed and the sprout, because in this the causal relation between the two is well known through perception. The causal relation between nescience and the silver, however, is not known at all, so an *infinite regress* is unavoidable. If, on the other hand, the second alternative is maintained—namely, that nescience is not originated—then an erroneous cognition, of which nescience is said to be the material cause, will always be there until there arises the knowledge of Brahman. In summary, neither of the two alternatives can be accepted.

6.44.3.1 In response, *PP* observes that the beginningless nescience is the material cause of silver. Regarding the transformation of nescience into the form of silver, a defect, such as film (*kāca*), constitutes the auxiliary cause.[16] It thus makes sense to say that erroneous cognitions are occasional. The material cause of objects such as ether is primal nescience and of silver is modal nescience, which accounts for the distinction between the two.

6.44.3.2 At this juncture, PP reminds us that we must not forget that, for the Advaitins, the consciousness conditioned by the object becomes identical with the witness-consciousness. Nescience, that has for its adjectival feature the specific nature of shell and is present in consciousness, undergoes modification in the form of silver and in the form of the knowledge of silver, that is nothing but a mode of nescience. The auxiliary cause, namely, latent impressions, which operates in conjunction with nescience, is revived because of the knowledge of similarity. With this in mind, our author states—*pramātṛ caitanya abhinnā*—that is, the consciousness conditioned by the content is non-different from the witness-consciousness.[17] The identity of witness-consciousness with the consciousness conditioned by the shell is for the purpose of construing the definition of the perceptibility of an object in the case of illusory objects.

6.45 *pariṇāmo nāma upādānasamasattākakāryāpattiḥ. vivarto nāma upādānaviṣamasattākakāryāpattiḥ. prātibhāsikaṃ rajataṃ cāvidyāpekṣayā pariṇāmaḥ, caitanyāpekṣayā vivartaḥ, iti cocyate. avidyāpariṇāmarūpañ ca tad rajatam avidyādhiṣṭhāna idamavacchinnacaitanye vartate. asmanmate sarvasyāpi kāryasya svopādānāvidyādhiṣṭhānāśritatvaniyamāt.*

6.45 *Transformation is the name for the production of an effect that has the same level of existence [reality] as its material cause. Transfiguration is the production of an effect that has an unequal existence [different level of reality] from its material cause. The illusory silver is transformation in the context of nescience, and transfiguration in the context of consciousness, so it has been said [according to our doctrine]. And this silver, which is a transformation of nescience, exists in the consciousness conditioned by the 'this' element, because according to our [Advaitin] doctrine, all effects necessarily reside in the substratum of nescience which is their [effects] material cause.*

6.45 Introducing the distinction that *VP* makes between the two notions that are necessary to understand the nature of the modification that consciousness *vis-à-vis* nescience undergoes (that is, transformation and transfiguration), *PP* points out that both major schools of Advaita locate the modal nescience in the cognizer-consciousness. To allow nescience conditioned by the shell to undergo transformation in the form of silver, it is said that the object-consciousness is identical with the cognizer-consciousness. But there is one important difference. The Vivaraṇa tradition, unlike that of Bhāmatī,[18] distinctly holds that consciousness acting as the substratum of nescience is the transfigurative material cause of the object. To allow consciousness conditioned by the shell to become the transfigurative material cause, the modal nescience present in the cognizer-consciousness has been explained as being located in the object-consciousness. *PP* favors the Vivaraṇa view. It maintains that nescience is the direct material cause of the superimposition of silver. This means that it is present in the consciousness conditioned by the shell, that, in turn, implies that silver is transformation in relation to nescience but transfiguration in relation to consciousness.

6.45.1 Explaining the above distinction, *PP* further observes that nescience is the transformative material cause of objects such as pitchers, and the consciousness that is associated with the pitcher is the transfigurative material cause. Similar considerations also apply to the snake-rope illusion and the rope-conditioned consciousness. It must be remembered that the nescience, which is the transfigurative material cause of the snake is only modal nescience and not primal nescience. *PP* states this in rejection of the statement made in *AB* to the effect that transformation and transfiguration involve a reference to two levels of reality, absolute and nonabsolute.[19] The view of *AB* is propounded as applying alike to shell-silver as well as to its cause, namely, nescience. It is based on the view that erroneous cognitions, like shell-silver, are the manifestations of primal nescience.

6.45.2 *PP*'s thesis of silver as the transformation of nescience is very instructive. Nescience is the material cause of actual objects, like pitchers, and also of illusory objects, such as silver. Opponents raise an objection here. According to the Advaitins, for objects such as pitchers, there is the requirement of the parts of the pitcher. Similarly, if silver is the effect of nescience, it too will have to satisfy the same requirement. So how could the silver, although illusory, arise without the parts of silver?

PP says that it is true that there is the requirement of the parts, namely, the pitcher sherds, in case of objects such as a pitchers. They serve as the limiting condition of the consciousness, because the pitcher is superimposed upon the consciousness conditioned by the pitcher-sherds. Silver, however, is not superimposed upon the consciousness conditioned by its parts but rather on the consciousness conditioned by the 'this' element. Therefore, there is no requirement for the parts of the silver. The *VP* text *svopādana avidyā adhiṣṭhāna āśritatvaniyamād iti*, *PP* explains, signifies that illusory cognition is a cognition that has for its content something that possesses a reality different from the reality of its substratum.[20]

6.46 *nanu caitanyaniṣṭharajatasya katham idaṃ rajatam iti*

purovartinā tādātmyam?

ucyate, yathā nyāyamate ātmaniṣṭhasya sukhādeḥ śarīraniṣṭhatvenopalambhaḥ, śarīrasya sukhādyadhikaraṇatāvacchedakatvāt, tathā caitanyamātrasya rajataṃ pratyanadhiṣṭhānatayā idamavacchinnacaitanyasya tadadhiṣṭhānatvenedamo 'vacchedakatayā, rajatasya purovartisaṁsargapratyaya upapadyate.

tasya ca viṣayacaitanyasya tadantaḥkaraṇopahitacaitanyābhinnatayā viṣayacaitanyādhyastam api rajataṃ sākṣiṇy adhyastaṃ kevalasākṣivedyam, sukhādivad ananyavedyam iti cocyate.

6.46 *[Objection]: How can there be identity of the silver, that has consciousness as its substratum, with the object present, in the form "'his is silver'?*

It is said in response that just as in the Nyāya system, happiness and the like, located in the self, are experienced as present in the body, because the body delimits [its] being the locus of pleasure, and so on; in the same way, pure consciousness in itself is not the locus of silver, it is only the consciousness conditioned by the 'this' element, [that serves as the locus of the silver]; for 'this' being the determining characteristic [being the substratum of the illusory characteristic], the cognition of the relation of silver with the presented content is intelligible.

And because that consciousness conditioned by the object is nondifferent from the consciousness that has the internal organ as its limiting adjunct, the silver, although superimposed on the consciousness conditioned by the object, is spoken of as being superimposed on the witness-consciousness and being cognizable by the witness-consciousness alone, and like happiness, and so on, not being cognizable by another person.

6.46 The thesis of an indeterminable silver as the content of an erroneous cognition allows for the contingency of cognizing that silver has arisen and has ceased to be. The cognition of origination and decease of illusory silver conflicts with the sublating cognition that there is the absence of silver in all three divisions of time. In addition, it is asked: Is the origination or destruction assumed at the time of the erroneous cognition or at the time of sublation? It cannot be the former, because the cognition of identity with the 'this' element that arose earlier and did not cease will serve as the counteracting factor. The latter is not the case either, because the knowledge of absolute negation, like the knowledge of counter-correlate, is the counteracting factor in the comprehension of origination as well as the destruction of silver.

6.46.1 *PP* further elucidates this point, and in so doing reformulates the text of *VP*. The silver that is superimposed upon the consciousness is conditioned by the 'this' element. The superimposed identity, however, does not imply that a real identity exists between the two. Speaking from the vantage point of experience, however, we must admit an identity between the 'this' element and silver, because the 'this' element is intelligible even on the basis of the identity between the consciousness conditioned by the 'this' and silver. One cannot argue that because the 'this' element is the limiting condition of the consciousness, the silver that is located in the consciousness also should be located in the 'this' element and must not be treated as superimposed thereon. In other words, it is not necessary to hold that an object that exists in the conditioned consciousness also must exist in the limiting condition.[21]

6.46.2 *PP* draws the attention of the reader to the distinction made in earlier Advaitin treatises between two similar and yet distinguishable notions of substratum *(adhiṣṭhāna)* and support (*ādhāra*).[22] If we admit that silver is the effect of primal nescience, then it is only pure consciousness that can be said to be its substratum, but the consciousness conditioned by the 'this' element, however, is its support. The commentary on *Siddhāntbindu* also supports such a view.[23] It makes a distinction between the consciousness conditioned by the nescience and the consciousness conditioned by the mind. Between these two, it is the consciousness conditioned by the mind that is said to be the *ādhāra*, and Brahman, pure consciousness, is the *adhiṣṭhāna*. Thus, according to the view that silver is the effect of primal nescience, because the consciousness conditioned by the 'this' element is the support as well as the limiting condition of consciousness of silver, an identity manifests between the 'this' element and the silver. The *VP* text *saṁsargapratyaya* signifies such a cognition of identity.

6.46.3 With respect to the erroneous perceptual cognition 'this is silver', it might be asked whether the cognition is introspective or external. Because silver is not an internal state of mind like happiness, its cognition cannot be introspective. Similarly, because the silver is only illusory, it cannot be a species of external cognition either. Before the cognition of silver, it surely did not exist. Therefore, there could not be any sense-contact with it, nor a mental mode assuming its form. This explanation also rejects the view that silver is known by the witness-consciousness, because without its relation through the avenue of the mental mode, one cannot maintain that an object is manifested by the witness-consciousness. It may, however, be manifested by *Īśvarasākṣin* who transcends nescience, through a mode of nescience in the form of silver but it cannot be manifested by the *jīvasākṣin* either.

To reject the above contention, the author states, *tasya ceti*. The consciousness conditioned by the content is nondifferent from the consciousness qualified by the internal organ. Silver, although superimposed on the consciousness conditioned by the content, is spoken of as being superimposed on the witness-consciousness. It is cognizable only by the witness-consciousness and, like happiness and the like, cannot be cognized by another person.

6.47 *nanu sākṣiṇiy adhyastatve 'ahaṃ rajatam' iti pratyayaḥ syāt, "ahaṃ sukhī" itivat.*

iti ced ucyate; na hi sukhādīnām antaḥkaraṇāvacchinnacaitanyaniṣṭhāvidyākāryatvaprayuktam "ahaṃ sukhī" iti jñānam; sukhādīnām ghaṭādivac chuddhacaitanya evādhyāsāt. kintu yasya yadākārānubhavāhitasaṁskārasahakṛtāvidyākāryatvaṃ tasya tadākārānubhavaviṣayatvam ity evānugataṃ niyāmakam.

tathā ca idamākārānubhavāhitasaṁskārasahakṛtāvidyākāryatvāt, ghaṭāder idamākārānubhavaviṣayatvam; ahamākārānubhavāhitasaṁskārasahitāvidyākāryatvād antaḥkaraṇādeṛ ahamanubhavaviṣayatvam; śarīrendriyāder ubhayavidhānubhavāhitasaṁskārasahitāvidyākāryatvād ubhayavidhānubhavaviṣayatvam. tathā ca ubhayavidho 'nubhavaḥ, "idam śarīram,""ayaṃ dehaḥ," "ahaṃ manuṣyaḥ," "ahaṃ brāhmaṇaḥ," "idaṃ cakṣuh," "ahaṃ kāṇaḥ," "idaṃ śrotram," "ahaṃ badhiraḥ" iti.

prakṛte ca prātibhāsikarajatasya pramātṛcaitanyābhinnedamavacchinnacaitanyaniṣṭhāvidyākāryatve 'pi "idaṃ rajatam" iti satyasthalīyedamākārānubhavāhitasaṁskārajanyatvāt idamākārānubhava viṣayatā, na tu "ahaṃ rajatam" iti ahamākārānubhavaviṣayateti anusandheyam.

6.47 *[Objection]: Now, if there is superimposition on the witness-consciousness, then the cognition would be of the form 'I am silver' like 'I am happy'.*[24]

It is said in reply that the cognition 'I am happy' is not determined [produced] by happiness, and the like, which, being the product of nescience, has as its substratum the consciousness conditioned by the internal organ, because happiness, and so on, like a pitcher, are superimposed on pure consciousness itself. But the universal rule is that something is the content of experience in a particular form when it is produced by nescience associated with the residual latent impressions generated by an experience of that particular form.

So a pitcher and the like are the contents of an experience in the form of 'this', because they are the effects of nescience associated with the latent impressions generated by an experience in the form of 'this'. The internal organ (the mind and the buddhi) are the contents of an experience in the form of 'I', because they are the effects of nescience associated with the latent impression generated by an experience in the form of 'I'. The body, the sense organs, and the like are the effects of an experience in the form of both 'this' and 'I', because they are the products of nescience associated with the latent impressions of an experience in both the forms. Accordingly, there are two types of experiences: This is a body'- I am the body', 'I am a man'-'I am a Brāhmaṇa', and 'this is the eye'-'I am one-eyed', 'this is an ear'-'I am deaf'.

In the example under consideration, it should be borne in mind that although the illusory silver is the product of nescience located in the consciousness conditioned by 'this', which is not different from the consciousness conditioned by the cognizer, it serves as a content [an object] with respect to the experience assuming the form 'this', but not with respect to the experience assuming the form of 'I', as in 'I am silver', because it is generated by latent impression assuming the form 'this' in a true [experience] 'this is silver'.

6.47 *PP* makes use of the distinction made earlier between the substratum and the support to further elucidate the distinction between an erroneous perceptual cognition like 'this is silver' and an introspective cognition like 'I am happy'. In an erroneous cognition like 'this is silver', the 'this' element is also manifested with the silver. The question that is asked in this context is whether the 'this' element may be considered as the delimiting condition of consciousness, that serves as the substratum of the superimposition of silver. Or is it the delimiting condition of the consciousness that serves as the support of the superimposition of silver? If silver is superimposed upon the witness-consciousness, then there will be the manifestation of the identity of mind in the form of 'I' with the silver, to the effect 'I am the silver'.

6.47.1 *PP* maintains that the illustrative example 'I am happy' exemplifies cognitions of the form 'I am the silver'. In the cognition 'I am happy' there is the state of being the content of the cognition 'I', and that state of being exists in happiness through the relation of identity. The same is the case here. Happiness is an attribute of the mind, and between the substance and an attribute there is identity. Silver, on the other hand, is not an attribute of the mind. If one wants to express the experience of identity between the two, one could do so only by using a word that expresses the sense of possession, as in the example 'the pitcher possesses color'.

6.47.2 Rejecting the position maintained by *AB*,[25] that because there is no cognition of silver with regard to the witness-consciousness, silver is only superimposed upon the consciousness conditioned by the 'this' element and not upon the witness-consciousness, *PP* reiterates the position that he has consistently held in this regard—the definition of the perceptuality of silver will not unduly be applicable to the instance of silver unless there is a superimposition of identity with the silver. The silver is superimposed upon the witness-consciousness, although there is absence of the cognition of silver in the form 'I am silver'. This is based upon the contention that silver is not the effect of nescience associated with the auxiliary factor of latent impressions borne out of earlier experience of identity with the witness-consciousness. The main contention of *PP* is that there cannot be manifestation of an object, illusory or otherwise, without relation to the witness-consciousness. Thus it is significant to assert that the silver that is superimposed upon the consciousness conditioned by the object is also superimposed upon the witness-consciousness.

6.47.3 This explanation, *PP* maintains, is based on *Siddhantābindu̥ṭīka* (*SBT*),[26] that clearly explains what is involved in the erroneous cognition of the form 'this is silver'. It maintains that silver is an effect of primal nescience, and so the identity of the 'this' element with the silver is not caused by 'this' element being the substratum of the superimposition of silver, because silver, like a pitcher, is superimposed upon pure consciousness. However, pitcher sherds, being the limiting condition of the consciousness which is the substratum of the pitcher, are identical with the pitcher. Similarly, the identity of silver with the 'this' element is based upon the 'this' element being the limiting condition of the consciousness that serves as the substratum of the superimposition of silver. Thus silver is superimposed upon the witness-consciousness because there is identity between the witness consciousness and the consciousness conditioned by the silver. Unlike the mental states of happiness and pain, which are superimposed upon the consciousness conditioned by the mind, silver is not superimposed upon the consciousness conditioned by the mind. Thus there is no possibility of a cognition in the form 'I am the silver'. This also explains the absence of a cognition of the form 'I am a pitcher'.

6.47.4 In this context *PP* discusses another point of great significance, drawing, as he does elsewhere, from the text *Siddhāntabindu.* He raises the question: When an object is superimposed upon the consciousness conditioned by the object, and it is also superimposed upon the witness-consciousness, why is it held that it is only the former and not the latter that is said to be the substratum of the object? The response is that in every erroneous cognition it is only the nescience, aided by the latent impressions arising from the experience of a particular form, that is considered to be the cause. There is the superimposition of an effect upon the consciousness conditioned by that effect, arising from nescience and aided by the latent impressions produced by a particular form of experience. It cannot be argued that because 'A' is the limiting condition of the consciousness that is the superimposition of the substratum of 'X', 'A' will have to be the object of experience in the form of 'X'. In the case of the consciousness associated with the mind, the body as such is not superimposed, but it is superimposed through the superimposition of its qualities such as 'stoutness', 'leanness', and so on. Therefore, there is no cognition in the form 'I am the body'. Thus, although silver is superimposed upon the witness-consciousness, there is no cognition of the form 'I am the silver', because there is no superimposition of silver upon the consciousness conditioned by the mind. And there is the superimposition of mental states such as happiness and pain on the witness-consciousness that transcend the mind. The effect of primal nescience is superimposed only on pure consciousness, because only such a consciousness is the content of primal nescience. The consciousness conditioned by the mind is not the content of primal nescience.

6.47.5 The question is raised why the cognition 'I am happy' is not caused by happiness being the effect of ignorance, that resides in the consciousness conditioned by the mind. In this cognition, happiness is superimposed upon pure consciousness, the locus of primal nescience. At the time of cognition of happiness, the consciousness conditioned by happiness becomes identical with the witness-consciousness. Having this future identity in mind, the consciousness conditioned by happiness itself is spoken of as the witness-consciousness. This may be contrasted with the case of an erroneous cognition, in which what is essential is that it must arise from latent impressions. This is the significance of the term '*smṛtirūpah*' in the definition of *adhyāsa.*[27]

6.47.6 In the case of the erroneous cognition 'this is silver', because the effect of nescience in association with latent impressions is not there, there is no experience in the form 'I am silver'. Consequently, when the objects are superimposed upon pure consciousness, there is an experience in the form 'this'. Only in the case of the superimposition of the mind upon the self is there the experience in the form of 'I'. The body is superimposed directly upon pure consciousness and not on the mind. The superimposition of the body upon the consciousness here refers only to the attribute of the body. The sense organ, on the other hand, is superimposed upon pure consciousness, not because of its attributes but because of the consciousness conditioned by the mind.

There is the experience 'this is silver' and not 'I am silver', even though indeterminate silver is superimposed upon the individual self, because the consciousness conditioned by the 'this' element is the support of silver. Because we previously had the experience 'this is silver' and not 'I am silver', the erroneous cognition invariably takes the form of the experience 'there is silver' and not 'I am silver'.

6.48 *nanv evam api mithyārajatasya sākṣāt sākṣisambandhitayā bhānasambhave rajatagocarajñānābhāsarūpāvidyāvṛtter abhyupagamaḥ kimarthaḥ?*

iti ced ucyate; svagocaravṛttyupahitacaitanyabhinnasattākatvābhāvasya viṣayāparokṣatvarūpatayā rajatasya aparokṣatvasiddhaye tad-abhyupagamāt.

6.48 *[Objection]: Now, even then, because the false silver can be perceived as being directly related do we the witness-consciousness alone, why to recognize a mental mode of nescience which is of the nature of an apparent cognition having silver as its content?*[28]

It is said in response that it is assumed to establish the immediacy of silver, because the immediacy of a content consists in its not having a level of existence [reality] different from that of the consciousness conditioned by the mental mode which is its own (sva) content.

6.48 As stated earlier, in the case of the erroneous cognition 'this is silver', there is a mental mode in the form of 'this', and there is a mode of nescience in the form of silver. The objection that *VP* anticipates in this context is very pertinent. Because the witness-consciousness manifests both the valid and the erroneous cognitions, the illusory silver must also be in contact with the witness-consciousness. Therefore the witness-consciousness itself may be admitted to be the manifesting factor of consciousness, and there is no necessity to admit a mode of nescience in the form of silver. Because objects, such as pitchers, are not related directly to the witness-consciousness without a mental mode, there is the need of admitting a mental mode assuming the form of the pitcher. In the case of an erroneous cognition, however, the concealment by nescience that gives rise to the notion that the object does not exist itself is not existent.

VP explains the need for admitting the operation of the mode of nescience, which assumes the form of silver in the passage under consideration: "It is admitted for the sake of establishing the immediacy of silver. And the immediacy of silver consists in not having a level of reality different from the consciousness qualified" peripherally by the mode whose object is the silver itself.

P P's elucidation greatly reduces the opacity of the text. The criterion of the perceptuality of consciousness consists in its immediacy, that is, in the object not having any independent reality apart from the cognizer-consciousness, that is associated with the mental mode assuming the form of the object. Consciousness conditioned by the mind, consciousness conditioned by the 'this' element, and the consciousness conditioned by the mental mode assuming the form of 'this' all three located in one and the same place, are said to be identical. Similarly, silver, the conditioning factor of the 'this' element, and the consciousness conditioned by the mode of nescience in the form of silver, also are said to be identical with the three mentioned above. This explains the earlier claim that what is superimposed upon the cognizer-consciousness is manifested by the witness-consciousness. The important point to note about the observation made by *PP* (contrary to the observation of *AB*) is that by the term 'consciousness' as used in *VP* is meant the consciousness that transcends nescience, whereas the term 'cognizer' refers only to the witness-consciousness.

6.49 *nanv idaṁvṛtte rajatākāravṛtteś ca pratyekam ekaikaviṣayatve gurumatavadviśiṣṭajñānānabhyupagame kuto bhramajñānasiddhiḥ?*

iti cen na; vṛttidvayapratibimbitacaitanyasyaikasya satyamithyāvastutādātmyāvagāhitvena bhramatvasvīkārāt. ata eva sākṣijñānasya satyāsatyaviṣayatayā prāmāṇyāniyamād aprāmāṇyoktiḥ sāmpradāyikānām.

6.49 *[Objection]: Now, if a mental mode in the form of 'this' and a mental mode in the form of 'silver', each have a separate content, and because, in the opinion of the Gūrū [Prābhākara] a cognition implying a relation [between the two mental modes] is not allowed, how can one account for (establish or prove) erroneous cognition?*

If such is said, [the reply is] "no." Erroneous cognition must be admitted, because the consciousness, although one, is reflected in both mental modes and comprehends the identity between the real and the false objects. Therefore, because the cognition of the witness-consciousness has for its object both an existent and nonexistent [real and a nonreal] content, and thus lacks invariable validity [valid with respect to 'this' and not valid with respect to silver], the followers of the tradition declare it to be without authority.

6.49 *VP* draws a pointed distinction between the Advaita analysis of 'this is silver' and that of the theorists, alluded to earlier, who analyze such an experience as entailing two cognitions with distinct contents, each valid in itself. Explaining this point, *PP* observes that the Advaitins admit two modes: a mental mode in the form of 'this', and a mode of nescience in the form of silver. The opponent here quickly points out that one and the same cognition cannot have two different objects, 'this' and silver. If two different objects are admitted, his theory would become indistinguishable from that of the 'no-error' theorists mentioned earlier.[29] According to the latter, in the erroneous cognition 'this is silver', there is the perceptual experience of 'this' and recollection in the form of silver. Error, if it may be called error at all, is the nonapprehension of the distinction between the two.

6.49.1 The reply here is significant. It is true that the Advaitins admit two modes: one of mind having 'this' as its content and another of nescience having silver as its content. But there is no difference in the cognitions, because there is a mutual superimposition between the two. Furthermore, the consciousness manifested by the two is one only, because the mode of nescience in the form of silver arises only as conditioned by the mental mode assuming the form 'this'. Erroneous cognition lies in the consciousness reflected in these two modes—consciousness comprehends the identity of the real object with the erroneous one. Furthermore, we must remember that, according to the Advaitins, *vṛtti* is not knowledge, it is insentient. It is only the consciousness conditioned by the *vṛtti* element that has been spoken of as knowledge.

6.49.2 Validity with respect to cognition through manifestation of the witness-consciousness does not imply that there also is validity. Validity with respect to the witness-consciousness could be achieved when the identity is not sublated later on. In the instance of 'this is silver', because there is sublation as 'this is not silver', there can be no validity regarding silver. That is why the cognition of the witness-consciousness is held to be lacking in authority in the tradition of Advaita. *PP* draws from Śaṁkara 's commentary here, in which it is clearly stated that the usages 'I' and 'this is mine' are a blend of the real and not real.[30] The Advaitins, says *PP*, accordingly maintain that Brahman alone is real as knowledge and all other cognitions are not real.

6.50 *nanu siddhānte deśāntarīyarajatam apy avidyākāryam adhyastaṃ ceti kathaṃ śuktirūpyasya tato vailakṣaṇyam?*

iti cen na. tvanmate satyatvāviśeṣe 'pi keṣāñcit kṣaṇikatvaṃ keṣāñcit sthāyitvam ity atra yad eva niyāmakaṃ tad eva svabhāvaviśeṣādikaṃ mamāpi. yad vā ghaṭādyadhyāse avidyaiva doṣatvena hetuḥ; śuktirūpyādhyāse tu kācādayo 'pi doṣaḥ. tathā ca āgantukadoṣajanyatvaṃ prātibhāsikatve prayojakam. ata eva svapnopalabdharathādīnam āgantukanidrādoṣajanyatvāt prātibhāsikatvam.

6.50 *[Objection]: Because according to your [Vedānta] conclusive view the silver present elsewhere is also a product of nescience and is superimposed, how does it differ from the shell-silver?*

It is said in response, "no." In your system although everything possesses equal existence [i.e., the different levels of reality are not admitted], some objects are momentary and others are permanent; that itself, that is, one's unique nature being the rule, works for us as well. Or else, in the superimposition of a pitcher, and so on, nescience, as the sole defect, alone is the cause, whereas in the superimposition of silver on the shell, there are additional defects like the cataract and the like in the eye. So the determinant of something being illusory is its being generated by an adventitious defect. Therefore chariots and similar objects cognized in a dream are illusory, because they are generated by an adventitious defect, sleep.

6.50 Now the question arises: If both the pitcher and the shell-silver are modifications of nescience, what then is the distinction between the two? *PP* argues that the actual pitcher is the effect of primal nescience, while the illusory object, for example, silver, is the effect of modal nescience. This explanation, however, will not be accepted by those who maintain that illusory objects are the effects of primal nescience. Therefore, *PP* explains that the shell-silver is superimposed upon the consciousness conditioned by the 'this' element, and the actual silver is superimposed upon pure consciousness. This explains the difference between the two. Such an explanation is also in keeping with the view that shell-silver is an effect of modal nescience. The text '*kathaṁ*' means 'objection', and when *VP* asks how could there be difference, he is suggesting that there could be no difference.

The author of *VP* proposes another way of distinguishing between the actual silver and the illusory silver. The superimposition of the actual silver is caused by nescience, whereas superimposition of the illusory silver is caused by nescience as well as a defect in the sense organ. In other words, the actual objects (empirically real objects) arise only from nescience, but the illusory objects have some other factors as the cause in addition to nescience.

Notes

1. In the inferential cognition 'the mountain is fiery', both the mountain and the smoke are perceptual, whereas the fire is not; it is being inferred. So if perceptuality is articulated only in the context of content, then fire would be excluded from its scope. On the other hand, if perceptuality is articulated in the context of cognition, then if all knowledge in itself is perceptual according to Vedānta, the cognition of fire would be included in its purview. This, in short, is the distinction between the perceptuality of cognition with regard to itself and its contents.
2. *ataḥ saṁsārakālīnabādhaviṣayeti prātibhāsikaviśeṣaṇam*. *PP*, 101.
3. Although most of us experience illusion at some time in our lives, it is difficult to say with certainty why it happens. It occurs without any effort on the part of the individual experiencing it. When we perceive a shell as silver, we say that we have perceived wrongly and reject our perception as false. The questions immediately arise: In what does the falsity of a false perception consist? What is the referent of the falsehood or falsity? Does it refer to the apprehension, or the content that is apprehended in the erroneous cognition? It is safe to say that falsity in an erroneous cognition focuses more on the nature of the content apprehended than on the apprehension itself. True, the previous apprehension also is called into question in the rectification that follows. But it is called into question only as a consequence of a rejection of content. All discussions in the context of erroneous perception turn out to be discussions about the nature and status of content misperceived. In other words, different theories of erroneous perception are debates about the nature and status of content rather than the fact of subjective apprehension.

Generally, five different theories about erroneous apprehension have been recognized in Indian philosophy: the Prābhākara theory of *akhyāti* (nonapprehension), the Yogācāra theory of *ātmakhyāti* (apprehension of the subjective), the Mādhyamika theory of *asatkhyāti* (apprehension of the nonexistent), the Nyāya theory of *anyathākhyāti* (misapprehension), and the Advaita theory of *anirvacanīyakhyāti* (apprehension of the ideterminate). Of these five theories, *VP* singles out the Nyāya theory. *PP*, however, in its discussion, also includes the remaining four theories.

There is a vast and growing literature of secondary works on the subject in the recent writings of Indian philosophy. For example, see Bijaynanda Kar, *The Theories of Error in Indian Philosophy* (India: Ajanta Publications, 1978).

4. This radical view is held by Prābhākara, who interprets the *Mīmāṁsā-Sūtras* in an extreme way, thus parting company with the more moderate interpretation of it by Kumārila. The relevant section of the Śabara's *Mīmāṁsā-Sūtras* is the passage in 1.1.4: ""That Cognition is real Perception which appears when there is contact of the Sense organs with the object perceived'; that is to say, when the Sense organ are in contact with the Object actually perceived, the resultant Cognition of the man is real Perception—and it is not real Perception when the Object perceived is different from that with which the Sense organ is in contact. (Therefore, in a case where the Shell is cognised as Silver, what is cognised is the Silver, while what is in contact with the sense organ is the Shell; hence this is not a case of real Perception at all). "*Pūrva Mīmāṁsā*, trans. Ganganath Jha, Library of Indian Philosophy and Religion Series, no. 1 (Banaras: Banaras Hindu University, 1964), 80.

Thus a wrong cognition is a cognition of a thing as something which it is not. In the erroneous cognition of silver, one does not perceive the silver, one simply remembers it. The perception of 'this' is characterized by features that are common to both the silver and the shell. So error may be described as an erroneous or incomplete cognition. Error, therefore, is nonapprehension and not misapprehension.

5. The notion of nondiscrimination or noncognition of distinction between remembrance and perception is logically opaque. For what is distinction other than the nature of distinct objects? The proposition that a piece of cloth is distinct from a pitcher signifies that the negation of each obtains in the locus of the other. Distinction is reciprocal negation (*anonyābhava*). Therefore, along with the manifestation of the cognition and their objects, distinction also becomes manifest, the distinction being nothing more than the correlates themselves. It is incoherent to argue that although the distincts are perceived the distinction itself is not perceived. The Prābhākara thesis is that in the case of the erroneous perceiving of shell as 'this is silver', perception and recollection, respectively, of 'this' and 'silver' are not known to be different. This is inconsistent with his own admission that a distinction between one unit of knowledge and another is but of the nature of knowledge itself, and that knowledge is self-revealing. With respect to cognitions and their contents, differences are necessarily cognized along with the revelation of the nature of cognitions as well as the contents. In short, Prābhākara cannot explain the precise nature of nondiscrimination. Additionally, we must remember that nondiscrimination is not a necessary condition for the occurrence of an erroneous cognition.

For a more comprehensive account of the logical, epistemological, and linguistic account of the problems connected with the notion of 'nonapprehension of difference', (*bhedāgraha*) see A. K. Ray Chaudhuri, *The Doctrine of Māyā* (Calcutta: Dasgupta and Co. Ltd., 1950) 16–24. Also see P. K. Sundaram, *Advaita Epistemology*, 314.

6. *grahaṇanibandhanau hi tasya vyavahāravyapadeśau katham agrahaṇamātrāt bhavetām iti. PP*, 102.

7. Padmapāda's critique of the Prābhākara theory of error focuses on the technical label by which the theory is known, namely *akhyāti* (*a-khyāti*), which means 'no-knowledge'. *PPD*, 1st *Varṇaka*,11.26. The translator of *PPD* distinguishes the various meanings of the negative particle in the term *akhyāti*. In Sanskrit, the negative prefix has several meanings: negation, otherness, opposition. The question here is, does 'no-knowledge' mean 'a simple negation of knowledge' or 'something other than knowledge' or 'the contradictory of knowledge'? It is not a simple negation

of knowledge, first, because illusion is admitted to be a case of knowledge and not simply a negation of knowledge; and second, if 'no-knowledge' literally were taken to signify a simple negation of knowledge, then the term would be extended in its scope to refer to deep sleep that is characterized by a total absence of knowledge.

Again, if the negation in 'no knowledge' is taken to signify 'otherness', then the illusory cognition, thus understood, would lead to action in relation to a false object or a cognition of 'several undifferenced objects'. Explaining that neither of these two alternatives would hold, the translator records: "[T]he first alternative is faulty because in the case of those who have no desire to possess 'the silver' there is illusion, but because it is not the hetu to prompt action it would not be akhyāti. The second alternative also fails. The word 'undifferentiated' (avivikta) cannot mean identity, for when we use an expression 'this is silver' (idaṃ rajatam) two distinct words are uttered and the objects 'idaṁ' and 'rajatam' appear as distincts; and as such the cognition 'this is silver' will not be then cognition of things undifferentiated."

Nor is the the third meaning of negation, namely, that negation is a contrary opposite of knowledge, untenable. Cognition of cloth is opposed to pitcher-cognition, the two being reciprocally different, and one may arise after the other. The scope of *akhyāti* according to this sense of negation would extend to such cases. The point is that if no knowledge simply stands for a case of cognition that stands in contrary opposition to an earlier cognition, any sequence of two instances of cognition, one following the other, would qualify as an instance of illusory cognition. Thus the translator concludes that the definition of *akhyāti* fails. *Ibid.*, 20–21.

8. This is the Buddhist theory of *ātmakhyāti*: Three schools of Buddhism, —the Sautrāntika, the Vaibhāṣika, and the Yogācāra (Vijñānavāda)—may be said to subscribe to this doctrine. *PP*'s criticism is directed against the Yogācāra formulation of *ātmakhyāti*. According to Vijñānavādins, illusion consists in the wrong ascription of independent existence to an idea. In the illusory cognition of rope as snake, the snake is real as an idea but its 'thisness' as indicative of externality to consciousness is unreal. The Vijñānavādin generalizes such an understanding of error and speaks of consciousness alone as 'Vijñāna' as real, and the phenomenal world as its false construction. In short, the apparent ascription of external over internal states of consciousness accounts for the erroneous cognitions. The subjective idea of silver is wrongly thought to be presented outside.

9. See introduction, n. 62, for the Buddhist doctrine of momentariness. Also see section 9 for Śaṁkara's critique of Vijñānavāda Buddhism.

10. The point of the objection here is that error is not possible, or, alternately, cognition would forfeit its character as self-manifest. If illusory silver presents itself even in its form as 'this', as a case of knowledge, then such knowledge should be self-evident. Where, then, is error? The admission of error-sublation amounts to admitting that one cognition depends on or judges another cognition. If there are no objects but only cognition, and if cognitions *prima facie* are self-manifest, as Vijñānavādins uphold, then it makes no sense to say that an erroneous cognition is sublated by another cognition.

11. *PP* next very briefly mentions the Mādhyamika theory of *asatkhyāti*. It holds that in the erroneous cognition, say, of the shell-silver, the silver is apprehended as real. However, it does not exist at all. Neither silver nor shell is real. On their view nonexistent shell appears as nonexistent silver. One becomes aware of the nonexistence of silver only when the erroneous perception is corrected.

PP does not enter into a long critique of *asatkhyāti*. After criticizing the Yogācāra view, *PP* simply states that by this (the criticism of Yogācāra), the *asatkhyāti* should be taken to have been rejected. Śaṁkara condemns Śūnyavāda and its implied *asat-*

khyāti in just one sentence: It is not possible to negate the world without the acceptance of another reality; to negate an error is to accept the general truth on which it is based. *BSB* 2.2.31. The author of *PP*, following Advaitins, may have been so convinced of the positive character of an erroneous cognition that he felt that the Buddhist theory of *asatkhyāti* was not worth discussing. As pointed out earlier, the notion of ignorance in Advaita Vedānta is positive. The distinction between the existence and the nonexistence in the final analysis is a function of consciousness. Reality—pure existence—was, is, and will be.

Modern interpreters of *śūnyavāda* acknowledge that the Vedāntic critique of it as nihilism, as implying the denial of all existence, is well-known. Murti, the well-known Buddhist scholar, brings out the ontological weight of *śūnyavāda*. He observes: "In fact, the Mādhyamika does not deny the real; he simply denies *doctrines* about the real. For him, the real as transcendent to thought can be reached only by the denial of the determinations which systems of philosophy ascribe to it. When the entire conceptual activity of reason is dissolved by criticism, there is a Prajñā-Pāramita. The *Aṣṭasāhasrikā* declares in the clearest terms that Prajñāpāramita is not to be construed as a doctrine of Element, of Groups, and so on These conceptual devices do not obtain in reality, the nonapprehension of things (vo 'nupalambaḥ sarvadharmāṇām) is Prajñāpāramita." T. R. V. Murti, *The Central Philosophy of Buddhism*, 218.

12. *satkhyātir nāma jñānaviṣayasya satyatvam. tarhi bhramatvaṃ katham? iti cet, viṣayavyavahārabādhāt bhramatvam. tad upapādayāmaḥ—pañcīkaraṇaprakriyayā pṛthivyādiṣu sarvatra sarvabhūtānāṃ vidyamānatvāt, ata eva śuktikādau rajatāṃśasya vidyamānatvāj jñānaviṣayasya satyatvam. tatra rajatāṃśasya svalpatvāt tatra na vyavahāra iti tajjñānam bhramaḥ. śuktyaṃśabhūyastvajñānāt bhramānivṛttiḥ.* YMD, 14–15.

13. Hiriyanna refers to the significance of the twofold explanations as amounting to distinguishing between two classes of objects: One public, cognized by all (e.g., the illusion of the mirage), and the other private, special to particular individuals (e.g., a yellow conch, and a dream elephant). Hiriyanna, *Outlines of Indian Philosophy*, 392–93.

The abovementioned twofold explanation should not, however, mislead one, as Hiriyanna himself concedes, into believing that there are different levels of reality—an admission that would make Rāmānuja's epistemology very similar to Śaṁkara's. In fact, it is in the context of rejecting such a distinction that Rāmānuja articulates his theory of *satkhyāti*. A corollary of their thesis is that knowledge implies both subject and object (*Śrī Bhāṣya* 2.2.29). It is the subject that knows the object with the help of its essential attribute (*dharmabhūta jñāna*). All knowledge is characterized by attributes, and there is no knowledge devoid of attributes (*saviśeṣa vastu viṣayatvāt sarva pramāṇam*, *Śrī Bhāṣya* 1.1.1). Rāmānuja's view has been described as *satkhyāti*, which means what exists (*sat*) is alone cognized.

14. *PP* next rejects the Naiyāyika theory of *anyathākhyāti*. The author quotes from Bhāmatī to substantiate his position: *ataḥ āpaṇasthārūpyādīnāṃ saṁsargamātram atra kalpyata ity anyathākhyātir evāṅgīkaraṇīyā. etena—śaṁkhapītam ādibhramo 'pi—vyākhyātaḥ tad uktaṃ bhāmatyām: "nahi sarpādibhāvena rajjvādayo na pratibhāsante, pratibhāsamānā vā bhavanti tad ātmānas taddharmāṇa vā. tathāsati maruṣu marīcīcayam uccāvacam uccalattan gataraṅgamālābhyarṇam avatīrṇā mandākinīty abhisandhāya pravṛttas tattoyamāpīyāpi pipāsām upaśamayed" iti. PP*, 105. This statement, which intended to reject *satkhyāti*, according to *PP*, also rejects the Nyāya theory. *PP* argues that the Naiyāyika theory also amounts to arguing that one could drink water from the mirage to quench one's thirst, given that the parts of the sand in a mirage are also present in the water. This, as would be obvious to one familiar with the Nyāya theory, is misrepresenting their position .

To explain the erroneous cognition of a silver, for example, the Naiyāyikas assume a relation of identity between the object before us and the remote silver. The silver cognized in an illusion is not unreal, because then it would not be perceived at all. The relation of inherence that exists between the silver and the silverness also is apprehended in the 'this' and 'silverness'. The silver perceived in a jewelry store sometime in the past is perceived through *jñāna lakṣaṇa sannikarṣa*, one of the extra-empirical contacts recognized by the Naiyāyikas. Thus the shell is mistaken for the silver. Falsity consists in associating silver with the shell where it does not exist. Neither of them is unreal. The aim of Nyāya theory is to demonstrate that error, like truth, has an objective referent. It is neither perception of nonexistence (*asatkhyāti*) nor noknowledge (*akhyāti*); it is wrong perception. All knowledge claims, irrespective of whether true or false, are referential. It is only the false predictions of '*that*' as '*what*' (i.e., silver) which is corrected subsequently, but never the '*that*' itself. See *VP* passage 43.

15. *anirvacanīyatvaṃ ca sadasadvilakṣaṇatvam sac cen na bādhyetāsac cen na pratīyeteti khyātibādhāny athānupapattyā tu sadasadvilakṣaṇatvasiddhiḥ sattvaṃ cātra bādhyatvaṃ kva cid apy upadhāu sattvena pratītyanarhabhinnatvaṃ veti na doṣah. PP*, 108. Madhusūdana explains what is entailed in describing an erroneous cognition as indescribable: " [W]e do not assert 'indescribability' merely on the ground of absence of description; we base it upon absence of description as real; and this is certainly present in the phenomenal world, in whose case sublating causes are present." AS, chap. 1, sec. 26, *Indian Thought* 9, nos. 2 & 3 (1917): 232.

16. *Vivaraṇaprameyasaṅgraha* explains why the defects, such as *kāca* cannot serve as the material cause: "It is invariable for the superimposition and the material cause to have the same locus. Here, however, superimposition is located in the self, while defects are located in the sense organs etc; hence material causality does not belong to those defects." *VPS*, 31.

17. *PP*, 110.

18. *SLS* lists the three positions regarding the material causality of Brahman as follows: "Vācaspati Miśra, however, says thus: Brahman, that has been made the content of the māyā located in the jīva, is the material cause, since of itself it illusorily manifests itself in the form of the world, the locus of inertness; hence māyā is merely an accessory, not a subsidiary cause persistent in the effect." *SLS*, 160.

"The author of the *Saṅkṣepaśārīraka*, however, says thus: Brahman alone is the material cause; since, in the case of the immutable, independent causality is unintelligible, māyā is the subsidiary cause; the subsidiary, though not the cause, is yet present in the effect, since there is seen in the pot persistence of the softness, and so on (of the clay), as of the clay (itself)." *SLS*, 159–60.

"Even the refutation of the material causality of the associated (Brahman) in the *Saṅkṣepaśārīraka* is with the view of refuting the material causality of what is qualified by māyā, but does not have for purport the refutation of the material causality of intelligence in the form of the Lord, as distinguished (from māyā)..." *SLS*, 154–55.

19. *pariṇāmavivartalakṣaṇayoḥ pāramārthikāpāramārthikasattādvaividhyābhiprāyakatvād avidyāgatāyā apāramārthikasattāyāḥ samāyāḥ śuktirajatādīnām iti pakṣam anusṛtyaiveti mantavyam. PP*, 111

20. *Ibid.*, 112.

21. Madhusūdana explains this point further: "We do not admit that the 'Consciousness circumscribed by the Projection in the form of silver' is the substratum of the misconception of silver; in fact, what forms the substratum of the misconception of silver is Consciousness circumscribed by the notion of 'this'; and it is by mere chance that 'the Consciousness circumscribed by the Mental Projection in the shape of silver'

also becomes a substratum of it. But this does not make this latter a necessary condition for the misconception." *AS*, *Indian Thought* 9, nos. 2 & 3 (1917): 220.

22. For an analysis of the distinction between substratum (*adhiṣṭhāna*) and support (*ādhāra*), see chap. 1, n. 14.

23. *avidyāmanoviśiṣṭacaitanyayor antaḥkaraṇataddharmān prati manoviśiṣṭacaitanyasya kāṇatvādīn pratyadhyāsādhāratvāt tadadhyāsādhiṣṭhānasya ca brahmacaitanyasyendriyādhyāsepy adhiṣṭhānatvād iti*. *PP*, 114.

24. The Naiyāyikas argue that the Advaitin thesis would give rise to a cognition of the form 'I am silver'. The Advaitins maintain that silver is an effect of nescience and the consciousness conditioned by the internal organ is its substratum. Because the internal organ has assumed modification in the form of the object, the consciousness conditioned by the object and the cognizer-consciousness have become nondifferent. This is very similar to a cognition of a mental state such as 'I am happy'. Thus it makes perfect sense to say that there would be a cognition of the form 'I am silver' like the cognitions 'I am happy' and 'I am miserable'. The author of *VP* maintains that such is not the case. In such cases one resorts to the inner nature of things, and that is considered to be final. It is in the nature of silver to always presents itself in the form 'this is silver' and not as 'I am silver'.

25. *idam avacchinnacaitanya eva rajatasyādhyāsaḥ, na tu sākṣiṇy api; sākṣiṇaṃ prati rajatatvabuddhyabhāvāt. atah idaṃ rajatam ity eva pratīti rucitā , na tu ahaṃ rajatam iti rajatasya sākṣiṇy adhyastatāpratipādanaṃ tu sākṣiṇo 'dhyastarajatākāravṛttimatvād eva na tu paramārthas tasya rajatādhyāsaviṣayatvād ity asvarasāda aha—ahaṃ rajatavān iti vā pratītiḥ syād iti*. *PP*, 115.

26. *ajñānaviśiṣṭacaitanye 'haṁkārādhyāsaḥ tadviśiṣṭe ca dharmapuraskāreṇaivāhamkārādhyāsaḥ, tadviśiṣṭe kāmasaṁkalpādī nāmadhyāsaḥ, tadviśiṣṭe ca dharmapuraskāreṇaivāhaṃ manuṣya ity adhyāsaḥ, na tu svarūpatah ahaṃ deha iti pratītyabhāvād iti*. *Ibid.*, 116.

27. Śaṁkara, *Adhyāsabhāṣya.*

28. Opponents ask: Because the illusory silver can be cognized as being directly related to the witness-consciousness in your system, why assume a mental mode in the form of an apparent cognition with regards to silver?

29. *PP*, 121.

30. *satyāsatyaviṣayatayeti. ata evoktaṃ bhāṣye -"satyānṛte mithunīkvatyāham [mithunīkṛtyāham] idaṃ mamedam iti naisargiko 'yaṃ lokavyavāharaḥ iti." Ibid.*, 122.

7

Dream Perception

7.51 *nanu svapnasthale pūrvānubhūtarathādeḥ smaraṇamātreṇaiva vyavahāropapattau na rathādisṛṣṭikalpanam, gauravāt.*

iti cen na. rathādeḥ smṛtimātrābhyupagame "rathaṃ paśyāmi, svapne ratham adrākṣam" ityādyanubhavavirodhāpatteḥ, "atha rathān rathayogān pathaḥ sṛjate" iti rathādisṛṣṭipratipādakaśrutivirodhāpatteś ca. tasmāt, suktirūpyavat svapnopalabdharathādayo 'pi prātibhāsikā yāvatpratibhāsam avatiṣṭhante.

7.51 *[Objection]: Because in the case of dreams simple recollection of formerly experienced [in the waking state] chariots, and so on, makes dealings [with chariots, and so on] intelligible, there is no need to assume the creation of a chariot and the like because of prolixity [cumbrous].*

If such is the case [the answer is], "no." If the recollection of chariots, and so on, alone is admitted, it would contradict experiences such as 'I see a chariot', 'I saw a chariot in the dream', and the like. Furthermore, it would contradict śruti [texts] which establish the creation of chariots, and so on, like 'but he projects from himself chariots, [the horses] yoked to chariots, and roads' (BU 4.3.10). Therefore, even the chariots cognized in a dream, like the shell-silver, are also illusory and appear so long as the appearance lasts.

7.51 Discussion of the distinction between an actual object, as arising from nescience, and illusory objects, as arising from the factors apart from nescience, leads to the topic of dream objects. *PP*'s preamble to the observations of *VP* in this regard is very instructive. Dream objects are the effects of primal nescience. Because dream objects are superimposed upon the conditioned pure consciousness—the consciousness that transcends the individual consciousness and is devoid of any modal ignorance—it is entirely appropriate to articulate the criteria of illusory objects in terms of some defects apart from nescience. This also explains the status of dream objects in the system of Advaita.[1] Dream objects are viewed as illusory, because they have sleep as a defect apart from the primal nescience.

7.51.1 It might be objected that if we view the dream objects to be the effects of primal nescience, then the dream objects could cease to exist only if their cause, the primal nescience, ceases to exists. According to the Advaitin thesis, the primal nescience ceases to exist only when the knowledge of Brahman arises. In other words, the opponents contend that because the dream objects are the effects of primal nescience and primal nescience endures till the onset of Brahman knowledge, the dream objects also should endure till that time. This, however, is not the case. The experience of dream objects, in fact, notoriously terminates on waking up. Therefore the Advaitin thesis goes against our everyday experiences.

7.51.1.1 *PP* treats this objection in a refreshing manner. In the snake-rope illusion, for example, the erroneous cognition vanishes when one realizes that it is a rope and not a snake. Similarly, the dream objects also cease to exist because the immediately succeeding state, namely, the waking state. Accordingly, the possibility of admitting the presence of dream objects in the waking state does not even arise.

7.51.1.2 *PP* also proposes an alternative answer to the aforementioned objection to make the explanation of dream objects conform to the distinction made between two kinds of nescience, namely, the primal nescience and the modal nescience. Sleep, which is only a derivative of the primal nescience, is the material cause of the dream objects, and modal ignorance, which is a derivative of primal nescience, is the material cause of the shell-silver. Dream objects are the transfigurations of the consciousness conditioned by the mind and not the transfigurations of pure consciousness. The point to note here is the assertion of parity between dream objects and illusory objects; the silver appearing in erroneous cognitions arises from a defect. Objects appearing in dreams, such as a chariot, arise because of the defect of sleep, epistemologically speaking, and hence are illusory.

7.51.2 It is asked that because the perception of a chariot in a dream, for example, could be explained as a case of recollection of the previous experience of chariot, why assume that it arises from the defect of sleep to account for their illusory nature?

7.51.2.1 The answer provided in *VP* is plain enough. The experience of a dream may be articulated in the words 'I see a chariot', which one may verbalize from within the dream experience, or it may take the form 'I saw a chariot in my dream', which one may verbalize in retrospect after waking up. Dream experience is not a species of recollection.

7.51.2.2 *PP*'s explanation in this regard is very much to the point. By what criterion is something deemed illusory? The answer that is proposed also is the definition given of the illusory objects—it is the existence of those objects only at the time of the erroneous perception. Recollection, however, does not possess this feature. It could exist even after the erroneous perception has ceased to exist.[2]

7.51.3 To account for the perceptual experience of silver in the form 'I perceive the silver', in the case of the erroneous cognition of shell as silver, it is appropriate to assume the creation of an indeterminable silver. In the case of dream objects, however, the sense of sight does not function, and consequently, mind cannot undergo modification, and there can be no perceptual experience of the dream objects. Dream perceptions are still a part of the dream experience and should not be assimilated into the category of the erroneous perceptions that form a part of waking life.[3] *PP* quotes from *SLS* to substantiate his point.[4] The perceptual experience of an elephant arises from sense-contact with an empirically cognized elephant and not from the contact with the elephant, which was perceived in one's dream. Alternately, it makes no sense to say that the elephant that exists elsewhere, say in a zoo, alone is manifested in a dream.

7.52 *nanu svapnarathādyadhiṣṭhānatayopalabhyamānadeśaviśeṣasyāpi tadā asannikṛṣṭatayānirvacanīyaprātibhāsikadeśo bhyupagantavyaḥ; tathā ca adhyāsaḥ kutra?*

iti cen na; caitanyasya svayaṃprakāśasya rathādyadhiṣṭhānatvāt. pratīyamāno rathādir astīty eva pratīyata iti sadrūpeṇa prakāśamānam caitanyam evādhiṣṭhānam. deśaviśeṣo 'pi cidadhyastaḥ prātibhāsikaḥ. rathādāv indriyagrāhyatvam api prātibhāsikam, tadā sarvendriyāṇām uparamāt.

"ahaṃ gajaḥ" ityādipratītyāpādanan tu pūrvavat nirasanīyam. svapnagajādayaḥ sākṣān māyāpariṇāmā iti kecit. antaḥkaraṇadvārā tatpariṇāmā ity anye.

7.52 *[Objection]: Now, because the particular location in a dream cognized as the support of the chariot, and so on, is not in sense-contact at that time [at the time of dreaming], an indeterminable illusory location has to be assumed, and so where does the superimposition [of dream chariot] take place?*[5]

If this is said [the answer is], "no." The chariot, and so forth [in a dream], is indeed cognized as existent, because the self-luminous consciousness is the substratum of chariot and the like. The chariots, and so forth [in a dream], are indeed experienced as existent, and so it is the consciousness manifesting itself as existent that is [serves as] the substratum. Even the particular location [where a chariot is dreamt to exist] is superimposed on the consciousness and is [therefore] only illusory. Sense-cognizedness of the chariot also is illusory, because all sense organs are at rest at that time [during the time the dream occurs].

As for the possibility of an experience of the form 'I am an elephant' and so on, it should be refuted in the manner stated already. Some maintain that the elephants and the like seen in a dream are a direct transformation of nescience. Others hold that they are its transformation through the medium of the internal organ.

7.52 The *pūrvapakṣins,* calling into question the Advaitin analysis of dream objects, raise the following objections: What is the substratum of dream objects, like chariots? Is it pure consciousness or is it the particular place wherein the chariot is located in the dream experience? Regarding the first alternative, it is further asked whether the substratum is the unconditioned consciousness itself, or if consciousness is of some other sort. It also is asked: Is it consciousness that serves as the original or the consciousness that is reflected that serves as the substratum of dream objects? The consciousness that serves as the original (*bimba caitanya*) cannot be the substratum of dream objects, because it is concealed by ignorance. Such a consciousness cannot become the content of any knowledge. The consciousness that is reflected, as the Advaitins themselves concede, cannot become the substratum. The individual consciousness cannot serve as the substratum either, because that would make the cognition 'I am an elephant' intelligible. So by the process of elimination the Advaitins must accept that the specific place that serves as the locus of such objects as chariots in the dream is the substratum of the dream objects.

The opponent here quickly notes that the specific place cannot be regarded as the locus either because, in this regard, the question arises whether the specific place is inside the body or outside the body. It cannot be said to be present outside the body during the state of dreaming, because the objects cannot be perceived without the functioning of the sense organs, and admittedly sense organs cease to function in the state of dreaming. On the other hand, the specific place cannot be considered to be inside the body, because large objects, such as large roads, cannot exist inside the body. For these reasons, we must assume that the specific place wherein the chariot moves is indeterminably created. Moreover, because they have been indeterminably created or fancied, they cannot become the content of ignorance and so cannot serve as the substratum either. In short, the dream objects do not have any substratum.

7.52.1 The reply to these objections may be summarily set forth steering through the tangle of objections and answers proposed in *PP* and keeping close to the conclusive view in *VP*. The particular location cognized as the substratum of the dream chariot is still only a part of the dream and hence cannot serve as the substratum. The consciousness that is unconditioned and reflected in nescience is the real substratum of the chariot and other dream objects. *VP* clearly states that it is self-luminous consciousness that serves as the substratum.[6] To the extent that the chariot cognized in a dream is cognized as an existent object, the substratum is but the consciousness manifested as the dream reality. Other Advaitins concur with this general position, except that some of them would qualify such a consciousness serving as the substratum of the dream objects as also manifested by the mental mode. It is, of course, a case of the functioning of the mental mode being different from the one that is required in the ordinary wakeful perceptions. In a dream there is no 'going out' of the body; consequently the functioning of the senses is not required. Treating the substratum as consciousness defined by the mental mode or by a sense of 'I'—defined in the sense of limiting adjunct—helps to avoid the unwelcome contingence of dream experiences taking the form 'I am an elephant'.

7.52.2 The author of *PP* refines the statement about consciousness being the substratum of dream objects in the following manner. It is true that the specific place where the chariot runs is also fancied and thus cannot serve as the substratum; however, the consciousness that is unconditioned and reflected in *avidyā* could definitely serve as its locus. Consciousness reflected in nescience, although known in its general aspect and thus self-luminous, is not known in its specific aspect.[7] In other words, in its specific nature, it is concealed by nescience, that is why the Advaitins maintain that it is only the consciousness conditioned by the mental mode that is opposed to ignorance and not pure consciousness as such. Therefore, the charge that on the Advaitin thesis there is no substratum of the dream objects is not valid.

PP also adds that both pure consciousness reflected in the mental mode, which is said to be self-luminous, and the consciousness conditioned by the 'I' sense (*ahaṃ padārtha*) reflected in ignorance, which is said to be the individual self (*jīva*), could serve as the substratum of the dream objects. This also explains the notion that the consciousness that transcends the mind (*sākṣin*) also could serve as the substratum. Mind is only a distinguishing factor and not an adjectival feature, and so there is no possibility of the dream experience being of the form 'I am an elephant'.

7.52.3 Illusory objects are the effects of nescience associated with the latent impressions. For one to have the erroneous cognition 'this is silver', one must have the previous experience of silver. To have a previous experience, the Advaitins maintain, is one of the necessary conditions but not sufficient to give rise to erroneous cognitions, the sufficient factor being nescience. Thus only the objects experienced in our everyday lives can be manifested in the erroneous cognition. One may make the same claim regarding dream cognitions. In ordinary life when I see an elephant, I use the expression 'this is an elephant' and not 'I am an elephant'. Similarly, in the dream cognitions there is the experience 'this is an elephant'. *PP* adds another point of interest. The dream world is sublated by the waking experience because the consciousness that is reflected in the nescience is only the substratum of modal ignorance. Therefore, as soon as the knowledge of the empirical individual self arises, the dream world becomes sublated.

7.53 *nanu gajādeḥ śuddhacaitanyādhyastatva idānīṃ tatsākṣātkārābhāvena jāgaraṇe pi svapnopalabdhagajādayo nurvarteran?*

ucyate. kāryavināśo hi dvividhaḥ. kaścid upādānena saha, kaścit tu vidyamāna eva upādāne. ādyo bādhaḥ. dvitīyas tu nivṛttiḥ. ādyasya kāraṇam adhiṣṭhānatattvasākṣātkārāḥ, tena vinā upādānabhūtāyā avidyāyā anivṛtteḥ. dvitīye virodhivṛttyutpattiḥ doṣanivṛttiś ca.

tad iha brahmasākṣātkārābhāvāt svapnaprapañco mā bādhiṣṭa. musalaprahāreṇa ghaṭāder iva virodhipratyayāntarodayena svajanakībhūtanidrādidoṣanāśena vā gajādinivṛttau ko virodhaḥ?

evañ ca śuktirūpyasya śuktyavacchinnacaitanyaniṣṭhatūlāvidyākāryatvapakṣe śuktir iti jñānena tadajñānena saha rajatasya bādhaḥ. mūlāvidyākāryatvapakṣe tu mūlāvidyāyā brahmasākṣātkāramātranivartyatayā śuktitvajñānenānivartyatayā tatra śuktijñānāt nivṛttimātram musalaprahāreṇa ghaṭasyeva.

7.53 *[Objection]: Now, if the elephants, and so on, are superimposed on pure consciousness, in the absence of realization of that [consciousness] in the present [in the waking state], the objects cognized in a dream should continue to be cognized even in the waking state.*

It is said in reply that the destruction of an effect indeed is of two kinds. One is the removal of it [effect] along with its material cause; the second, however, is even when its material cause continues to be known as existing. The first is sublation; the second, however, is cessation (removal). The cause of the first is the realization of the reality of the substratum, because in the absence of that there is no removal of nescience that is the material cause. In the second, it is the generation of a contrary mental mode or the removal of the defects.

Thus although in the awakened state the dream world may not be sublated because of the absence of Brahman realization, yet like the destruction of a pitcher and the like by the blows of a pestle, what is the contradiction involved in maintaining that the cessation of elephant, and so on [seen in a dream], is either because of the generation of a contrary mental mode, or caused by the destruction of defects like sleep which cause them [the dream cognitions]?

Thus according to the view that shell-silver is a product of modal nescience present in the consciousness conditioned by the shell, there is the sublation of silver together with the nescience by the knowledge that it is a shell. According to the view that it [the shell silver] is a product of primal nescience that is only destroyed by the knowledge of Brahman and not removable by the knowledge of shellness, there is simply the removal (not sublation) through the knowledge that it is a shell, as of a pitcher by the blows of a pestle.

7.53 Opponents contend that the Advaitins clearly maintain that the consciousness reflected in nescience is equal to pure consciousness that serves as the original. Thus when it is admitted that the dream objects are superimposed upon the consciousness reflected in nescience, it amounts to saying that pure consciousness alone is the substratum of the dream world. In that case there will be no distinction between the waking and the dreaming state. So the opponents object that if the dream objects, like elephants, are taken to be the instances of the superimposition on the substratum of pure consciousness, then the dream cognized objects should persist, even in the waking state, because in the waking state there is no intuition of pure consciousness and the consequent removal of nescience. In short, there will be no distinction between the waking and the dreaming world.

7.53.1 It is said in response that in the cases of dream objects, although there is no sublation, there can be destruction or termination, wherein the cause remains while the effect is destroyed.[8] The dream world is destroyed because of a contrary mental state in the form of a waking state, while its material cause, nescience, continues to exist.

The absence of an effect even in the form of its cause is technically known as 'cancellation' (*bādha*). Existence of an effect, no longer as an effect but in the form of its cause, is technically known as 'destruction' or 'termination' (*nivṛtti*).[9] When a pitcher is broken, there is the absence of pitcherness in the pitcher sherds. Similarly, the dream objects cease to exist upon waking up. In the erroneous cognition of shell-silver, the silver ceases to exist when there is the knowledge of the true nature of the shell. This, technically speaking, is not cancellation. Cancellation in such cases is admitted only by those who maintain that silver is an effect of modal nescience.

7.53.2 The definition of the perceptibility of an object is its unsublatability, and such a definition does not go so far as to include the erroneous cognition of shell-silver, because shell-silver is not unsublatable. An object, according to Advaita, is sublatable if it is the counter-correlate (*pratiyogin*) of the absence in the three divisions of time as such, or as an an absolutely real entity.[10] In other words, it is the counter-correlate of sublation or cancellation.

7.53.3 On the view that the silver is the effect of the primal nescience, unsublatability means that the object must be different from the one that is the effect of nescience. It does not mean that it is not the counter-correlate of the mental mode, because if that is admitted then the definition of the perceptibility of an object will be inapplicable. An object is not the counter-correlate of its destruction in the form of its cause. This feature, however, exists in the case of the shell-silver during the time of phenomenal existence. If by the term 'unsublatable' is meant that an object is not the counter-correlate of destruction in the form of its cause, only then will the definition of the perceptibility of an object unduly extend to the case of shell-silver.

7.54 *nanu śuktau rajatasya pratibhāsasamaye prātibhāsikasattābhyupagame "nedaṃ rajatam" iti traikālikaniṣedhajñānaṃ na syāt, kintu 'idānīm idaṃ na rajatam' iti, "idānīṃ ghaṭaḥ śyāmo na" itivat.*

iti cen na. na hi tatra rajatatvāvacchinnapratiyogikābhāvo niṣe-

dhadhīviṣayaḥ; kintu laukikapāramārthikatvāvacchinnaprātibhāsikarajatapratiyogitākaḥ; vyadhikaraṇadharmāvacchinnapratiyogitākābhāvābhyupagamāt.

nanu prātibhāsike rajate pāramārthikatvam avagatam na vā? anavagate pratiyogitāvacchedakāvacchinnajñānābhāvād abhāvapratyakṣānupapattiḥ; avagate aparokṣāvabhāsasya tātkālikaviṣayasattāniyatatvād rajate pāramārthikatvam api anirvacanīyaṃ rajatavad evotpannam iti tadavacchinnarajatasattve tadavacchinnābhāvas tatra kathaṃ vartate?

iti cen na; pāramārthikatvasyādhiṣṭhānaniṣṭhasya rajate pratibhāsasam bhavenarajataniṣṭhapāramārthikatvotpattyanabhyupagamāt. yatrāropyam asannikṛṣṭaṃ tatraiva prātibhāsikavastūtpatter aṅgīkārāt.

ata eveindriyasannikṛṣṭatayā japākusumagatalauhityasya sphaṭike bhānasambhavān na sphaṭike 'nirvacanīyalauhityotpattiḥ.

nanv evaṃ yatra japākusumaṃ dravyāntaravyavadhānād asannikṛṣṭam, tatra lauhityapratītyā prātibhāsikaṃ lauhityaṃ svīkriyatām.

iti cen na; iṣṭatvāt. evaṃ pratyakṣabhramāntareṣv api pratyakṣasāmānyalakṣaṇānugamo yathārthapratyakṣalakṣaṇāsadbhāvaś ca darśanīyaḥ.

7.54 *[Objection]: Now, if at the time of the appearance of silver in a shell an illusory existence is admitted, then there would be no [subsequent] cognition of its negation in the three divisions of time [past, present, and future]; but it would be of the form 'now, this is not silver', like [the cognition of the form] 'now [after baking], the pitcher is not black'.*[11]

This is not the case, because the content of the negative [sublating] cognition then is not the nonexistence, and so forth, whose counter-correlate is conditioned by silverness; rather, it is that whose counter-correlate is [simply] illusory silver characterized by empirical reality, because we admit that kind of nonexistence whose counter-correlate is conditioned by a distinguishing attribute present in a substratum other than its own (vyadhikaraṇa).[12]

[Objection]: Now, in the case of the illusory silver, is real existence cognized or not? If not cognized, then because of the nonexistence of the cognition of the counter-correlate with that which conditions counter-correlatedness, there cannot be any perception of its nonexistence; if cognized, then because in the case of the immediate presentation the contemporaneous existence of the content is a necessary concomitant, there is, in the silver also, real existence, which is indeterminable and produced just as the silver [itself] is; how could

nonexistence [of the silver] conditioned by the real existence occur in that [the illusory silver]?

If such is said [the answer is], "no," for because it is possible for the real existence belonging to the substratum [shell] to appear in the silver, the production of a real existence present in the silver is not admitted; because the production of an illusory object is admitted only where the superimposed thing is not in sense-contact.

Hence, there being the possibility of the cognition in the crystal of the redness belonging to a hibiscus flower, because of its being in contact with the organ, there is no production of an indeterminable redness in the crystal.

[Objection]: Now where the hibiscus flower is not in sense-contact because of the intervention of some other object, the result of the cognition of redness, an illusory redness must be admitted.

If such is said, [the Advaitins respond] "no" [objection], for we accept it. Similarly, in other instances of erroneous perception, it is noticed that the general definition of perception is applicable and the definition of true perception is inapplicable.

7.54 It might be objected that the Advaitin contention—that cognitions such as 'this is not silver' and 'there is no silver' comprehend the absence of silver in the three divisions of time—has not been established so far. The Advaitins maintain that this objection is without any basis. Indeed, they admit the existence of silver in the three divisions of time. The sublating cognition 'this is not silver' only comprehends that the object before me is not silver, and nothing more.

7.54.1 *PP*'s general comment about the soundness of the theory of the indeterminable origin of silver deserves to be kept in mind for appreciating the points that are discussed in the subsequent sections of *VP*. The silver is indeterminable in the sense that it is different from the real and the unreal, not to speak of its being different from both at once. It does manifest as silver in the shell, and yet it does not have an independent existence. Negation of silver as in 'this is not silver', must be understood in the sense of negation of silver as an independent, that is, an absolutely real entity. What is negated, in other words, is not an illusory silver, but only the absolutely real silver.

7.54.2 The term *'tatra'* in the text signifies that in the two types of cognitions, 'this is not silver' and 'there is no silver here', the absence of silverness as such, which is the defining characteristic of silver, is not established because silverness exists in the actual silver as well as, phenomenologically speaking, in the illusory silver. True, there is the existence of the activity on the part of the one who desires silver by the knowledge of the illusory silver. But the existence of silverness need not be admitted to substantiate this point. A sense of identification between the illusory silver and the actual silver will suffice. Furthermore, silverness does not form the essential nature of the counter-correlate. In the Nyāya terminology, it is known as '*vyadhikaraṇa*'. The Neologicians maintain that there is only one silverness, and it is common to both the empirically real silver and the illusory silver. And, as common to both, silverness exists in the counter-correlate of the nonexistence of silver.

7.54.3 In this context, *PP* explains the position of the Neologicians with great clarity. What is involved in the assertion that there is the nonexistence or the absence of a pitcher here? According to the Neologicians, the pitcher is the *pratiyogin* (counter-correlate), the nonexistence is the *anuyogin,* and *pratiyogitā* (counter-correlatedness) exists in the pitcher. The Advaitins use this distinction to explain the nonexistence or the absence of silver. When it is said that 'there is the absence of silver here', silver is the *pratiyogin,* and *pratiyogitā* exists in the silver. Reality here is the delimiting condition (*avacchedaka*) of the counter-correlatedness: it is conditioned by *laukika viśeṣaṇatā*, that is, it is conditioned by empirical reality. In other words, the experience 'this is not silver' comprehends the absence of silver, in which the silver is the *pratiyogin* that is conditioned by the empirical reality.

7.54.3.1 Because it is held that the counter-correlatedness that exists in the counter-correlate is conditioned by absolute reality, one might say that the Advaitins also admit the theory of nonexistence, whose counter-correlate is conditioned by a feature that does not exist in it. This amounts to saying that the counter-correlate of an *abhāva* may be conditioned by a feature that does not exist in the counter-correlate. Although absolute reality is not a qualifying attribute of the shell-silver, the counter-correlate, namely, the shell-silver that is the counter-correlate of its absence, is definitely conditioned by reality. The Advaitins maintain that when a pitcher is negated in the relation of contact, it also is negated in the relation of inherence. When, for example, it is said 'Caitra with the tuft of hair on the crown of his head is lost or destroyed', the negatum is the 'tuft of hair' and not Caitra. Caitra is not the negatum in this instance. Similarly, when a pitcher is negated in the relation of inherence (in a pitcher there is color that exists in the pitcher through the relation of inherence; the content of such an experience is the absence of color. The counter-correlate is contact and the delimiting factor of that counter-correlate is contactness), only the relation is negated and not the pitcher. When a pitcher is negated, it is negated in all of its possible aspects. So the Advaitins maintain that if the pitcher could be negated in one relation, it would also be negated in any other relation. Similarly, in the cognition, 'there is no pitcher here as a cloth', the counter-correlate of the cognition of nonexistence is conditioned by a feature that does not co-exist with it. But, because the substantive feature, the pitcher, exists on the floor, its absence cannot be predicated with reference to it. Such a cognition merely comprehends the absence of a feature that does not co-exist with the *pratiyogitā* in the substantive, the pitcher. Similarly, the knowledge of the absence of shell-silver as real merely comprehends the absence of reality in the silver. So there is no unintelligibility with respect to silver being the counter-correlate of its absence in the three divisions of time.

7.54.3.2 It might be argued that when reality is negated in the silver, it is silver as associated with the reality that is negated. That which is not the adjectival feature of a *pratiyogin* cannot be the conditioning factor of *pratiyogitā*, which exists in the *pratiyogin*. At the time of the determined cognition 'a pitcher is not a cloth', there does not result the experience 'a pitcher does not exist as a cloth'. That cognition that is noticed in the form 'there is no pitcher here as cloth' comprehends only the nonexistence of the pitcher as associated with the features pitcherness and clothness. It is indeed true that clothness is contradicted in the pitcher. Yet the knowledge of clothness in the pitcher is erroneous.

7.54.3.2.1 Accordingly, it must be held that in the shell-silver there is illusory reality. When it is thus clear that at the time of the erroneous cognition reality is manifest, silver cannot be absent in the three divisions of time. How, then, could the sublating cognition 'this is not silver' comprehend the absence of silver as real in the three divisions of time? It is true that at the time of the erroneous cognition of silver, the indeterminable silver exists concomitantly and yet there is the absence of empirical reality in it. This empirical reality serves as the delimiting factor, or the determinant, of the counter-correlatedness that exists in the silver. Thus the adjectival feature *laukika*, that means empirical reality, becomes significant.

7.54.3.2.2 It might be argued that the cognition 'this is not silver' is perceptual in nature. Such a cognition of absence does not have for its content an absence whose counter-correlate is associated with the feature that does not co-exist with it. Therefore, it is not plausible to maintain that the cognition 'this is not silver' refers to the absence of silver in the three divisions of time. If the cognition 'the pitcher does not exist as a cloth' is admitted to be inferential in nature, there is no conflict. If it is regarded as perceptual, then it must be held that it comprehends the absence of 'clothness' in the pitcher; or, it must be admitted to comprehend the absence of the pitcher as associated with the superimposed feature, clothness. In any event, the contention that the perceptual cognition 'this is not silver' comprehends the absence of silver that is associated with empirical reality cannot be accepted.

7.54.3.2.3 For the Advaitins, the cause of the knowledge of nonexistence is the knowledge of the counter-correlate that possesses an identity with the factor that conditions the state of being a reality, that in turn determines the state of being a counter-correlate. It is true that such an identity is not noticed in the case of silver. Because it is not noticed does not, however, mean that it does not exist. In fact, it exists without any contradiction. The counter-correlate is manifested as identical with a particular factor, and that factor alone is considered to be the condition that delimits the state of being a counter-correlate. In the cognition 'the pitcher does not exist as a cloth', clothness being remote is also superimposed. This, however, is an entirely different issue. Even if we admit that in the shell-silver there does not arise reality in the silver, it does not constitute any defect.

7.54.3.2.4 In this context, we must remember precise nature of superimposition that is involved. *PP* makes extra efforts to clarify the issues involved. Just as the mere *relation* of the 'this' element present in the substratum is superimposed on the silver, it is only the relation of reality that is superimposed. Reality as such is not superimposed upon the silver. It does not comprehend an independent existence in the silver, because only one level of reality is admitted. What is superimposed upon the silver is not reality itself but its relatedness. The distinctions made earlier between the two notions of substratum and support might be useful here. What is involved in superimposition as a term is the support and not the substratum. In the experience of 'this is silver', the 'isness' comprehends or connotes the relation of identity with silver, and not an independent existence of silver in an ontic sense. It is not necessary, therefore, to hold that silver possesses a silverness that is common both to the actual as well as the illusory silver. As explained earlier, it is not necessary to admit reality with respect to silver to account for the activity of the one who desires it after perceiving it as 'this is silver'. A mere superimposition of the relation of identity will suffice.

PP here reminds the reader that most Advaitins admit an indeterminate creation of five factors in the case of an erroneous cognition, namely, the identity with the 'this' element, the relation to the state of being a 'this' element, silver, identity with the silver, and relation to silverness. They do not admit an origination of silver that is common to both the actual and the illusory silver. For example, in the case of the experience 'crystal is red', in that the the identity of the color red with the crystal arises through a reflected image of the red flower in the crystal, the state of being a red color is not admitted to be originated unless the two are present in places remote from each other. On the theory of one level of reality, the expression 'negation in the three divisions of time' simply implies the absence of the relation of reality to silver. Therefore, even if one does not have the knowledge of reality in the silver, it does not create any problem for our system.

7.54.3.2.5 The text *rajate pratibhāsasaṃbhaveneti* means that there is a possibility of manifestation in relation to silver. The essence of the point that has been made is that it is not reality that is cognized in silver, but only that its relation is comprehended. Therefore, the cognition of absence is intelligible, as we could have the knowledge of the counter-correlate associated with a factor that conditions the state of being a counter-correlate. Thus it makes perfect sense to say that reality is not noticed in silver; only the relation of reality is known. Such is the analysis of 'this is silver'. The experience 'this is not silver' is also a perceptual cognition of the absence of silver, in which again reality as such is not involved, but reality in its relational aspect (i.e., the relation of absence) is involved. Even according to the theory of three grades of reality, in the negation of 'silver' in the three divisions of time, what is negated as real is not silver as such but its relation with reality. Therefore, there is no contradiction.

7.54.3.2.6 *PP* explains the nature of the Advaitin thesis with clarity. Regarding the knowledge of the absence of the counter-correlate conditioned by an attribute that is not present in the thing that is negated, the knowledge of the counter-correlate associated with the factor that conditions the state of being a counter-correlate is not the cause. The knowledge of silver that is associated with reality does not become valid. It is erroneous, and in the erroneous cognition it is only the indeterminable silver that is manifested as real. This reality cannot be considered to be a feature that exists in a particular substratum where it does not actually exist. Thus there is no possibility of our having the cognition of counter-correlate conditioned by a feature that exists in the counter-correlate. *Laghucandrikā* also supports such a position: there is the nonexistence whose *pratiyogin* is conditioned by a factor that does not exist in the counter-correlate; it is admitted that it is only the knowledge of a counter-correlate conditioned by the factor that conditions the state of being a counter-correlate.[13]

In short, even if we admit an *abhāva* whose counter-correlate is conditioned by a contrary feature, the knowledge of the counter-correlate as associated with a contrary feature is not the cause of the perception of nonexistence. Thus even if reality is not admitted in silver, there does not arise any defect. Whatever it may be, it is only according to the view that reality is not noticed in the silver; the conclusive view is presented and not according to the standpoint that reality is noticed in the silver.

7.54.4 It might be objected that in the cognition 'the crystal is red', there is no need to admit an indeterminable redness because of the proximity of the rose to the crystal. The two exist in proximity to each other, and the redness present in the one is superimposed upon the other, resulting in the cognition 'the crystal is red'. The redness is in sense-contact, although located in the rose and not in the crystal. The error of the cognition here consists in the transference and not in creation of a novel content, i.e., an indeterminate redness.

7.54.4.1 *VP* explains that the above objection does not pose any threat to the Advaitins' position. In the cognitions in which the objects superimposed are present by the mere admission of the superimposition of the relation, the Advaitins accept a relational theory of error in that the content of error is an elsewhere existent brought into a relation with the locus to which it does not belong.[14]

7.54.4.2 *PP* here is not slow to add nuances to the conditional nature of the acceptance of such a theory. In the erroneous cognition 'this is silver', silver is not in proximity, and so both silver as well as its identity is superimposed upon the object in front of us. In the cognition of crystal as red, redness is in proximity, and so its manifestation as an adjectival feature would hold good by the superimposition of the mere relation. If, however, the redness that is present in the flower is not in proximity, because it is impeded by another substance, then the origination of an indeterminable redness must be admitted.

7.55 *uktaṃ pratyakṣaṃ prakārāntareṇa dvividham, indriyajanyaṃ tadajanyaṃ ceti. tatrendriyājanyaṃ sukhādipratyakṣam, manasa indriyatvanirākaraṇāt.*

indriyāṇi pañca, ghrāṇarasanacakṣuḥśrotratvagātmakāni. sarvāṇi cendriyāṇi svasvaviṣayasaṃyuktāny eva pratyakṣajñānaṃ janayanti.

tatra ghrāṇarasanatvagātmakānīndriyāṇi svasthānasthitāny eva gandharasasparśopalambhāñ janayanti. cakṣuḥśrotre tu svata eva viṣayadeśaṃ gatvā svasvaviṣayaṃ gṛhṇītah.

śrotrasyāpi cakṣurādivat paricchinnatayā bheryādideśagamana-sambhavāt. ata evānubhavo "bherīśabdo mayā śrutaḥ' iti." anyathā vīcītaraṅgādinyāyena karṇa śaṣkulīpradeśe'nantaśabdotpattikalpanāgauravam "bherīśabdo mayā śrutaḥ" iti pratyakṣasya bhramatvakalpanāgauravañ ca syāt.

tad evaṃ vyākhyātam pratyakṣam.

iti pratyakṣaparicchedaḥ.

7.55 *Perception, already explained, is twofold in another way: sense-generated and not sense-generated. Among these, that which is not caused by sense organs is the perception of happiness, and so forth, because the view that mind is a sense organ has [already] been refuted.*

The sense organs are five: smell, taste, sight, hearing, and touch. All these senses give rise to perceptual knowledge only when they are conjoined with their respective contents.

Of these [organs], the senses of smell, taste, and touch give rise to the cognitions of smell, taste, and touch remaining only in their own locations. Senses of sight and hearing, however, apprehend their respective objects by themselves going to the location of those [respective] contents.

For the sense of hearing also, being limited like the sense of sight, it is possible to reach the location of the drum, and so on, and so the experience 'the drum-sound is heard by me'. Otherwise, there would be the prolixity of assuming, on the analogy of ripples, waves, and so on, the generation of innumerable sounds till it reaches the place of the ear cavity, and the [additional] prolixity of assuming the falsity of the perception 'the drum-sound is heard by me'.

Thus perception has been explained.

Here ends the chapter on perception.

7.55 The issue of the senses and the role that they play in the perceptual process is discussed as a kind of sequel to the discussion of perceptuality and its criterion in relation to consciousness. The relevance of the account of senses, as made of physical elements partaking their characteristics, to the issue of perception is the extent that they serve as avenues by which to reach the place of the object. The account given here of the senses addresses the main question of the possibility of their 'reaching' their respective places. The senses, being extremely clear substances, reach the place of their objects at the quickest interval of time and pervade the object.

7.55.1 It might be argued that the sense of sight, being finite, conceivably can reach its specific place, but the sense of hearing being of the nature of ether is infinite and all pervasive, and therefore cannot be interpreted or understood in terms of reaching the place of the object, namely, sound. Philosophers such as Kumārila respond that ether being all pervasive can be present in the far-off places also, and so there will be the possibility of hearing even the remote sounds. The ether is partless, but to maintain that *one part of the space is the sense of hearing and another is not so*, it is held that that part of the space which is associated with the merit and demerit of the individual soul constitutes the sense of hearing. The author of *VP* rejects this position, because it is inconsistent with the view that the ether is partless.

7.55.2 The space conditioned by the ear cavity, it may be argued, is the sense of hearing. Even then, argues *PP*, thinking along the lines of *VP*, the ether conditioned by the ear cavity, being a finite entity, cannot conceivably reach the place of the object. The view that the quarters constitute the sense of hearing does not accommodate the position that the sense of hearing reaches the place of the object. The position finally defended by *VP* is that the sense of hearing being limited, like the sense of sight, can reach the place of the object.

7.55.3 *PP* concludes the account with a suggestion as to why the author of *VP* strains after providing an account of the auditory sense and chooses it to illustrate the thesis of sense functioning by reaching out to the object. Perceptual knowledge, according to Advaita, particularly of the tradition that the author of *VP* defends, could arise from verbal testimony and is useful in leading to the removal of nescience covering Brahman. After the rise of the direct knowledge of Brahman, the perceptual cognition of empirical objects, which are ascertained to be nonreal, is sublated. Even if the theory that verbal testimony gives rise to perceptual knowledge is not admitted, the stated results will hold good. Hearing the verbal testimony initiates the process leading to the removal of nescience and identity with Brahman.

Notes

1. The analysis of dreaming and its relationship to the waking state has been a continuing exercise for philosophers, both east and west, since the beginning of philosophy. Whether philosophers are concerned with forecasting the future by means of dreams or simply with distinguishing dreaming from the nondreaming state, they

have been unable to escape the problem. Some will conclude, perhaps solipsistically, that there is no real difference between these states. Then there are others who maintain that there is no real criterion for distinguishing between the dreaming and the waking states. Bertrand Russell maintained that "it is obviously possible that what we call waking life may be only an unusually persistent and recurrent nightmare." *Our Knowledge of the External World* (London: George Allen & Unwin, 1980), 101. In a later work, he narrates one of his dreams and notices that his dream perception of a ruined church was "an experience intrinsically indistinguishable from that of seeing a ruined church when awake. It follows that the experience which I call 'seeing a church' is not conclusive evidence that there is a church, since it may occur when there is no such external object as I suppose in my dream. It may be said that, though when dreaming I may *think* that I am awake, when I wake up I *know* that I am awake. But I do not see how we are to have any such certainty; I have frequently dreamed that I woke up.... I do not believe that I am now dreaming, but I cannot prove that I am not. I am, however, quite certain that I am having certain experiences, whether they be those of a dream or those of waking life." *Human Knowledge* (London: George Allen & Unwin, Ltd., 1948), 171–72. Others may propose criteria, consistency of experience, for example, to distinguish between these states. But any one who is concerned with consciousness, and the analysis of our mental states, cannot forego the analysis.

Phenomenology of dream consciousness plays a central role in Śaṃkara's philosophy. He uses it to demonstrate the continuity of consistency and persistence of self-awareness in the different states of consciousness. The independence of the subject, the experiencer, from the object experienced is never more obvious than in a dream state. No matter how deeply we are involved in our dreams, we retains our independence from them. Upon returning to waking consciousness, we affirm 'I had a dream'. Śaṃkara states: "[T]he topic of dream is introduced for revealing the self-effulgence of the witnessing self as a distinct fact. This is done because in the waking state we have the existence of the contact between the objects and senses and an admixture of the light of sun, and so on, so that the self-effulgence of the self cannot be distinguished from them." Gambhirānanda, *Brahma-Sūtra-Bhāṣya*, 593. The dream experiences, in other words, attest to the persistence and continuity of consciousness.

The dream perception points to the reality that a person in his true being is self-manifest, self-existent consciousness, unchangeable in the midst of all the variations and changes. This self persists in the waking, dreaming, and dreamless sleep. The self within is essentially one with the all-pervading consciousness.

2. *svāpanikapratītivyavahārayo rupāpattyeti arthaḥ. yathāśrute tu smṛtiviṣayatvasya pratītikālamātrasthāyitvarūpaprātibhāsikatvāprayojakatvād asaṅgateḥ. etena "prātibhāsikatveti pratītikālamātrasthāyitveti arthaḥ. PP*, 124.

3. *māyāmātraṃ tu kārtsnyenānabhivyaktasvarūpatvāt* . But the dream world is a mere appearance or illusion because of its not being a manifestation in its entirety (spanning all attributes of waking reality). Śaṃkara explains that in a dream, the requisite environment, time, and other necessary materials, and the nonliability of obliteration associated with real things cannot be possible. *na hi paramārtha-vastu-viṣayāṇi-deśa-kāla-nimittāny abādhaś ca svapne sambhāvyante. BSB*, 3.2.3.

Commenting on the above aphorism, Radhakrishnan observes: "Dream states are not bound by the rules of space-time, cause and non-contradiction. We cannot find space for chariots and the like in the limited confines of the body. The dreamer sees things at long distances.... Lying asleep at night he dreams that it is the day. Besides, how can he without materials make chariots and the like? Within the dream itself there is self-contradiction. A chariot becomes a man and a man a tree. Objects appear to exist in dreams as silver does in a mother-of-pearl. What we see in dreams is only an appearance. Radhakrishnan, *The Brahma-Sūtra*, 443–44. The point of significance about dream-experiences for Advaita, in short, is that dream-experience is not intrinsically different from the waking experience. Dream objects are traces of the waking experience with greater latitude and freedom in their combination and sequence. The waking state, however, endures till the Brahman-realization, whereas the dream state is sublated by everyday experiences. In short, dream experiences, although rooted in waking life, are not real in the same sense as the contents of waking life.

4. *asmāt jāgradgajādyanubhava eva cakṣurādijanyaḥ, na tu svāpnagajādyanubhavaḥ iti*. *PP*, 125. *PP* refers to the passages in *SLS* in which the author refers to an objection which in effect blurs the distinction between wakeful and dream experiences. The point of the objection is, in dream as in waking, one experiences an elephant, that is, sees with the 'eyes' open. It is therefore on a par with the illusory cognition, for example, 'I see the silver with my eyes'. The wakeful experience of seeing an elephant in a zoo, therefore, is not structurally different from the dream and illusory experiences. In reply, it is observed: "...though there is parity in respect of the cognition of the concomitance of co-presence and so on, it is only the waking experience of elephant and so on, that is generated by the sense of sight and so on, not the dream experience of elephant and so on" *SLS*, vol. 1, chap. 2, 3.62, 297–98.

5. Opponents maintain that in the absence of the substratum the superimposition of dream objects, such as chariots and the like, cannot take place. They contend that the "superimposition of the dream world on undefined intelligence or on intelligence as conditioned by individuation, do not stand to reason; for, on the first (view), the dream elephant and so on, since they occupy space other than that of the witness conditioned by individuation, cannot, like happiness and so on, be manifested by that, independently of relation to a psychosis of the internal organ; and the sense of sight and so on being quiescent, the rise of a psychosis is impossible; hence, there cannot be manifestation by that, in dependence on the relation to that (psychosis); (while), on the second (view), there would be the contingence of (the experience) 'I am an elephant' as of 'This is silver', or of 'I possess an elephant' as of 'I am happy'." *SLS*, chap. 12, 3.5411, 289–90.

6. To the objection that the location cognized as the substratum of the dream chariots is nothing other than the indeterminable phenomenal reality, the author of *VP* observes that the substratum of such dream objects is consciousness—it is consciousness manifest as reality. What *VP* means to say is that the self-luminosity of consciousness as substratum extends only to its existence aspect. All presentations, in dream as well as in waking conditions, come as existents, as when one says, 'the pitcher exists' or 'the dream chariot exists'. But this admission should not be construed, as the author of *SM* does, to mean that of the three aspects of consciousness, reality, and bliss, the latter two are veiled and have to be realized through the help of Vedānta *śravana*. The general Advaita position in this regard seems to be that whatever is self-manifest must be manifest as consciousness and also as bliss. Bliss, existence, and eternality are not different from the nature of consciousness. Vācaspati argues along these lines when he says: "Of the self that is but of the one essence of intelligence, there is not, verily anything unapprehended, when the element of intelligence is apprehended. Bliss, eternality, pervasiveness etc. are not, indeed, different from its nature as intelligence such that they are not apprehended along with the apprehension of that element. While being certainly apprehended, yet because of posited difference, they appear as if not discriminated, and hence not apprehended." *Catussūtrī*, *Adhyāsabhāṣya*, 40. For a discussion of these and other related issues, see *SLS*, chap. 2, 3.51-3.62; and S. S. Śāstrī, chap. 1, n. 25.

7. *satyam deśaviśeṣaḥ kalpito nādhiṣṭhānam, caitanyam tu anavacchinnama-*

vidyāpratibimbam vādhiṣṭhānam iti bhavaty eva tasya ca sāmānyarūpeṇa jñātasyāpi viśeṣarūpeṇajñānam api sambhavaty eva. vṛttyavacchinnacaitanyam evājñānavirodhi [ḥ]; na svarūpacaitanyam iti rūpāntareṇāvaraṇam apy upapadyate. evaṃ ca na niradhiṣṭhānatāvada ity āśayena samādhatte. PP, 128.

8. Dream perception, although real to the dreamer, is contradicted by the waking experience. A dream is very similar to memory in that both are caused by latent impressions. However, whereas memory in principle is presentative, a dream in principle is representative. Dreaming is more like an erroneous cognition. However, there is one very vital difference between the two. In an erroneous cognition, mind is joined with the sense organs and, in a sense, also with the external object. Such a sense-contact is not present in dreaming. The objects that appear in a dream, no matter how real they appear to be, disappear upon waking. In Advaita literature, dreams are treated on a par with illusory cognitions. In both, the issue revolves around the substratum (*adhiṣṭhāna*) of such experiences. Some maintain that the wakeful self, the 'I' of waking consciousness, is the substratum of dream experiences. The argument adduced is that like an empirical illusion, in a dream experience, when the knowledge of substratum arises, the dream experience is terminated or cancelled. The obvious objection to this position is that the 'I' of wakeful conciousness is not present in dreams. The position of *VP* as well as Vivaraṇa is that the witness-consciousness is the real substratum. The witness-consciousness continues to remain unknown on waking up, as in a dream experience. Thus, technically speaking, wakeful experience does not cancel (*bādha*) dream, it only points to a removal, a cessation (*nivṛtti*) of dream experience. This shows a subtle line of distinction between empirical illusions characteristic of wakeful life and dream experiences.

9. *kāraṇātmanā vināsaḥ kāraṇarūpeṇāpy abhāvo bādhaḥ; kāraṇātmanā 'vasthānāṃ nivṛttir iti vibhāga iti bhāvaḥ. PP*, 130.

10. The counter-correlate (*pratiyogin*) of a negation or nonexistence is that whose existence is denied. In the cognition 'this is not silver', silver is the counter-correlate and it possesses counter-correlatedness (*pratiyogitā*) as its attribute.

The *pratiyogin* of an absence means the thing that is absent. When 'A' is absent, 'A' is the *pratiyogin*, and when 'B 'is absent, 'B' is the *pratiyogin*. In other words, 'A' and 'B' are *pratiyogin*s of their respective absences. In the Nyāya terminology, *pratiyogitā* resides in both 'A' and 'B.' "Absolute existence (*atyantābhāva*) is that absence 'which abides through the three modes of time' (*traikālika*) and 'the facthood of whose negatum' (*pratiyogitā*) is specified (*avachinna*) by a 'relation' (*saṃsarga*)'; e.g. 'There is no pot on the ground'." *TSD*, 380.

11. Advaitins, unlike the Naiyāyikas, maintain that in illusory perceptions we do not perceive an object as another, but cognize an illusory reality produced at that time and place. This reality, the Advaitins further contend, is indefinable and different from the empirical reality. Similarly, during sleep in dream perceptions as well, illusory realities are produced at the time and the place very much like the illusory perceptions of waking stage. Illusory realities (e.g., elephants and chariots) are created, and these dream objects persist so long the dream cognition endures.

Opponents maintain that if an illusory existence is admitted for silver during the appearance of the shell-silver, then the sublating cognition of its negation would take the form '*now*, this is not silver', and would not express the negation of shell-silver in the three divisions of time, past, present, and future.

In response *VP* holds that the sublating cognition 'this is not silver', does not negate the actual silver with which we are familiar in our day-to-day activities, nor does it negate the illusory silver, but merely the existence of that illusory silver which was cognized during the erroneous cognition and assumed the characteristic of an empirical silver. The illusory silver never was actual silver, is not, and will not be so in the future. So the cognition 'this is not silver' negates the silver in the three divisions of time.

12. When one says 'a chair does not exist as a table', one is denying the existence of a chair that then becomes the counter-correlate of this negation. A table is different from a chair and has a different substratum from that of a chair. The property of a table (i.e., tableness), is the distinguishing attribute of the counter-correlatedness of this negation. Therefore the nonexistence in this instance is *vyadhikaraṇa dharma avacchina pratiyogitāka abhāva*, because it will always be found to be present in a chair. *Self and Falsity in Advaita Vedānta* (Calcutta: Progressive Publishers, 1955), 154.

Similarly, in the erroneous cognition of the shell-silver, when one has the subsequent cognition in the form 'this is not silver', it is realized that the absence of illusory silver characterized by empirical reality always will be present in the shell, because, although the shell may erroneously appear to be silver, it is never the empirically real silver. Empirical objects like silver, table, chair, do not possess the absolute reality but they exist so long as one does not realize Brahman. Dreams and the like, on the other hand, are sublated as soon as one returns to the waking state.

13. *na vyadhikaraṇadharmāvacchinnatvavādinām asmākaṃmate pratiyogitāvacchedakāvacchinnapratiyogijñānam kāraṇam iti. PP*, 135. Also see *Laghucandrikā*, schap. on *pratyakṣabādhoddhārah*, 117–45.

14. *VP* maintains that when the content that is being apprehended is in sense contact, although existent in another locus, there is no need to admit an indeterminable creation. In instances like the reflection in the mirror and crystal appearing as red, there is simply a confusion between two things. Because the confused object is in proximity, the error occurs in transposing or transferring. The redness, although present in the rose, is mistakenly transferred to the silver. So *VP* maintains that when the superimposed is in sense contact, we accept the Nyāya theory of *anyathākhyāti*. *PP* further adds that if redness is in proximity but is being impeded by another object, then the origination of an indeterminable redness must be admitted. In this context, we must keep in mind that all the Advaitins do not subscribe to this view. The generally accepted view is that the redness of the crystal is indeterminable.

Select Bibliography

Recommended General Works on Indian Philosophy

Chatterjee, Satischandra, and Datta, Dhirendramohan. *An Introduction to Indian Philosophy*. Calcutta: University of Calcutta, 1960.

Dasgupta, Surendranath. *A History of Indian Philosophy*. 5 vols. Cambridge: Cambridge University Press, 1922–55.

______________. *Indian Idealism*. Cambridge: Cambridge University Press, 1933.

Edgerton, Franklin. *The Beginnings of Indian Philosophy*. London: George Allen & Unwin Ltd., 1965.

Hiriyanna, Mysore. *The Essentials of Indian Philosophy*. London: George Allen & Unwin, 1932.

______________. *Outlines of Indian Philosophy*. Bombay: George Allen & Unwin, Pvt. Ltd., 1973.

Potter, Karl. *Presuppositions of India's Philosophies*. Englewood Cliffs, N.J.: Prentice Hall, Inc., 1963.

Prasad, Jwala. *History of Indian Epistemology*. Delhi: Munshi Ram Manoharlal, 1958.

Puligandala, R. *Fundamentals of Indian Philosophy*. New York: Abingdon Press, 1975.

Radhakrishnan, Sarvepalli. *Indian Philosophy*. 2 vols. London: George Allen & Unwin, 1923, 1927.

Radhakrishnan, Sarvepalli and Moore, Charles A., eds. *A Sourcebook in Indian Philosophy*. Princeton, N.J.: Princeton University Press, 1957.

Sharma, Chandradhar. *Indian Philosophy: A Critical Survey*. New York: Barnes & Noble, Inc., 1962.

Smart, Ninian. *Doctrine and Argument in Indian Philosophy*. London: George Allen & Unwin, 1964.

Zimmer, Heinrich. *Philosophies of India*. Edited by Joseph Campbell. London: Routledge & Kegan Paul, 1952.

Primary Sources

Ādidevānanda, Swāmī, trans. *Yatīndramatadīpikā*. Madras: Sri Ramakrishna Math, 1949.

Alaston, William P. and Nakhnikian, George, eds. *The Idea of Phenomenology* by Edmund Husserl. The Hague: Martinus Nijhoff, 1966.

Alston, A. J., trans. *The Naiṣkarmya Siddhi of Śrī Sureśvara*. London: Shanti Sadan, 1959.

Apte, V. M., trans. *Brahma-Sūtra-Śhānkara-Bhāshya*. Bombay: Popular Book

Depot, 1960.

Athalye, Yashwant Vasudev, trans. *Tarka-Saṃgraha of Annaṃbhaṭṭa with Dīpikā and Govardhana's Nyāya-Bodhinī*. Bombay Sanskrit and Prakrit Series, 55. Bombay: R. N. Dandekar, 1963.

Bhattacharya, Gopinath, trans. *Tarkasaṃgraha Dīpikā on Tarkasaṃgraha*. Calcutta: Progressive Publishers, 1976.

Bhattacharya, Kamleshwar, trans. *Vigrahavyāvarttani*. Delhi: Motilal Banarsidass, 1986.

Bühler, George, trans. *The Laws of Manu*. The Sacred Books of the East, vol. 25. New York: Dover Publications, Inc., 1969.

Devanji, Prahlad Chandrashekha, trans. *Siddhāntabindu of Madhusūdana with the Commentary of Purushottama*. Gaekwad Oriental Series, vol. 64. Baroda: Oriental Institute, 1933.

Gambhirānanda, Swāmī, trans. *Brahma-Sūtra-Bhāṣya of Śrī Śaṅkarācārya*. Calcutta: Advaita Ashrama, 1983.

_______________, trans. and ed. *Eight Upaniṣads with the commentary of Śaṅkarācārya*. 2 vols. Calcutta: Advaita Ashrama, 1965.

Granoff, Phyllis, trans. Śrī Harṣa's *Khaṇḍanakhaṇḍakhādya* Dodrecht, Holland: D. Reidel Publishing Co., 1978.

Hiriyanna, Mysore, ed. *The Naiṣkarmya-Siddhi of Sureśvarācārya with the Candrikā of Jnānottama*. Bombay Sanskrit and Prakrit Series no. 38. Poona: Bhandarkar Oriental Research Institute, 1980.

Hume, Robert Ernest, trans. *The Thirteen Principal Upanishads*. Oxford: Oxford University Press, 1967.

Jagadānanda, Swāmī, trans. *Upadeśa Sāhasrī of* Śrī *Śankarāchārya* ("A Thousand Teachings"). Mylapore, Madras: Sri Ramakrishna Math, 1961.

Jha, Ganganath, trans. *Advaitasiddhi* of Madhusūdana Sarasvatī. *Indian Thought*, vol. 6, 1914; vol. 7, 1915; vol. 8, 1916; vol. 9, 1917.

_______________, trans. Kumārila's *Śloka Vārtika*. Sri Garib Das Oriental Series, no. 8. Delhi: Sri Satguru Publications, 1983.

_______________, trans. *The Nyaya-Sūtras of Gauṭama*. 5 vols. Delhi: Motilal Banarsidass, 1984.

Karmarkar, Raghunath Damodar, trans. and ed. *Kāvyaprakāśa of Mammaṭa*. Poona: Bhandarkar Oriental Institute, 1933.

Lauer, Quentin, trans. *Edmund Husserl's Phenomenology and the Crisis of Science*. New York: Harper Torchbook, 1965.

Mādhavānanda, Swāmī, trans. *Bhāṣā-Pariccheda with Siddhānta-Muktāvalī*. Calcutta: Advaita Ashrama, 1977.

_______________, trans. *The Bṛhadāraṇyaka Upaniṣad: with the Commentary of Śaṅkarācārya*. Mayavati, Almora, Himalayas: Advaita Ashrama, 1950.

_______________.trans. and ed. *Vedānta Paribhāṣā* by Dharmarāja Adhvarīndra. Mayavati: Advaita Ashrama, 1983.

Mahadevan, T. M. P., ed. and trans. *The Saṃbandha-Vārtika of Sureśvarācārya*. Madras: University of Madras, 1958.

Mohanty, J. N. *Gangeśa Theory of Truth*. Shantiniketan: Centre of Advanced Study in Philosophy, 1966.

Nikhilānanda, Swami, trans. *The Māṇḍūkhyopaniṣad with Gauḍapāda's Kārikā and*

Śaṅkara's Commentary. Mysore: Sri Ramakrishnan, Ashrama, 1955.

_____________, trans. *Self-Knowledge: An English Translation of Śaṅkarāchārya's Ātmabodha*. Mylapore, Madras: Sri Ramakrishna Math, 1947.

_____________, trans. *Vedāntasāra: or the Essence of Vedānta of Sadānanda Yogīndra*. Mayavati, Almora, Himalayas: Advaita Ashrama, 1949.

Nyāyapañcanana, Kṛṣṇanātha. *Āśubodhinī*, a commentary on *Vedānta Paribhāṣā*. Calcutta: n.p., 1852.

Radhakrishnan, Sarvepalli, trans. *The Brahma Sūtra: The Philosophy of Spiritual Life*. New York: Greenwood Press, 1968.

_____________, trans. *The Principal Upaniṣads*. New York: Harper & Bros., 1953.

Sadhuna, Govindasinha. Ramakṛṣṇadhvarīndra's *Śikhāmaṇi with Vedānta Paribhāṣā*. Bombay: Shree Venkatashwar Publishers, 1968.

Sarasvatī,Brahmānanda: *Laghucandrikā*. Kumbakonam: Vidya Press, n.d.

Śāstrī, Anantakṛṣṇa, ed. *Brahmasūtra-Śaṅkara-Bhāṣyam*. Calcutta Sanskrit Series, 3 parts. Calcutta: The Metropolitan Printing and Publishing House, Ltd., 1941.

_____________, ed. *Paribhāṣā Prakāśikā*, a commentary on *Vedānta Paribhāṣā*. Calcutta: University of Calcutta, 1927.

Śāstrī, Śrī Gaurinath, trans. *Kiraṇāvalī*. Banaras: Research Institute, 1980. The book has been translated into Hindi.

Śāstrī, Kuppuswami, ed. *Brahmasiddhi*. Madras: Madras Government Press, 1937.

_____________, trans. *A Primer of Indian Logic*. Madras: Kuppuswami Research Institute, 1961.

Śāstrī, Srirama, trans. *The Pañcapādikā of Padmapāda*. Madras Government Oriental Series, vol. 155. Madras: Government Oriental Manuscript Library, 1958.

Śāstrī, S. S. Suryanarayana, trans. *Siddhāntaleśasaṅgraha of Appayya Dīkṣita*. Madras: University of Madras, 1935.

_____________, trans. and ed. *Vedānta Paribhāṣā by* Dharmarāja Adhvarīndra. Adyar: The Adyar Library, 1942.

Śāstrī, S. S. Suryanarayana, and Raja, C. Kunhan, ed. and trans. *The Bhāmatī of Vācaspati: on Śaṅkara's Brahmasūtrabhāṣya (Catussūtrī)*. Madras: Theosophical Publishing House, 1933.

Śāstrī, S. S. Suryanarayana, and Sen, Saileswar, trans. *Vivaraṇaprameyasaṅgraha*. Madras: The Sri Vidya Press, 1941.

Shastri, Hari Prasad, trans. *Pañcadaśī. A Treatise on Advaita Metaphysics by Swāmī Vidyāraṇya*. London: Shanti Sadan, 1956.

Smith, Colin M., trans. Merleau-Ponty's *Phenomenology of Perception*. London: Routledge & Kegan Paul, 1962.

Sprung, Marvin, trans. *The Lucid Exposition of the Middle Way*. London: Routledge & Keagan, Paul, 1979.

Tailanga, G. S., ed. Vācaspati Miśra's *Nyāyavārtikatātparyaṭīka*. Vizianagram Sanskrit Series, no. 9, 1896.

Thibaut, George, trans. *The Vedānta-Sūtras with the Commentary of Śaṅkarācārya*. Vols. 34 and 38 of *Sacred Books of the East*. Edited by Max Muller. Oxford: The Clarendon Press, 1890, 1896.

Vācaspati, Bhāmatī with Kalaptaru and Parimala. Bombay: Nirnayasagar Press, 1917.

van Buitenen, J. A. B., trans. *Vedārthasaṃgraha*. Deccan College Monograph Series, 16. Poona: Deccan College Postgraduate and Research Institute, 1956.

Veezhinattan, N., ed. *The Saṃksepaśāriraka of Sarvajñātman*. Madras: University of Madras, 1985.

Venkataramiah, D., trans. *The Pañcapādikā of Padmapāda*. Gaekwad Oriental Series, vol. 107. Baroda: Oriental Institute, 1948.

Yogīndrananda, ed. and trans. Citsukha's, *Tattavapradīpikā with Pratyaksvarūpa's Nayaṇaprasādini* Banaras: Shuddarsana Prakasana Pratisthana, 1956.

Secondary Sources

Alaston, William P., and Nakhnikian, eds. *Readings in Twentieth Century Philosophy*. London: The Free Press of Glencoe, 1963.

Arapura, J. G. "*Māyā* and the Discourse about Brahman." In *The Problem of Two Truths in Advaita Vedānta and Buddhism*, edited by Marvin Sprung. Dodrecht-Holland: D. Reidel Publishing Company, 1973.

Belvalkar, S. K. *Vedānta Philosophy*. Poona: Bilrakunja Publishing House, 1929.

Bhaduri, Sadananda. *Studies in Nyāya-Vaiśeṣika Metaphysics*. Poona: Bhandarkar Oriental Research Institute, 1947.

Bhattacharya, Asutosh Sastri. *Studies in Post-Śaṅkara Dialectics*. Calcutta: University of Calcutta, 1936.

Bhattacharyya, Kalidas. *A Modern Understanding of Advaita*. Ahmedabad, India: L. D. Institute of Technology, 1975.

Bhattacharyya, Kokileswar. *An Introduction to Advaita Philosophy*. Calcutta: University of Calcutta, 1924.

Bhattacharyya, K. C. *Studies in Vedāntism*. Calcutta: University of Calcutta, 1909.

Cane, P. V. *A Brief Sketch of the Pūrva-Mīmāmsā System*. Poona: Aryabhushan Press, 1924.

Carman, John B. *Theology of Rāmānuja*. New Haven, Conn.: Yale University Press, 1974.

Chakraborty, Nirod Baran. *The Advaita Concept of Falsity—A Critical Study*. Calcutta College Sanskrit Series no. 57. Calcutta: The Principal, Sanskrit College, 1967.

Chatterjee, A. K., and Dravid, R. R. *The Concept of Sākṣi in Advaita Vedānta*. Banaras: Banaras Hindu University, 1979.

Chatterjee, Tara. "The Concept of Sākṣin." *The Journal of Indian Philosophy*, Vol. 10 (1988).

Chaudhuri, Anil Kumar Ray. "The Concept of Sākṣin." *Our Heritage*, Vol. 1, 1953.

______________. *The Doctrine of Māyā*. Calcutta: Dasgupta & Co., Ltd., 1950.

______________. *Self and Falsity in Advaita Vedānta*. Calcutta: Progressive Publishers, 1955.

Chisholm, Roderick M. *Realism and the Background of Phenomenology*. New York: The Free Press, 1964.

Coward, Harold G., ed. *Studies in Indian Thought*. Delhi: Motilal Banarsidass, 1983.

Datta, Dhirendra Mohan. "Inward and Outward in Advaita Vedānta." *The Philosophical Quarterly*, 30 (October 1957): 165–72.

______________. *The Six Ways of Knowing: A Critical Study of the Vedānta*

Theory of Knowledge. 2d rev. ed. Calcutta: The University of Calcutta, 1960.

______________. "Some Realistic Aspects of Indian Philosophy." In *Recent Indian Philosophy*, edited by Kalidas Bhattacharyya. Calcutta: Progressive Publishers, 1963.

de Bary, William Theodore, ed. *The Buddhist Tradition in India, China, and Japan*. New York: The Modern Library, 1969.

Deutsch, Eliot. *Advaita Vedānta: A Philosophical Reconstruction*. Honolulu: East-West Center Press, 1968.

Deutsch, Eliot, and van Buitenen, J. A. B., eds. *A Sourcebook of Advaita Vedānta*. Honolulu: University Press of Hawaii, 1971.

Devaraja, N. K. *An Introduction to Śaṅkara's Theory of Knowledge*. Delhi: Motilal Banarsidass, 1962.

Dravid, Raja Ram. *The Problem of Universals in Indian Philosophy*. Delhi: Motilal Banarsidass, 1972.

Farber, Marvin. *Foundations of Phenomenology*. Cambridge, Mass.: Harvard University Press, 1943.

Guenther, Herbert V. *Buddhist Philosophy in Theory and Practice*. Maryland: Penguin Books, 1972.

Gupta, Bina. "Are *Hetvābhāsas* Formal Fallacies?" *Journal of Indiaṇ Philosophy* 8 (1980).

Gupta, Bina, and Wilcox, William C. "'*Tat tvam asi*': An Important Identity Statement or a Mere Tautology." *Philosophy East and West* 34, no. 1, (1984).

Hacker, Paul. "Śaṃkara's Conception of Man." In *Kleine Schriften*. Wiesbaden: F. Steiner, 1978.

Hasurkar, S. S. *Vācaspati Miśra on Advaita Vedānta*. Darbhanga: Mithila Institute, 1958.

Jhalakīkar,Bhīmācārya. *Nyāyakośa*. Bombay Sanskrit and Prakrit Series, no. 49. Poona: The Bhandarkar Oriental Institute, 1978.

Kar, Bijayananda. *The Theories of Error in Indian Philosophy*. India: Ajanta Publications, 1978.

Kockelmans, J. ed. *Phenomenology*. Garden City, N.Y.: Doubleday & Co., 1967.

Larson, Gerald, M. *Classical Sāṃkhya*. Delhi: Motilal Banarsidass, 1969.

Mahadevan, T. M. P. *The Philosophy of Advaita*. New Delhi: Arnold-Heinemann Publishers, 1976.

______________. *Superimposition in Advaita Vedānta*. New Delhi: Sterling Publishers Private Ltd., 1985.

Maitra, Sushil Kumar. *Fundamental Questions of Indian Logic and Metaphysics*. Calcutta: University of Calcutta, 1974.

Malkani, G. R. *Vedāntic Epistemology*. Amalner: The Indian Institute of Philosophy, 1953.

Malkani, G. R., Das, R., and Murti, T. R. V. *Ajñāna*. London: Luzac & Co., 1933.

Matilal, Bimal K. *Nyāya-Vaiśeṣika*. A History of Indian Literature Series, vol. 6, edited by Jan Gonda. Wiesbaden: Otto Harrassowitz, 1977.

______________. *Perception*. Oxford: Claredon Press, 1986.

Mondal, Pradyot Kumar. "Some Aspects of Perception in Old Nyāya." *Journal of Indian Philosophy* 10, (1982).

Mukherjee, A. C. *The Nature of Self*. Allahabad, India: The Indian Press Ltd., 1938.

Murti, T. R. V. *The Central Philosophy of Buddhism*. London: George Allen & Unwin, 1960.

Pereira, José, ed. *Hindu Theology: A Reader*. New York: Doubleday, 1976.

Phillips, Stephen H. "Padmapāda's Illusion Argument." *Philosophy East and West* 37 (January 1987).

Potter, Karl. *Encyclopaedia of Indian Philosophies*. 4 vol. Delhi: Motilal Banarsidass, 1981.

______________. "Some Thoughts on the Nyāya Conception of Meaning." *Journal of Indian Philosophy* 3 (1975).

______________. "*Vedāntaparibhāṣā* as Systematic Reconstruction," in *Perspectives on Vedānta*, edited by S. Rama Rao Pappu. Leiden: E. J. Brill, 1988.

Price, H. H. *Perception*. London: Methuen & Co. Ltd., 1961.

Radhakrishnan, E. P. "The Pañcapādikā Literature." *Poona Orientalist* 6 (1941–1942).

Radhakrishnan, S. *An Idealist View of Life*. India: George Allen & Unwin, 1971.

______________, ed. Ganganatha Jha's *Pūrva Mīmāṃsā*. Library of Indian Philosophy and Religion Series, vol. 1. Banaras: Banaras Hindu University, 1964.

Raju, P. T. *Idealistic Thought of India*. Cambridge, Mass.: Harvard University Press, 1953.

Randle, H. N. "A Note on Indian Syllogism." *Mind* 33 (1926).

Russell, Bertrand. *Human Knowledge*. London: George Allen & Unwin, Ltd., 1948.

______________. *Our Knowledge of the External World*. London: George Allen & Unwin, 1980.

Sarma, V. A. *Citsukha's Contribution to Advaita*. Mysore, India: Kavyalaya Publishers, 1976.

Satprakāshānanda, Swāmī. *Methods of Knowledge*. Calcutta: Advaita Ashrama, 1975.

Sengupta, Bratindra Kumar. *A Critique of the Vivaraṇa School*. Calcutta: Dr. Bratindra Kumar Sengupta, 1959.

Singh, Ram Pratap. *The Vedānta of Śaṃkara—A Metaphysic of Value*, vol. I. Jaipur: Bharat Publishing House, 1949.

Sinha, J. N. *Indian Epistemology of Perception*. India: Sinha Publishing House, 1969.

______________. *Indian Psychology*. 2 vols. Calcutta: Sinha Publishing House, 1958.

Sircar, Mahendranath. *Comparative Studies in Vedāntism*. Bombay: Humphrey Milford, 1927.

Sivaraman, Krishna. *Śaivism in Philosophical Perspective*. Delhi: Motilal Banarsidass, 1973.

Srinivasan, T. M., and Sreelakshmi, B. G., eds. *Sense Perception in Science and Śāstras*. Sringeri: Sri Sharda Trust, 1986.

Stcherbatsky, F. Th. *Buddhist Logic*. 2 vols. New York: Dover Publications, 1962.

Sundaram, P. K. *Advaita Epistemology*. Madras: University of Madras, 1968.

Takakusu, Junjiro. *The Essentials of Buddhist Philosophy*. Delhi: Motilal Banarsidass, 1978.

Takakusu, Junjiro. *The Essentials of Buddhist Philosophy*. Delhi: Motilal Banarsidass, 1978.

Upadhyaya, Veeramani Prasad. *Lights on Vedānta*. ("Chowkhamba Sanskrit Series," vol. 6) Varanasi, 1959.

Index

A

Q–R

S

T

U